The Leader's SMARTbook

Second Revised Edition

&## Training Management
Leadership
Team Building

The Lightning Press
Norman M. Wade

The Lightning Press

2227 Arrowhead Blvd
Lakeland, FL 33813
24-hour Voicemail/Fax/Order: 1-800-997-8827
E-mail: SMARTbooks@TheLightningPress.com
www.TheLightningPress.com

The Leader's SMARTbook
(2nd Revised Edition)

Training Management, Leadership and Team Building

Compiled, Edited, and Illustrated by Norman M. Wade

Copyright © 2003 Norman M. Wade

ISBN: 0-9742486-1-4

This is the second revised edition of The Leader's SMARTbook. The major change in this edition is the incorporation of the Army's new "FM 7-0 Training the Force, Oct. 2002" which replaced the previous "FM 25-100 Training the Force, Nov. 1988" included in our first edition.

Printed and bound in the United States of America.

Second Revised Edition to "The Leader's SMARTbook"

Updated to the new FM 7-0!

This is the second revised edition of The Leader's SMARTbook. The major change in this edition is the incorporation of the Army's new "FM 7-0 Training the Force, Oct. 2002" which replaced the previous "FM 25-100 Training the Force, Nov. 1988" included in our first edition.

FM 7-0 is the Army's capstone training doctrine and is applicable to all units, at all levels, and in all components. While the examples in this manual are principally focused at division and below, FM 7-0 provides the essential fundamentals for all individual, leader, and unit training. Training for warfighting is our number one priority in peace and in war.

FM 7-0 provides the training and leader development methodology that forms the foundation for developing competent and confident soldiers and units that will win decisively in any environment. Training is the means to achieve tactical and technical competence for specific tasks, conditions, and standards. Leader Development is the deliberate, continuous, sequential, and progressive process, based on Army values, that develops soldiers and civilians into competent and confident leaders capable of decisive action.

FM 7-0 provides the Training Management Cycle and the necessary guidelines on how to plan, execute, and assess training and leader development. Understanding "How the Army Trains the Army" to fight is key to successful joint, interagency, multinational (JIM), and combined arms operations. Effective training leads to units that execute the Army's core competencies and capabilities.

SMARTbook Features

Chapters and sections are organized in the same fashion as the source manuals where possible. For example, chapter one from a reference equates to section one in The Leader's SMARTbook; chapter two is section two, etc. Furthermore, the text is as close to the original source text as possible to replicate approved doctrinal publications and procedures.

The Leader's SMARTbook can be used as a study guide, as a basic lesson plan to conduct opportunity training, and as a quick reference guide during actual tactical operations and training exercises such as practical exercises (PEs), field training exercises (FTXs), and command post exercises (CPXs).

SMARTregister for Updates

Keep your SMARTbooks up-to-date! The Lightning Press will provide free e-mail notification of updates, revisions and changes to our SMARTbooks. Users can register their SMARTbooks online at www.TheLightningPress.com. Updates and their prices will be announced by e-mail as significant changes or revised editions are published.

The Leader's SMARTbook (2nd Rev. Ed.)

References

The following references were used to compile The Leader's SMARTbook. All references are available to the general public and designated as "approved for public release; distribution is unlimited." The Leader's SMARTbook does not contain classified or sensitive information restricted from public release.

Field Manuals

FM 7-0 (NEW!)	Oct 2002	Training the Force
FM 22-100	Aug 1999	Army Leadership
FM 22-101	3 Jun 1985	Leadership Counseling
FM 22-102	2 Mar 1987	Soldier Team Development
FM 25-4	10 Sep 1984	How to Conduct Training Exercises
FM 25-5	25 Jan 1985	Training for Mobilization and War
FM 25-101	Sep 1990	Battle Focused Training
FM 101-5	30 Sep 1997	Staff Organization and Operations

Training Circulars

TC 22-6	Nov 1990	The Army Noncomissioned Officer Guide
TC 25-8	25 Feb 1982	Training Ranges
TC 25-10	26 Aug 1996	A Leader's Guide to Lane Training
TC 25-20	30 Sep 1993	A Leader's Guide to After-Action Reviews
TC 25-30	27 Apr 1994	A Leader's Guide to Company Training Meetings

Center for Army Lessons Learned (CALL) Publications

CALL 92-3	Mar 1992	Fratricide Risk Assessment for Company Leadership
CALL 98-5	May 1998	Rehearsals
CALL 91-1	Jan 1991	Rehearsals

Other Publications

BCBL	1995	Battle Command Techniques and Procedures
IMSC	Oct 1996	Command, Leadership, and Effective Staff Support by the Information Management Support Center
ALDH	Draft 2000	The Army Leadership Development Handbook - Draft

The Leader's SMARTbook (2nd Rev. Ed.)
Table of Contents

Chap 1

Training the Force (FM 7-0)

Chap 2

Company-Level Training Mgmt

After-Action Reviews (AARs)

Chap 3

The Army Leader: Be, Know, Do

Levels of Leadership

Combat-Ready Teams

Chap 7

Developmental Counseling

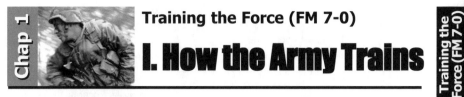
Ref: FM 7-0 Training the Force, chap. 1.

I. The Training Imperative

Every soldier, noncommissioned officer (NCO), warrant officer, and officer has one primary mission—to be trained and ready to fight and win our Nation's wars. Success in battle does not happen by accident; it is a direct result of tough, realistic, and challenging training. The Army exists to deter war, or if deterrence fails, to reestablish peace through victory in combat wherever U.S. interests are challenged. To accomplish this, the Army's forces must be able to perform their assigned strategic, operational, and tactical missions. For deterrence to be effective, potential enemies must know with certainty that the Army has the credible, demonstrable capability to mobilize, deploy, fight, sustain, and win any conflict. Training is the process that melds human and materiel resources into these required capabilities. The Army has an obligation to the American people to ensure its soldiers go into battle with the assurance of success and survival. This is an obligation that only rigorous and realistic training, conducted to standard, can fulfill.

We train the way we fight because our historical experiences show the direct correlation between realistic training and success on the battlefield. Today's leaders must apply the lessons of history in planning training for tomorrow's battles. We can trace the connection between training and success in battle to our Army's earliest experiences during the American Revolution. Over tv centuries later, the correlation between tough, realistic training and success or the battlefield remains the same. During Operation Enduring Freedom, and Operation Anaconda in Afghanistan, the U.S. Army deployed a trained and ready force on short notice to a contemporary battlefield fighting against a coalition of rebel forces on difficult terrain.

These units trained to their wartime mission, and developed company grade officers, NCOs, and soldiers who knew their jobs and were confident they could act boldly and decisively. Their confidence, and technical and tactical competence gave them the ability to adapt to the mission and harsh environment with resounding success. Airmobile infantry quickly perfected methods of routing rebel forces from heavily fortified caves. Special forces teams rode horses with their host nation counterparts—learning to call in tactical air support with devastating accuracy while on the move. Staffs quickly learned how to integrate Special Operations Forces (SOF) and conventional force operations. Engineer units cleared mine fields that were as old as many of their soldiers involved in the clearing process. Again, American soldiers had met the enemy and decisively defeated them.

II. The Strategic Environment

In an era of complex national security requirements, the Army's strategic responsibilities now embrace a wider range of missions that present even greater challenges in our training environment. To "train the way we fight," commanders and leaders at all levels must conduct training with respect to a wide variety of operational missions across the full spectrum of operations. These operations may include combined arms, joint, multinational, and interagency considerations, and span the entire breadth of terrain and environmental possibilities. Commanders must strive to set the daily training conditions as closely as possible to those expected for actual operations.

The operational missions of the Army include not only war, but also military operations other than war (MOOTW). Operations may be conducted as major combat operations, a small-scale contingency, or a peacetime military engagement. Offensive and defensive operations normally dominate military operations in war along with some small-scale contingencies. Stability operations and support operations dominate in MOOTW. Commanders at all echelons may combine different types of operations simultaneously and sequentially to accomplish missions in war and MOOTW. Throughout this document, we will emphasize the primary function of the Army—to fight and win our Nation's wars. Implicit in the emphasis is the mounting importance of MOOTW. These missions also require training; future conflict will likely involve a mix of combat and MOOTW, often concurrently. The range of possible missions complicates training. Army forces cannot train for every possible mission; they train for war and prepare for specific missions as time and circumstances permit. The nature of world crises requires Army forces to simultaneously train, deploy, and execute. Therefore, at Army level, warfighting will encompass the full spectrum of operations that the Army may be called upon to execute. Warfighting in units is refined and focused on assigned wartime missions or directed change of missions.

Contingency operations in the 1990s normally followed a sequence of alert, train, deployment, extended build-up, and shaping operations followed by a period of decisive operations. To be truly responsive and meet our commitments, Army forces must be deployable and capable of rapidly concentrating combat power in an operational area with minimal additional training. Our forces today use a train, alert, deploy sequence. We cannot count on the time or opportunity to correct or make up training deficiencies after deployment. Maintaining forces that are ready now, places increased emphasis on training and the priority of training. This concept is a key link between operational and training doctrine. Units train to be ready for war based on the requirements of a precise and specific mission; in the process, they develop a foundation of combat skills, which can be refined based on the requirements of the assigned mission. Upon alert, commanders assess and refine from this foundation of skills. In the train, alert, deploy process commanders use whatever time the alert cycle provides to continue to refine mission-focused training. Training continues during time available between alert notification and deployment, between deployment and employment, and even during employment as units adapt to the specific battlefield environment and assimilate combat replacements.

III. Joint, Interagency, Multinational (JIM) Training

The purpose of joint training is to prepare the Army to execute missions as a part of a joint force in the conduct of joint military operations and across the full spectrum of conflict. Employing Army forces at the right place and time allows combatant commanders to conduct decisive land operations along with air, sea, and space-based operations. The Army provides to a joint force commander (JFC) trained and ready forces that expand the commander's range of military options. Army commanders tailor and train forces to react quickly to any crisis.

Commanders of major Army headquarters may serve as the joint force land component commander (JFLCC), a combined forces commander (CFC), or as the joint task force commander (JTFC). To perform these assignments organizations conduct joint training.

- **Joint training** uses joint doctrine, tactics, techniques, and procedures, and the training involves more than one Service component. However, two or more Services training together using their respective service doctrine, tactics, techniques, and procedures are Service-sponsored interoperability training. Although, not classified as joint training, Service sponsored interoperability is a vital component of joint proficiency and readiness.

- **Multinational training** is based on applicable multinational, joint and/or service doctrine and is designed to prepare organizations for combined operations with allied nations.

- **Interagency training** is based on applicable standard operating procedures; and, is designed to prepare the Army to operate in conjunction with government agencies.

IV. How the Army Trains the Army

Training is a team effort and the entire Army—Department of the Army, major Army commands (MACOMs), the institutional training base, units, the combat training centers (CTC), each individual soldier and the civilian work force—has a role that contributes to force readiness. Department of the Army and MACOMs are responsible for resourcing the Army to train. The institutional Army including schools, training centers, and NCO academies, for example, train soldiers and leaders to take their place in units in the Army by teaching the doctrine and tactics, techniques, and procedures (TTP). Units, leaders, and individuals train to standard on their assigned missions, first as an organic unit and then as an integrated component of a team. Operational deployments, and major training opportunities such as major training exercises, CTCs, CTC-like training, and external evaluations (EXEVAL) provide rigorous, realistic, and stressful training and operational experience under actual or simulated combat and operational conditions to enhance unit readiness and produce bold, innovative leaders. Simultaneously, individual soldiers, NCOs, warrant officers, officers, and the civilian work force are responsible for training themselves through personal self-development. Training is a continuous, lifelong endeavor that produces competent, confident, disciplined, and adaptive soldiers and leaders with the warrior ethos in our Army. Commanders have the ultimate responsibility to train soldiers and develop leaders who can adjust to change with confidence and exploit new situations, technology, and developments to their advantage. The result of this Army-wide team effort is a training and leader development system that is unrivaled in the world. Effective training produces the force—soldiers, leaders, and units—that can successfully execute any assigned mission.

V. Leader Training and Development

The Army is a profession, the Profession of Arms. Warfighting in defense of U. S. values and interests is the core competency of this profession. As a profession, the development of each member becomes the foundation, involving a lifelong devotion to duty both while in uniform and upon return to the civilian life. Professional development involves more than mastering technical skills. What is uniquely distinct to the military profession is its emphasis on not only what is to be accomplished, but how it is accomplished and with the full realization that the profession of arms may require of its members, the supreme sacrifice. Professional development extends to inculcating the Army values of Loyalty, Duty, Respect, Selfless Service, Integrity, Honor, and Personal Courage in every soldier to create a warrior ethos based on camaraderie and service to our Nation. Professional education provides the foundation involving a variety of training domains ranging from

Army Training and Leader Development Model

Ref: FM 7-0, pp. 1-5 to 1-12.

The Army Training and Leader Development Model centers on developing trained and ready units led by competent and confident leaders. The model identifies three core domains that shape the critical learning experiences throughout a soldier's and leader's career are the operational, institutional, and self-development domains.

Army Training and Leader Development Model

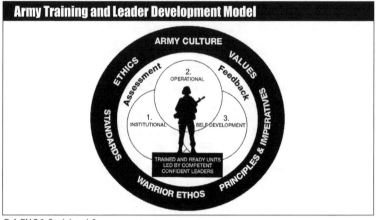

Ref: FM 7-0, fig. 1-1, p. 1-6.

1. The Institutional Domain

The institutional domain focuses on educating and training soldiers and leaders on the key knowledge, skills, and attributes required to operate in any environment. It includes individual, unit and joint schools, and advanced education.

A. Initial Military Training (IMT)

This training provides the basic skills, knowledge, and task proficiency to become a soldier and subsequently to succeed as members of a small Army unit, contribute to unit mission accomplishment, and survive on the battle-field. IMT is the foundation training given to all personnel upon entering the Army. It provides an ordered transition from being a civilian to becoming a soldier, motivation to become a dedicated and productive member of the Army, and qualification on critical soldier skills & knowledge.

B. Professional Military Education (PME)

PME develops Army leaders. Officer, warrant officer, and NCO training and education is a continuous, career-long, learning process that integrates structured programs of instruction—resident at the institution and non-resident via distributed learning at home station. PME is progressive and sequential, provides a doctrinal foundation, and builds on previous training, education and operational experiences. PME provides hands-on technical, tactical, and leader training focused to ensure leaders are prepared for success in their next assignment and higher-level responsibility.

- **Officer Education System (OES)**. Army officers must lead and fight; be tactically and technically competent; possess leader skills; understand how the Army operates as a service, as well as a component of a joint, multinational, or interagency organization; demonstrate confidence, integrity, critical judgment, and responsibility; operate in a complex, uncertain, and rapidly changing environment; build effective teams amid continuous organizational and technological change; and solve problems creatively. OES develops officers who are self-aware and adaptive to lead Army units to mission success.

- **Warrant Officer Education System (WOES).** Warrant officers are the Army's technical experts. WOES develops a corps of highly specialized experts and trainers who are fully competent and proficient operators, maintainers, administrators, and managers of the Army's equipment, support activities, and technical systems.
- **NCO Education System (NCOES).** NCOES trains NCOs to lead and train soldiers, crews, and subordinate leaders who work and fight under their leadership. NCOES provides hands-on technical, tactical, and leader training focused to ensure that NCOs are prepared for success in their next assignment and higher-level responsibility.
- **Functional Training.** In addition to the preceding PME courses, there are functional courses available in both resident and non-resident distributed learning modes that enhance functional skills for specific duty positions. Examples are Battalion S2, Battalion Motor Officer, First Sergeant, Battle Staff NCO, and Airborne courses.

2. The Operational Domain

The operational domain includes home station training, combat training center rotations, joint training exercises, and operational deployments that satisfy national objectives. Each of these actions provides foundational experiences for soldiers, leaders, and unit development.

The unit commander is responsible for the wartime readiness of all elements in the formation. The commander is, therefore, the primary trainer of the organization, responsible for ensuring that all training is conducted in accordance with the unit's mission essential task list (METL) to the Army standard. This is the commander's number one priority.

A great strength of the U.S. Army is its professional NCO Corps who take pride in being responsible for the individual training of soldiers, crews, and small teams. They ensure the continuation of the soldierization process of new soldiers when they arrive in the unit. Within the unit, the NCO support channel (leadership chain) parallels and complements the chain of command. It is a channel of communication and supervision from the command sergeant major (CSM) to first sergeant and then to other NCOs and enlisted personnel. In addition, NCOs train soldiers to the non-negotiable standards published in MTPs and soldiers training publications (STP).

Unit training consists of three components: collective training that is derived directly from METL and MTPs, leader development that is embedded in the collective training tasks and in discrete individual leader focused training, and individual training that establishes, improves, and sustains individual soldier proficiency in tasks directly related to the unit METL.

3. The Self-Development Domain

The self-development domain, both structured and informal, focuses on taking those actions necessary to reduce or eliminate the gap between operational and institutional experiences. Throughout this lifelong learning and experience process, there is formal and informal assessment and feedback of performance to prepare leaders for their next level of responsibility.

Self-development is continuous and should be emphasized in both institutional and operational assignments. Successful self-development requires a team effort. Self-development starts with an assessment of individual strengths, weaknesses, potential, and developmental needs. Commanders and leaders provide feedback to enable subordinates to determine the reasons for their strengths and weaknesses. Together, they prioritize self-development goals and determine courses of action to improve performance.

institutional schooling, self-study, and operational experience to personal interaction with superiors, peers, and subordinates. All of these interactions are essential in developing and understanding training and leader development for warfighting.

Competent and confident leaders are a prerequisite to the successful training of ready units. It is important to understand that leader training and leader development are integral parts of unit readiness. Leaders are inherently soldiers first and should be technically and tactically proficient in basic soldier skills. They are also adaptive, capable of sensing their environment, adjusting the plan when appropriate, and properly applying the proficiency acquired through training.

Leader development is the deliberate, continuous, sequential, and progressive process, grounded in Army values, that grows soldiers and civilians into competent and confident leaders capable of decisive action. Leader development is achieved through the lifelong synthesis of the knowledge, skills, and experiences gained through institutional training and education, organizational training, operational experience, and self-development. Commanders play the key role in leader development that ideally produces tactically and technically competent, confident, and adaptive leaders who act with boldness and initiative in dynamic, complex situations to execute mission-type orders achieving the commander's intent.

VI. The Role of MACOMS, Corps, Divisions, USAR Regional Commands and ARNG Area Commands in Training

These commands, whether oriented along operational, functional, or specialty missions, have unique responsibilities for managing and supporting training. Their most important contribution to training is to establish stability in the training environment by maintaining focus on warfighting tasks, identifying and providing resources, protecting planned training, and providing feedback that produces good training and develops good trainers and leaders.

The corps' and divisions' fundamental basis for organization and operations is combined arms operations. They conduct these operations increasingly in JIM environments. Corps commanders' training focus is on warfighting, to include joint operations, and training division cdrs and corps separate commands and brigades.

VII. Reserve Component Training

The RC represent a large portion of the Army's deterrence and warfighting power. They are an integral part of the force. However, available training time has a significant impact on RC training. RC units have a limited number of available training days. Geographic dispersion of units also impacts RC training. An average reserve battalion is spread over a 150- to 300-mile radius. Additionally, most reserve units travel an average of 150 miles to the nearest training area. Individual soldiers often travel an average of 40 miles to their training sites.

RC units have premobilization readiness and postmobilization training requirements. Premobilization readiness plans must be developed and approved for the current fiscal and training year. Similarly, postmobilization plans must be developed and approved for units with deployment missions. For example, the RC focuses premobilization training for infantry, armor and cavalry units on platoon and lower level maneuver and collective tasks and drills. Postmobilization training focuses on platoon gunnery, company team, and higher-level collective tasks. IMT and professional military education requirements for individual reserve officers and soldiers approximate that of the active Army with training provided by the institution. In sum, RC units focus on fewer tasks done to standard during premobilization training.

II. Battle Focused Training

Ref: FM 7-0 Training the Force, chap. 2.

Commanders train their units to be combat ready. Training is their number one priority. Commanders achieve this using tough, realistic, and challenging training. At every echelon, commanders must train their unit to the Army standard. Battle focus enables the commander to train units for success on the battlefield. Using the Army Training Management Cycle, the commander continuously plans, executes, and assesses the state of training in the unit. This cycle provides the framework for commanders to develop their unit's METL, establish training priorities, and allocate resources.

I. Principles of Training

There are 10 principles of training.

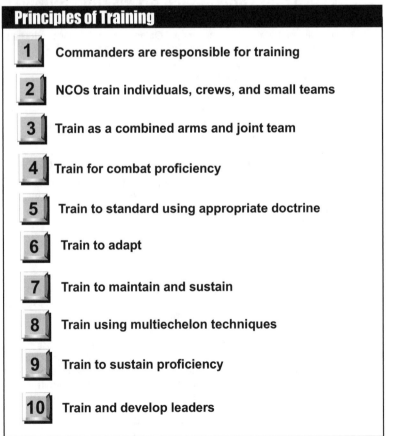

Principles of Training

1. Commanders are responsible for training

2. NCOs train individuals, crews, and small teams

3. Train as a combined arms and joint team

4. Train for combat proficiency

5. Train to standard using appropriate doctrine

6. Train to adapt

7. Train to maintain and sustain

8. Train using multiechelon techniques

9. Train to sustain proficiency

10. Train and develop leaders

Ref: FM 7-0, fig. 2-1, p. 2-1.

1. Commanders are Responsible for Training

Commanders are responsible for the training and performance of their soldiers and units. They are the primary training managers and trainers for their organization, are actively engaged in the training process, and adhere to the 10 principles of training. To accomplish their training responsibility, commanders must—

- Be present at training to maximum extent possible
- Base training on mission requirements
- Train to applicable Army standards
- Assess current levels of proficiency
- Provide the required resources
- Develop and execute training plans that result in proficient individuals, leaders, and units

Commanders delegate authority to NCOs in the support channel as the primary trainers of individuals, crews, and small teams. Commanders hold NCOs responsible for conducting standards-based, performance-oriented, battle-focused training and provide feedback on individual, crew, and team proficiency.

2. NCOS Train Individuals, Crews, and Small Teams

NCOs continue the soldierization process of newly assigned enlisted soldiers, and begin their professional development. NCOs are responsible for conducting standards-based, performance-oriented, battle-focused training. They–

- Identify specific individual, crew, and small team tasks that support the unit's collective mission essential tasks
- Plan, prepare, rehearse, and execute training
- Evaluate training and conduct AARs to provide feedback to the commander on individual, crew, and small team proficiency. Senior NCOs coach junior NCOs to master a wide range of individual tasks

3. Train as a Combined Arms and Joint Team

The Army provides a JFC with trained and ready forces that expand the command's range of military options in full spectrum operations. Army commanders tailor and train forces to react quickly to any crisis. Army forces provide a JFC the capability to—

- Seize areas previously denied by the enemy.
- Dominate land operations.
- Provide support to civil authorities.

Army forces seldom operate unilaterally. Joint interdependence from the individual, crew, and small team to the operational level requires training to develop experienced, adaptive leaders, soldiers, and organizations prepared to operate with joint, and multinational forces and to provide interagency unity of effort.

The fundamental basis for the organization and operation of Army forces is combined arms. Combined arms is the integrated application of several arms to achieve an effect on the enemy that is greater than if each arm was used against the enemy separately or in sequence. Integration involves arrangement of battlefield actions in time, space, and purpose to produce maximum relative effects of combat power at a decisive place and time. Through force tailored organizations, commanders and their staffs integrate and synchronize the battlefield operating systems (BOS) to achieve combined arms effects and accomplish the mission.

Today's Army doctrine requires teamwork at all echelons. Well-trained Army combined arms teams can readily perform in JIM environments. When committed to battle, each unit must be prepared to execute operations without additional training or lengthy adjustment periods. Leaders must regularly practice of habitually associated combat arms, combat support, and combat service support capabilities. Teams can only achieve combined arms proficiency and cohesiveness when they train together. Similarly, peacetime relationships must mirror wartime task organization to the greatest extent possible.

Commanders are responsible for training all warfighting systems. The full integration of the combined arms team is attained through the task organization approach to training management. Task organizing is a temporary grouping of forces designed to accomplish a particular mission. This approach acknowledges that the maneuver commander integrates and synchronizes the BOS. In short, the maneuver commander, assisted by higher echelon leaders, forges the combined arms team.

The commander of the task-organized force must develop a training plan that addresses two complementary challenges. The commander's training plan must achieve combined arms proficiency and ensure functional training proficiency of the combat arms, combat support, and combat service support units of the task force. Combined arms proficiency requires effective integration of BOS functions.

4. Train for Combat Proficiency

The goal of all training is to achieve the standard. This develops and sustains combat capable warfighting organizations. To achieve this, units must train to standard under realistic conditions. Achieving standards requires hard work by commanders, staff officers, unit leaders, and soldiers. Within the confines of safety and common sense, commanders and leaders must be willing to accept less than perfect results initially and demand realism in training. They must integrate such realistic conditions as imperfect intelligence; reduced communications; smoke; noise; rules of engagement; simulated nuclear, biological, and chemical environments; battlefield debris; loss of key leaders; civilians on the battlefield; JIM requirements; and varying extremes in weather. They must seize every opportunity to move soldiers out of the classroom into the field; fire weapons; maneuver as a combined arms team; and incorporate protective measures against enemy actions. Although CTCs provide the most realistic and challenging training experience in the Army, they must not be viewed as an "end point" in the unit-training life cycle. Rather, they provide a "go to war experience" by which commanders can assess their METL proficiency and determine the effectiveness of their training program.

A. Realistic

Tough, realistic, and intellectually and physically challenging training excites and motivates soldiers and leaders. Realistic training builds competence and confidence by developing and honing skills, and inspires excellence by fostering initiative, enthusiasm, and eagerness to learn. Successful completion of each training phase increases the capability and motivation of individuals and units for more sophisticated and challenging achievement.

B. Performance-Oriented

Units become proficient in the performance of critical tasks and missions by practicing the tasks and missions. Soldiers learn best by doing, using an experiential, hands-on approach. Commanders and subordinate leaders plan training that will provide these opportunities. All training assets and resources, to include training aids, devices, simulators, and simulations (TADSS), must be included in the unit's training strategy.

5. Train to Standard Using Appropriate Doctrine

Training must be done to the Army standard and conform to Army doctrine. If mission tasks involve emerging doctrine or non-standard tasks, commanders establish the tasks, conditions and standards using mission orders and guidance, lessons learned from similar operations, and their professional judgment. The next higher commander approves the creation of the standards for these tasks. FM 3-0 provides the doctrinal foundations; supporting doctrinal manuals describe common TTP that permit commanders and organizations to adjust rapidly to changing situations. Doctrine provides a basis for a common vocabulary across the force. In units, new soldiers will have little time to learn non-standard procedures. Therefore, units must train to the Army standard contained in the MTP and STPs, while applying Army doctrine and current regulatory guidance. When serving as a joint headquarters and conducting joint training Army organizations use joint doctrine and TTP.

6. Train to Adapt

Commanders train and develop adaptive leaders and units, and prepare their subordinates to operate in positions of increased responsibility. Repetitive, standards-based training provides relevant experience. Commanders intensify training experiences by varying training conditions. Training experiences coupled with timely feedback builds competence. Leaders build unit, staff and soldier confidence when they consistently demonstrate competence. Competence, confidence, and discipline promote initiative and enable leaders to adapt to changing situations and conditions. They improvise with the resources at hand, exploit opportunities and accomplish their mission in the absence of orders.

7. Train to Maintain and Sustain

Soldier and equipment maintenance is a vital part of every training program. Soldiers and leaders are responsible for maintaining all assigned equipment and supplies in a high state of readiness to support training or operational missions. Units must be capable of fighting for sustained periods of time with the equipment they are issued. Soldiers must become experts in both the operation and maintenance of their equipment. This link between training and sustainment is vital to mission success.

8. Train Using Multiechelon Techniques

Multiechelon training is the most effective and efficient way of sustaining proficiency on mission essential tasks with limited time and resources. Commanders use multiechelon training to—

- Train leaders, battle staffs, units, and individuals at each echelon of the organization simultaneously
- Maximize use of allocated resources and available time
- Reduce the effects of personnel turbulence. Large-scale training events provide an excellent opportunity for valuable individual, leader, crew, and small unit training

All multiechelon training techniques—

- Require detailed planning and coordination by commanders and leaders at each echelon
- Maintain battle focus by linking individual and collective battle tasks with unit METL tasks, within large-scale training event METL tasks
- Habitually train at least two echelons simultaneously on selected METL tasks

9. Train to Sustain Proficiency

Once individuals and units have trained to a required level of proficiency, leaders must structure individual and collective training plans to re-train critical tasks at the minimum frequency necessary to sustain proficiency. Sustainment training is the key to maintaining unit proficiency through personnel turbulence and operational deployments. MTP and individual training plans are tools to help achieve and sustain collective and individual proficiency. Sustainment training must occur often enough to train new soldiers and minimize skill decay. Army units train to accomplish their missions by frequent sustainment training on critical tasks. Infrequent "peaking" of training for an event (CTC rotation, for example) does not sustain wartime proficiency. Battle focused training is training on wartime tasks. Many of the METL tasks that a unit trains on for its wartime mission are the same as required for a stability operation or support operation that they might execute.

The Band of Excellence

The Band of Excellence is the range of proficiency within which a unit is capable of executing its wartime METL tasks. For RC units the Band of Excellence is the range of proficiency within which a unit is capable of executing its premobilization tasks. Training to sustain proficiency in the Band of Excellence includes training leaders, battle staffs, and small lethal units. Personnel turbulence and availability of resources pose a continuous challenge to maintaining METL proficiency within the Band of Excellence.

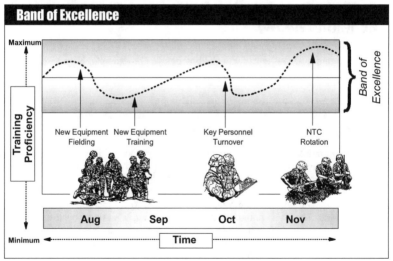

Ref: FM 7-0, fig. 2-4, p. 2-9 (modified).

10. Train and Develop Leaders

Commanders have a duty and execute a vital role in leader training and leader development. They teach subordinates how to fight and how to train. They mentor, guide, listen to, and "think with" subordinates. They train leaders to plan training in detail, prepare for training thoroughly, execute training aggressively, and evaluate short-term training proficiency in terms of desired long-term results. Training and developing leaders is an embedded component of every training event. Nothing is more important to the Army than building confident, competent, adaptive leaders for tomorrow.

II. Commanders and Training

Ref: FM 7-0, pp. 2-10 to 2-13.

Effective training is the number one priority of commanders. The commander is the primary trainer and responsible for the wartime readiness of their formation. In wartime, training continues with a priority second only to combat or to the support of combat operations. Commanders and senior leaders must extract the greatest training value from every training opportunity. Effective training requires the commander's continuous personal time and energy to accomplish the following—

A. Develop and Communicate a Clear Vision

The senior leader's training vision provides the direction, purpose, and motivation necessary to prepare individuals and organizations to win in battle. It is based on a comprehensive understanding of—

• Mission, doctrine, and history

• Enemy/threat capabilities

• Operational environment

• Organizational and personnel strengths and weaknesses

• Training environment

B. Train One Echelon Below and Evaluate Two Echelons Below

Commanders are responsible for training their own unit and one echelon below. Commanders evaluate units two echelons below. For example, brigade commanders train battalions and evaluate companies; battalion commanders train companies and evaluate platoons.

C. Require Subordinates to Understand and Perform their Roles in Training

Since good training results from leader involvement, one of the commander's principal roles in training is to teach subordinate trainers how to train and how to fight. The commander provides the continuing leadership that focuses on the organization's wartime mission. The commander assigns officers the primary responsibility for collective training and NCOs the primary responsibility for individual, crew, and small team training. The commander, as the primary trainer, uses multiechelon techniques to meld leader, battle staff, and individual training requirements into collective training events, while recognizing the overlap in training responsibilities. Commanders teach, coach, and mentor subordinates throughout.

D. Train All Elements to be Proficient on their Mission Essential Tasks

Commanders must integrate and train to Army standard all BOS, within and supporting their command, on their selected mission essential tasks. An important requirement for all leaders is to project training plans far enough into the future and to coordinate resources with sufficient lead time.

E. Develop Subordinates

Competent and confident leaders build cohesive organizations with a strong chain of command, high morale, and good discipline. Therefore, commanders create leader development programs that develop warfighter professionalism— skills and knowledge. They develop their subordinates' confidence and empower them to make independent, situational-based decisions on the battlefield. Commanders assist subordinates with a self-development program and share experienced insights that encourage subordinates to study and learn their profession. They train leaders to plan training in detail, prepare for training thoroughly, execute aggressively, and evaluate short-term training proficiency in terms of desired long-term results.

F. Involve Themselves Personally In Planning, Preparing, Executing, and Assessing Training

The senior commander resources training and protects subordinate commanders' training time. They are actively involved in planning for future training. They create a sense of stability throughout the organization by protecting approved training plans from training distracters. Senior commanders protect the time of subordinate commanders allowing them to be present at training as much as possible. Subordinate commanders are responsible for executing the approved training to standard. Senior commanders are present during the conduct of training as much as possible and provide experienced feedback to all participants.

G. Demand Training Standards are Achieved

Leaders anticipate that some tasks will not be performed to standard. Therefore, they design time into training events to allow additional training on tasks not performed to standard. It is more important to train to standard on a limited number of critical tasks, rather than attempting and failing to achieve the standard on too many tasks, rationalizing that corrective action will occur during some later training period. Soldiers will remember the enforced standard, not the one that was discussed.

H. Ensure Proper Task and Event Discipline

Senior leaders ensure junior leaders plan the correct task-to-time ratio. Too many tasks guarantee nothing will get trained to standard and no time is allocated for retraining. Too many events result in improper preparation and recovery.

I. Foster a Command Climate that is Conducive to Good Training

Commanders create a climate that rewards subordinates who are bold and innovative trainers. They challenge the organization and each individual to train to full potential. Patience and coaching are essential ingredients to ultimate achievement of the Army standard.

J. Eliminate Training Distractions

The commander who has planned and resourced a training event is responsible to ensure participation by the maximum number of soldiers. Administrative support burdens cannot be ignored, however, they can be managed using an effective time management system. Senior commanders must support subordinate commanders' efforts to train effectively by eliminating training distracters and reinforcing the requirement for all assigned personnel to be present during training.

III. Top-Down/Bottom-Up Approach

The top-down/bottom-up approach to training is a team effort in which senior leaders provide training focus, direction and resources, and junior leaders provide feedback on unit training proficiency, identify specific unit training needs, and execute training to standard in accordance with the approved plan. It is a team effort that maintains training focus, establishes training priorities, and enables effective communication between command echelons.

IV. Battle Focus

Battle focus is a concept used to derive peacetime training requirements from assigned and anticipated missions. The priority of training in units is to train to standard on the wartime mission. Battle focus guides the planning, preparation, execution, and assessment of each organization's training program to ensure its members train as they are going to fight. Battle focus is critical throughout the entire training process and is used by commanders to allocate resources for training based on wartime and operational mission requirements. Battle focus enables commanders and staffs at all echelons to structure a training program that copes with non-mission related requirements while focusing on mission essential training activities. It is recognition that a unit cannot attain proficiency to standard on every task whether due to time or other resource constraints. However, commanders can achieve a successful training program by consciously focusing on a reduced number of critical tasks that are essential to mission accomplishment.

V. Army Training Management Cycle

The foundation of the training process is the Army Training Management Cycle, and is detailed in subsequent sections of this chapter.

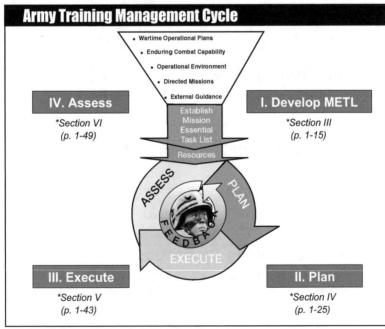

Army Training Management Cycle

- Wartime Operational Plans
- Enduring Combat Capability
- Operational Environment
- Directed Missions
- External Guidance

IV. Assess
Section VI
(p. 1-49)

Establish Mission Essential Task List

Resources

I. Develop METL
Section III
(p. 1-15)

ASSESS
PLAN
FEEDBACK
EXECUTE

III. Execute
Section V
(p. 1-43)

II. Plan
Section IV
(p. 1-25)

Ref: FM 7-0, fig. 2-7, p. 2-15.

Ref: FM 7-0 Training the Force, chap. 3.

I. METL Development Process

A mission essential task is a collective task in which an organization has to be proficient to accomplish an appropriate portion of its wartime operational mission. Army organizations, whether they are AC or RC, Modification Table of Organization and Equipment (MTOE) or Table of Distribution and Allowances (TDA), cannot achieve and sustain proficiency on every possible training task. The commander must identify those tasks that are essential to accomplishing the organization's wartime operational mission. Battle-focused METL identifies those tasks that are essential to the accomplishment of the unit's wartime operational mission and provides the foundation for the unit's training program.

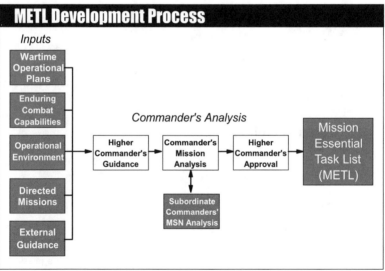

Ref: FM 7-0, Fig. 3-1, p. 3-3.

All company level and above units develop a METL that is approved by its designated wartime commander. Detachments, organized with a commander and under a distinct MTOE or TDA, also develop a METL.

METL development is the catalyst that keeps Army training focused on wartime operational missions. Applying the METL development-

- Focuses the unit's training on essential tasks
- Provides a forum for professional discussion and leader development among senior, subordinate and adjacent (peer) commanders concerning the linkage between mission and training
- Enables subordinate commanders and key NCOs to crosswalk collective, leader and individual tasks to the mission
- Leads to "buy-in" and commitment of unit leaders to the organization's training plan

A. Inputs to METL Development

There are five primary inputs to METL development.

1. Wartime Operational Plans

The most critical inputs to METL development are the organization's wartime operational and contingency plans. The missions and related information provided in these plans are key to determining essential training tasks.

2. Enduring Combat Capabilities

The fundamental reason for the organization and operation of Army forces is to generate effects of combined arms in order to contribute to successful execution of wartime operational missions. To do this, Army commanders form combat, CS, and CSS forces into cohesive teams through training for combat proficiency. Enduring combat capabilities are the unique contribution each unit makes to ensure the Army successfully accomplishes any mission anytime anywhere.

3. Operational Environment

The operational environment has six dimensions; Threat, Political, Unified Action, Land Combat Operations, Information, and Technology. Each dimension affects how Army forces combine, sequence, and conduct military operations. Commanders tailor forces, employ diverse capabilities, and support different missions to succeed in this complex environment.

4. Directed Missions

Army organizations are frequently directed to conduct a mission other than its assigned wartime operational mission. These missions range from major combat operations to providing humanitarian assistance or other types of stability and support operations.

5. External Guidance

External guidance serves as an additional source of training tasks that relate to an organization's wartime operational mission. Some examples are-

- Higher headquarters directives
- MTP
- Force integration plans
- Army Universal Task List (AUTL)
- Universal Joint Task List (UJTL)

In some cases, external guidance identifies tasks that make up the mission (for example, MTPs). In others, they specify additional tasks that relate to the mission (for example, mobilization plans, directed stability operations or support operations).

In similar type organizations, METL may vary significantly because of different missions or geographical locations. For example, a power projection organization may identify strategic deployment requirements as critical deployment tasks while a forward-deployed organization may identify tactical deployment requirements (such as rapid assembly and tactical road marches) as critical deployment tasks. Geography may also influence the selection of different mission essential tasks for units with missions in tropical, cold, or desert environments.

B. Commander's Analysis

The commander's analysis of wartime operational plans, and others primary input to the METL, identify those tasks critical for wartime mission accomplishment. Higher commanders provide guidance to help their subordinate commanders focus this analysis. Commanders coordinate the results of their analysis with subordinate and adjacent commanders. The higher commander approves the METL. This process provides the means to coordinate, link, and integrate a wartime operational mission focused METL throughout the organization.

To illustrate the METL development process, the following brigade wartime mission statement forms the start point for determining the most important training tasks: At C-day, H-hour, Brigade deploys: On order, conducts combat operations assigned by higher headquarters.

The commander reviews the wartime operational mission statement and other primary input to the METL, and identifies all of the training tasks. Together, these five sources provide the total list of possible training tasks. The commander then narrows down the list of all derived tasks to those tasks critical for mission accomplishment. These tasks become the brigade's METL.

II. Battle Tasks

After review and approval of subordinate organizations' METL, the senior commander selects battle tasks. A battle task is a staff or subordinate organization mission essential task that is so critical that its accomplishment will determine the success of the next higher organization's mission essential task. Battle tasks are selected for each METL task. Battle tasks define the training tasks that—

- Integrate the BOS
- Receive the highest priority for resources such as ammunition, training areas and facilities, materiel, and funds
- Receive emphasis during evaluations directed by senior headquarters

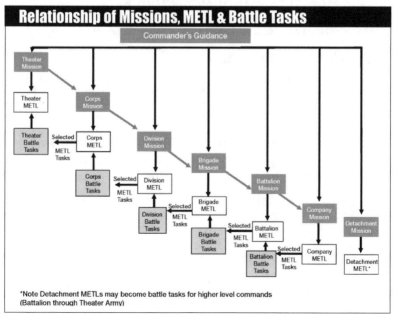

Relationship of Missions, METL & Battle Tasks

*Note Detachment METLs may become battle tasks for higher level commands (Battalion through Theater Army)

Ref: FM 7-0, fig. 3-10, p. 3-14.

III. METL Development Fundamentals

Ref: FM 7-0, pp. 3-5 to 3-8.

The following fundamentals apply to METL development-

- The METL is derived from the organization's wartime plans and related tasks in external guidance
- Mission essential tasks must apply to the entire organization. METL does not include tasks assigned solely to subordinate organizations
- Each organization's METL must support and complement the METL of higher headquarters
- The availability of resources does not affect METL development. The METL is an unconstrained statement of the tasks required to accomplish wartime missions.
- Commanders direct operations and integrate the BOS through plans and orders.

A. Reserve Component METL Development

The METL development process is the same for AC and RC organizations. RC METL development recognizes that RC units have less than 20 percent of the training time available to their AC counterparts. Therefore, battle focus is essential so that RC commanders can concentrate their time on the most critical wartime training requirements. RC units often operate under a chain of command different from their wartime chain of command. The associate AC chain of command assigns missions, provides wartime mission guidance, and approves METLs. The state adjutant general or regional support groups review and coordinate RC METLs. They resource training and ensure that mission training tasks are executed and evaluated. Continental U.S. Armies (CONUSAs) approve the METL for selected RC units. The peacetime chain of command approves the remainder of RC unit METLs.

B. Echelon Above Division/Echelon Above Corps (EAD/EAC) METL Development

In a similar manner, commanders of EAD/EAC organizations must use the battle focus concept and METL development process to focus their training.

C. TDA METL Development

Battle focus is equally applicable to TDA organizations. Senior leaders of TDA organizations derive METL from critical peacetime or wartime missions. Mission essential tasks may be either critical training tasks or operational activities. In short, they represent the tasks required to accomplish the TDA organization's mission.

D. METL Development for Directed Missions

When an organization is directed to conduct a mission other than its assigned wartime operational mission (such as a stability operation or support operation), the training management cycle still applies. Directed missions can span the full spectrum of operations. For MTOE organizations, directed missions could range from major combat operations to providing humanitarian assistance or other types of stability operations and support operations. For TDA organizations, directed missions can range from mobilization to installation force protection operations.

Using their wartime METL as the foundation, commanders who are directed to change their mission conduct a mission analysis, identify METL tasks, and assess training proficiency for the directed mission. The mission analysis of the newly assigned mission could change the unit's METL, training focus, and the strategy to achieve proficiency for METL tasks.

In cases where mission tasks involve emerging doctrine or nonstandard tasks, commanders establish tasks, conditions, and standards using mission orders and guidance, lessons learned from similar operations, and their professional judgment. Senior commanders approve the established standards for these tasks as part of the normal METL approval process. If time permits prior to deployment, units should execute a mission rehearsal exercise (MRE) with all participating units.

Upon redeployment from a directed mission, commanders conduct a mission analysis consistent with the training management cycle to reestablish proficiency in the unit's wartime operational METL. Senior commanders must take into account the additional time this reintegration process may take. Battle focus guides the planning, preparation, execution, and assessment of each organization's training program to ensure its members train as they will fight.

E. Joint METL (JMETL) Development

Army organizations often provide Army forces within joint force formations. The missions and JMETL of such formations are derived from the Universal Joint Task List by the joint force commander and service component commanders, and are approved by the combatant commander.

A selected Army headquarters may be designated as a JTF headquarters, joint forces land component headquarters (JFLC) or Army Forces (ARFOR) headquarters. This requires the designated Army headquarters to develop a JMETL. The Army headquarters commander crosswalks the JMETL with the current Army headquarters and subordinate unit METLs. Joint training manuals provide an overview of the joint training system (JTS), and assists in-

• Developing joint training requirements

• Planning joint training

• Executing joint training

• Assessing joint proficiency

F. Staff METL Development

Staff elements at each headquarters develop a METL to address mission essential tasks in their areas of responsibility. In addition to staff METLs, organizations may develop a METL for each separate command post (for example tactical, main, and rear). The organization's commander or chief of staff approves the staff METL. Organizations that conduct daily support functions also prepare a METL. The METL for these support organizations must address the differences between peacetime and wartime operating conditions. For example, a CSS unit may operate during peacetime from a permanent facility with some major supplies provided via contract transportation and automation systems operated using commercial telephone systems. A wartime environment, however, may require support missions to be accomplished under austere conditions on an active battlefield.

G. Task-Organized Units

The METL for units habitually task organized must be coordinated during the development process. This requirement reinforces the training fundamental that combined arms teams will train as they fight. A key component of the senior commander's METL approval process is determining if each subordinate organization has properly coordinated its METL. A support organization's METL must identify these wartime requirements and include them in their training plans.

IV. METL Linked Training Strategy
Ref: FM 7-0, pp. 3-10 to 3-13.

The METL provides the foundation for the organization's training plans. The METL is stabilized once approved. The commander is responsible for developing a training strategy that will maintain unit proficiency for all tasks designated as mission essential.

Commanders involve subordinate commanders and their CSM/1SG in METL development to create a team approach to battle focused training. Subordinate participation develops a common understanding of the organization's critical wartime requirements so METLs throughout the organization are mutually support-ing. Subordinate commanders can subsequently apply insights gained during preparation of the next higher headquarters' METL to the development of their own METL. The CSM/1SG and key NCOs must understand the organization's collective METL so that they can integrate individual tasks into each collective mission essential task during METL based training.

After the commander designates the collective mission essential tasks required to accomplish the organization's wartime operational mission, the CSM/1SG, in conjunction with key NCOs, develop a supporting individual task list for each mission essential task. Soldier training publications and MTPs are major source documents for selecting appropriate individual tasks.

There should be no attempt to prioritize tasks within the METL. All METL tasks are equally essential to ensure mission accomplishment. However, all tasks may not require equal training time or resources. The commander allocates training re-sources to ensure the organization's METL proficiency remains within the Band of Excellence.

Commanders realize when allocating training time and resources that there are some non-mission related requirements that are critical to the health, welfare, individual readiness, and cohesiveness of a well trained unit. Commanders must carefully select, in conjunction with the CSM/1SG, which non-mission related requirements are critical to the unit. They emphasize the priority of METL training and find opportunities to include non-mission related requirements in the training plan.

Commanders develop effective training strategies when they crosswalk collective, leader and individual tasks to each METL task with subordinate commanders, CSMs/1SGs, and other key officer and NCO leaders.

Training Objectives

After mission essential tasks are selected, commanders identify supporting training objectives for each task. The resulting training consists of—

A. Task
A clearly defined and measurable activity accomplished by organizations and individuals.

B. Condition(s)
The circumstances and environment in which a task is to be performed.

C. Standard
The minimum acceptable proficiency required in the performance of a particular training task.

The conditions and standards for many major collective training tasks are identified in applicable MTPs.

Development of Training Objectives

Ref: TC 25-101, p. 2-20 to 2-24.

After identifying battalion and company METLs, supporting platoon and squad collective tasks, and supporting soldier and leader tasks, leaders establish supporting conditions and standards for each task. The resulting training objective describes the desired outcome of a training activity.

Local conditions vary. Commanders must therefore modify conditions statements to fit their training environments and assessments of their units' level of proficiency. The goal is to create as realistic and demanding a training environment as possible with the resources available.

To adapt a conditions statement, the commander should take the following steps:

1. Read the existing MTP or SM statement. (It is deliberately general because a more specific conditions statement may not apply to all units.)

2. Read the applicable references with suggested support requirements and identify the resources needed to train the task.

3. Consider the local situation — ammunition available, OPFOR, time, terrain, ranges, TADSS, and weather conditions.

4. Prepare a revised conditions statement. Conditions prescribed should be realistic and practical. If conditions are considerably different from those stated in the MTP, the commander must consider whether the standards can be met or should be modified. Regardless, the conditions should be adjusted so that the standards remain appropriate to the task.

The conditions statement will include comments on one or more of the following:

- Status and capability of threat forces
- Equipment, material, tools, or other resources allocated for use in performing the task
- References, checklists, and other memory aids for use during actual task performance
- Physical or environmental conditions; for example, darkness, dense tropical forests, cold weather, or NBC conditions
- Assistance available during performance of the task
- Time allocated for task performance
- Restrictions or limitations

The standards for most tasks may be found in applicable MTPs and SMs. These standards for task performance are the minimum Army standards. For tasks without published training objectives, the following documents will assist in their development:

- DA Pamphlet 350-38
- Deployment or mobilization plans
- General defense plans
- Army, major Army command (MACOM), and local regulations
- Local standing operating procedures (SOPs)
- Equipment TMs and FMs

CS and CSS unit commanders should structure daily operations so they replicate how business will be conducted during war. For example, a counterintelligence team from the military intelligence (MI) battalion supports the brigade's operational security (OPSEC) program in garrison through OPSEC awareness and vulnerability assessments; the FSB will routinely have maintenance support teams from the maintenance company operate with supported unit's organic personnel.

V. Battalion / Company-Level METL Development

Ref: TC 25-101, p. 2-8 to 2-16.

Battalion-Level METL Development Process

1, The battalion commander receives the brigade mission and METL and analyzes the mission to identify specified and implied tasks. He also reviews war plans and external directives to help identify those tasks.

2. Restates the unit's wartime mission.

3. Determines and selects the tasks critical for wartime mission accomplishment, which becomes the unit's METL.

4. Gets and approves the unit's METL from the brigade commander.

5. Provides the approved METL to his staff and company commanders.

Using the same procedures, the battalion staff and company commanders select METL tasks which are approved by the battalion commander.

Ref: FM 25-101, p. 2-3.

The METL is not prioritized. It may be changed or adjusted if wartime missions change. Cdrs reexamine the METL periodically to ensure it still supports the wartime mission.

The METL must support and complement the METL of the next higher headquarters and the supported wartime unit for CS and CSS units. This is especially important for battalion and lower units assigned to echelons above division; for example, a supply and services company, general support.

Key points about the METL:

- Must be understood by the CSM and key NCOs so that they can integrate soldier tasks
- Must apply to the entire unit
- May vary for like units because of different wartime missions or locations
- Must be briefed to and approved by the next higher wartime commander. Some RC units may be unable to conduct in-person briefings to their higher wartime headquarters. In those cases, commanders must use other means such as messages or mail to get their METL approved.

Other points concerning METL development:

- Company is the lowest level unit that prepares a METL
- Battalion staffs develop staff METLs which are approved by the battalion commander. Battalion commanders must ensure staff, supporting slice, and company METLs are properly coordinated and mutually supporting.
- Commanders create a team approach to METL development by involving all subordinate leaders
- Combat task organizations may be tailored as heavy, light, special operations, or any combination to meet specific mission require-merits. When mission, enemy, terrain, troops, and time available (METT-T) dictate changes in a force mix, such as heavy and light, cdrs must understand each unit's capabilities and limitations when reexamining METL. The same applies to joint/combined operations.

Integration of Soldier, Leader & Collective Training
Ref: TC 25-101, p. 2-8 to 2-16.

Company is the lowest level to have a METL. From the company mission and METL, the platoon leader and platoon sergeant would determine their collective tasks.

1. Selection of Platoon and Squad Collective Tasks
The following process can be used:

- Use mission-to-collective task matrixes found in applicable ARTEP-MTPs to determine platoon collective tasks that support each company mission essential task.

- Determine which collective tasks support more than one company mission essential task to identify high payoff tasks.

- Present selected platoon collective tasks to the commander to obtain his guidance and approval. The commander uses mission, enemy, terrain, troops, and time available (METT-T) analysis, resource availability, and unit status analysis to select the most important platoon tasks.

2. Selection of Leader and Soldier Tasks
Leader tasks can be found in the appropriate soldier training publication (STP), MQS, MTP or SM. CS and CSS leaders may have similar documents available. When no published leader tasks exist, they must develop them using doctrinal manuals, other proponent school publications, and common task manuals. Leaders must determine which subordinate leader tasks will be incorporated into collective training.

Unit leaders select soldier tasks to support squad and platoon collective tasks using collective-to-soldier task matrixes found in appropriate ARTEP MTPs. They do this for each skill level withing the unit.

The CSM and key NCOs review and refine the supporting soldier tasks for each skill level in every MOS within the unit. They pay particular attention to low-density MOS tasks. Leader books are a valuable tool to track tasks for which subordinates must be proficient.

The leaders also identify tasks essential to both the soldiers' duty positions and to duty positions for which they are being cross trained.

Task Approval Matrix for Leader/Soldier Tasks

Soldier to be trained	Task Selection	Review	Approve
1SG	CSM	Co Cdr	Bn Cdr
PSG	1SG	Plt Ldr/Co Cdr	Bn Cdr
Sqd Ldr	PSG	Plt Ldr/1SG	Co Cdr
Tm Ldr	Sqd Ldr	PSG/Plt Ldr	Co Cdr
Soldier	Tm Ldr	Sqd Ldr/PSG	Plt Ldr

Ref: FM 25-101, fig. 2-18, p. 2-11.

VI. The Battlefield Operating Systems (BOSs)

Ref: FM 7-0, pp. 3-8 to 3-9.

A tool that the commander may use to organize his battle tasks is the battlefield operating systems (BOS). The seven BOS are the major functions which occur on the battlefield. All BOS are not equal in all operations, nor do they apply for all tasks. They also are not end in themselves. Mission accomplishment and overall unit performance are what count.

Intelligence

The intelligence system plans, directs, collects, processes, produces, and disseminates intelligence on the threat and the environment; performs intelligence preparation of the battlefield; and other intelligence tasks.

Maneuver

Commanders maneuver forces to create the conditions for tactical and operational success. Maneuver involves movement to achieve positions of advantage with respect to enemy forces. Through maneuver, friendly forces gain the ability to destroy enemy forces or hinder enemy movement by direct and indirect application of firepower or threat of its application.

Fire Support

Fire support consists of fires that directly support land, maritime, amphibious, and special operations forces in engaging enemy forces, combat formations, and facilities in pursuit of tactical and operational objectives. Fire support integrates and synchronizes fires and effects to delay, disrupt, or destroy enemy forces, systems, and facilities. The fire support system includes the collective and coordinated use of target acquisition data, indirect fire weapons, fixed-winged aircraft, electronic warfare, and other lethal and nonlethal means to attack targets.

Air Defense

Air defense protects the force from air and missile attack and aerial surveillance. It prevents enemies from interdicting friendly forces while freeing commanders to synchronize maneuver and fire power.

Mobility/Countermobility/Survivability (MCS)

Mobility operations preserve the freedom of maneuver for friendly forces. Mobility missions include breaching obstacles, increasing battlefield circulation, improving or building roads, providing bridge and raft support, and identifying routes around contaminated areas. Counter-mobility denies mobility to enemy forces. Survivability operations protect friendly forces from the effects of enemy weapon systems and from natural occurrences. NBC defense measures are essential survivability tasks.

Combat Service Support (CSS)

Combat service support (CSS) provides the physical means with which forces operate, from the production base and replacement centers in the continental United States to soldiers engaged in close combat. CSS includes many technical specialties and functional activities. It includes maximizing the use of host nation infrastructure and contracted support.

Command and Control (C2)

Command and control (C2) has two components -the commander and the C2 system. The C2 system supports the commander's ability to make informed decisions, delegate authority, and synchronize the BOS. Moreover, the C2 system supports the commander's ability to adjust plans for future operations, even while focusing on current operations. Reliable communications are central to C2 systems.

Ref: FM 7-0 Training the Force, chap. 4.

The Planning Process

Planning is an extension of the battle focus concept that links organizational METL with the subsequent preparation, execution, and evaluation of training. A relatively centralized process, planning develops mutually supporting METL based training at all echelons within an organization. The planning process ensures continuous coordination from long-range planning, through short-range and near-term planning, and ultimately leads to training execution. The commander's assessment provides direction and focus to the planning process.

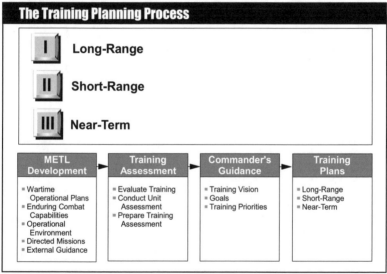

Ref: FM 7-0, fig. 4.1, p. 4-2.

The commander applies two principal inputs at the start of the planning process-the METL and the training assessment. Commanders identify tasks that support the METL. The training assessment compares the organization's current level of training proficiency with the desired level of warfighting proficiency. This desired level is defined in MTPs and other doctrinal literature. Commanders may make conscious decisions, based on their training assessment, to defer training for some tasks in which they are currently well trained. The commander uses subordinate input in making the final determination of the organization's current proficiency on each task. Cdrs assess METL task proficiency as-

- **"T" (trained)** - The unit is trained and has demonstrated its proficiency in accomplishing the task to wartime standards
- **"P" (needs practice)** - The unit needs to practice the task. Performance has demonstrated that the unit does not achieve the standard without some difficulty or has failed to perform some task steps to standard
- **"U" (untrained)** - The unit cannot demonstrate an ability to achieve wartime proficiency

Comparison of Training Plans

I. Long-Range	II. Short-Range	III. Near-Term
■ Disseminate METL and battle tasks ■ Establish training objective for each mission essential task ■ Schedule projected major training events ■ Identify long lead time resources and allocate major resources such as major training area rotations ■ Identify available training support system products and services and identify new services and identify new requirements ■ Coordinate long-range calendars with all supporting agencies to eliminate training detractors ■ Publish long-range guidance and planning calendar ■ Provide basis for command operating budget input ■ Provide long-range training input to higher headquarters	■ Refine and expand upon appropriate portions of long-range plan ■ Cross reference each training event with specific training objectives ■ Identify and allocate short lead time resources such as local training facilities ■ Coordinate short-range calendar with all support agencies ■ Publish short-range guidance and planning calendar ■ Provide input to unit training meetings	■ Refine and expand upon short-range plan through conduct of training meetings ■ Determine best sequence for training ■ Provide specific guidance for trainers ■ Allocate training support system products and services, including training aids, devices, simulators, simulations, and similar resources to specific trainers ■ Publish detailed training schedules ■ Provide basis for executing and evaluating training

Ref: FM 7-0, Fig. 4-3, p. 4-5.

CS and CSS Training

CS and CSS units support combined arms unit training every day through execution of core warfighting functional tasks. Combat arms unit commanders recognize their units cannot conduct combined arms training without their task organized CS and CSS units. For example, combat arms unit commanders recognize their units cannot train without operational equipment, fuel, rations, water, and other supplies and services provided by their supporting CSS units. CS and CSS unit commanders integrate their unit training plans with their supported combat arms units. CS and CSS units daily perform their core warfighting functional tasks, at the section, team, and individual technical MOS level. For example, maintenance support teams routinely perform organizational and direct support automotive, turret, armament, and communications-electronic maintenance and periodic services, as well as provide repair parts support to their supported combat arms units.

Garrison Training

Garrison commanders' training plans incorporate mobilization, postmobilization, deployment, redeployment, and demobilization requirements. Garrison commanders plan and schedule periodic mobilization exercises (MOBEXs), emergency deployment readiness exercises (EDREs), and other contingency plan exercises to sustain proficiency on Title X related tasks outlined in current Army and MACOM regulations. Garrison commanders coordinate their training plans with their supported corps, divisional, and tenant organizations. Garrisons routinely support scheduled unit training deployments and exercise certain deployment tasks such as "operating departure/ arrival airfield control groups and seaports of embarkation and debarkation."

Training Plans

Ref: FM 7-0, chap. 4, pp. 4-4 to 4-6.

Properly developed training plans will-

Maintain a consistent battle focus

Each headquarters in the organization involves its subordinate headquarters in the development of training plans. Based on the higher headquarters' plans, subordinate commanders prepare plans that have a battle focus that is consistent throughout the organization.

Be coordinated with habitually task organized supporting organizations

Brigade combat team and battalion task force commanders plan for coordinated combined arms training of their wartime task organizations. Commanders of habitually task-organized units actively participate in this process and develop complementary training plans. Corps and division commanders require integrated training plans and monitor coordination efforts during the planning process.

Focus on the correct time horizon

Long-range training plans in the AC extend out at least one year. The RC long-range plans consider a minimum of two years. Short-range training plans in the AC normally focus on an upcoming quarter (three months) while RC short-range training plans typically use a one-year planning horizon. Near-term planning for the AC starts approximately eight weeks prior to the execution of training with the RC starting approximately four months prior.

Be concerned with future proficiency

Training plans must focus on raising or sustaining the proficiency of mission essential tasks to the Army standard.

Incorporate risk management into all training plans

The nature of the military profession is inherently dangerous. Commanders must train their units to tough standards under the most realistic conditions possible. Application of the risk management process will not detract from this training goal, but will enhance execution of highly effective, realistic training. Risk management is the process of identifying, assessing, and controlling risks arising from operational factors and making decisions that balance risk costs with mission training benefits. Leaders and soldiers at all echelons use risk management to conserve combat power and resources. Leaders and staffs continuously identify hazards and assess both accident and tactical risks. They then develop and coordinate control measures to mitigate or eliminate hazards. Risk management is a continuous process for each mission or training event. It must be integral to military decisions, tied into each training plan, and become a continuous part of preparation for training.

Establish organizational stability

Changes disrupt training and frustrate subordinate leaders and soldiers. Planning allows organizations to anticipate and incorporate change in a coordinated manner. Stability and predictability are the result of locking in training plans. Senior commanders are responsible to protect subordinate units from change.

Make the most efficient use of resources

The planning process allocates limited time and other resources for training that contributes most to achieving and sustaining wartime proficiency levels.

I. Long-Range Planning

Senior commanders publish their training guidance document sufficiently in advance to provide adequate planning time for both their wartime units and supporting peacetime organizations. Guidance at these senior command echelons is critical to the development and integration of a large number of subordinate AC and RC long-range training plans. Therefore, long lead times are the norm. Each headquarters follows these time lines to allow subordinates adequate time to prepare their plans.

A. Command Training Guidance (CTG)

The CTG is published to document the organization's long-range training plan. It is the training analog of the organization's war plan. It must be read and understood by all commanders, staff officers, and senior NCOs. The CTG is used as a ready reference for the planning, preparation, execution, and evaluation of training throughout the long-range planning period. Examples of topics normally addressed in the CTG are-

- Commander's training philosophy
- METL and associated battle tasks
- Combined arms training
- JIM training, as applicable
- Major training events and exercises
- Organizational Inspection Program (OIP)
- Leader training.
- Battle staff training
- Individual training
- Self development
- Standardization
- Training evaluation and feedback
- New equipment training and other force integration considerations
- Resource allocations
- Training management
- Risk management

B. Long-Range Planning Calendar

Commanders publish the long-range planning calendar concurrently with their CTG. The calendar graphically depicts the schedule of events described in the CTG. Any known major training events or deployments scheduled beyond the normal planning window appear on the long-range planning calendar. To provide extended planning guidance for RC organizations, AC and RC planners routinely forecast major events that require RC participation for up to five years into the future. They include major events, such as annual training periods and overseas deployments for training (ODT), on their long-range planning calendars. Upon publication and approval by higher headquarters, long-range planning calendars are "locked in" to provide planning stability to subordinate organizations. This means that only the approving commander can change a long-range planning calendar. The senior commander agrees to allocate and protect the requisite resources, including time, and the subordinate commanders agree to conduct training to standard in accordance with the published calendar.

Long-Range Planning Cycle

Active Component (AC)

Action	Planning Guidance Publication Date	Future Planning Horizon
MACOM publishes training guidance and major event calendar	18 months prior to start of a 2-year period	Up to 10 years or more
Corps publishes training guidance and major event calendar	12 months prior to start of a 2-year period	5 to 7 years
Division, separate brigade, regiment, and separate group publish CTG and long-range calendar	8 months prior to FY start	CTG at least 1 year, calendar at least 2 years
Installation and community publish long-range calendar	7 months prior to FY start	At least 1 year
Brigade and group publish CTG and long-range calendar	6 months prior to FY start	CTG at least 1 year, calendar at least 18 months
Battalion, squadron, and separate company publish long-range calendar	4 months prior to FY start	At least 1 year

Reserve Component (RC)

Action	Planning Guidance Publication Date	Future Planning Horizon
Division, separate brigade, regiment, and separate group publish CTG and long-range calendar	12 months prior to FY start	CTG at least 2 years, calendar at least 5 years
Brigade and separate battalion publish CTG and long-range calendar	10 months prior to FY start	At least 5 years
Battalion, squadron, and separate company publish long-range calendar	6 months prior to FY start	At least 3 years

Ref: FM 7-0. fig.4-4, p. 4-7 and fig. 4-5, p. 4-8.

Commanders coordinate long-range planning calendars with subordinate commanders, installation support agencies, and any other organizations that can generate training distracters if not fully integrated into the training organization's long-range plan.

Senior leaders at all echelons eliminate nonessential activities that detract from METL based training. In peacetime, however, certain activities occur that do not directly relate to an organization's wartime mission but are important to other Army priorities. An example of this is AC support of ROTC summer training; for the RC, state-directed requirements for Army National Guard units. Senior leaders limit these peacetime activities to the maximum extent possible. Those that are absolutely essential are included in long-range planning documents. When assigned these activities, commanders continually seek mission related training opportunities.

During long-range planning, commanders organize training time to support METL training and concentrate training distracters in support periods. In addition to individual requirements such as leave and medical appointments, units may have temporary duty details and other support functions at the installation level. Failure to consider these requirements early in the planning process can cause disruption to planned mission essential training.

C. Training Events

Commanders link training strategies to executable training plans by designing and scheduling training events. During long-range planning, commanders and their staffs make a broad assessment of the number, type, and duration of training events required to accomplish METL training. The event itself is only a tool to achieve and sustain proficiency on the METL within the Band of Excellence. METL proficiency is the objective. In the subsequent development of short-range training plans, senior commanders fully define training events in terms of METL based training objectives, scenarios, resources, and coordinating instructions. Through training events, senior commanders-

- Develop mission-related scenarios
- Focus the entire organization on several METL tasks
- Integrate all BOS into coordinated combined arms training

Training events are the common building blocks that support an integrated set of METL-related training requirements. Included in long-range training plans, training events form the framework for resource allocation and provide early planning guidance to subordinate commanders and staffs.

By developing and coordinating training events, the organization is able to bring together the training areas and facilities, TSS products and services, OPFOR, observer/controllers, evaluators, and other resources that create the most realistic and battle focused training.

During planning, senior commanders allocate maximum training time to subordinates. Some large-scale training events, however, must be planned so senior commanders can exercise and integrate all BOS within their wartime organizations. The training value of these large-scale exercises to the entire command is increased when subordinate headquarters participate in developing multiechelon training objectives and scenarios. Subordinate commanders use higher headquarters training guidance, their unit METL, and their unit battle tasks to develop their unit training plan. The next higher commander approves, protects, and resources that plan.

The Army has increasingly emphasized externally supported training events in which a headquarters senior to the unit being trained provides assistance in the form of detailed planning, additional resources, and evaluation. Support provided by the higher headquarters usually includes a METL derived scenario with associated training and evaluation outlines (T&EO), an OPFOR, observer/controllers, and evaluation support. The Army's CTCs are prime examples of training opportunities that provide combined arms battle focused training that is externally supported. CTCs provide training events based on each participating organization's METL and conducted under realistic and stressful conditions. Externally supported training events can also be conducted at home station to enable units to focus exclusively on the execution of training.

Organizations can only obtain the full training benefits of externally supported events through carefully planned preparatory training. Therefore, a priority during long-range planning is to develop METL based training programs designed to assist leaders and units in achieving and sustaining METL task proficiency in the Band of Excellence. METL proficiency is the goal, not the completion of the event.

D. Training and Time Management

Ref: FM 7-0, pp. 4-9 to 4-12.

The purpose of time management is to achieve and sustain technical and tactical competence and maintain training proficiency within the Band of Excellence. Time management systems identify, focus, and protect prime time training periods and the resources to support the training so subordinate organizations are able to concentrate on mission essential training. Specific activities will vary between installations according to the local situation and requirements. Time management periods are depicted on applicable long-range planning calendars. One technique, illustrated below, is the "Green-Amber-Red" time management system.

"Green-Amber-Red" Time Management System

Green Cycle

- Training focus primarily on collective tasks with individual and leader tasks integrated during multiechelon training
- Maximum soldier attendance at prime time, mission essential training
- Coincides with availability of major resources and key training facilities or devices
- Administrative and support requirements that keep personnel from participating in training eliminated to the maximum extent possible
- Leaves and passes limited to the minimum essential

Amber Cycle

- Small unit, crew, leader and individual soldier training emphasized
- Provides time for soldier attendance at education and training courses
- Some sub-organizations may be able to schedule collective training
- Scheduling of periodic maintenance services
- Selected personnel diverted to support requirements when all available personnel in organizations in red period are completely committed to support requirements

Red Cycle

- Maximize self development
- Diverts the minimum essential number of personnel to perform administrative and support rqmts
- Sub-organizations take advantage of all training opportunities to conduct individual, leader, and crew training
- Support missions/details accomplished with unit integrity to exercise the chain of command and provide individual training opportunities for first line supervisors, as time permits. Unit taskings can be used to reduce the number of permanent special duty personnel within installations and communities.
- Leaves and passes maximized. When appropriate, block leave may be scheduled.
- Routine medical, dental, and administrative appointments coordinated and scheduled with installation support facilities

Ref: FM 7-0, fig. 4-6, p. 4-11.

A "Green-Red" time management system may be more appropriate for some organizations. Although support requirements vary greatly from installation to installation, the time management system can be modified to accommodate these particular situations. The primary purpose of the time management system is to identify and protect prime time training periods for subordinate organizations.

Likewise, commanders can utilize the Green-Amber-Red or Green-Red time management system for internal organizational use. For example, it may be feasible for organizations in Red periods to meet all support requirements with only a portion of their subordinate units at any given time. In this case, the remaining subordinate units are free to train. A subordinate unit could be assigned an internal Green period. In this manner, organizations can optimize small unit, crew, leader, and individual soldier unit training opportunities.

Preparing the Long-Range Calendar
Ref: TC 25-101, p. 3-7 to 3-8.

3. Long-Range Calendar

Step 1. Post the time mangagement system

Step 2. Post required training events

Step 3. Schedule other requirements

Step 4. Schedule unit-controlled exercises and other training

Ref: FM 25-101, pp. 3-7 to 3-8.

Step 1. Post the time management system

Posting the time management system first highlights prime-time training periods available to the unit, and support periods. Commanders then focus their resource and exercise planning to take advantage of prime-time training. NOTE: Holiday periods to include host-nation holidays must be posted.

Step 2. Post required training events on the calendar

These are requirements that are directed by higher headquarters. These events provide excellent training opportunities for the battalion commander and subordinate leaders. They must take full advantage of these events to select training objectives to be accomplished. The dates of these events should be annotated. If exact dates are unknown, block window periods. Examples of required training events are—

- MAPEX, TEWT, CPX, CFX, FCX, FTX and CTC training rotations
- External evaluations
- Gunnery periods
- Security reaction force duty
- Reserve Officers' Training Corps (ROTC) support
- OPFOR support and training
- RC support (for AC units)

Step 3. Schedule other requirements

Identify other requirements that impact on training. Reduce training distracters by identifying required events early in the planning process. Some examples are-

- Announced inspections, such as technical validation inspections (TVIs), nuclear surety inspections (NSIs), and command inspection program (CIP)
- New equipment fielding to include new equipment training (NET)
- Community and installation support events; for example, parades and displays
- Directed administrative rqmts, such as panographic x-rays and HIV screening

Step 4. Schedule unit-controlled exercises and other training

On the basis of his strategy, the commander schedules events which will improve or sustain METL proficiency, in conjunction with higher headquarters' directed-training requirements. The long-range planning calendar is staffed with outside agencies that can impact on training. It is coordinated with subordinate and higher commanders, installation commanders, and supporting slice units.

E. Live, Virtual, and Constructive (L-V-C) Training

Commanders use a mix of live, virtual, and constructive (L-V-C) training to achieve and sustain unit and staff proficiency on selected METL tasks and supporting unit and staff battle tasks within the Band of Excellence. The goal is to train mission essential tasks to standard and sustain a wartime readiness posture. Battalion level units attain and sustain warfighting proficiency and develop soldier fieldcraft primarily through live training. Brigades and higher units rely more on V-C training events to attain and sustain their warfighting proficiency. In general, commanders at battalion level and lower plan and execute standards based in V-C simulations to-

- Prepare for live "in the dirt" training
- Rehearse selected staff and unit battle tasks and squad, team and crew drills
- Retrain on selected unit battle tasks, supporting squad, team and crew critical tasks, and leader and individual soldier tasks evaluated as either "P" (needs practice) or "U" (untrained)

Battalion commanders leverage V-C training events to accelerate junior leader mastery of tasks directly related to developing tactical competence, confidence, and proficiency that support their unit's METL or supporting critical collective tasks. Similarly, battalion and company commanders look to their CSM, 1SGs and key NCO leaders to leverage V-C training events to accelerate junior NCO and soldier mastery of individual tasks directly related to developing their technical competence, confidence, and proficiency that support their small unit, crew, leader, and individual soldier tasks.

The commander selects the tools that will result in the unit receiving the best training based on available resources. Virtual and constructive training cannot replace all live training. They can, however, supplement, enhance, and complement live training to sustain unit proficiency within the Band of Excellence.

Battalion task force through division/corps/Army forces/joint forces commanders must sustain their battle staffs' wartime proficiency. Leaders and staffs achieve and sustain proficiency primarily through repetitive execution of battle staff drills to standard. Brigade and battalion/task forces may execute live, virtual, and constructive training. The use of virtual and constructive training provides excellent training opportunities for leader training. The repetitive nature of these tools makes them invaluable in training adaptive leaders. Commanders can run multiple iterations of a task, changing only the conditions, to help mature the decision-making and judgment abilities of subordinate leaders.

The intent is to train to standard. It is the commander's responsibility to be familiar with all three of these tools and to select the most applicable within allocated L-V-C resources and available training time. The commander, when planning training, must determine the appropriate mix that meets the unit training requirements and objectives. Units may conduct training using L-V-C training, simultaneously.

F. Training Resources

The commander uses his assessment of METL and battle tasks to determine the resource priorities for training requirements. During both longrange and short-range planning, constrained resources may require deletion of low-priority training requirements, substitution of less costly training alternatives, or a request for additional resources to execute METL training not resourced, and lower priority training. To the extent possible, commanders confirm resources before publishing training plans.

A METL-based events approach to resource planning is used for the allocation of time, facilities, ammunition, funds, fuel products, and other resources. For example, a reasonably close approximation of the future petroleum, oil, and lubricants (POL) (Class III) and repair parts (Class IX) resource requirements (the most significant operations and maintenance costs in a tank battalion) can be calculated for a training event.

The same procedure is followed to determine the costs for each projected training event and totaled into an aggregate training cost for the year.

There is a relationship between the number of miles or hours that an item of equipment, such as a tank, is operated and the dollars required to purchase the repair parts and POL for that piece of equipment. Funding authority to purchase the projected repair parts, fuel products, and other items necessary to support the training mission is allocated to units based on operating tempo (OPTEMPO). The OPTEMPO of an organization is the average annual miles or hours of operation for its major equipment systems. The total annual training cost of the desired list of training events, which represents an OPTEMPO of 800 miles per tank, is then compared with budget projections to determine if the desired training can be fully resourced. If the battalion is not projected to receive sufficient resources to finance the projected list of events, the commander may have to revise the list of events.

The Army relies on live FTXs to provide realistic training. Live fire exercises (LFX), STXs, deployment exercises, and battle drills must be conducted under conditions that replicate actual combat as nearly as possible. This is especially true at battalion level and below. Virtual and constructive training cannot replace live training. They can, however, supplement, enhance, and complement live training to sustain unit proficiency within the Band of Excellence. Based on resources available (such as time, ammunition, simulations, and range availability), commanders determine the right mix and frequency of live, virtual, and constructive training to ensure efficient use of allocated training resources. Brigade size and larger organizations normally plan and execute more virtual and constructive training.

Live, virtual, and constructive training opportunities are integral components of a commander's training strategy to develop competent, confident, and adaptive leaders, battle staffs, and units. A resource analysis allows leaders at all echelons to make training trade-offs, within various budget and program levels, that best support the commander's training strategy.

The unit may be required to conduct fewer FTXs and LFXs (which require higher densities of equipment and higher resource expenditures) and add a mix of simulation exercises to stay within resource constraints and maintain training proficiency within the Band of Excellence. The commander determines the effect these substitutions will have on attaining desired levels of training proficiency. He then provides this information to the next higher commander who will either provide additional resources or approve the constrained resource plan.

By summing up fiscal resource projections of subordinate units, commanders at higher echelons are able to estimate resource requirements necessary to support their training strategies. Similar analyses are conducted to estimate ammunition, facilities, and other resources. Upon completion of the trade-off analysis, the commander includes the resulting events and associated resources in the long-range training plan.

A significant resource consideration in RC planning is the allocation of available training time. Limited training time requires RC commanders to prioritize training requirements. They may have to train fewer tasks so that the Army standard can be attained. RC commanders compensate for lack of training time by carefully distributing requirements over longer periods of time and identifying selected training tasks for execution during postmobilization training.

II. Short-Range Planning

Short-range training plans define in greater detail the broad guidance on training events and other activities contained in the long-range training guidance and long-range calendar. They refine the allocation of resources to subordinate organizations and provide a common basis for preparing nearterm training plans.

A. Short-Range Training Guidance

Each echelon from division through battalion publishes short-range training guidance that enables the commander and staff to prioritize and refine mission essential training guidance contained in the long-range CTG. Commanders must publish the short-range training guidance with sufficient lead time to ensure subordinate units have time to develop their own shortrange training plans. The AC division provides quarterly training guidance (QTG) to subordinate commands and installations at least 90 days prior to the start of each quarter. After receiving guidance from higher headquarters, subordinate units down to battalion sequentially publish their QTG. The RC process is conceptually the same as the AC process; except, the guidance normally is published annually as yearly training guidance (YTG). Additionally, RC unit commanders are required to develop a postmobilization training plan to complete training to the level organized. This plan should be updated concurrently with the yearly training plan.

An important aspect of the quarterly and yearly training guidance is the role of the NCO. Within the framework of the commander's guidance, the CSM/1SG and key NCOs provide planning recommendations on the organization's individual training program. They identify the individual training tasks that must be integrated into collective mission essential tasks during the short-range planning period. Examples of topics normally addressed in QTG and YTG are-

- Commander's assessment of METL proficiency
- Training priorities and strategy to improve and sustain METL proficiency
- Combined arms training
- Organizational inspection program
- JIM training, as applicable
- A cross reference of training events and associated METL training objectives
- Individual training
- Leader development and leader training
- Self development
- Training of trainers and evaluators
- Training evaluation and feedback
- Force integration
- Resource guidance
- Training management
- Risk management

B. Short-Range Planning Calendar

The short-range planning calendar refines the long-range planning calendar and provides the time lines necessary for small unit leaders to prepare near-term training schedules.

In preparing a short-range calendar, details are added to further define the major training events contained on the long-range planning calendar. Some examples of these details include-

- The principal daily activities of major training events
- Home station training conducted in preparation for major training events and evaluations
- Other mandatory training that supports METL and warfighting such as command inspections as part of the OIP, Army Physical Fitness Test, weapons qualification, or periodic equipment maintenance and services
- Significant non-training events or activities that must be considered when scheduling training. Examples are national or local holidays and installation support missions.

The short-range training calendar is coordinated with appropriate installation support agencies to create a common training and support focus between supported and supporting organizations.

Short-Range Planning Cycle

Active Component (AC)

Frequency	Action	Planning Guidance Publication Date	Future Planning Horizon
Quarterly	Division, separate brigade, regiment, group or similar level cmd publishes **QTG**	3 months prior to start of quarter	3 months
	Brigade or group publish **QTG**	2 months prior to start of quarter	3 months
	Battalion, squadron and separate company publish **QTG**	6 weeks prior to start of quarter	3 months
	Conduct **QTB**	Prior to start of quarter	3+ months

Reserve Component (RC)

Frequency	Action	Planning Guidance Publication Date	Future Planning Horizon
Annually	Division, separate brigade, regiment, group or similar level command publishes **YTG**	6-8 months prior to FY start	1 year
	Brigade and separate battalion publish **YTG**	4-6 months prior to FY start	1 year
	Battalion, squadron and separate company publish **YTG**	3-4 months prior to FY start	1 year
	Conduct **YTB**	Prior to FY start	1+ years

Ref: FM 7-0, fig. 4-15, p. 4-22 and fig. 4-16, p. 4-23.

C. Training Events

Major training events are identified and scheduled during the longrange planning process. Short-range planning refines major training events. A major aspect of designing short-range training events is allocation of time to ensure the planned training is conducted to standard. Detailed information on training events may appear in the organization's short-range training guidance or in separate documents such as exercise directives or memorandums of instruction.

D. Multiechelon Training

Limited time and other resources do not permit developing sequential training programs in which each echelon from lower to higher is successively trained to reach interim "peaks" in proficiency. Therefore, leaders use a multiechelon training approach to plan training events. Multiechelon training allows simultaneous training and evaluation on any combination of individual and collective tasks at more than one echelon. Multiechelon training is the most efficient and effective way to train and sustain proficiency on mission essential tasks within limited periods of training time.

The designation of control and evaluation organizations is an important aspect of externally supported training exercises. This allows the units performing training to focus on execution of training while other organizations provide the necessary control, evaluation, and administrative support. Multiechelon training occurs when-

- An entire organization focuses on a single METL task
- Different echelons of an organization conduct training on related METL tasks simultaneously. The battalion task force headquarters and company headquarters participate in a constructive battle simulation while tank platoons concurrently conduct platoon STXs in virtual simulations. Mechanized platoons concurrently conduct squad live fire exercises and crew proficiency training to prepare for the platoon hasty attack LFXs on "Day 8". It addresses some RC unique training considerations such as the use of the CONUSA, division (training support), and AC support of RC training.

Larger scale training events also provide an opportunity for valuable individual, crew, battle staff, and small unit training. These exercises can result in unproductive training for soldiers at lower echelons unless senior leaders plan multiechelon training down to the smallest participating units. This is the best method to maintain battle focus on the large unit METL tasks as well as on supporting collective and individual battle tasks for even the smallest participating units.

E. Training Resources

In short-range planning, commanders allocate training resources to subordinate organizations for specific training activities. As required, adjustments are made from the initial resource projections contained in longrange plans. The key requirement for division and brigade commanders is to coordinate short-range training plans with the various resource processes that support training. Examples of these processes are Program Budget Advisory Committee (PBAC) meetings, ammunition forecasts, and training area and facility scheduling conferences. A significant resource to assist the commander in planning training is the TSS. The TSS is a collection of resources that supports training and leverages available technology to replicate combat conditions and enhance training. Examples of TSS training support products are-

- Facilities such as ranges, training areas, firing points, urban training sites, digital training facilities, and mission support and training facilities ??Training products such as MTP, training support packages, multimedia products, and distance learning through electronically stored and delivered course content and programs of instruction

- TADSS such as tactical engagement simulations, instrumentation at the CTC and home station, embedded training capabilities, MILES, and warfighter Simulation
- Training services such as the Center for Army Lessons Learned, proponent schools, installation support, and CTC

F. Train the Trainers

Training the trainers is a critical step in preparation for training. The leaders, trainers, and evaluators involved in any training event must know, understand, and be proficient on the specified tasks. Leaders, trainers, and evaluators must be trained to standard if the training event is to be done to standard.

In addition to leader training, specific trainer training must also be identified and planned. All leaders are trainers, but all trainers are not necessarily leaders. A specialist or subject matter expert may be necessary to conduct the instruction for a particular collective or individual task. It is essential that these trainers be allocated sufficient time to prepare the specified training.

An overlap in training responsibilities, frequently overlooked by leaders when planning, is the case where a subordinate leader is the primary trainer as well as the leader of an element undergoing a collective training event. Senior leaders must consciously allocate sufficient time for subordinates to prepare for these responsibilities.

Training leaders, trainers, and evaluators to standard supports, enhances, and enables collective training when properly planned and conducted before the training event. Commanders must plan, resource, and ensure timely accomplishment of trainer training.

G. Short-Range Training Briefings

The short-range training briefing is a conference conducted by senior commanders to review and approve the training plans of subordinate units. It is conducted before the time period addressed in the QTG or YTG. AC units conduct a Quarterly Training Briefing (QTB). RC units conduct the Yearly Training Briefing (YTB).

Division commanders receive the short-range training briefing from subordinate brigades and all battalions in the division. The brigade commander and CSM personally present the overview of the brigade training plan; battalion commanders and CSMs present detailed briefings of their training plans. All habitually associated commanders participate in preparing and conducting the training briefing.

The training briefing is a highlight of the senior commander's leader development program. It provides the commander an opportunity to coach and teach subordinates on the fine points of his philosophy and strategies in all aspects of warfighting, to include doctrine, training, force integration, and leader development. It enables subordinate commanders, some of whom may be new to the organization, to gain a better understanding of how their mission essential training relates to the battle focused training programs of their senior commanders and peers.

Training briefings produce a contract between the senior commander and each subordinate commander. As a result of this contract, the senior commander agrees to provide resources, including time, and protect the subordinate unit from unprogrammed taskings. The subordinate commander agrees to execute the approved training plan and conduct training to standard. This shared responsibility helps maintain priorities, achieve unity of effort, and synchronize actions to achieve quality training and efficient resourcing.

Quarterly / Yearly Training Briefing
Ref: FM 7-0, pp. 4-28 to 4-29.

The Quarterly Training Briefing (QTB; active component) or Yearly Training Briefing (YTB; reserve component), as appropriate, is the forum where contracts for that training period are discussed and confirmed. Training guidance flows from the top-down and requirements for planning and execution of tasks flow from the bottom-up.

The senior commander specifies the format and content of the briefing in the QTG or YTG. However, the briefing guidance should be flexible enough to provide subordinate commanders and CSMs the latitude to highlight their initiatives and priorities. Units should refrain from discussing readiness issues not directly related to training. Such statistical, logistical, manning, or other management data is more appropriate to other readiness review forums and distracts from the overall training focus of the QTB or YTB.

During the training briefing, the subordinate commanders, as a minimum, usually address the following specific areas-

- Brief training that was planned and briefed at previous QTB or YTB, but was not conducted and why
- The organization's METL and assessment of proficiency levels
- A discussion of the unit's training focus and objectives for the upcoming training period
- A presentation of the organization's short-range planning calendar
- A description of upcoming training events
- Officer leader development program with emphasis on warfighting skill development
- Self development
- Risk management
- Plans for preparing trainers and evaluators
- Force integration plans for the upcoming period
- Resource allocation

Each CSM normally follows the commander's presentation. The CSM provides an analysis of the organization's individual training proficiency and discusses the organization's planned individual training and education. Example discussion topics include-

- Individual training proficiency feedback received concerning previous short-range planning period
- An assessment of the organization's current individual training proficiency
- Individual training events planned during the upcoming short-range planning period and strategy to prepare soldiers for these evaluations
- A description of METL derived individual tasks to be integrated with upcoming collective mission essential tasks
- Marksmanship and physical fitness programs
- NCO leader development program with emphasis on warfighting skill development
- Self development
- NCO/enlisted schools

III. Near-Term Planning

Near-term planning is primarily conducted at battalion and subordinate command levels. It is conducted to-

- Schedule and execute training objectives specified in the short-range training plan to the Army standard
- Provide specific guidance to trainers
- Make final coordination for the allocation of resources to be used in training
- Complete final coordination with other units that will participate in training as part of the task organizations
- Prepare detailed training schedules

Near-term planning covers a six- to eight-week period prior to the conduct of training for AC units and a four-month period prior to training for RC units. Formal near-term planning culminates when the unit publishes its training schedule.

Near-Term Planning Cycle

Note: Training schedules are developed at company level and approved by battalion commanders. Training schedules are typed and reproduced at battalion level

Active Component (AC)

Frequency	Action	Planning Guidance Publication Date
Weekly	Battalion training meetings and subsequent draft training schedules	6-8 weeks prior to execution
	Battalion publishes training schedules	4-6 weeks prior to execution

Reserve Component (RC)

Frequency	Action	Planning Guidance Publication Date
Monthly	Battalion training meetings and subsequent draft training schedules	4 months prior to execution
	Battalion publishes training schedules	3 months prior to execution

Ref: FM 7-0, fig. 4-21, p. 4-30 and fig. 4-22, p. 4-31.

A. Training Meetings

Training meetings are the key to near-term planning. Training meetings create the bottom-up flow of information regarding specific training proficiency needs of the small unit, battle staff, and individual soldier. Normally platoons, companies, and battalions conduct weekly training meetings. At battalion level, training meetings primarily cover training management issues. At company and platoon level, they are directly concerned with the specifics of training execution and must include pre-execution checks. During training meetings, nothing is discussed but training. All key leaders of the unit must attend.

B. Training Schedules

Near-term planning results in detailed training schedules. Training is considered "locked in" when the battalion commander signs the training schedule. At a minimum, it should-

- Specify when training starts and where it takes place
- Allocate adequate time for scheduled training and additional training as required to correct anticipated deficiencies
- Specify individual, leader, and collective tasks to be trained
- Provide concurrent training topics that will efficiently use available training time
- Specify who conducts the training and who evaluates the training
- Provide administrative information concerning uniform, weapons, equipment, references, and safety precautions

Senior commanders establish policies to minimize changes to the training schedule. Training is locked in when training schedules are published. Command responsibility is established as follows-

- The company commander drafts the training schedule
- The battalion commander approves and signs the schedule and provides necessary administrative support
- The brigade commander reviews each training schedule published in his command
- The division commander reviews selected training schedules in detail and the complete list of training highlights developed by the division staff

Senior commanders provide feedback to subordinates on training schedule quality and subsequently attend as much training as possible to ensure that mission essential tasks are accomplished to standard.

Training Schedule Development

Week T-6
- Based on assessment, identify collective and soldier tasks
- Prepare draft tng schedule
- Submit requests for TADDS, tng areas and other requirements
- Request Class I, III, IV and V
- Begin pre-execution checks

Week T-5
- Finalize and approve tng objectives (Cdr)
- Confirm support requests
- Identify trainer rehearsal requirments
- Resolve and eliminate training distractors
- Provide soldier tasks for integration (key NCOs)

Week T-4
- Sign and lock in training schedules; post in company area
- Lock in resources
- Identify and brief trainers and assistant trainers on responsibilities

Week T-3
- Begin rehearsals
- Ensure training distractors are under control

Week T-2
- Fight hard to stop changes
- Intensify rehearsals and preparation
- Conduct back briefs
- Begin gathering training aids and supplies

Week T-1
- Complete pre-execution checks
- Obtain training aids
- Complete rehearsals
- Stop changes to scheduled training
- Brief soldiers on training

Week T (Current)
- Conduct precombat checks
- Execute training
- Conduct AARs

Ref: FM 25-101, fig. 3-29, p. 3-32.

Battalion Training Meetings

Ref: TC 25-101, p. 3-28 to 3-30.

Note: For guidance on company-level training meetings, see chapter 2.

The primary focus of training meetings at battalion level is training management issues for the next six weeks. Coordination meetings should be held to resolve resource issues prior to the battalion training meeting. At company level, training meetings focus on the specifics of training to be conducted.

Suggested Participants

This section recommends participants for battalion and company training meetings.

At battalion level, participants may include—

- Battalion commander
- Command sergeant major
- Battalion executive officer
- Company commanders and first sergeants
- Specialty platoon leaders (medical, support, scouts, mortar, signal as required)
- Slice leaders (FSO, engineer, AD, GSR, and MST)
- Operations officer from the FSB or main support battalion (MSB)
- Battalion staff (S1, S2, S3, and S4)
- Special staff (chaplain, chemical officer, BMO, and physician's assistant)
- Battalion operations sergeant

When appropriate, RC commanders may want to include participants from the readiness group and AC 'partnership unit. When geographical dispersion precludes the company attending battalion training meetings, essential training information must be exchanged. Units should consider mail or other means to exchange critical information.

Suggested Agenda

Training meetings at each echelon review past training. Further, they refine and plan training for the next six weeks

At battalion level, the following agenda may be used:

- Review of QTC or YTC
- Past training (briefed by company commanders), to include—
    - Assess training conducted since the last meeting
    - Review reasons for training planned, but not conducted
    - Update the current status of training proficiency
- Near-term training, to include—
    - Discuss new guidance received from higher commanders
    - Lock in training scheduled for next four to six weeks (next three months for RC)
    - Review and complete pre-execution checks (document training distracters from higher headquarters)
    - Issue commander's guidance for training scheduled six to eight weeks out (four months out for RC)
    - Review preparations for multiechelon training
    - Review the short-range plan
    - Review projected resources

V. Execution

Ref: FM 7-0 Training the Force, chap. 5.

I. Execution of Training

All good training, regardless of the specific collective, leader, and individual tasks being executed, must comply with certain common requirements. These include adequate preparation, effective presentation and practice, and thorough evaluation. The execution of training includes preparation for training, conduct of training, and recovery from training.

The training execution process is applicable at all echelons, from a high level staff participating in a joint training exercise to a first line leader's individual training of his team.

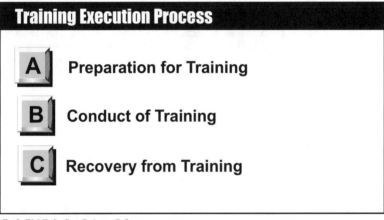

Training Execution Process

A **Preparation for Training**

B **Conduct of Training**

C **Recovery from Training**

Ref: FM 7-0, fig. 5-1, p. 5-2.

A. Preparation for Training

Formal near-term planning for training culminates with the publication of the unit training schedule. Informal planning, detailed coordination, and preparation for executing the training continue until the training is performed. Commanders and other trainers use training meetings to assign responsibility for preparation of all scheduled training. Preparation for training includes selecting tasks to be trained, planning the conduct of the training, training the trainers, reconnaissance of the site, issuing the training execution plan, and conducting rehearsals and pre-execution checks. Pre-execution checks are preliminary actions commanders and trainers use to identify responsibility for these and other training support tasks. They are used to monitor preparation activities and to follow-up to ensure planned training is conducted to standard. Pre-execution checks are a critical portion of any training meeting. During preparation for training, battalion and company commanders identify and eliminate potential training distracters that develop within their organizations. They also stress personnel accountability to ensure maximum attendance at training.

Subordinate leaders, as a result of the bottom-up feed from internal training meetings, identify and select the collective, leader, and individual tasks necessary to support the identified training objectives. Commanders develop the tentative plan to include requirements for preparatory training, concurrent training, and training resources. At a minimum, the training plan should include confirmation of training areas and locations, training ammunition allocations, training simulations and simulators availability, transportation requirements, soldier support items, a risk management analysis, assignment of responsibility for the training, designation of trainers responsible for approved training, and final coordination. The time and other necessary resources for retraining must also be an integral part of the original training plan.

Leaders, trainers, evaluators, observer/controllers, and OPFOR are identified, trained to standard, and rehearsed prior to the conduct of the training. Leaders and trainers are coached on how to train, given time to prepare, and rehearsed so that training will be challenging and doctrinally correct. Commanders ensure that trainers and evaluators are not only tactically and technically competent on their training tasks, but also understand how the training relates to the organization's METL. Properly prepared trainers, evaluators, and leaders project confidence and enthusiasm to those being trained. Trainer and leader training is a critical event in the preparation phase of training. These individuals must demonstrate proficiency on the selected tasks prior to the conduct of training.

Commanders, with their subordinate leaders and trainers, conduct site reconnaissance; identify additional training support requirements; and refine and issue the training execution plan. The training plan should identify all elements necessary to ensure the conduct of training to standard. Rehearsals are essential to the execution of good training. Realistic, standards based performance oriented training requires rehearsals for trainers, support personnel, evaluators, observer/controllers, and OPFOR.

B. Conduct of Training

Ideally, training is executed using the crawl-walk-run approach. This allows and promotes an objective, standards-based approach to training. Training starts at the basic level. Crawl events are relatively simple to conduct and require minimum support from the unit. After the crawl stage, training becomes incrementally more difficult, requiring more resources from the unit and home station, and increasing the level of realism. At the run stage, the level of difficulty for the training event intensifies. Run stage training requires optimum resources and ideally approaches the level of realism expected in combat. Progression from the walk to the run stage for a particular task may occur during a one-day training exercise or may require a succession of training periods over time. Achievement of the Army standard determines progression between stages.

In crawl-walk-run training, the tasks and the standards remain the same, however, the conditions under which they are trained change. Commanders may change the conditions for example, by increasing the difficulty of the conditions under which the task is being performed, increasing the tempo of the task training, increasing the number of tasks being trained, or by increasing the number of personnel involved in the training. Whichever approach is used, it is important that all leaders and soldiers involved understand which stage they are currently training and understand the Army standard.

An AAR is conducted immediately after training and may indicate that additional training is needed. Any task that was not conducted to standard should be retrained. Retraining should be conducted at the earliest opportunity. Commanders should program time and other resources for retraining as an integral part of their long, short-, and near-term training planning cycle. Training is incomplete until the task is trained to standard. Soldiers will remember the standard enforced, not the one discussed.

Trainers use the appropriate combination of demonstrations, conferences, discussions, and practice activities to present training. Using the crawl-walk-run approach, they inform individuals being trained of the training objectives (tasks, conditions, and standards) and applicable evaluation methods. They immediately follow presentation with practice to convert information into usable individual and collective skills. The amount of detail included in practice depends on experience levels. If individuals or organizations are receiving initial training on a mission essential task, trainers emphasize the basic conditions. If those receiving the instruction are receiving sustainment training on a task, trainers raise the level of detail and realism until the conditions replicate the wartime environment as closely as possible. Trainers challenge those with considerable experience to perform multiple training tasks within a given training scenario. Properly presented and executed training is realistic, safe, accurate, well structured, efficient, and effective:

- **Realistic** training requires organizations to train the way they will fight or support within all dimensions of the battlefield/space. Realistic training includes all available elements of combined arms teams and, as appropriate, joint, multinational, and interagency teams. It optimizes the use of TSS products to replicate the stresses, sounds, and conditions of combat.

- **Safe training** is the predictable result of performing to established tactical and technical standards. Through the risk management process, leaders at all echelons ensure that safety requirements are integral and not add-on considerations to all aspects of planning, executing, and evaluating training.

- **Accurate** training complies with Army operational and training doctrine and is technically correct. Field manuals, MTPs, battle drills, and other training publications provide factual information to trainers to facilitate conduct of training, coach subordinate trainers, and evaluate training results.

- **Well-structured** training contains a mixture of initial and sustainment training. It also consists of a mix of individual and leader tasks that are integrated into METL collective tasks. Soldiers and leaders increase proficiency in individual tasks while training on collective mission essential tasks.

- **Efficient** training ensures that training resources are expended properly. Efficiently executed training makes full use of every participant's time. Commanders monitor physical and financial resource execution through PBACs, range conferences, and similar forums. They use the feedback received during these forums to adjust resources within their commands to sustain METL proficiency within the Band of Excellence. Continuing advances in training technology enhance the commander's ability to hone warfighting skills and are increasingly required to balance constraints to training, such as environmental protection considerations and availability of training areas and ranges. Similarly, TSS products and services, such as TADSS, not only provide a means for initial and sustainment training on warfighting fundamentals, but also provide relatively inexpensive preparation for resource intensive training events. Although TSS products provide excellent virtual and constructive training supplements, there is no substitute for the more robust experience of live training.

- **Effective** training builds proficiency, teamwork, confidence, and cohesiveness. Effective training is competitive. Although individuals and organizations may sometimes compete against one another, they should always compete to achieve the prescribed standard. If they do not initially achieve the standard, trainers take corrective actions so that the proper performance level results.

Effective Training

Ref: FM 7-0, chap. 5, pp. 5-5 to 5-6.

Effective training builds proficiency, teamwork, confidence, and cohesiveness. Effective training is competitive. Although individuals and organizations may sometimes compete against one another, they should always compete to achieve the prescribed standard.

Training and Evaluation Outline (T&EO)

Effective collective, leader, and individual training are guided by the use of T&EOs. The T&EO provides summary information concerning collective training objectives as well as individual and leader training tasks that support the collective training objectives.

Individual Training

The individual soldier is the heart of any unit's ability to conduct its mission. The ability to perform individual/leader skills to standard is founded in the institutional training base, but it is honed and maintained by effective, periodic repetition of tasks.

Leader Training

Leaders spend virtually all available training time supervising the training of subordinates. Often, they do not increase their own understanding of how to fight as combat or support leaders. Therefore, senior commanders view leader training as a continuous process that encompasses more than periodic officer and NCO professional development classes. Senior commanders establish a positive training environment that encourages subordinates to become adaptive leaders capable of independent thinking on the move, and of timely decision making based on broad, effects-based intent guidance, mission orders, and a shared vision of the battlefield.

Battle Rosters

Battle rosters are maintained at battalion level and below to track key training information on selected mission essential systems. They track such pertinent training data as crew stability and manning levels, and qualification status. A key aspect of battle rosters is the designation of qualified back-up operators or crewmembers assigned in other positions in the organization. During the execution of training, battle rostered crewmembers train with their designated crews at available opportunities. Commanders must discipline the battle roster system.

Battle Staff Training

Battle staff training develops and sustains planning, coordination, execution, and other staff functions related to wartime mission requirements. Commanders train battle staffs primarily through a mix of constructive and virtual simulations. Battle staffs train to integrate and coordinate the BOS internally within their own headquarters, horizontally with other staffs at the same organizational level, and vertically with higher and subordinate organizational staffs.

JIM (Joint, Interagency, Mulitinational) Training

Joint training is conducted using approved joint doctrine and TTPs, and must be consistent with assigned joint missions and priorities. When assigned as a JFC, Army commanders establish joint training objectives and plans, execute and evaluate joint training, and assess training proficiency. Multinational training optimizes contributions of member forces by matching their missions with their capabilities, and uses available training assistance programs.

C. Recovery from Training

The recovery process is an extension of training and, once completed, it signifies the end of the training event. At a minimum, recovery includes conduct of maintenance training, turn-in of training support items, and the conduct of AARs that review the overall effectiveness of the training.

Maintenance training is the conduct of post operations preventive maintenance checks and services, accountability of organizational and individual equipment, and final inspections. Class IV, Class V, TADSS and other support items are maintained, accounted for, and turned-in. Training sites and facilities are closed out.

AARs conducted during recovery focus on collective, leader, and individual task performance, and on the planning, preparation and conduct of the training. Unit AARs focus on individual and collective task performance, and identify shortcomings and the training required to correct deficiencies. AARs with leaders focus on tactical judgment. These AARs contribute to leader learning and provide opportunities for leader development. AARs with trainers, evaluators, observer/controllers, and OPFOR provide additional opportunities for leader development.

The AARs conducted during recovery along with the AARs that took place during the conduct of training enhance future training . They provide the feedback that contributes to the development of training plans to correct identified deficiencies. Finally, these AARs contribute to the commander's overall evaluation of training effectiveness and unit assessment. However, they are not in themselves the end state of recovery. Recovery from training is complete when the unit is again prepared to conduct its assigned mission.

II. Role of Commanders and Senior Leaders

Although planning for training is relatively centralized to align training priorities at all echelons of an organization, the execution of training is decentralized. Decentralization tailors training execution to available resources and promotes bottom-up communication of unique wartime mission related strengths and weaknesses of each individual, leader, and unit.

Senior commanders must personally observe and evaluate the execution of training at all echelons to the maximum extent possible. From their observations of training and other feedback, they provide guidance and direct changes that lead to improved training and increased readiness.

By personally visiting training, senior commanders communicate to subordinate units and leaders the paramount importance of training. In addition to observing and evaluating the training of their headquarters and immediate subordinate commands, senior commanders also observe and evaluate the quality of training at all echelons down to the lowest levels of the organization. They receive feedback from subordinate leaders and soldiers during training visits. Through feedback, senior commanders identify and resolve systemic problems in planning, leadership, management, support, and other functions.

The most beneficial senior commander and staff visits to training are unannounced or short notice. They observe training as experienced by soldiers and prevent excessive visitor preparation by subordinate organizations (this, in itself, can become a training distracter). Senior commanders assign coordination of training support for subordinate units as a priority requirement for organizational staffs. Training support and coordination of training resources are key to successful training execution. Senior commanders check the adequacy of external training support during every training visit and require prompt and effective corrective action to resolve support deficiencies.

III. Role of Noncommissioned Officers

The difference in our Army and every other army in the world is that we have a proud, professional NCO Corps that takes pride in, and accepts responsibility for, the care and individual training of soldiers. CSM/1SG and key NCOs select and train specific individual tasks that support the units' collective mission essential tasks. NCOs are indispensable throughout the training process. Commanders approve the tasks selected and supervise and evaluate training with the officers and NCOs throughout the training execution process.

NCOs are responsible for individual, crew, and small team training. They continue the soldierization process of newly assigned enlisted soldiers and begin their professional development. In units, individual skill training is presented by the first-line leader, and not presented to large numbers of soldiers by committee. The first-line leader is responsible to train individual tasks to soldiers in their squads, crews, teams, and equivalent small units. The first-line leader and senior NCOs emphasize standards-based, performance-oriented training to ensure soldiers achieve the Army standard. NCO leaders conduct cross training to ensure critical wartime skills within the unit. The CSMs, 1SG, and other senior NCOs coach junior NCOs to master a wide range of individual tasks. Commanders allocate training time for NCOs to conduct individual training and require that individual tasks be included in all collective METL training. NCOs are responsible for conducting individual training to standard and must be able to explain how individual task training relates to the collective mission essential tasks.

Individual, crew, and small team tasks to be trained are based on the small unit leader's evaluation of training deficiencies. These tasks are input as the NCO's bottom-up feed at the weekly training meeting, approved by the commander, and incorporated into the unit training plans and subsequent training schedules. NCO leaders plan, prepare, rehearse, execute, and conduct AARs for the approved training and provide feedback during weekly training meetings. Commanders may, as required, approve the conduct of training that may not have a strictly tactical focus but sustains soldier readiness. For example, lowdensity occupational specialty soldiers may be consolidated periodically for training under the senior functional NCO to sustain proficiency.

VI. Assessment

Ref: FM 7-0 Training the Force, chap. 6.

Assessment is the commander's responsibility. It is the commander's judgment of the organization's ability to accomplish its wartime operational mission.

I. Assessment

Assessment is the commander's responsibility. It is the commander's judgment of the organization's ability to accomplish its wartime operational mission. Assessment is a continuous process that includes evaluating training, conducting an organizational assessment, and preparing a training assessment. The commander uses his experience, feedback from training evaluations, and other evaluations and reports to arrive at his assessment. Assessment is both the end and the beginning of the training management cycle.

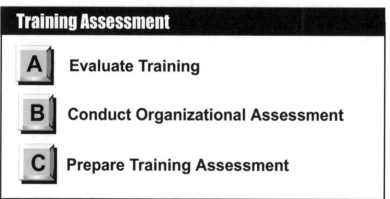

Training Assessment

A   **Evaluate Training**

B   **Conduct Organizational Assessment**

C   **Prepare Training Assessment**

Ref: FM 7-0, p. 6-1.

Training assessment is more than just training evaluation, and encompasses a wide variety of inputs. Assessments include such diverse systems as training, force integration, logistics, and personnel. They provide the link between the unit's performance and the Army standard. Evaluation of training is, however, a major component of assessment. Training evaluations provide the commander with feedback on the demonstrated training proficiency of soldiers, leaders, battle staffs, and units. Commanders cannot personally observe all training in their organization and, therefore, gather feedback from their senior staff officers and NCOs.

II. Organizational Assessment

Battalion and higher echelon commanders must be concerned with broader concepts. Accordingly, they perform organizational assessments that aggregate a large number of evaluations. These commanders establish an organizational assessment program that-

- Fixes responsibility within the staff and subordinate units for gathering and analyzing evaluation data and preparing recommendations
- Concentrates on the effectiveness of leader and organization training

- Utilizes the CSM and other senior NCOs to gather feedback on the individual, crew, and team training
- Allows the senior commander to monitor outcomes and take action to reshape priorities, policies, or plans to overcome assessed weaknesses and sustain demonstrated strengths

CTC take-home packages are an excellent source of feedback to include in an organizational assessment.

III. Evaluations

Evaluations can be informal, formal, internal, external, or any combination, thereof-

- **Informal evaluations** take place when a leader conducts training with his unit, for example when a squad leader trains his squad to assault an objective. Another example would be whenever a leader visits ongoing training, for instance when a battalion commander observes company training. This type of evaluation provides real time feedback on the training environment and the proficiency resulting from training.
- **Formal evaluations** are resourced with dedicated evaluators and are generally scheduled in the long-range or short-range training plans. Formal evaluations are normally highlighted during short-range training briefings. To the maximum extent possible, headquarters two echelons higher conduct formal external evaluations; for example, division commanders evaluate battalions, brigade commanders evaluate companies, and battalion commanders evaluate platoons.
- **Internal evaluations** are planned, resourced, and conducted by the organization undergoing the evaluation.
- **External evaluations** are planned, resourced, and conducted by a headquarters at an echelon higher in the chain of cmd than the organization undergoing the evaluation or a headquarters outside the chain of command.

Evaluation of individual and small unit training normally includes every soldier and leader involved in the training. For large-scale training events, evaluators sample a number of individuals and subordinate organizations to determine the likelihood of the entire organization to be able to perform specific mission essential tasks to standard.

IV. Evaluation of Training

Training evaluations are a critical component of any training assessment. Evaluation measures the demonstrated ability of soldiers, commanders, leaders, battle staffs, and units against the Army standard.

All training must be evaluated to measure performance levels against the established Army standard. The evaluation can be as fundamental as an informal, internal evaluation performed by the leader conducting the training. Evaluation is conducted specifically to enable the unit or individual undergoing the training to know whether the training standard has been achieved. Commanders must establish a climate that encourages candid and accurate feedback for the purpose of developing leaders and trained units.

Evaluation of training is not a test; it is not used to find reasons to punish leaders and soldiers. Evaluation tells the unit or the soldier whether or not they achieved the Army standard and, therefore, assists them in determining the overall effectiveness of their training plans. Evaluation produces disciplined soldiers, leaders and units. Training without evaluation is a waste of time and resources.

Leaders use evaluations as an opportunity to coach and mentor subordinates. A key element in developing leaders is immediate, positive feedback that coaches and leads subordinate leaders to achieve the Army standard.

V. The After Action Review (AAR)

Ref: FM 7-0, chap. 6, pp. 6-4 to 6-5.

Editor's Note: See chap. 3, for a complete chapter on AARs.

The AAR, whether formal or informal, provides feedback for all training. It is a structured review process that allows participating soldiers, leaders, and units to discover for themselves what happened during the training, why it happened, and how it can be done better. The AAR is a professional discussion that requires the active participation of those being trained. The AAR is not a critique and has the following advantages over a critique:

- Focuses directly on key METL derived training objectives
- Emphasizes meeting Army standards rather than pronouncing judgment of success or failure
- Uses "leading questions" to encourage participants to self-discover important lessons from the training event
- Allows a large number of individuals and leaders to participate so more of the training can be recalled and more lessons learned can be shared

The AAR consists of four parts-

1. Review what was supposed to happen (training plans)

The evaluator, along with the participants, reviews what was supposed to happen based on the commander's intent for the training event, unit-training plan, training objectives, and applicable T&EOs.

2. Establish what happened

The evaluator and the participants determine what actually happened during performance of the training task. A factual and indisputable account is vital to the effectiveness of the discussion that follows. For force-on-force training, OPFOR members assist in describing the flow of the training event and discuss training outcomes from their points of view.

3. Determine what was right or wrong with what happened

The participants establish the strong and weak points of their performance. The evaluator plays a critical role in guiding the discussions so conclusions reached by participants are doctrinally sound, consistent with Army standards, and relevant to the wartime mission.

4. Determine how the task should be done differently the next time

The evaluator assists the chain of command undergoing the training to lead the group in determining exactly how participants will perform differently the next time the task is performed.

Leaders understand that not all tasks will be performed to standard and in their initial planning, allocate time and other resources for retraining. Retraining allows the participants to apply the lessons learned during the AAR and implement corrective action. Retraining should be conducted at the earliest opportunity to translate observation and evaluation into training to standard. Commanders must ensure that units understand that training is incomplete until the Army standard is achieved.

The AAR is often "tiered" as a multiechelon leader development technique. Following an AAR with all participants, senior trainers may use the AAR for an extended professional discussion with selected leaders. These discussions usually include a more specific AAR of leader contributions to the observed training results.

VI. Evaluators

Commanders must plan for formal evaluation and must ensure the evaluators are trained. These evaluators must also be trained as facilitators to conduct AARs that elicit maximum participation from those being trained. External evaluators will be certified in the tasks they are evaluating and normally will not be dual-hatted as a participant in the training being executed. In addition to being able to plan, prepare, and conduct AARs, effective evaluators must also-

- Be familiar with the evaluated organization's METL
- Be trained (tactically and technically proficient) and rehearsed in the tasks evaluated
- Know the evaluation standards
- Follow the tactical and field SOPs for the organization being evaluated
- Apply relevant information about the evaluated unit, such as wartime missions, personnel turbulence, leader fill, and equipment status

Unit leaders, officers and NCOs, must be trained to conduct informal, internal evaluations as well. They must be able to plan, prepare, and conduct AARs effectively. This means they must-

- Be familiar with their organization's METL and how it supports their higher headquarters' METL
- Be tactically and technically proficient in the tasks evaluated

Not only do the individuals and units receiving the training learn from the evaluator, but also the evaluator learns while observing the evaluated unit.

VII. The Role of Senior Commanders and Leaders

Senior commanders ensure that evaluations take place at each echelon in the organization. Commanders use this feedback to teach, coach, and mentor their subordinates. They ensure that every training event is evaluated as part of training execution and that every trainer conducts evaluations. Senior commanders use evaluations to focus command attention by requiring evaluation of specific mission essential and battle tasks. They also take advantage of evaluation information to develop appropriate lessons learned for distribution throughout their commands.

The use of evaluation data can have a strong effect on the command climate of the organization. Therefore, senior commanders make on-the-spot corrections, underwrite honest mistakes, and create an environment for aggressive action to correct training deficiencies, through retraining.

Senior commanders use training evaluations as one component of a feedback system. These feedback systems allow the senior commander to make changes that lead to superior training results and to teach, coach and mentor subordinate leaders. Some sources of training feedback include-

- Training plan assessments
- Quarterly training briefing (AC)
- Yearly training briefing (RC)
- PBAC
- Range conferences
- Evaluation data
- Staff visits
- Leader development discussions
- Personal observations
- CTC take home packages

VII. Training Exercises

Ref: FM 25-101, app. C.

Training Exercises

1 Map Exercise (MAPEX)

2 Tactical Exercise Without Troops (TEWT)

3 Fire Coordination Exercise (FCX)

4 Command Post Exercise (CPX)

5 Situational Training Exercise (STX)

6 Command Field Exercise (CFX)

7 Logistical Coordination Exercise (LCX)

8 Field Training Exercise (FTX)

9 Live Fire Exercise (LFX)

Ref: FM 25-101, app. C.

Commanders select a particular training exercise or combination of exercises based on specific training objectives and on available resources. When selecting exercises, commanders must consider several key questions:

- Who will be trained (soldiers, leaders, or units)?
- What are the training objectives?
- Which, if any, of the training exercises are most suitable to accomplish each objective?
- What are the available resources (time, training areas, equipment, money)?
- Which of the training exercises or combination will help meet the training objectives within the available training resources?

Realism vs. Level of Resourcing
Ref: FM 25-101, fig. C-1, p. C-2.

Suggested Exercise Participants
Ref: FM 25-101, pp. C-6 to C-9.

1. MAPEX
Battalion & Task Force Level
- Battalion cdr, CSM and XO
- Primary staff (S1, S2, S3, S4)
- Company cdrs & 1SGs
- Battalion motor officer
- Slice cdrs and leaders

Company & Team Level
- Company cdr, 1SG, and XO
- Platoon Leaders
- FIST chief
- Support leaders & co HQs personnel as appropriate
- Platoon sergeants

Platoon Level
- Platoon leader
- Platoon sergeant
- Squad ldrs & vehicle cdrs

2. TEWT
Battalion Level
- Battalion cdr, CSM and XO
- Primary and special staff
- Slice cdrs and leaders
- Company cdrs, XOs, plt ldrs

Company Level
- Company cdr, 1SG, and XO
- Platoon Leaders
- FIST chief
- Platoon sergeants

3. FCX
Battalion Level
- Battalion cdr
- S3, FSO, ALO
- Company cdrs and plt ldrs
- Squad and team leaders
- Slice leaders if applicable
- Weapon system personnel

Company Level
- Company cdr
- Platoon Leaders
- Squad and team leaders

Platoon Level
- Platoon leader
- Squad leader
- Team and section leaders
- Weapon system personnel

4. CPX
Battalion Level
- Battalion cdr, CSM and XO
- Battalion staff
- Company cdrs and plt ldrs
- Bn slice and spt leaders

Company Level
- Company cdr, 1SG, and XO
- Platoon ldrs and plt sgts
- FIST chief

5. LCX
Battalion Level
- Battalion XO
- S1 and S4 sections
- Bn motor officer and NCO
- Spt platoon leader
- Personnel services NCO
- Medical platoon leader

Company Level
- Company XO and 1SG
- Platoon ldrs, plt sgts
- Squad leaders
- Unit supply sgt & co medic
- Key soldiers

Exercise Selection Matrix
Ref: FM 25-101, fig. C-2, pp. C-4 to C-5.

Intelligence

	1 MAPEX	2 TEWT	3 FCX	4 CPX	5 LCX	6 STX	7 CFX	8 FTX	9 LFX
Collect Information			X		X	X	X	X	
Process Information	X	X	X	X	X	X	X	X	
Prepare Intel Reports	X	X	X	X		X	X	X	

Maneuver

	1 MAPEX	2 TEWT	3 FCX	4 CPX	5 LCX	6 STX	7 CFX	8 FTX	9 LFX
Move	X	X	X	X		X	X	X	X
Engage Enemy									X
Control Terrain						X		X	X

Fire Support

	1 MAPEX	2 TEWT	3 FCX	4 CPX	5 LCX	6 STX	7 CFX	8 FTX	9 LFX
Process Ground Tgts	X	X	X	X		X	X	X	X
Engage Ground			X	X		X	X	X	X

Mobility, Countermobility & Survivability

	1 MAPEX	2 TEWT	3 FCX	4 CPX	5 LCX	6 STX	7 CFX	8 FTX	9 LFX
Provide Mobility						X		X	
Provide Countermobility	X	X	X	X		X	X	X	
Enhance Survivability		X	X	X		X	X	X	

Air Defense

	1 MAPEX	2 TEWT	3 FCX	4 CPX	5 LCX	6 STX	7 CFX	8 FTX	9 LFX
Process Air Targets		X	X	X		X	X	X	X
Attack Enemy Air Targets			X					X	
Deny Airspace	X	X	X	X		X	X	X	

Combat Service Support

	1 MAPEX	2 TEWT	3 FCX	4 CPX	5 LCX	6 STX	7 CFX	8 FTX	9 LFX
Arm	X	X	X	X	X	X	X	X	X
Fuel	X	X	X	X	X	X	X	X	X
Fix	X	X	X	X	X	X	X	X	X
Man the Force				X	X	X	X	X	
Distribution				X	X	X	X	X	X
Provide Sustainment Engineering	X	X		X	X	X	X	X	X
Provide Military Police Spt				X		X	X	X	X

Combat Service Support

	1 MAPEX	2 TEWT	3 FCX	4 CPX	5 LCX	6 STX	7 CFX	8 FTX	9 LFX
Acquire & Communicate Information and Maintain Status	X	X	X	X	X	X	X	X	X
Assess Situation	X	X	X	X	X	X	X	X	X
Determine Actions	X	X	X	X	X	X	X	X	X
Direct and Lead Subordinate Forces	X	X	X	X	X	X	X	X	X

1. Map Exercise (MAPEX)

The MAPEX portrays military maps and overlays. It requires situations on a minimum number of support personnel and may be conducted in garrison or in the field. When conducted in garrison, it is low-cost in terms of training dollars and facilities; it is an excellent training tool for a resource-constrained unit. Communications equipment may be used. A MAPEX helps the commander train his staff and leaders in planning, coordinating, and ex- ecuting operations tasks on map boards, chalkboards, training mock-ups, and sand tables. It is an excellent training tool before conducting other more costly exercises. A MAPEX trains the following:

- Functioning as an effective team
- Exchanging information
- Preparing estimates
- Giving appraisals
- Making recommendations and decisions
- Preparing plans
- Issuing orders
- Coordinating execution of orders

A MAPEX can be conducted internally at platoon, company, and battalion level or externally with a brigade or division MAPEX.

2. Tactical Exercise Without Troops (TEWT)

The TEWT is conducted on actual terrain with unit leaders and staffs, without soldiers. A TEWT allows the battalion TF or company commander to train his staff and subordinate leaders. It also allows him to analyze, plan, and present how he would conduct an operation on the actual terrain.

TEWTs are normally conducted internally. Because only the battle staff and selected support personnel are involved, the TEWT is an inexpensive way to familiarize leaders with the area of operations. A TEWT can be used:

- To analyze terrain
- To employ units according to terrain analysis
- To emplace weapons systems to best support the unit's mission
- To prepare and validate plans
- To plan CS and CSS operations

3. Fire Coordination Exercise (FCX)

The FCX is used to train the combined arms team chain of command and related fire control elements to rapidly synchronize fires on the battlefield.

The exercise can use reduced-scale targets and ranges to depict combat situations. The chain of command must respond in the form of maneuver and fire coordination techniques and procedures. Commanders use FCXs:

- To develop the chain of command into a team
- To synchronize fires within the combined arms team
- To train the chain of command prior to a live fire exercise
- To exercise the communications net
- To assist in integrating new weapons system
- To portray a rapidly changing situation for the chain of command to react to

FCXs are normally used to train platoon- through battalion-level. The entire task force chain of command can be trained.

4. Command Post Exercise (CPX)

The CPX may be conducted in garrison or in the field. It requires the establishment of the command post. When compared with the MAPEX or TEWT, it represents a greater commitment of soldiers' time and resources. A CPX an expanded MAPEX for staff and all commanders to lead and control tactical operations by using tactical communications systems. Of ten the CPX is driven by a simulation or is part a larger exercise. Normal battlefield distances between CPs may be reduced. A CPX trains commanders and staff—

- To build teamwork and cohesion
- To exchange information by proper reporting IAW tactical SOPs
- To prepare estimates, plans, and orders
- To establish and employ tactical communications
- To displace headquarters and command posts
- To integrate synchronized BOS

Battalions and companies may participate in a CPX as part of a larger force (brigade, division, and corps); they also may conduct internal CPXs.

5. Logistical Coordination Exercise (LCX)

LCXs allow leaders to become proficient at conducting unit sustainment operations such as supply, transportation, medical, personnel replacement, maintenance, and graves registration. LCXs provide a valuable, hands-on opportunity to deal with combat-related challenges of these activities. Most important, leaders can develop the SOPs so essential to their effective accomplishment. An LCX—

- Clarifies key elements of the battalion or TF logistics apparatus
- Exercises the flow of logistical information
- Incorporates a tactical war game that produces a wide variety of logistical requirements
- Allows plenty of opportunity for instruction and critique
- Exercises the communications network

As the primary leaders and soldiers train for the exercise, the interplay of CSS activities can be fully examined. Unit SOPs can be developed, modified, and verified. As proficiency in logistical operations is attained, LCX can be tied to other task force exercises to complete the integration of CSS with other combat operations.

6. Situational Training Exercise (STX)

STXs are mission-related, limited exercises designed to train one collective task, or a group of related tasks and drills, through practice. STXs teach the standard, preferred method for carrying out the task. They are more flexible than drills and usually include drills, leader tasks, and soldier tasks. STXs may be modified, based on the unit. METL, or expanded to meet special mission requirements. To ensure standardization, service schools develop STXs to teach the doctrinally preferred way to perform specific missions or tasks.

The company commander trains STXs and other similar exercises while platoons execute combat and crew drills. The battalion commander does the same for company exercises. The battalion commander assigns his staff to evaluate and assist with the STX. The STX's final objective is to prepare units for larger-scale exercises.

Prerequisite training for the STX is progressive with heavy emphasis on drills. "Close-in" or local training follows with drills executed in a tactical setting using MILES. Using TEWTs, sand tables, and simulation, the STX should bring C2 elements to a high level of proficiency.

An STX may be conducted like a CFX. The maneuver elements participate with slice elements (represented with only a portion of their personnel and equipment). An FA battery, for example, may be represented by a single howitzer section and fire direction center (FDC). An air cavalry troop may be represented by two or three helicopters. Vehicles that are destroyed must be evacuated under combat conditions. Calls for fire must be computed and "shot."

7. Command Field Exercise (CFX)

The CFX lies on a scale between the CPX and FTX. Available resources determine where the CFX fits on the scale. The CFX can also be a backup for the FTX if maneuver damage, weather, or other factors prohibit the planned FTX. The CFX is an FTX with reduced unit and vehicle density, but with full C2, CS, and CSS elements. For example, the platoon leader in his vehicle represents the entire platoon.

CFXs are excellent vehicles for training leaders and staff with full command, control, communications, and logistical systems. They are less expensive and exercise intersystem linkages and real distances. They sharpen unit skills in such areas as-

- Intelligence
- Fire support
- Slice integration
- CSS
- Rear area operations
- Command, control, and communications

A CFX can train as much, or as little, of the task force as necessary, depending on the commander's assessment and training objectives.

8. Field Training Exercise (FTX)

FTXs are conducted under simulated combat conditions in the field. FTXs fully integrate the total force in a realistic combat environment. They involve combat arms, CS, and CSS units. FTXs encompass such training as battle drills, crew drills, and STXs to reinforce soldier and collective training integration. They are used to train the commander, staff, subordinate units, and slice elements—

- To move and maneuver units realistically
- To employ organic weapons systems effectively
- To build teamwork and cohesion
- To plan and coordinate supporting fires
- To plan and coordinate logistical activities to support tactical operations

9. Live Fire Exercise (LFX)

LFXs are resource-intensive; player units maneuver and employ organic and supporting weapons systems using full-service ammunition. LFXs integrate all combat arms, CS, and CSS elements. The extensive range and resource requirements usually limit them to platoon and company team levels. Consequently, their principal focus is unit and weapons integration at company team level. LFXs provide realistic training on collective and soldier skills in such areas as—

- Fire control and distribution
- Command and control in a noisy, confusing environment
- Individual movement techniques
- Integration of all fire support assets
- Small-unit tactics
- Weapons, demolitions, and other pyrotechnics not used in other exercises
- Safety awareness

Company-Level Training Mgmt

Ref: TC 25-30, chap. 1.

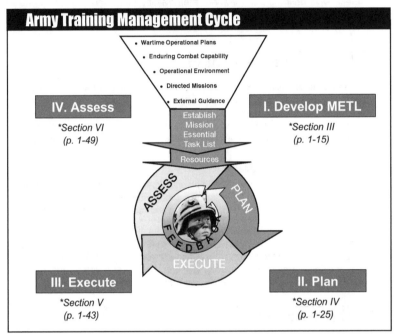

Army Training Management Cycle

- Wartime Operational Plans
- Enduring Combat Capability
- Operational Environment
- Directed Missions
- External Guidance

Establish Mission Essential Task List

Resources

IV. Assess
Section VI
(p. 1-49)

I. Develop METL
Section III
(p. 1-15)

ASSESS — PLAN — FEEDBA — EXECUTE

III. Execute
Section V
(p. 1-43)

II. Plan
Section IV
(p. 1-25)

Ref: FM 7-0, fig. 2-7, p. 2-15.

Effective training is the Army's number one priority during peacetime. Training management is the process used by Army leaders to identify training requirements and then plan, resource, execute and evaluate training. At the company level, as at all levels of command, the training meeting is an essential element of the training management process. Training meetings are periodic meetings conducted by leaders to review past training, plan and prepare future training, and exchange timely training information.

Battle-Focused Training

Battle focus is the process of deriving peacetime training requirements from wartime missions. The purpose of developing a "battle focus" approach to training is to allow cdrs to achieve a successful training program by consciously narrowing the focus of the unit's training efforts to a reduced number of vital tasks that are essential to mission accomplishment. Once the cdr has developed a battle focus approach to training, the next step is to ensure scarce resources of time and training dollars are not wasted.

Training Management Cycle

For a more detailed discussion of METL development, see Chapter 1, p. 1-15.

The training management cycle begins with the assignment of a wartime mission and the establishment of a mission essential task list (METL). Once the METL is developed, it becomes the training focus for the unit, or the "where we want to be" in terms of training proficiency. The training management cycle continues with a training assessment. This assessment is a "where we are" check in terms of training proficiency for the unit. These two basic elements of the training management cycle define the framework of the training plan. Knowing where you are (training assessment) and knowing where you are going (METL) are half the battle to conducting effective training.

A. Long-Range Planning

At the company level, long-range planning encompasses training that is planned for and resourced 12 months (active component) to 36 months (reserve components) in advance. Example resources that are planned for include training areas, ammunition, and fuel. By conducting long-range planning, units can predict their needs and coordinate for support well in advance of the planned training.

Planning Calendars

Long-range plans are translated into planning calendars for use by subordinate units in their planning process. An AC battalion calendar covers one training year, normally coinciding with a fiscal year (FY). An RC battalion calendar covers three training years.

This "planning horizon" allows companies to plan and prepare appropriately for major training events. It also allows soldiers to make plans for leave, military schooling, or specialty training without conflicting with major training events. Planning calendars provide specific information on training events. Generally, each separate event has a beginning and ending date, as well as a brief description of the activity.

B. Short-Range Planning

Short-range planning is a refinement of the long-range plan. The short-range plan defines in specific detail the broad general guidance found in the long-range plan. The short-range plan begins with a training assessment, and results in specific command training guidance (CTG).

Short-range planning at the battalion and company level has a planning horizon of 3 months (AC) and 12 months (RC). For AC battalions, short-range plans are prepared for each quarter, and are published 6 weeks before the start of the quarter. For RC bns, yearly guidance is published 3 - 4 months before the start of the training year.

Command Guidance

Command guidance is the product of the short-range plan. At the company level, command guidance comes from the battalion commander. The commander's training guidance is a document that describes the training strategy and assigns specific training objectives and priorities for the next quarter (AC) or year (RC). Battalion commanders base their command training guidance on input from brigade and higher commanders, along with planning recommendations from subordinate leaders. Command training guidance is very specific in nature, and normally addresses topics such as—

- Commander's assessment of METL proficiency
- Training priorities

Company Training Meeting Responsibilities
Ref: TC 25-30, p. 1-3 to 1-7.

Battalion Commander and Staff

The battalion command and his staff play a key role in the successful execution of company-level training. Besides providing command guidance and long-range training plans, the battalion commander sets the tone for establishing a safe, realistic training program that achieves the unit's training objectives. Most importantly, the battalion commander is the key leader with the power to protect companies from training detractors. The Command Sergeant Major (CSM) is personally responsible for advising the commander on all matters pertaining to enlisted soldiers. Additionally, the CSM, with other NCO leaders, helps integrate collective and individual soldier training tasks.

Company Commander

The company commander is the training manager for the company. Company commanders personally train platoon leaders with their platoons, and evaluate section, squad, team, and crew leaders with their units. If training needs to be scheduled, it is the company commander's responsibility to see that it gets put on the training schedule.

Executive Officer (XO)

The XO must be aware of command guidance, understand how to schedule training, and request the appropriate resources. Additionally, the XO is usually tasked with significant additional duties that can have a major impact on the training schedule.

Platoon Leader/ Platoon Sergeant

Platoon leaders and platoon sergeants (PSGs) are responsible for the training proficiency of their platoons. They assess the training proficiency with input from section/ squad leaders to identify the individual soldier and collective tasks that need training.
The platoon leader—
  • Assesses the training proficiency of collective tasks
  • Plans training
  • Rehearses trainers
  • Evaluates leader, team, and crew-level collective training
  • Conducts platoon training meetings
The platoon sergeant—
  • Assesses and evaluates the training proficiency of individual soldier tasks
  • Plans conduct of training
  • Selects individual soldier training tasks
  • Selects opportunity training
  • Provides input to the platoon leader's collective task assessment
  • Assigns and rehearses trainers
  • Conducts preexecution checks and ensures sldrs are prepared for & attend training

First Sergeant

As the senior enlisted soldier, the 1SG is charged with maintaining a high level of proficiency on soldier tasks and the NCO leader development program. First Sergeants keep tabs on the "training pulse" of the company. 1SGs also have formal responsibilities during Quarterly Training Briefs (QTBs) and discuss specific training topics, such as—
  • CTT survival skills
  • An assessment of the unit's battle focused soldier and NCO leader training programs
  • Soldier training proficiency feedback from current training events
  • Company education, Army Physical Fitness Test (APFT), weapon qualification data, reenlistment status and overweight programs

Other Leaders

Slice leaders must keep the company commander informed of their training needs, and their ability to help the unit with specialty training.

- Integration of slice training (other units that habitually fight and train together)
- Impact of time management systems on scheduled training (duty company, for example)
- Integration of soldier, leader, and collective training
- Evaluations, inspections, and feedback

Quarterly/Yearly Training Briefings

Each quarter for active component units (yearly for RC units) company commanders and first sergeants brief their brigade commanders on training-related issues. The briefings discuss past, present, and future training expectations. At this briefing, company commanders seek the approval of their training plans. Once approved, the brigade commander agrees to provide appropriate resources, and then promises to ruthlessly protect the company from unprogrammed training detractors.

Quarterly and yearly training briefings (YTBs) are high priority events and impact the entire chain of command. It is important that all primary leaders (1SG, platoon leader/PSG) and slice leaders attend the training briefing with the company commander. The briefing is designed to create confidence throughout the chain of command by ensuring that leaders at all levels understand the intent of the senior commanders. As a result, company commanders can make effective, independent training decisions as they execute the approved training plan.

C. Near-Term Planning

Near-term planning identifies specific actions required to execute the short-range plan. Near-term planning covers a four- to six-week period before the execution of training for AC units (four-month period for RC units). Near-term planning is conducted weekly AC units (monthly for RC) and consists of training meetings at battalion and company levels.

Training Meetings

Training meetings are conducted weekly (monthly for RC) at platoon and company level and are the primary forum for providing guidance for forming the training schedules.

I. Planning for Tng Mtgs

Ref: TC 25-30, chap. 2.

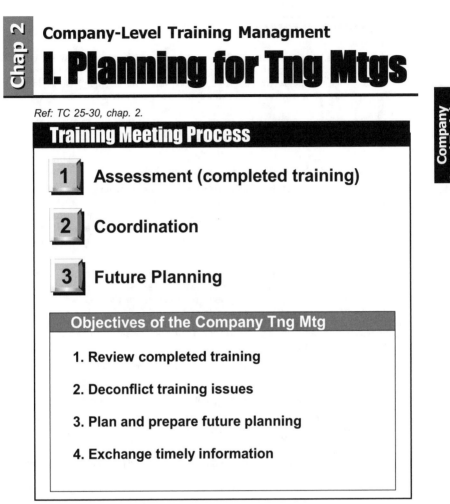

Training Meeting Process

1 Assessment (completed training)

2 Coordination

3 Future Planning

Objectives of the Company Tng Mtg

1. Review completed training

2. Deconflict training issues

3. Plan and prepare future planning

4. Exchange timely information

Ref: TC 25-30, chap. 4.

1. Assessment

The assessment phase seeks to describe the effectiveness of the training conducted since the last training meeting. Leaders from all subordinate units brief changes in training status. The commander takes this information, combines it with his personal observations, and comes up with a commander's assessment.

2. Coordination

With the formulation of the commander's assessment complete, the next phase is the coordination of future training that has already been planned. Detailed and specific instructions are added to events that already appear on the training schedule. Individual subordinate leaders may brief the company leadership on specific training exercises or events.

3 Future Planning

With coordination complete, the final phase of the training meeting process is to plan for future training. Subordinate leaders work with the commander to develop future training plans that support the assessment conducted in Phase I (assessment). During this phase the company commander ensures that scarce training time is effectively used.

Training Meeting Time and Place

When To Conduct the Training Meeting

Training meetings should be conducted on the same day and time each week when in garrison. Selection of a particular day to conduct the meeting depends on when the battalion conducts its training meeting. Logically, the company training meeting should follow the battalion training meeting by not more than two days. This allows for the information gleaned from this meeting to be incorporated into the company meeting before it becomes outdated.

Selection of a time to conduct training meetings depends on several factors. Main considerations include: enabling attendees to make the meeting, minimizing training disruptions, and allowing subordinate leaders time to brief their soldiers without delaying their normal release time.

For RC companies, selecting a time to conduct training meetings is more difficult. There are three alternatives:

- Conduct the meeting during a regularly scheduled drill session
- Conduct the meeting during an Additional Training Assembly (ATA)
- Conduct the meeting during a "for points only" or nonpaid assembly

For most companies, scheduling the meeting during the last period of the monthly drill is the best solution. However, commanders must select the time that best supports their needs.

Regardless of when the meeting is conducted, both AC and RC commanders must strive to hold the meeting on the same day and time each week or month. This allows subordinate leaders to plan and prepare for company training meetings, and plan their platoon meetings accordingly.

Training Meeting Location

Commanders select locations for training meetings based on the following factors: size, accessibility, and environmental considerations. With the large number of attendees for the typical training meeting, it is important to select a location that will fit everyone comfortably. A room in the company area may be sufficient, or possibly a conference room in the battalion headquarters. Other possible locations include an empty motor pool bay or outside if the weather permits.

The site selected should be easily accessible to all attendees, and preferably at the same location each meeting. This is particularly important for RC companies since subordinate or slice units may not all be based at the same location. Confusion and delays can be avoided if attendees do not have to search for the meeting place each month.

Environmental considerations that impact on the effectiveness of the meeting include weather and noise. A room that is excessively hot or cold, or lacks proper ventilation is inappropriate for a meeting place.

Company Training Meeting Attendees

Ref: TC 25-30, p. 2-2 to 2-4.

Attendance for selected leaders is mandatory for Company Training Meetings.

Company Commander

The commander is responsible for the efficient conduct of the training meeting. Although all ldrs participate, the cdr leads the meeting and provides direction and focus.

Executive Officer

The XO runs the training meeting in the commander's absence. Additionally the XO helps coordinate training for all the soldiers in sections or attachments without platoon leaders or PSGs. If assigned as maintenance officers, XOs assist the commander with coordinating maintenance-related activities that need to be addressed during training meetings.

First Sergeant

The ISG is the senior enlisted soldier in the company, and a personal advisor to the commander on all issues that effect individual soldier training in the unit. During the training meeting the ISG has the key task of helping the commander with individual soldier training assessments. Additionally, the ISG provides guidance and advice on training plans, also helping review preexecution checks discussed during the training meeting. In the role of advisor, the ISG helps in the leader development of both officers and NCOs by actively participating in the formulation of effective training plans for platoons.

Platoon Leaders

Platoon leaders brief the collective task proficiency of their platoon during the assessment phase of the training meeting. During the coordination phase of the training meeting, platoon leaders provide details on upcoming training. During the future planning phase they request and recommend collective training tasks they want to train.

Platoon Sergeants

Platoon sergeants brief individual soldier task proficiency during the assessment phase of the meeting if required by the commander. During the coordination phase, PSGs brief specific essential preexecution checks for upcoming training. During the future planning phase, PSGs recommend individual soldier tasks for opportunity training.

Master Gunners/Other Key Staff NCOs

Master gunners or other key staff NCOs advise the commander on specialist training. For example, the master gunner works with the ISG to track individual and crew-served weapon qualification, and helps the leaders with gunnery training assessments.

Maintenance Team Chiefs

Maintenance team chiefs coordinate the maintenance efforts of the company and work with the cdr and XO to ensure that timely support is provided whenever necessary. Additionally, the maintenance team chief recommends maintenance-related training for the company and informs the commander of scheduled services and inspections.

Supply Sergeants

Supply sergeants advise the commander on supply-related issues, inspections, and inventories. They also work with the XO and 1SG to coordinate support from outside sources.

External-Slice and Attachments

To "train like you fight," cdrs must fully integrate the training of all habitually associated (slice) units such as attached infantry, armor, engineer, or fire support leaders.

Special

Reserve Component companies may have readiness group (RG) and resident training detachment (RTD) personnel attend their training meetings.

Training Meeting Frequency

Garrison and Field Locations

Training meetings are held each week for AC companies/platoons and each month for RC companies/platoons. In a garrison environment this is generally easy to do. During extended deployments or field training exercises it may be more difficult. Commanders must strive to find the time, even in the field, to conduct training meetings. The planning cycle does not stop simply because it is not convenient to hold a meeting.

Company Huddles

Company huddles are daily gatherings of key leaders, usually before the first duty formation, to conduct a quick discussion of the day's training. As such, topics are limited to the following:

- Last minute changes to training
- Final pre-execution check review
- Special or new command guidance
- Maintenance/personnel status changes

Reserve Component companies conduct huddles before each drill, and every day during multiple unit training assemblies (MUTAs). Company huddles allow commanders to manage training on a daily basis, without calling impromptu training meetings. Company huddles usually last no more than five to ten minutes.

Ref: TC 25-30, chap. 3.

Commander's Assessment

The commander's assessment determines the training strengths and weaknesses of the unit. AC commanders' assessments generally review the training conducted in the past week. RC commanders' assessments focus on training that occurred during the most recent drill period.

Commanders use the T (trained) -P (needs practice) -U (un-trained) rating scale to assess training proficiency on METL tasks.

Commander's Assessment

Trained
"T" means the unit is trained and has demonstrated proficiency in accomplishing the task to wartime standards

Needs Practice
"P" means the unit needs to practice the task. Performance has demonstrated that the unit does not achieve the standard without some difficulty or has failed to perform some task steps to standard

Untrained
"U" means the unit cannot demonstrate an ability to achieve wartime proficiency

Ref: FM 7-0, p. 4-3.

Sources Of Input

Commanders and leaders at all levels use many sources to develop their training assessments. Possibly the best source is through personal observation. Personal observation allows leaders to see firsthand the training strengths and weaknesses. Sources include:

- Local external evaluations
- Combat Training Center (CTC) take-home packages
- After-action reviews (FTXs, gunnery, etc.)
- Annual training (AT) reports
- Common Task Test results
- Unit/mobile conduct-of-fire trainer (UCOFT/MCOFT)
- Maintenance and logistic evaluations
- APFT scores
- Weapon qualification records

Training Meeting Work Sheets

Purpose

The purpose of the training meeting work sheet is to help the commander maintain focus during the training meeting. The commander partially fills out the work sheet prior to the training meeting with notes and general plans for future training. During the meeting the work sheet is used to record training notes and assessment results.

Format

The recommended format for the training meeting work sheet a simple two-column form. Each column is then broken down into week-long blocks. The left side of the work sheet is reserved for the commander's notes and "reminders" of issues to address during the meeting. The right side of the work sheet is filled out during the meeting and is used to help complete future training schedules.

NOTE: The training meeting work sheet is an informal training management tool used by the company commander. It should not be inspected.

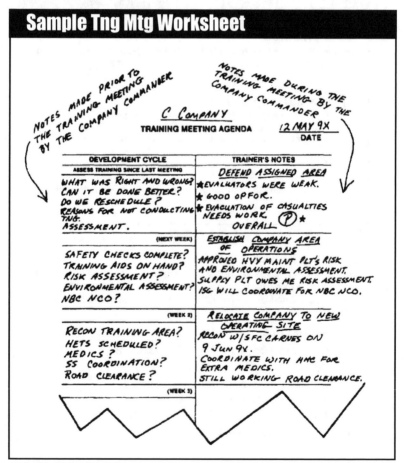

Sample Tng Mtg Worksheet

Ref: TC 25-30, fig. 3-3. p. 3-4.

What to Bring to the Training Meeting

Ref: TC 25-30, pp. 3-4 to 3-9.

The key to success is leaders having everything at their fingertips so that they can effectively participate in the meeting process.

Commander
- Company battle rosters
- Training meeting work sheet
- Mission essential task list with current assessment
- Most current Command Tng Guidance
- Long- and short-range calendars
- Company training schedules
  — Past week/month
  — Approved future schedules
- Applicable manuals
- Applicable OPORDs, MOIs, and training support requests

Executive Officer
- Maintenance schedule
- Inspection schedule
- Current DA Form 2406
- Supply inventory schedule
- Headquarters and headquarters company (HHC) training schedules
- Status of resources requested for training

First Sergeant
- Leader book
- Company battle rosters
- Company duty rosters
- Battalion duty schedules
- Taskings
- Appointment schedules
- Schools schedules
- Inspection schedules
- Miscellaneous information (APFT, height/weight data)

Plt Leader/Plt Sergeant
- Leader book
- Platoon assessment work sheets
- Training schedules
- Preexecution checklists
- Training and evaluation outlines (TEO) for future training
- Platoon battle rosters
- Future training work sheets

Master Gunner
- Leader book
- Training schedules

- Battle rosters
- Individual/crew weapon qualification records
- Unit Conduct-of-Fire Trainer (UCOFT) training results
- Gunnery training plans

Battle Staff NCO
- Training schedules
- Maintenance schedule
- Staff inspection schedule
- Maintenance Team Chief
- Leader book
- Battle roster
- Training schedules
- Maintenance schedule
- Inspection schedule
- Current DA Form 2406

Supply Sergeant
- Leader book
- Training schedules
- Supply inventory schedules (10 percent inventories)
- Inspection schedules

Training NCO
- Training schedule
- Battle roster
- SDT schedules
- Schools information

NBC NCO
- Leader book
- Training schedules
- NBC equipment services schedule
- Inspection schedule

Slice Leaders/Attachments
- Leader books
- Training schedules (own unit and company)
- Applicable SOPs
- Command training guidance
- Long- and short-range training calendars

Food Service NCO
- Leader book
- Training schedule
- Mess equipment service schedule
- Inspection schedule

Homework

Key leaders have "homework" to do before each training meeting. This homework includes specific tasks that require attention on a weekly basis. Preparing in advance of the meeting ensures leaders waste no time during the actual training meeting.

Commander

The company commander reviews the past week's (current drill for the RC) training and makes a tentative assessment prior to the meeting. Coordination with higher headquarters (includes battalion commander's latest training guidance) and adjacent units is finalized as much as possible for near-term training events. Other tasks include:

- Update training calendars
- See that platoon leaders are prepared for the training meeting
- Discuss training plans with the XO and ISG and seek any advice he may have to make training more effective
- Fill out left side of training meeting worksheet

Executive Officer

The XO ensures that the supply sergeant and maintenance team chief are prepared for the training meeting. In the maintenance arena, the XO sees that all service schedules are coordinated with the battalion motor officer. Additionally, the XO works closely with the S4 and support platoon leader for all classes of supply for training.

First Sergeant

The ISG works with platoon sergeants and other NCOs to ensure that platoons are prepared for the training meeting. Random reviews of leader books gives the 1SG a unique insight into the proficiency of individual soldiers. Information gleaned from this review helps the 1SG give the commander a better insight into soldier task proficiency.

Platoon Leader/Platoon Sergeant

The platoon leader and PSG have the most to gain from the company training meeting. They, particularly the PSG, must coordinate all of the details that support training that they want on the training schedule. For example, platoon leaders and PSGs would conduct the following coordination for land navigation training:

- Is a training area available?
- Can medics support?
- Develop TEOs
- Check with 1SG for duty roster conflicts
- Coordinate with the supply sergeant

The objective for PSGs is to do as much as possible to see that the training event is not "shot down" during the training meeting.

Ref: TC 25-30, chap. 4.

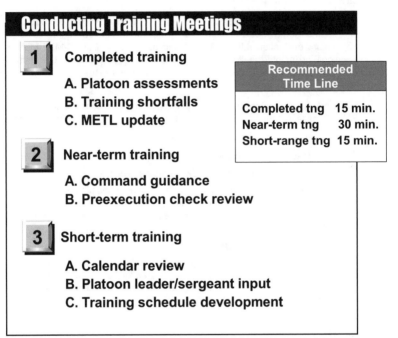

Conducting Training Meetings

1 Completed training

   A. Platoon assessments

   B. Training shortfalls

   C. METL update

2 Near-term training

   A. Command guidance

   B. Preexecution check review

3 Short-term training

   A. Calendar review

   B. Platoon leader/sergeant input

   C. Training schedule development

Recommended Time Line	
Completed tng	15 min.
Near-term tng	30 min.
Short-range tng	15 min.

Ref: TC 25-30, chap. 4.

Agenda

Components

There are three phases to company training meetings. They are completed training, near-term training, and short-range training. Commanders begin the meeting by discussing the training conducted since the last meeting, and progress through preexecution checks for near-term training. They finish by planning future training.

Time Requirements

Training meeting length should not exceed one hour. There are occasions or situations where meetings may last more than one hour. The key is for the commander to achieve the meeting objectives as quickly and efficiently as possible.

1. Completed Training

A. Platoon Assessments

Training meetings begin with platoon leaders and platoon sergeants assessing collective and soldier training since the last training meeting. This assessment is a detailed "go and no go" snapshot of all training conducted by the platoon. The sources of the platoon assessment may be formal, such as a platoon training evaluation extract from an ARTEP Mission Training Plan (MTP), or informal, such as comments gathered from an after-action review (AAR).

For example, if an interrogation platoon conducted training on establishing an operations site, the most logical source for giving an assessment of the training would be the training and evaluation outlines (TEO) found in ARTEP 34-298-1O-MTP, Mission Training Plan for Interrogation Platoon, Military Intelligence Battalion, Light Infantry Division. Based on the TEO extract, the platoon leader's assessment would sound like this:

"The interrogation platoon trained on establishing an operations site during last week's FTX. My assessment that we are a "GO" for the task, with the following shortcomings:

- Weak local security during occupation
- OPs need to improve camouflage skills
- Everyone needs to learn the proper tactical symbols to post on the SITMAP"

To assist in briefing this assessment, the platoon leader and platoon sergeant can prepare a simple one-page acetate-covered poster that graphically portrays the assessment. This poster can be used over again for each training meeting.

B. Training Shortfalls

As each platoon completes the training assessment, training shortfalls are addressed. A training shortfall is when training has been planned for, but not conducted. Platoon leaders must explain to the commander the reasons for not executing training, and what the plans are to makeup the missed training.

C. METL Update

After all platoons complete their training assessments and discuss any training shortfalls, the cdr then updates the company training assessment. Just as with the platoon assessment, this only deals with training conducted since the last meeting.

The primary source for the training assessment is the input from platoon leaders and personal observations of training.

The commander updates his training assessment for each METL task using a training assessment work sheet. The work sheet can take any form, but should contain the following information:

- A listing of each METL task
- Current training status of each METL task broken down by Battlefield Operating System (BOS)
- An overall assessment of each METL task
- A strategy to improve or sustain training proficiency

The general definition of "needs practice" assists when deciding upon an assessment, but the final decision of whether a task is a T, P, or U always comes down to a judgment call. Cdrs must honestly assess the ability of their company to execute METL tasks.

2. Near-Term Training

A. Command Guidance

The next step in the training meeting process is to apply new command guidance. Command guidance usually comes in the form of new or unscheduled requirements. Commanders must limit the discussion of new command guidance to training-related issues.

B. Pre-execution Check Review

One of the most important parts of the training meeting is the discussion of pre-execution checks. Pre-execution checks include the informal planning and detailed coordination conducted during the preparation for training. By reviewing key pre-execution checks the commander ensures that training events are fully planned for and coordinated with all elements of the company.

The AC commanders look four to six weeks out when reviewing pre-execution checks. For RC commanders, the time period is the next three months. Within these training windows, commanders review pre-execution checks in reverse order. The last week (AC) or month (RC) first, working down until the next training period is covered in detail.

Commanders focus on specific details when reviewing pre-execution checks. For example, if the training schedule reflected that a platoon would conduct land navigation training, the commander would look for the following level of detail:

- Have TEOs been prepared?
- Have lessons learned from the last land navigation training been incorporated?
- Has the training area been confirmed?
- Has transportation been requested?
- Has class I been coordinated?
- Are enough maps and compasses available?
- Have leaders conducted a risk and environment assessment?
- Have "lessons learned" been incorporated?

This is just a partial list, but enough to give an idea of what level of detail is discussed during preexecution check review. The closer the training is to being executed, the more detail required when reviewing pre-execution checks.

In reality, pre-execution checks would be discussed for every major training event. Habitually recurring events such as PT, motor stables, and barracks maintenance normally do not need to be reviewed during the training meeting. Pre-execution checks are briefed by the primary trainer as indicated on the training schedule. If this trainer is an NCO other than the platoon sergeant, then the platoon sergeant would brief the pre-execution checks during the training meeting. For almost every training event for platoons and below, the platoon sergeant is the key coordinator. The platoon sergeant coordinates the efforts of other NCOs in the platoon and ensures that training is thoroughly prepared.

For reserve component companies, the pre-execution check review process is almost identical to that for AC companies. Since the training window is generally three months long (usually six training days) the level of detail can be much higher.

3. Short-Term Training

A. Calendar Review

Before planning any new training, the commander must first check the battalion long-range training calendar. Any events indicated on the battalion calendar or found in command training guidance are put on the company training schedule first. After these events are accounted for, the commander can then begin planning company training.

B. Platoon Leader/Platoon Sergeant Input

Based on their training assessments, platoon leaders and platoon sergeants develop plans to improve training proficiency. These plans are prepared and briefed to the commander during the training meeting.

One method of preparing all the necessary information required to "win a slot" on the training schedule is to use a training event work sheet. The work sheet contains all of the information necessary to convince the commander that the particular training event fits into the overall company training plan.

C. Training Schedule Development

Commanders receive input from all platoons and other elements of the company before formulating the draft training schedule. Because of support limitations or other conflicts, the commander may have to disapprove a training event that a platoon requested, or move it to another week (AC) or month (RC). Once all conflicts are resolved, the commander develops a rough draft of the next training schedule. When formulating the training schedule the commander needs to keep the two "rules" of successful company training management in mind.

Rule Number One

The first rule is that commanders do not put anything on the training schedule that they do not intend to execute. Commanders must avoid the temptation of scheduling events they know cannot or will not be executed just to satisfy cyclic training requirements. If a commander does not intend to execute the training, then it should not be on the training schedule.

Rule Number Two

The second rule is that commanders do not need to fill up every minute of the training schedule. Filling up every minute on the training schedule often leaves subordinate leaders with little room to "maneuver" during the training day. Even the best units often must react to short notice, high priority taskings. With this in mind commanders should leave uncommitted time on the training schedule. Doing this allows for the following occurrences:

- Reaction time for short-notice taskings
- Time for immediate retraining
- Preparation time for training
- Make-up training for soldiers on sick call, etc.

IV. Preparing for Training

Ref: TC 25-30, chap. 5.

Preparing for Training

1 Prepare yourself for training

2 Prepare the resources

3 Prepare the training support personnel

4 Prepare the soldier

Certifying Leaders & Trainers

A. Trainer

B. Certifier

C. Validator

Training preparation duties

	Trainer	Certifier	Validator
Individual	SL/TC	PSG	1SG
Section/Crew/Squad	PL/PSG	CO CDR/1SG	BN CDR/CSM
Platoon	CO CDR	BN CDR	BDE CDR
Company	BN CDR	BDE CDR	ADC

Ref: TC 25-30, fig. 5-1, p. 5-2.

Ref: TC 25-30, chap. 5.

Certifying Leaders and Trainers

A key element in executing successful training is the preparation and certification of trainers and leaders. Time must be dedicated on the training schedule to train, rehearse, and certify leaders and trainers.

A. Trainer

- Conducts collective and individual training
- Provides evaluation on TEOs
- Conducts risk assessment
- Conducts environmental assessment; considers environmental constraints
- Assesses training and directs collective training on weak subtasks
- Conducts leader training

B. Certifier

- Senior trainer, conducts leader training
- Provides assessment through capstone events
- Certifies that the trainer is prepared for training
- Reviews risk and environmental assessment

C. Validator

- Conducts sample assessments of a task in a unit

Guidance for Trainers

The proper execution of training is a difficult but rewarding process. Trainers use a four-step process when preparing for training.

1. Prepare Yourself for Training

Trainers must know how to perform the task being trained. This requires the trainer to master the task through study and practice. After mastering the actual task, trainers must rehearse the training exactly as it is to be presented.

Before conducting training, trainers must know how to train others to perform the task. Good trainers ensure that training is performance oriented (hands-on). That means getting enough training aids so that every soldier can practice the task.

2. Prepare the Resources

Once a training event is scheduled, the trainer must arrange for training aids to support the training. When looking at training aids, the trainer takes the following actions:

- Identify and request training aids, devices, simulators, and simulations (TADSS)
- Get the equipment and materials before rehearsal
- Operate the equipment to become familiar with it and check it for completeness and functionality during rehearsal

For the active component, the platoon sergeant is the key to acquiring the appropriate training aids. Once the TADSS are identified, the trainer works with the platoon sergeant to develop a schedule to accomplish all of the required inspections and rehearsals prior to the training event.

For reserve component companies the resource preparation process is more complicated. There are generally three "scenarios" that exist for TADSS support. They are:

Scenario 1

The training aids may be on hand at the Armory/Reserve Training Center. In this case the trainer can request the training aid and rehearse before training execution without much difficulty.

Scenario 2

The training aid is only available from the unit's training support installation. In this case the trainer coordinates with the unit training NCO (full time Active Guard Reserve (AGR)) to pickup the training aid a month in advance of training execution.

Scenario 3

The training aid is only available from the unit's support installation and is an item that is in high demand (such as MILES equipment). This type of equipment cannot sit idle for a full month. As in scenario 2, the trainer coordinates with the unit training NCO for TADSS support. The training NCO would then draw the equipment a week in advance, inspect it, and make it available for the trainer to rehearse when time permits.

It is obvious that an RC trainer may not be able to conduct extensive rehearsals.

3. Prepare the Training Support Personnel

Trainers must ensure that support personnel are fully prepared to support the training event. Trainers do this by ensuring that the following actions occur:

- Training support personnel understand their mission
- Evaluators or OCs know their roles
- Support personnel are equipped and prepared to perform the tasks to standard
- Support personnel participate in recons and rehearsals

4. Prepare the Soldier

Soldiers need to be ready for training to achieve the maximum training benefit. Posting a copy of the training schedule is not sufficient to ensure soldiers are fully ready for training. The platoon sergeant assists trainers by—

- Identifying soldiers to be trained
- Ensuring subordinate leaders assess levels of training proficiency for each soldier (leader books)
- Training any prerequisite tasks or skills first
- Motivating soldiers by telling them the tasks to be trained and expected performance standards

Platoon sergeants do not necessarily physically execute each of these tasks. They are the catalyst to see that the chain of command sees that every effort is taken to prepare soldiers for training. This often includes after-duty-hours training for soldiers to ensure that they can get the maximum benefit from scheduled training.

Evaluation Plan

Each training event is evaluated during training execution. The purpose of a training evaluation is to provide feedback to the chain of command. This feedback is used to assess METL task proficiency, shape future training plans, and enhance leader development.

Planning for evaluations

Planning for evaluations begins when the company training schedule is signed and approved. Companies are primarily involved with planning and resourcing evaluations for sections, squads, crews, and individual soldiers. Other evaluations, such as those for platoon STX lanes, would be planned and resourced at battalion level.

Types of evaluations

Evaluations can be informal or formal and internal or external. Key points for each type of evaluation follow.

Informal evaluations are most commonly used at battalion level and below. Internal evaluations are planned, resourced, and conducted by the unit undergoing the evaluation. They are—

- Conducted by all leaders in the chain of command
- Continuous
- Used to provide immediate feedback on training proficiency

Formal evaluations are usually scheduled on the long-range and short-range calendars. These include ARTEP external evaluations, operational readiness evaluations (ORE), and technical validation inspections (TVIs). They are—

- Sometimes unannounced, such as an EDRE
- Normally highlighted during QTBs and YTBs
- Resourced with dedicated evaluators or OCs

External evaluations are also planned and resourced. However, they are normally conducted by he headquarters two levels above the unit being evaluated. For example, division evaluates battalions; brigade evaluates companies; battalion evaluates platoons; and company evaluates sections, squads, teams, or crews.

These evaluations can be combined to meet the particular needs of the units or soldiers being evaluated. Regardless of the type of evaluation, leaders must be present at all training, personally supervising and evaluating.

After-Action Reviews

An after-action review is a professional discussion of an event, focused on performance standards, that allows soldiers to discover for themselves what happened, why it happened, and how to improve on weaknesses and sustain strengths in the future. Leaders use AARs as a primary source for their training assessments.

Note: See chapter 3, AARs.

Ref: TC 25-30, app. A.

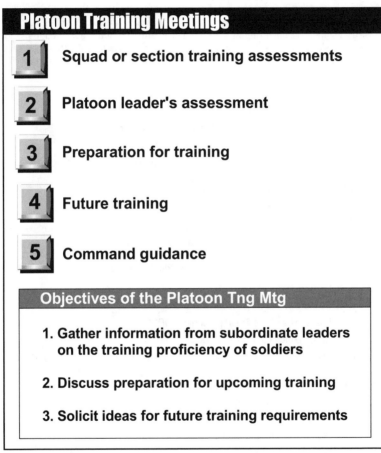

Platoon Training Meetings

1 Squad or section training assessments

2 Platoon leader's assessment

3 Preparation for training

4 Future training

5 Command guidance

Objectives of the Platoon Tng Mtg

1. Gather information from subordinate leaders on the training proficiency of soldiers

2. Discuss preparation for upcoming training

3. Solicit ideas for future training requirements

Ref: TC 25-30, app. A.

Platoons follow an established agenda when executing training meetings. This allows for a quick and efficient meeting, very similar to the system used for the issuing of an operation order (OPORD) for a tactical operation.

1. Squad or Section Training Assessments

Squad leaders give the platoon leader their assessments of the training they conducted since the last platoon meeting. This does not need to be an elaborate briefing. Since the platoon leader normally attends all training, squad leaders will only have to highlight what went right and what went wrong for the squad.

The purpose of the squad or section assessment is to get honest input directly from the fret-line leader. If the squad can perform the task to standard, then that is what needs to come out during the discussion. Likewise, if the squad leader feels the squad cannot perform a task to standard, that needs to be said. The platoon leader must establish an atmosphere where this can occur.

2. Platoon Leader's Assessment

Upon completion of squad assessments the platoon leader gives his assessment of the status of platoon collective tasks that support the company METL. This assessment is based upon squad assessments, personal observations, and discussions with the PSG. Upon announcing his assessment, other leaders update their leader books with the appropriate new entry for collective task proficiency. Elements include:

- Platoon collective task title
- Company METL that it supports
- Assessment (T-P-U, or GO/NO GO as appropriate)
- Brief description of the "why" for the assessment
- Plan to improve, if possible at this time (may be delayed until next meeting)

3. Preparation For Training

This phase of the platoon meeting belongs to the PSG. After the platoon leader has developed and received approval for a training plan, it is up to the PSG to see that the training is thoroughly prepared and executed. In this capacity, the PSG must personally ensure preexecution checks are completed and that nothing that could effect the quality of the training is left to chance. To do this, the PSG ensures that his NCOs-

1. Prepare themselves
2. Prepare the training resources (TADSS)
3. Prepare training support personnel (OPFOR)
4. Prepare their soldiers (prerequisite training)

Much of this review is discussed one-on-one between the PSG and the primary NCO trainer. However, during the platoon meeting squad leaders brief specifics of their training, ensuring to cover, at a minimum—

- Key pre-execution checks
- Rehearsal plan
- "Homework" requirements
- Any unresolved problems

PSGs maintain the tempo of the meeting by prompting squad leaders with questions and suggestions on the training being discussed. If the PSG or platoon leader is not satisfied that tng is prepared to standard, the discussion is continued after the meeting.

4. Short-Range Training

The platoon leader next solicits recommendations for future training from the NCOs. This is the chance for squad leaders to ask for time on the training schedule to correct training deficiencies. Squad leaders use the data in their leader books to select the individual and collective tasks that require attention.

The platoon leader and the platoon sergeant evaluate this input after the meeting and decide the specific tasks (individual and collective) that they feel require attention. The platoon leader then develops a detailed plan and briefs it to the company commander either one-on-one or during the company training meeting.

5. Command Guidance

Although command guidance is generally passed to subordinates as soon as it is received, the platoon meeting is a good time for a recap. The platoon leader briefs new training guidance, specific guidance or command directives from the 1SG or CSM.

Organization

Platoon training meetings are organized very similar to company training meetings, only less formal in nature. They are held every week (every month for RC during inactive duty training) and generally last about 30 minutes. Only key leaders attend; each squad- or section-level unit is represented by a single NCO. Keeping the number of leaders to an essential minimum allows for a more candid and efficient exchange of information. A typical list of attendees for a platoon meeting are listed below.

- Platoon leader
- Platoon sergeant
- Squad leaders/section leaders

Some platoons do not neatly fit the mold of infantry or armor platoons. For these platoons the platoon leader and PSG together decide who should attend the meeting, keeping in mind that the objective is to have each section represented by one NCO. For example, a maintenance platoon without a platoon leader may have a list of attendees that resembles the list shown below.

- Platoon sergeant
- Recovery section sergeant
- Services section sergeant
- Maintenance team chief
- PLL section sergeant

Whatever the composition of the list of participants, the platoon sergeant ensures that all NCOs are prepared for the meeting. This means everyone being on time and properly equipped. At a minimum, NCOs need to bring the following to a platoon meeting:

- Leader book
- Paper and pencil/pen
- Training schedules
- Calendar

When the meeting is conducted in the field the leaders assemble in a convenient location: in the back of a Bradley Fighting Vehicle, under a tree, or in a tent. The key is the meeting is informal. Elaborate training aids and other props are not necessary for a successful meeting.

Tips for a Successful Meeting

Good, efficient meetings come in many shapes and forms. The techniques listed below apply to all types of platoons, both active and reserve:

- Conduct the meetings the same time and place each week and make them mandatory
- Try a "standing meeting" (do not use chairs) if the meetings are lasting too long
- Enforce the use of leader books
- Listen when it is time to listen
- Do not wait until the meeting to conduct essential coordination
- Focus on training issues, leave administrative details until after the meeting
- Discuss one-on-one issues after the meeting

VI. Leader's Books

Ref: TC 25-30, app. B.

Leaders are responsible for providing training assessments to the chain of command on their soldiers and units. Commanders use these assessments to make training decisions. The purpose of the leader book is to give leaders a tool that efficiently tracks soldier and unit training status.

The leader book is a tool maintained by leaders at all levels for recording and tracking soldier proficiency on mission-oriented tasks. The exact composition of leader books varies depending on the mission and type of unit. Specific uses are to–

- Track and evaluate soldiers' training status and proficiency on essential soldier tasks
- Provide administrative input to the chain of command on the proficiency of the unit; for example platoon, section, squad, team, or crew
- Conduct soldier performance counseling

Daily Evaluations and Soldier Counseling

Leaders books are an integral part of everyday training. Leaders habitually carry their leader books with them during the training day. Shortly after training is evaluated leaders update the appropriate section of their leader book. By keeping up with the current status of the training of their soldiers, ldrs can give timely and accurate assessments.

Company and Platoon Training Meetings

Leader books are "part of the uniform" for both company and platoon training meetings. Accurate leader books add credibility to training assessments, and form the basis for requesting training.

NOTE. Leader books should not be formally inspected, however, their periodic review by the chain of command is appropriate. Leaders should not lose sight of the purpose of leader books-that of being a self-designed tool to assist leaders in tracking the training proficiency of their soldiers. They come in many shapes and forms; there is no approved solution or format.

1. Soldier Administrative Data

Administrative soldier data sheets contain everything leaders need to know about their soldiers. The form can be SATS generated or one developed by the leader. Recommended information for soldier data sheets includes the following:

- Name, rank, age, and duty position
- Current weapon qualification
- APFT score/date
- Height/weight data
- Family data
- Special medical data

Knowing this type of information allows leaders to better provide training which meets their soldiers' personal needs.

2. Co METL/Plt Suporting Collective Task List

Leaders need to maintain copies of both company METL and platoon supporting collective task lists in their leader books. Having these lists and current assessments helps leaders to select the appropriate individual, and collective tasks that require training emphasis.

This form can be in any format that the leader chooses. A recommended technique is to list the task, the current assessment, and also a "why" for the assessment.

Common Task Test Proficiency

Common Task Test (CTT) proficiency is critical information for all leaders. GO/NO GO data should be recorded for each soldier, along with the date. Knowing this allows ldrs to select appropriate opportunity training. Since company HQs maintain individual soldiers' DA Forms 5164, leaders must develop their own system for tracking CTT proficiency.

Essential Soldier Task Poficiency

Leaders select and track the proficiency of MOS-specific tasks which support the company METL/platoon supporting collective task list. By knowing the exact status of these essential tasks leaders can quickly identify weaknesses and plan and conduct training to improve proficiency.

Unit Collective Task Proficiency

Leaders need to know the proficiency of their units to perform the collective tasks and drills that support the platoon supporting collective task list. Leaders derive section/squad/crew collective tasks from the applicable MTPs. Units without a published MTP must determine for themselves which collective tasks and drills support the platoon supporting collective tasks. In many cases the section/squad/crew collective task list will be identical to the platoon list.

SATS does not provide a collective task proficiency tracking form. Recommended information for collective task proficiency forms includes-

- Collective tasks
- Assessment blocks (T-P-U or GO/NO GO)
- Date training last executed
- Reason for assessment/strategy to improve

3. Soldier Counseling Forms and Status

Soldier counseling is an essential element of a leader's duties. The leader book is a natural focal point for performance counseling. The extent that counseling can be tracked with the leader book is the leader's decision. Some leaders may want to maintain the DA Form 2166-7-1, NCO Counseling Checklist/Record (MCSR), for each subordinate NCO. DA Form 4856-E, Developmental Counseling Form, may be maintained for each soldier.

After-Action Reviews (AARs)

Ref: TC 25-20, p. 1-1 to 1-5.

An after-action review (AAR) is a professional discussion of an event, focused on performance standards, that enables soldiers to discover for themselves what happened, why it happened, and how to sustain strengths and improve on weaknesses. It is a tool leaders and units can use to get maximum benefit from every mission or task. It provides:

- Candid insights into specific soldier, leader, and unit strengths and weaknesses from various perspectives
- Feedback and insight critical to battle-focused training
- Details often lacking in evaluation reports alone

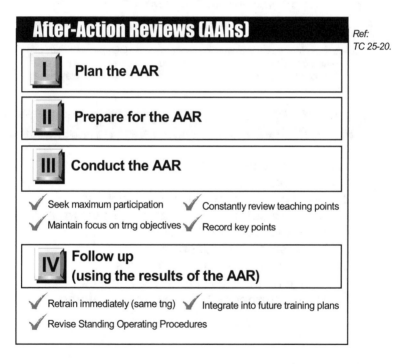

After-Action Reviews (AARs)

Ref: TC 25-20.

I Plan the AAR

II Prepare for the AAR

III Conduct the AAR

✓ Seek maximum participation ✓ Constantly review teaching points
✓ Maintain focus on trng objectives ✓ Record key points

IV Follow up
(using the results of the AAR)

✓ Retrain immediately (same tng) ✓ Integrate into future training plans
✓ Revise Standing Operating Procedures

Evaluation

Evaluation is the basis for the commander's unit-training assessment. No commander, no matter how skilled, will see as much as the individual soldiers and leaders who actually conduct the training. Leaders can better correct deficiencies and sustain strengths by carefully evaluating and comparing soldier, leader, and unit performance against the standard. The AAR is the keystone of the evaluation process.

Feedback

Feedback compares the actual output of a process with the intended outcome. By focusing on the task's standards and by describing specific observations, leaders and soldiers identify strengths and weaknesses and together decide how to improve their performances. This shared learning improves task proficiency and promotes unit bonding and esprit. Squad and platoon leaders will use the information to develop input for unit-training plans. The AAR is a valid and valuable technique regardless of branch, echelon, or training task.

Of course, AARs are not cure-alls for unit-training problems. Leaders must still make on-the-spot corrections and take responsibility for training their soldiers and units. However, AARs are a key part of the training process. The goal is to improve soldier, leader, and unit performance. The result is a more cohesive and proficient fighting force.

Because soldiers and leaders participating in an AAR actively discover what happened and why, they learn and remember more than they would from a critique alone. A critique only gives one viewpoint and frequently provides little opportunity for discussion of events by participants. Soldier observations and comments may not be encouraged. The climate of the critique, focusing only on what is wrong, prevents candid discussion of training events and stifles learning and team building.

To maximize the effectiveness of AARs, leaders should plan and rehearse before training begins. After-action review planning is a routine part of unit near-term planning (six to eight weeks out). During planning, leaders assign OC responsibilities and identify tentative times and locations for AARs. This ensures the allocation of time and resources to conduct AARs and reinforces the important role AARs play in realizing the full benefit of training.

AAR Key Points

1. **Are conducted during or immediately after each event**
2. **Focus on intended training objectives**
3. **Focus on soldier, leader and unit performance**
4. **Involve all participants in the discussion**
5. **Use open-ended questions**
6. **Are related to specific standards**
7. **Determine strengths and weaknesses**
8. **Link performance to subsequent training**

Ref: TC 25-20, fig. 1-1, p. 1-3.

Types of AARs

All AARs follow the same general format, involve the exchange of ideas and observations, and focus on improving training proficiency. How leaders conduct a particular AAR determines whether it is formal or informal. A formal AAR is resource-intensive and involves the planning, coordination, and preparation of supporting training aids, the AAR site, and support personnel. Informal AARs (usually for soldier, crew, squad, and platoon training) require less preparation and planning.

Types of After-Action Reviews

Formal Reviews	Informal Reviews
▪ Have external observers and controllers (OCs)	▪ Conducted by internal chain of command
▪ Take more time	▪ Take less time
▪ Use more complex training aids	▪ Use simple training aids
▪ Are scheduled beforehand	▪ Are conducted when needed
▪ Are conducted where best supported	▪ Are conducted at the training site

Ref: FM 25-20, fig. 1-3, p. 1-4.

Formal

Leaders plan formal AARs at the same time they finalize the near-term training plan (six to eight weeks before execution). Formal AARs require more planning and preparation than informal AARs. They may require site reconnaissance and selection, coordination for training aids (terrain models, map blow-ups, and so on), and selection and training of observers and controllers (OCs). Formal AARs are:

• Usually scheduled on the long-range and short-range calendars. These include ARTEP evaluations, expert infantry badge (EIB), expert field medic badge (EFMB), and technical validation inspections (TVIs).

• Sometimes unannounced, such as an emergency deployment readiness exercise (EDRE)

• Normally highlighted during quarterly training briefs (QTBs) and yearly training briefs (YTBs)

• Resourced with dedicated evaluators or OCs

The unit undergoing the evaluation plans, resources, and conducts internal evaluations. They also plan and resource external evaluations. However, the headquarters two levels above the unit being evaluated conducts theirs. For example, division evaluates battalion; brigade evaluates companies; battalion evaluates platoons; and company evaluates sections, squads, teams, or crews. Observers and controllers assist commanders in the evaluation process by collecting data and providing feedback.

Formal AARs are usually held at company level and above. An exception might be an AAR of crew, section, or small-unit performance after gunnery tables or after a platoon situational training exercise (STX). Squad and platoon AARs are held before the execution of formal company and higher echelon AARs. This allows all levels of the unit to benefit from an AAR experience. It also provides OCs and leaders with observations and trends to address during the formal AAR.

During formal AARs, the AAR leader (unit leader or OC) focuses the discussion of events on training objectives. At the end, the leader reviews key points and issues identified (reinforcing learning that took place during the discussion) and once again focuses on training objectives.

Informal

Leaders usually conduct informal AARs for soldier and small-unit training at platoon level and below. At company and battalion levels, leaders may conduct informal AARs when resources for formal AARs, including time, are unavailable. Informal AARs use the standard AAR format. Informal AARs are:

- Most commonly used at battalion level and below
- Conducted by all leaders in the chain of command
- Continuous
- Used to provide immediate feedback on training proficiency

Leaders may use informal AARs as on-the-spot coaching tools while reviewing soldier and unit performances during training. For example, after destroying an enemy observation post (OP) during a movement to contact, a squad leader could conduct an informal AAR to make corrections and reinforce strengths. Using nothing more than pinecones to represent squad members, he and his soldiers could discuss the contact from start to finish. The squad could quickly—

- Evaluate their performance against the Army standard (or unit standard if there is no published Army standard)
- Identify their strengths and weaknesses
- Decide how to improve their performance when training continues

Informal AARs provide immediate feedback to soldiers, leaders, and units during training. Ideas and solutions the leader gathers during informal AARs can be immediately put to use as the unit continues its training. Also, during lower echelon informal AARs, leaders often collect teaching points and trends they can use as discussion points during higher echelon formal AARs.

Informal AARs maximize training value because all unit members are actively involved. They learn what to do, how to do it better, and the importance of the roles they play in unit-task accomplishment. They then know how to execute the task to standard.

The most significant difference between formal AARs and informal AARs is that informal AARs require fewer training resources and few, if any, training aids. Although informal AARs may be part of the unit evaluation plan, they are more commonly conducted when the leader or OC feels the unit would benefit. Providing immediate feedback while the training is still fresh in soldiers' minds is a significant strength of informal AARs.

I. Planning the AAR

Ref: TC 25-20, p. 2-1 to 2-7.

Leaders are responsible for planning, executing, evaluating, and assessing training. Each training event is evaluated during training execution. A key element in an evaluation plan is the AAR plan. The AAR plan provides the foundation for successful AARs. Leaders develop an AAR plan for each training event. It contains:

- **Who** will observe the training and who will conduct the AAR
- **What** trainers should evaluate (training and evaluation outlines (TEOs))
- **Who** is to attend
- **When** and where the AAR will occur
- **What** training aids trainers will use

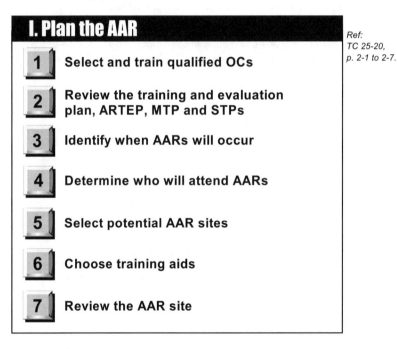

I. Plan the AAR

Ref: TC 25-20, p. 2-1 to 2-7.

1 Select and train qualified OCs

2 Review the training and evaluation plan, ARTEP, MTP and STPs

3 Identify when AARs will occur

4 Determine who will attend AARs

5 Select potential AAR sites

6 Choose training aids

7 Review the AAR site

Trainers use the AAR plan to identify critical places and events they must observe to provide the unit with a valid evaluation. Examples include unit maintenance collection points, passage points, and unit aid stations. By identifying these events and assigning responsibilities, unit leaders can be sure someone will be there to observe and take notes. This allows the training unit team to make the best use of its limited resources and conduct a first-class training event.

After-action review plans also designate who will observe and control a particular event. The term observer and controller refers to the individual tasked to observe training and provide control for the training exercise as well as to lead the AAR.

Example Exercise AAR Plan

Observer	1LT Jones
Element	1st Platoon
Priority tasks	Occupy, prepare and defend a battle position
Who attends	All
When held	One hour after contact broken
Location	Behind 2d squad GH44319218
Special requirements	LTC Smith will provide closing comments

Ref: FM 25-20, fig. 2-1, p. 2-3

1. Select and Train Observers and Controllers

When planning an AAR, trainers should select OCs who:

- Can perform the tasks to be trained to Army standards
- Are knowledgeable on the duties they are to observe
- Are knowledgeable on current TTPs

When using external OCs...

When using external OCs, trainers must ensure that OCs are at least equal in rank to the leader of the unit they will evaluate. If trainers must choose between experience and understanding of current TTPs or rank, they should go with experience. A staff sergeant with experience as a tank platoon sergeant can observe the platoon better than can a sergeant first class who has no platoon sergeant experience.

Use dedicated OCs

Observers should not have duties which would detract from their OC duties. If this is not possible, leaders in the chain of command should evaluate subordinate units and conduct the AARs. For example, squad leaders would evaluate the performance of soldiers in their squads and limit AAR discussion to individual actions. Platoon leaders or platoon sergeants would do the same for squads, company commanders or first sergeants for platoons, and so on. If possible, they should avoid evaluating their own duties and tasks. (It is hard to be objective about your own performance and to determine how it will affect your unit.)

Train the trainer

Trainers must train their small-unit leaders and OCs. Each OC leads AARs for the element he observes and provides input to the AAR leader for the next higher echelon. Leaders and OCs must be trained in the use of the methods, techniques, and proce-dures in this training circular. If possible, trainers should assign someone with AAR experience to accompany and assist an inexperienced AAR leader until he is proficient. The trainer must conduct AARs to help AAR leaders improve their performances. Inexperienced AAR leaders should observe properly conducted AARs before attempting to lead one. The trainer must include classes on small-group discussion techniques in OC instruction.

2. Review the Training and Evaluation Plan

Observers and controllers selected to observe training and lead AARs cannot observe and assess every action of every individual. Training and evaluation outlines provide tasks, conditions, and standards for the unit's training as well as the bottom line against which leaders can measure unit and soldier performance.

The steps in AMTPs and soldier's manuals provide the standard method for completing each task and help structure consistent observations. Using the evaluation plan, the OC can concentrate efforts on critical places and times where and when he can best evaluate unit performance. This ensures that feedback is directly focused on tasks being trained and provides the unit and its leaders with the information they need to improve or sustain proficiency.

3. Identify When AARs Will Occur

Leaders must schedule time to conduct AARs as an integrated part of overall training. When possible, they should plan for an AAR at the end of each critical phase or major training event. For example, a leader could plan a stopping point after issuing an operation order (OPORD), when the unit arrives at a new position, after it consolidates on an objective, and so on.

For planning purposes, leaders should allow approximately 30-45 minutes for platoon-level AARs, 1 hour for company-level AARs, and about 2 hours for battalion-level and above. Soldiers will receive better feedback on their performance and remember the lessons longer if the AAR is not rushed. Reviewers must fully address all key learning points. They must not waste time on dead-end issues.

4. Determine Who Will Attend AARs

The AAR plan specifies who must attend each AAR. Normally, only key players attend. At times, however, the more participants present, the better the feedback. Leaders must select as many participants as appropriate for the task and the AAR site.

At each echelon, an AAR has a primary set of participants. At squad and platoon levels, everyone should attend and participate. At company or higher levels, it may not be practical to have everyone attend because of continuing operations or training. In this case, friendly and OPFOR commanders, unit leaders, and other key players (fire support team (FIST) chief, radio telephone operator (RTO), and so on) may be the only participants.

5. Select Potential AAR Sites

Usually at or near the training exercise site

An AAR will usually occur at or near the training exercise site. Leaders should identify and inspect AAR sites and prepare a site diagram showing the placement of training aids and other equipment. Designated AAR sites also allow pre-positioning of training aids and rapid assembly of key personnel, minimizing wasted time.

Provide a comfortable AAR environment

The trainer should make soldiers attending the AAR as comfortable as possible (by removing helmets and so on), providing shelter from the elements (sun, cold, rain, snow), having refreshments (coffee, water), and creating an environment where participants can focus on the AAR without distractions. Participants should not face into the sun, and key leaders should have seats up front. Vehicle parking and equipment security areas should be far enough away from the AAR site to prevent distractions.

6. Choose Training Aids

Training aids add to an AAR's effectiveness. The trainer should choose them carefully and request them well in advance. Training aids should directly support discussion of the training and promote learning. Local training support center (TSC) catalogs list training aids available to each unit. Dry-erase boards, terrain models, and enlarged maps are all worthwhile under the right conditions.

Training Aids

Formal AARs	Informal AARs
▪ Terrain model	▪ Unit markers
▪ Enlarged map	▪ Pointer
▪ Models	▪ Unit maneuver graphics
▪ Dry-erase marker board	▪ Communications recordings
▪ Photographs	▪ Rocks and twigs
▪ Video camera and monitor	▪ Other field expedients

Ref: FM 25-20, fig. 2-2, p. 2-7.

To select the right training aids, trainers should ask:

- What points will I need to make during the AAR, and what training aids will help me make these points?
- Will the aid illustrate one or more of the main points?
- Can I use the actual terrain or equipment?
- Does the aid have any restrictions or special requirements, such as additional generators?
- Will participants be able to see and hear it?
- Is it really necessary for the discussion or just nice to have?

7. Review the AAR Plan

The AAR plan is only a guide. Leaders should review it regularly to make sure it is still on track and meets the training needs of their units.

Note: Remember that every change takes preparation and planning time away from subordinate OCs or leaders. This may impact the quality of feedback. The purpose of the AAR plan is to allow OCs and AAR leaders as much time as possible to prepare for the AAR. Frequent or unnecessary changes prevent that.

AAR Step II

II. Preparing for the AAR

Ref: TC 25-20, p. 3-1 to 3-7.

II. Prepare the AAR

Ref: TC 25-20, p. 3-1 to 3-7.

1	Review training objectives, orders, METL and doctrine
2	Identify key events OCs are to observe
3	Observe the training and take notes
4	Collect observations from other OCs
5	Organize observations (Identify key discussion or teaching points)
6	Reconnoiter the selected AAR site
7	Prepare the AAR site
8	Conduct rehearsal

1. Review Doctrine, Training Objectives, Orders and METL

Preparation is the key to the effective execution of any plan. Preparing for an AAR begins before the training and continues until the actual event. Observers and controllers should use the time before the training event to brush up on their knowledge. They must be tactically and technically proficient. Therefore, they should review current doctrine, technical information, and applicable unit SOPs to ensure they have the tools they need to properly observe unit and individual performances.

To gain understanding of both the focus of unit training and the exercise plan, OCs must also review the unit's training objectives, orders, and METL. The unit's training objectives focus on the specific actions and events which OCs must observe to provide valid observations and to effectively lead the unit in its discussion during the AAR. Orders, including OPORDs and fragmentary orders (FRAGOs), which the leader issues before and during training, establish initial conditions for tasks the units must perform. The METL contains the complete task, conditions, and standards for each task.

2. Identify Key Events Observers and Controllers are to Observe

Observers and controllers must focus their observations on the actions required to perform tasks to standard and to accomplish training objectives. To do this effectively, they must identify which events are critical to accomplishing each task and objective. By identifying key events, OCs can make sure they position themselves in the right place at the right time to observe the unit's actions. Examples of critical events include:

- Issuance of OPORDs and FRAGOs
- Troop-leading procedures (TLPs)
- Contact with opposing forces
- Resupply and reconstitution operations
- Intelligence preparation of the battlefield (IPB)
- Passage of lines

3. Observe the Training and Take Notes

All unit activities have three phases: planning, preparation, and execution. These phases can help the OC structure his observation plan and notetaking. He should keep an accurate written record of what he sees and hears and record events, actions, and observations by time sequence to prevent loss of valuable information and feedback. He can use any recording system (notebook, prepared forms, 3-by-5 cards) that fits his needs as long as it is reliable, sufficiently detailed (identifying times, places, and names), and consistent.

Example AAR Observation Worksheet

Training/exercise title:

Event:

Date/time:

Location of observation:

Observation (player/trainer action):

Discussion (tied to task / standard if possible):

Conclusions:

Recommendations (indicate how unit have executed the task(s) better or describe training the unit needs to improve):

Ref: FM 25-20, fig. 3-1, p. 3-3.

The OC should include the date-time group (DTG) of each observation so he can easily integrate his observations into those of other OCs. This will provide a comprehensive and detailed overview of what happened. When the OC has more time, he can review his notes and fill in any details he did not write down earlier.

One of the most difficult OC tasks is to determine when and where to position himself to observe training. The OC does not always need to stay close to the unit leader. Sometimes he can see more from locations where he can observe the performance of critical tasks or the overall flow of unit actions. However, he should not position himself where he would be a training distracter. He must look and act as a member of the unit (using individual and vehicle camouflage, movement techniques, cover and concealment, and so on). He must not compromise the unit's location or intent by being obvious. At all times, he should be professional, courteous, and low-key.

Another way to observe training is to monitor unit communications nets. Modern technology can quickly record radio transmissions using voice-activated tape recorders or video cameras. By listening to radio traffic, OCs can trace the dissemination of orders and messages as well as monitor information flow from subordinate units. When appropriate, OCs can monitor computer traffic on the Maneuver Control System (MCS) to determine unit actions or status and to identify the impact of inaccurate information on unit operations.

4. Collect Observations From Other Observers and Controllers

The AAR plan designates a time, place, or method to consolidate feedback from other OCs. The leader will need a complete picture of what happened during the training to conduct an effective AAR. Therefore, each OC must give him input. This input may come from subordinate units, combat support (CS) and combat service support (CSS) units, or adjacent units.

The leader may also receive input from OPFOR leaders, players, and OCs. The enemy's perspective is often useful in identifying why a unit was or was not successful. During formal AARs, the OPFOR leader briefs his plan and intent to set the stage for a discussion of what happened and why.

5. Organize Observations

After the leader has gathered all the information, he puts his notes in chronological sequence so he can understand the flow of events. Next, he selects and sequences key events in terms of their relevance to training objectives, identifying key discussion and/or teaching points.

6. Select and Reconnoiter the AAR Site

The leader selects potential AAR sites as part of the overall planning process. He should select areas near where the training occurred or where most of the critical events took place. However, he must be sure to reconnoiter alternate sites in case he finds he cannot use his first choice.

7. Prepare the AAR Site

The leader sets up the AAR site so participants can see the actual terrain or training aids. Horseshoe arrangements encourage discussion and allow everyone to see.

If possible, the leader should preposition training aids and equipment. If he cannot, he should place them nearby under the control of a responsible individual.

8. Conduct Rehearsal

After thorough preparation, the leader reviews the AAR format, rehearses at the AAR site, and gets ready to conduct the AAR. He should then announce to unit leaders the AAR start time and location. He must allow enough time for OCs to prepare and rehearse while unit leaders account for personnel and equipment, perform actions which their unit SOP requires, and move to the AAR site.

III. Conducting the AAR

Ref: TC 25-20, p. 4-1 to 4-8.

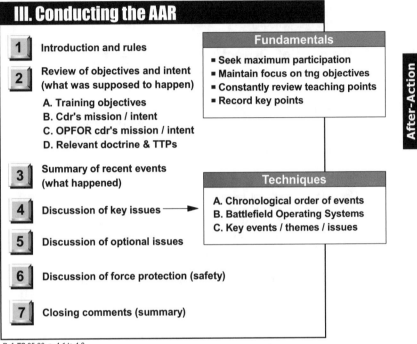

III. Conducting the AAR

1 Introduction and rules

2 Review of objectives and intent (what was supposed to happen)
- A. Training objectives
- B. Cdr's mission / intent
- C. OPFOR cdr's mission / intent
- D. Relevant doctrine & TTPs

3 Summary of recent events (what happened)

4 Discussion of key issues →

5 Discussion of optional issues

6 Discussion of force protection (safety)

7 Closing comments (summary)

Fundamentals
- Seek maximum participation
- Maintain focus on tng objectives
- Constantly review teaching points
- Record key points

Techniques
- A. Chronological order of events
- B. Battlefield Operating Systems
- C. Key events / themes / issues

After-Action Reviews (AARs)

Ref: TC 25-20, p. 4-1 to 4-8.

1. Introduction and Rules

The training exercise is over, AAR preparation is complete, and key players are at the designated AAR site. It is now time to conduct the AAR. The leader should begin with some type of "attention getter" — a joke, an appropriate anecdote, or a historical example that relates to the training, exercise, event, or conduct of the AAR. Then, if necessary, he reviews the purpose and sequence of the AAR. His introduction should include the following thoughts:

- An AAR is a dynamic, candid, professional discussion of training which focuses on unit performance against the Army standard for the tasks being trained. Everyone can, and should, participate if they have an insight, observation, or question which will help the unit identify and correct deficiencies or maintain strengths.

- An AAR is not a critique. No one, regardless of rank, position, or strength of personality, has all of the information or answers. After-action reviews maximize training benefits by allowing soldiers, regardless of rank, to learn from each other.

- An AAR does not grade success or failure. There are always weaknesses to improve and strengths to sustain.

Soldier participation is directly related to the atmosphere created during the introduction. The AAR leader should make a concerted effort to draw in and include soldiers who seem reluctant to participate. The following techniques can help the leader create an atmosphere conducive to maximum participation. He should:

- Enter the discussion only when necessary
- Reinforce the fact that it is permissible to disagree
- Focus on learning and encourage people to give honest opinions
- Use open-ended and leading questions to guide the discussion of soldier, leader, and unit performance

2. Review of Objectives and Intent (What Was Supposed to Happen)

A. Training objectives

The AAR leader should review unit training objectives for the training mission(s) the AAR will cover. He should also restate the tasks being reviewed as well as the conditions and standards for the tasks.

B. Commander's mission and intent

Using maps, operational graphics, terrain boards, and so on, the commander should restate the mission and his intent. Then, if necessary, the discussion leader should guide the discussion to ensure everyone understands the plan and the commander's intent. Another technique is to have subordinate leaders restate the mission and discuss their commander's intent.

C. OPFOR commander's mission and intent

In a formal AAR, the OPFOR commander explains his plan to defeat friendly forces. He uses the same training aids as the friendly force commander so participants can understand the relationship of both plans.

D. Relevant Doctrine, tactics, techniques and procedures (TTPs)

3. Summary of Recent Events (What Happened)

The AAR leader now guides the review using a logical sequence of events to describe and discuss what happened. He should not ask yes or no questions, but encourage participation and guide discussion by using open-ended and leading questions. An open-ended question has no specific answer and allows the person answering to reply based on what was significant to him. Open-ended questions are also much less likely to put him on the defensive. This is more effective in finding out what happened. For example, it is better to ask,

"SGT Johnson, what happened when your Bradley crested the hill?"

rather than—

"SGT Johnson, why didn't you engage the enemy tanks to your front?"

As the discussion expands and more soldiers add their perspectives, what really happened will become clear. Remember, this is not a critique or lecture; the OC does not tell the soldiers or leaders what was good or bad. However, the AAR leader must ensure specific issues are revealed, both positive and negative in nature. Skillful guidance of the discussion will ensure the AAR does not gloss over mistakes or unit weaknesses.

4. Discussion of Key Issues

The AAR is a problem-solving process. The purpose of discussion is for participants to discover strengths and weaknesses, propose solutions, and adopt a course of action to correct problems. Leaders can organize the discussion using one of the three techniques in the following paragraphs.

Discussion Techniques

A. Chronological Order of Events
This technique is logical, structured, and easy to understand. It follows the flow of training from start to finish and allows soldiers to see the effects of their actions on other units and events. By covering actions in the order they took place, soldiers and leaders are better able to recall what happened.

B. Battlefield Operating Systems (BOS)
To focus and structure the AAR, the leader can also use the battlefield operating systems (BOSs). By focusing on each BOS and discussing it across all phases of the training exercise, participants can identify systemic strengths and weaknesses. This technique is particularly useful in training staff sections whose duties and responsibilities directly relate to one or more BOS. However, leaders using this technique must be careful not to lose sight of the big picture. They must not get into long discussions about BOS which do not relate to mission accomplishment.

Battlefield Operating Systems (BOSs)

1. Intelligence
2. Maneuver
3. Fire support
4. Air defense
5. Mobility and survivability
6. Combat service support
7. Command and control

Ref: FM 100-5, p. 2-12.

C. Key Events/Themes/Issues

A key events discussion focuses on critical training events which directly support training objectives the chain of command identified before the exercise began. Keeping a tight focus on these events prevents the discussion from becoming sidetracked by issues which do not relate to training objectives. This technique is particularly effective when time is limited.

Fratricide

All incidents or near incidents of fratricide, whether inflicted by direct fire, indirect fire, or close air support (CAS), will be discussed in detail. The leader must focus on identifying the cause of the fratricide and develop SOPs and TTPs to prevent it in the future. Regardless of the environment (training or combat), the leader must swiftly deal with all fratricide incidents. As soon as possible after the event, an AAR should be held to discuss the circumstances surrounding the event, using the following discussion points:

- How and why did the incident occur?
- How were friendly personnel and equipment identified?
- What fire control measures were in place where the fratricide occurred and how effective were they?
- How did the commander's risk assessment and overall intent for the mission address the issue of fratricide?

Flexibility

One of the strengths of the AAR format is its flexibility. The leader could use the chronological format to structure the discussion, then, if a particular BOS seems to have systemic issues that the group needs to address, follow that BOS across the entire exercise. Once that topic is exhausted, the AAR could proceed using the chronological format. Each technique will generate discussion, identify unit strengths, weaknesses, and training the unit needs to improve proficiency. However, the leader must remember to:

- Be specific, avoiding generalizations
- Be thorough
- Not dwell on issues unrelated to mission accomplishment
- Focus on actions
- Relate performance to the accomplishment of training objectives
- Identify corrective action for areas of weakness
- Continually summarize

5. Discussion of Optional Issues

In addition to discussing key issues, the leader might also address several optional topics, included in the following paragraphs.

A. Soldier/Leader Skills

Through discussion, the unit can identify critical soldier and leader skills which affected unit or individual performance. The leader should note these skills for retraining or for future unit training. (Often it is best to discuss leader skills in a separate meeting or AAR specifically for that purpose. This allows for a candid discussion of leadership issues without wasting unit AAR time best spent on reviewing the entire training exercise.) The AAR leader for follow-on meetings should be a member of the unit so participants can candidly address key training issues without fear of airing dirty laundry in front of outsiders.

B. Tasks to Sustain/Improve

This technique focuses on identifying tasks on which the unit is proficient and tasks on which they need further training. The intent is to focus training on mission-essential tasks and supporting soldier, leader, and collective tasks which need improvement rather than training to known strengths. Although it is important to sustain proficiency on tasks whose standards the unit has met, it is more important to train to standard on new or deficient mission-essential tasks. Train to weakness, not to strength.

C. Statistics

Statistics are a double-edged sword. Effective feedback requires participants to measure, collect, and quantify performance during the training exercise. Statistics supply objective facts which reinforce observations of both strengths and weaknesses. The danger lies in statistics for statistics' sake. Chart after chart of ratios, bar graphs, and tables quickly obscures any meaning and lends itself to a "grading" of unit performance. This stifles discussion and degrades the AAR's value. Statistics and statistics-based charts should identify critical trends or issues and reinforce teaching points. (An example for an armored unit would be to link the number of rounds fired to the number of enemy vehicles destroyed. This would provide a good indication of unit gunnery skills.) Judicious use of statistic feedback supports observations and provides a focus to AAR discussions.

D. Other topics

Other topics which participants may need to discuss include troop-leading procedures, troop deployment and use of terrain, synchronization, enemy disposition and tactics, information dissemination and use, obstacle emplacement and breaching, vision of the battlefield, knowing the enemy, and so forth.

6. Discussion of Force Protection (Safety) Issues

Safety is every soldier's business and applies to everything a unit does in the field and in garrison. Safety should be specifically addressed in every AAR and discussed in detail when it impacts unit effectiveness or soldier health. The important thing is to treat safety precautions as integral parts of every operation.

7. Closing Comments (Summary)

During the summary, the AAR leader reviews and summarizes key points identified during the discussion. He should end the AAR on a positive note, linking conclusions to future training. He should then leave the immediate area to allow unit leaders and soldiers time to discuss the training in private.

IV. Following Up

Ref: TC 25-20, p. 5-1 to 5-3.

IV. Follow Up (Using the Results of the AAR)

 1 Identify tasks requiring retraining

 2 Fix the problem

- **Retrain immediately (same training event)**
- **Revise Standing Operating Procedures (SOPs)**
- **Integrate into future training plans**

3 Use to assist in making commander's assessment

Ref: TC 25-20, p. 5-1 to 5-3.

Benefits of AARs

The real benefits of AARs come from taking the results and applying them to future training. Leaders can use the information to assess performance and to immediately retrain units in tasks where there is weakness. Leaders can also use AARs to help assess unit METL proficiency. Immediately or shortly after the training event, leaders should conduct a trained-practiced-untrained (T-P-U) assessment and develop a future-training concept.

Leaders should not delay or reschedule retraining except when absolutely necessary. If the leader delays retraining, he must be sure the soldiers understand that they did not perform the task to standard and that retraining will occur later.

After-action reviews are the dynamic link between task performance and execution to standard. They provide commanders a critical assessment tool to use to plan soldier, leader, and unit training. Through the professional and candid discussion of events, soldiers can compare their performance against the standard and identify specific ways to improve proficiency.

Immediate Retraining (Same Training Exercise)

Retraining may be immediately necessary to address particularly weak areas. By applying its learning, a unit can improve its performance to meet the Army standard. However, the focus of this effort is not to get an A or B; it is to improve soldier and unit performance. By the end of an AAR, soldiers must clearly understand what was good, bad, or average about their performance.

After-Action Reviews (AARs)

Field Manuals 25-100 and 25-101 require leaders to schedule time for retraining as a normal part of the planning process. The unit must retrain on the tasks which they did not perform to standard before the unit can go to the next training event. The unit must always retrain and perform critical gate tasks derived from the Combined Arms Training Strategy (CATS) to standard before progressing to the next level of tasks. This reinforces the learning process by immediately correcting substandard performance. The unit must conduct any necessary retraining of supporting soldier or leader tasks before retraining on deficient collective tasks. This ensures that the unit can focus on performing the collective task. When there is not enough time to retrain the task or tasks, the leader must integrate it into the unit's training plan and reschedule it.

NOTE: Critical gate tasks are tasks grouped in a training event that a soldier or unit must perform and receive an evaluation for before progressing to more complex or difficult tasks or events. Commanders must prescribe the performance of the task to standard as a prerequisite for progressing to subsequent tasks or events.

Time or complexity of the mission may prevent retraining on some tasks during the same exercise. When this happens, leaders must reschedule the mission or training in accordance with FM 25-100 and FM 25-101. As part of this process, leaders must ensure that deficient supporting tasks found during the AAR are also scheduled and retrained.

Revised Standing Operating Procedures (SOPs)

After-action reviews may reveal problems with unit SOPs. If so, unit leaders must revise the SOP and make sure units implement the changes during any future training.

The AAR in Combat

Training does not stop when a unit goes into combat. Training is always an integral part of precombat and combat operations although limited time and proximity to the enemy may restrict the type and extent of training. Only training improves combat performance without imposing the stiff penalties combat inflicts on the untrained.

The AAR is one of the most effective techniques to use in a combat environment. An effective AAR takes little time, and leaders can conduct them almost anywhere consistent with unit security requirements. Conducting AARs helps overcome the steep learning curve that exists in a unit exposed to combat and helps the unit ensure that it does not repeat mistakes. It also helps them sustain strengths. By integrating training into combat operations and using tools such as AARs, leaders can dramatically increase their unit's chances for success on the battlefield.

The Army Leader
Be, Know, Do

Ref: FM 22-100, chap 1.

Leadership Dimensions

Leaders of character and competance...
act to achieve excellence by providing purpose, direction and motivation.

Values	Attributes	Skills	Actions[5]		
"Be"	"Be"	"Know"	"Do"		
Loyalty	Mental	Interpersonal	Influencing	Operating	Developing
Duty			Communicating	Planning / Preparing	Developing
Respect	Physical	Conceptual			
Selfless Service			Decision Making	Executing	Building
Honor	Emotional	Technical			
Integrity			Motivating	Assessing	Learning
Personal Courage		Tactical			

Ref: FM 22-100, Fig. B-1, p. B-1.

1. The mental attributes of an Army leader are will, self-discipline, initiative, judgment, self-confidence, intelligence and cultural awareness.

2. The physical attributes of an Army leader are health fitness, physical fitness, and military and professional bearing.

3. The emotional attributes of an Army leader are self-control, balance and stability.

4. The interpersonal, conceptual, technical and tactical skills are different for direct, organizational and strategic leaders.

5. The influencing, operating and improving actions are different for direct, organizational and strategic leaders.

Levels of Leadership

I. Direct
II. Organizational
III. Strategic
(Note: See chap. 5)

The Army's ultimate responsibility is to win the nation's wars. For you as an Army leader, leadership in combat is your primary mission and most important challenge. To meet this challenge, you must develop character and competence while achieving excellence. This chapter is about leadership. It focuses on character, competence, and excellence. It's about accomplishing the mission and taking care of people. It's about living up to your ultimate responsibility, leading your soldiers in combat and winning our nation's wars.

Be, Know, Do

Be

Army leadership begins with what the leader must BE, the values and attributes that shape a leader's character. It may be helpful to think of these as internal qualities: you possess them all the time, alone and with others. They define who you are; they give you a solid footing. These values and attributes are the same for all leaders, regardless of position, although you certainly refine your understanding of them as you become more experienced and assume positions of greater responsibility. For example, a sergeant major with combat experience has a deeper understanding of selfless service and personal courage than a new soldier does.

Know

Your skills are those things you KNOW how to do, your competence in everything from the technical side of your job to the people skills a leader requires. The skill categories of the Army leadership framework apply to all leaders. However, as you assume positions of greater responsibility, you must master additional skills in each category. Army leadership positions fall into one of three levels: direct, organizational, and strategic.

Do

But character and knowledge—while absolutely necessary—are not enough. You cannot be effective, you cannot be a leader, until you apply what you know, until you act and DO what you must. As with skills, you will learn more leadership actions as you serve in different positions. Because actions are the essence of leadership, the discussion begins with them. Leadership is influencing people—by providing purpose, direction, and motivation—while operating to accomplish the mission and improving the organization.

Leaders of Leaders

At any level, anyone responsible for supervising people or accomplishing a mission that involves other people is a leader. Anyone who influences others, motivating them to action or influencing their thinking or decision making, is a leader. It's not a function only of position; it's also a function of role. In addition, everyone in the Army—including every leader—fits somewhere in a chain of command. Everyone in the Army is also a follower or subordinate. There are, obviously, many leaders in an organization, and it's important to understand that you don't just lead subordinates— you lead other leaders. Even at the lowest level, you are a leader of leaders.

For example, a rifle company has four leadership levels: the company commander leads through platoon leaders, the platoon leaders through squad leaders, and the squad leaders through team leaders. At each level, the leader must let subordinate leaders do their jobs. Practicing this kind of decentralized execution based on mission orders in peacetime trains subordinates who will, in battle, exercise disciplined initiative in the absence of orders. They'll continue to fight when the radios are jammed, when the plan falls apart, when the enemy does something unexpected.

This decentralization does not mean that a commander never steps in and takes direct control. There will be times when a leader has to stop leading through subordinates, step forward, and say, "Follow me!" A situation like this may occur in combat, when things are falling apart.

More often, however, you should empower your subordinate leaders: give them a task, delegate the necessary authority, and let them do the work. Of course you need to check periodically. How else will you be able to critique, coach, and evaluate them? But the point is to "power down without powering off." Give your subordinate leaders the authority they need to get the job done. Then check on them frequently enough to keep track of what is going on but not so often that you get in their way. You can develop this skill through experience.

It takes personal courage to operate this way. But a leader must let subordinate leaders learn by doing. Is there a risk that, for instance, a squad leader—especially an inexperienced one—will make mistakes? Of course there is. But if your subordinate leaders are to grow, you must let them take risks. This means you must let go of some control and let your subordinate leaders do things on their own—within bounds established by mission orders and your expressed intent.

A company commander who routinely steps in and gives orders directly to squad leaders weakens the whole chain of command, denies squad leaders valuable learning experiences, and sends a signal to the whole company that the chain of command and NCO support channel can be bypassed at any time. On the other hand, successful accomplishment of specified and implied missions results from subordinate leaders at all levels exercising disciplined initiative within the commander's intent. Effective leaders strive to create an environment of trust and understanding that encourages their subordinates to seize the initiative and act.

Weak leaders who have not trained their subordinates sometimes say, "My organization can't do it without me." Many people, used to being at the center of the action, begin to feel as if they're indispensable. You have heard them: "I can't take a day off. I have to be here all the time. I must watch my subordinates' every move, or who knows what will happen?" But no one is irreplaceable. The Army is not going to stop functioning because one leader—no matter how senior, no matter how central—steps aside. In combat, the loss of a leader is a shock to a unit, but the unit must continue its mission. If leaders train their subordinates properly, one of them will take charge.

Strong commanders—those with personal courage—realize their subordinate leaders need room to work. This doesn't mean that you should let your subordinates make the same mistake over and over. Part of your responsibility as a leader is to help your subordinates succeed. You can achieve this through empowering and coaching. Train your subordinates to plan, prepare, execute, and assess will enough to operate independently. Provide sufficient purpose, direction, and motivation for them to operate in support of the overall plan.

Finally, check and make corrections. Take time to help your subordinates sort out what happened and why. Conduct AARs so your people don't just make mistakes, but learn from them. There is not a soldier out there, from private to general, who has not slipped up from time to time. Good soldiers, and especially good leaders, learn from those mistakes. Good leaders help their subordinates grow by teaching, coaching, and counseling.

Leadership and Command

Command is a specific and legal position unique to the military. It's where the buck stops. Like all leaders, commanders are responsible for the success of their organizations, but commanders have special accountability to their superiors, the institution, and the nation. Commanders must think deeply and creatively, for their concerns encompass yesterday's heritage, today's mission, and tomorrow's force. To maintain their balance among all the demands on them, they must exemplify Army values. The nation, as well as the members of the Army, hold commanders accountable for accomplishing the mission, keeping the institution sound, and caring for its people.

Command is a sacred trust. The legal and moral responsibilities of commanders exceed those of any other leader of similar position or authority. Nowhere else does a boss have to answer for how subordinates live and what they do after work. Our society and the institution look to commanders to make sure that missions succeed, that people receive the proper training and care, that values survive. On the one hand, the nation grants commanders special authority to be good stewards of its most precious resources: freedom and people. On the other hand, those citizens serving in the Army also trust their commanders to lead them well. NCOs probably have a more immediate impact on their people, but commanders set the policies that reward superior performance and personally punish misconduct. It's no wonder that organizations take on the personal stamp of their commanders. Those selected to command offer something beyond their formal authority: their personal example and public actions have tremendous moral force.

Subordinates

No one is only a leader; each of you is also a subordinate, and all members of the Army are part of a team. A technical supervisor leading a team of DA civilian specialists, for instance, isn't just the leader of that group. The team chief also works for someone else, and the team has a place in a larger organization.

Part of being a good subordinate is supporting your chain of command. And it's your responsibility to make sure your team supports the larger organization. Consider a leader whose team is responsible for handling the pay administration of a large organization. The chief knows that when the team makes a mistake or falls behind in its work, its customers—soldiers and DA civilians—pay the price in terms of late pay actions. One day a message from the boss introducing a new computer system for handling payroll changes arrives. The team chief looks hard at the new system and decides it will not work as well as the old one. The team will spend a lot of time installing the new system, all the while keeping up with their regular workload. Then they'll have to spend more time undoing the work once the new system fails. And the team chief believes it will fail—all his experience points to that.

But the team chief cannot simply say, "We'll let these actions pile up; that'll send a signal to the commander about just how bad the new system is and how important we are down here." The team does not exist in a vacuum; it's part of a larger organization that serves soldiers and DA civilians. For the good of the organization and the people in it, the team chief must make sure the job gets done.

Since the team chief disagrees with the boss's order and it affects both the team's mission and the welfare of its members, the team chief must tell the boss; he must have the moral courage to make his opinions known. Of course, the team chief must also have the right attitude; disagreement doesn't mean it's okay to be disrespectful. He must choose the time and place—usually in private—to explain his concerns to the boss fully and clearly. In addition, the team chief must go into the meeting knowing that, at some point, the discussion will be over and he must execute the boss's decision, whatever it is.

Once the boss has listened to all the arguments and made a decision, the team chief must support that decision as if it were his own. If he goes to the team and says, "I still don't think this is a good idea, but we're going to do it anyway," the team chief undermines the chain of command and teaches his people a bad lesson. Imagine what it would do to an organization's effectiveness if subordinates chose which orders to pursue vigorously and which ones to half step.

Both leaders understood the path to excellence: disciplined leaders with strong values produce disciplined soldiers with strong values. Together they become disciplined, cohesive units that train hard, fight honorably, and win decisively.

The Payoff: Excellence

Leaders of character and competence act to achieve excellence by developing a force that can fight and win the nation's wars and serve the common defense of the U.S.

You achieve excellence when your people are disciplined and committed to Army values. Individuals and organizations pursue excellence to improve, to get better and better. The Army is led by leaders of character who are good role models, consistently set the example, and accomplish the mission while improving their units. It is a cohesive organization of high-performing units characterized by the warrior ethos.

Army leaders get the job done. Sometimes it's on a large scale, such as GEN Meyer's role in making sure the Army was ready to fight. Other times it may be amid the terror of combat, as with COL Chamberlain at Gettysburg. However, most of you will not become Army Chief of Staff. Not all of you will face the challenge of combat. So it would be a mistake to think that the only time mission accomplishment and leadership are important is with the obvious examples—the general officer, the combat leader. The Army cannot accomplish its mission unless all Army leaders, soldiers, and DA civilians accomplish theirs—whether that means filling out a status report, repairing a vehicle, planning a budget, packing a parachute, maintaining pay records, or walking guard duty. The Army isn't a single general or a handful of combat heroes; it's hundreds of thousands of soldiers and DA civilians, tens of thousands of leaders, all striving to do the right things. Every soldier, every DA civilian, is important to the success of the Army.

Moral Excellence: Accomplishing the Mission with Character

The ultimate end of war, at least as America fights it, is to restore peace. For this reason the Army must accomplish its mission honorably. The Army fights to win, but with one eye on the kind of peace that will follow the war. The actions of Ulysses S. Grant, general in chief of the Union Army at the end of the Civil War, provide an example of balancing fighting to win with restoring the peace.

The Army must accomplish its mission honorably. FM 27-10 discusses the law of war and reminds you of the importance of restoring peace. The Army minimizes collateral damage and avoids harming noncombatants for practical as well as honorable reasons. No matter what, though, soldiers fight to win, to live or die with honor for the benefit of our country and its citizens.

Army leaders often make decisions amid uncertainty, without guidance or precedent, in situations dominated by fear and risk, and sometimes under the threat of sudden, violent death. At those times leaders fall back on their values and Army values and ask, What is right? The question is simple; the answer, often, is not. Having made the decision, the leader depends on self-discipline to see it through.

Achieving Collective Excellence

An excellent Army is the collection of small tasks done to standard, day in and day out. Good leaders know that each of these people is contributing in a small but important way to the business of the Army. At the end of the day, at the end of a career, those leaders, soldiers and DA civilians—the ones whose excellent work created an excellent Army—can look back confidently. Good leaders see excellence wherever and whenever it happens. Excellent leaders make certain all subordinates know the important roles they play. Look for everyday examples that occur under ordinary circumstances: the way a soldier digs a fighting position, prepares for guard duty, fixes a radio, lays an artillery battery; the way a DA civilian handles an action, takes care of customers, meets a deadline on short notice. Whether they commanded an invasion armada of thousands of soldiers or supervised a technical section of three people, they know they did the job well and made a difference.

Excellence in leadership does not mean perfection; on the contrary, an excellent leader allows subordinates room to learn from their mistakes as well as their successes. In such a climate, people work to improve and take the risks necessary to learn. They know that when they fall short—as they will—their leader will pick them up, give them new or more detailed instructions, and send them on their way again. This is the only way to improve the force, the only way to train leaders.

A leader who sets a standard of "zero defects, no mistakes" is also saying "Don't take any chances. Don't try anything you can't already do perfectly, and for heaven's sake, don't try anything new." That organization will not improve; in fact, its ability to perform the mission will deteriorate rapidly. Accomplishing the Army's mission requires leaders who are imaginative, flexible, and daring. Improving the Army for future missions requires leaders who are thoughtful and reflective. These qualities are incompatible with a "zero-defects" attitude.

Competent, confident leaders tolerate honest mistakes that do not result from negligence. The pursuit of excellence is not a game to achieve perfection; it involves trying, learning, trying again, and getting better each time. This in no way justifies or excuses failure. Even the best efforts and good intentions cannot take away an individual's responsibility for his actions.

Summary

Leadership in combat is your primary and most important challenge. It requires you to accept a set of values that contributes to a core of motivation and will. If you fail to accept and live these Army values, your soldiers may die unnecessarily. Army leaders of character and competence act to achieve excellence by developing a force that can fight and win the nation's wars and serve the common defense of the United States. The Army leadership framework identifies the dimensions of Army leadership: what the Army expects you, as one of its leaders, to BE, KNOW, and DO.

Leadership positions fall into one of three leadership levels: direct, organizational, and strategic. The perspective and focus of leaders change and the actions they must DO become more complex with greater consequences as they assume positions of greater responsibility. Nonetheless, they must live Army values and possess leader attributes.

Being a good subordinate is part of being a good leader. Everyone is part of a team, and all members have responsibilities that go with belonging to that team. But every soldier and DA civilian who is responsible for supervising people or accomplishing a mission that involves other people is a leader. All soldiers and DA civilians at one time or another must act as leaders.

Values and attributes make up a leader's character, the BE of Army leadership. Character embodies self-discipline and the will to win, among other things. It contributes to the motivation to persevere. From this motivation comes the lifelong work of mastering the skills that define competence, the KNOW of Army leadership. As you reflect on Army values and leadership attributes and develop the skills your position and experience require, you become a leader of character and competence, one who can act to achieve excellence, who can DO what is necessary to accomplish the mission and take care of your people. That is leadership—influencing people by providing purpose, direction, and motivation while operating to accomplish the mission and improving the organization. That is what makes a successful leader, one who lives the principles of BE, KNOW, DO.

Character: What a Leader Must BE

Ia. Army Values

Ref: FM 22-100, chap 2 and ALDH, chap. 1.

Ia. Army Values	
L	**Loyalty**
D	**Duty**
R	**Respect**
S	**Selfless Service**
H	**Honor**
I	**Integrity**
P	**Personal Courage**

Ref: FM 22-100, p. 2-3.

The Army is a value based organization. FM 22-100 (Military Leadership) identifies seven values that all leaders must possess: loyalty, duty, respect, selfless-service, honor, integrity, personal courage.

These values serve several functions. First, values help define the identity of America's Army. The trust that America's Army has among its members is dependent on individuals identifying with these values. The trust that the American people have in the Army depends on members of America's Army identifying with these values. Second, values help to define a person's character. Third, values will also provide guideposts--a compass--for personal character development and moral reasoning, resulting in good behavior.

Army values remind us and tell the rest of the world—the civilian government we serve, the nation we protect, even our enemies—who we are and what we stand for. The trust soldiers and DA civilians have for each other and the trust the American people have in us depends on how well we live up to Army values. They are the fundamental building blocks that enable us to discern right from wrong in any situation. Army values are consistent; they support one another. You can't follow one value and ignore another.

L. Loyalty

Bear true faith and allegiance to the Constitution, the Army, your unit, and other soldiers.

To be *loyal* is to be unswerving in allegiance to the Constitution and completely faithful to the lawful government. Our absolute allegiance and faithfulness prevents us from misplacing our loyalties. Loyalty to the unit is critical for generating confidence and trust, and for developing cooperative work relationships with others.

Loyalty is a two-way street: you should not expect loyalty without being prepared to give it as well. The loyalty of your people is a gift they give you when, and only when, you deserve it—when you train them well, treat them fairly, and live by the concepts you talk about. Leaders who are loyal to their subordinates never let them be misused.

Soldiers fight for each other—loyalty is commitment. Some of you will encounter the most important way of earning this loyalty: leading your soldiers well in combat. There's no loyalty fiercer than that of soldiers who trust their leader to take them through the dangers of combat. However, loyalty extends to all members of an organization—to your superiors and subordinates, as well as your peers.

A *loyal* individual does the following:
- Respects the Constitution and laws
- Puts obligations in order: the Constitution, the Army, the unit, and finally, self
- Observes higher Headquarters priorities
- Works within the system without manipulating it for personal advantage
- Shows faithfulness to unit and comrades
- Carries out tough orders without expressing personal criticism
- Defends soldiers against unfair treatment from outside or above

Developmental Activities/Actions
1. Increase loyalty to the unit by studying and exposing your soldiers to unit, installation, and Army history. Lead a field trip to local military museums or present a class/lead discussions regarding your unit history.

2. Discourage and correct others who "bad-mouth" the command.

3. Encourage sldrs to use their chain of cmd to resolve problems and/or concerns. Discourage use of the "rumor mill" which can undermine actions of the command.

4. Inform your cdr before publicizing and/or taking a problem to a higher commander.

5. Track all commitments you make to your soldiers and leaders Follow-up and take appropriate actions to fulfill commitments.

6. Take responsibility for difficult tasks or missions that your unit must accomplish. Pass along orders or guidance as if they were your own. Never try to persuade or inform people by saying, " well, I don't like it either, but we got to do it because that's what the old man wants." Never belittle plans, orders, or guidance from a higher headquarters.

7. Take tough issues to your commander before they become a problem for the unit. If you identify an issue that needs attention, then take action even if you know it may initially upset somebody in your chain of commander.

D. Duty

Fulfill your obligations

Duty delineates the sum total of all laws, rules, etc., that make up o ur organizational, civic, and moral obligations. Our values originate with duty because, at a minimum, we expect all members of the Army to fulfill their obligations. We often expect individuals to exceed their duty, especially in ethical matters.

Duty begins with everything required of you by law, regulation, and orders; but it includes much more than that. Professionals do their work not just to the minimum standard, but to the very best of their ability. Soldiers and DA civilians commit to excellence in all aspect of their professional responsibility so that when the job is done they can look back and say, "I couldn't have given any more."

Army leaders take the initiative, figuring out what needs to be done before being told what to do. What's more, they take full responsibility for their actions and those of their subordinates. Army leaders never shade the truth to make the unit look good—or even to make their subordinates feel good. Instead, they follow their higher duty to the Army and the nation.

A leader's duty is to take charge, even in unfamiliar circumstances. But duty isn't reserved for special occasions.

An individual who expresses the value of *duty* will, at a minimum, do the following:

- Carry out requirements of job/office
- Fulfill legal, civic, and moral obligations
- Sacrifice personal time in pursuit of excellence

Developmental Activities/Actions

1. Establish and maintain a tracking system for all requirements or missions you are tasked to accomplish.

2. Familiarize yourself with the Code of Conduct and lead a discussion concerning the Code with your soldiers and/or peers.

3. Prior to assuming a duty position read/study all applicable regulations and standard operating procedures (SOP).

4. Prior to assuming a duty position identify an officer known for setting high standards who has executed this duty in the past.

5. Volunteer for a tasking or holiday duty which no one desires.

6. Vote in the presidential and state election and assist subordinates to register.

7. Take the lead in being a good steward of supplies and resources such as photocopy machines and phones. Know the policies and set the example.

8. Familiarize yourself with the biographies or citations of Medal of Honor winners. Present a class or lead a discussion during an OPD session on their actions.

9. Seek out and use opportunities to demonstrate commitment to the military and/or civilian community. Offer to speak to in classrooms on post or community schools; invite school administrators, teachers, and students to your Organization Day, etc.

10. Identify the critical and most difficult tasks of an upcoming duty. Observe someone with a reputation for high standards execute those critical tasks.

R. Respect

Treat people as they should be treated.

Respect denotes the regard and recognition of the absolute dignity that every human being possesses. Respect also involves the notion of fairness. Although the Army wants rigorous and difficult training, Army leaders must execute this training while maintaining the dignity and self-esteem of all.

Respect for the individual forms the basis for the rule of law, the very essence of what makes America. In the Army, respect means recognizing and appreciating the inherent dignity and worth of all people. This value reminds you that your people are your greatest resource. Army leaders honor everyone's individual worth by treating all people with dignity and respect.

As an Army leader, you must also foster a climate in which everyone is treated with dignity and respect regardless of race, gender, creed, or religious belief. Fostering this climate begins with your example: how you live Army values shows your people how they should live them. In essence, Army leaders treat others as they wish to be treated.

An individual who consistently expresses *respect*:

- Recognizes dignity of all and demonstrates consideration for others
- Is discreet and tactful when correcting or questioning others
- Is courteous and polite; creates a climate of fairness
- Demonstrates concern for safety and well-being of others
- Values diversity and is sensitive to diversity issues
- Does not take advantage of position of authority when placed in charge of others

Developmental Activities/Actions

1. Lead or simply engage in discussions regarding respect with subordinate leaders.

2. Do things with peers who have different ethnic, religious, or racial backgrounds.

3. Keep a calendar of birth dates, enlistment dates, anniversaries, etc., and recognize people on significant dates, either verbally or with cards/notes.

4. When you meet someone for the first time, be quick to greet them - stand up, and shake hands, regardless of rank or other characteristics.

5. Memorize/learn the names, marital status, children, hometown, interests of your immediate subordinates and as many of your soldiers as you can.

6. Be aware of times when soldiers or NCOs are suffering in their personal lives. Express your genuine interest and concern with words, a visit, or a note.

7. Learn and use enough of the language of the country in which you work to be able to (at a minimum) use the basic forms of introductions and greetings.

8. Meet with an officer who has a good working relationship with diverse groups.

9. Visit the Equal Opportunity (EO) office and discuss their work.

10. Talk with minority peers about their experiences in the Army. Find out about their educational experience, hometown, friends and hobbies, and their family life.

11. Focus on identifying and correcting the problem instead of fixing blame.

S. Selfless Service

Put the welfare of the nation, the Army, and subordinates above your own.

Selfless-service signifies the proper ordering of priorities. Think of it as service before self. The welfare of the nation and the organization come before the individual. While the focus is on service to the nation, the value also requires that the service member properly takes care of family and self.

Selfless service doesn't mean that you neglect your family or yourself; in fact, such neglect weakens a leader and can cause the Army more harm than good.

An individual who properly expresses the value of *selfless service* does the following:

- Focuses priorities on service to the Nation
- Places needs of the Army above personal gain
- Ensures that soldiers' needs are met before attending to personal needs
- Balances mission, family, and personal needs
- Gives credit due others and accepts blame for the team

Developmental Activities/Actions

1. Focus recognition on the unit instead of yourself. Ensure soldiers are getting the credit for unit accomplishments. For example, put your soldiers in for timely PCS and impact awards. Trust that your leadership will reward you appropriately.

2. Learn about the experiences of those who have lived and demonstrated service before self. Invite war veterans to visit your unit or take soldiers to visit veterans in the local VA Hospital. Ask veterans to discuss situations they either witnessed or experienced where leaders, instead of putting themselves first, put others first. Ask them to describe the outcome/effect this had on soldiers.

3. Inspect the barracks after duty hours.

4. Volunteer at Army Community Service.

5. Set a goal to routinely complete work at a decent hour to attend a family evening event such as your child's athletic practice, scout meet, etc.

6. Learn about the selfless service demonstrated by Medal of Honor winners.

7. Put the needs of soldiers above your own. For example, follow behind soldiers through food lines; don't rush to the head of the line in order to "get back to work." In the field, ensure that security and communications have been established and soldiers' personal needs are being cared for before tending to your own.

8. Ensure your work schedule allows sufficient time for family and yourself. If necessary, be proactive by anticipating dates and events that are especially significant to you and/or your family. Note these on your personal planning calendar and plan ahead to minimize conflicts with other responsibilities. Plan your leave dates and coordinate them with your NCOs, peers, and supervisor.

9. Demonstrate an understanding of "achieving and maintaining a balance among mission, family, and personal needs" by setting the example for your soldiers. Llet soldiers see you engaging in and enjoying family and recreational activities.

10. Don't wait for an award ceremony to recognize soldier contribution - use every opportunity: AARs, unit meetings, gatherings to publicly recognize soldier accomplishments and their contributes to mission accomplishment.

The Army Leader

H. Honor

Live up to all the Army Values

Honor circumscribes the other six Army values. *Honor* provides the motive for action and provides the ability and will to make moral decisions based on deep personal values and conscience. Honor demands adherence to a public moral code, not protection of a reputation. *Honor* circumscribes the complex or the set of all the values that make up the public code for the Army (or for any organization). *Honor* and moral identity stand together because the honorable individual identifies with the group values. Significantly, honor provides the motive for action. *Honor* demands adherence to a public moral code, not protection of a reputation.

Honor provides the "moral compass" for character and personal conduct in the Army. Though many people struggle to define the term, most recognize instinctively those with a keen sense of right and wrong, those who live such that their words and deeds are above reproach. The expression "honorable person," therefore, refers to both the character traits an individual actually possesses and the fact that the community recognizes and respects them.

How you conduct yourself and meet your obligations defines who you are as a person; how the Army meets the nation's commitments defines the Army as an institution. For you as an Army leader, honor means putting Army values above self-interest, above career and comfort. For all soldiers, it means putting Army values above self-preservation as well. This honor is essential for creating a bond of trust among members of the Army and between the Army and the nation it serves. Army leaders have the strength of will to live according to Army values, even though the temptations to do otherwise are strong, especially in the face of personal danger. The military's highest award is the Medal of Honor. Its recipients didn't do just what was required of them; they went beyond the expected, above and beyond the call of duty. Some gave their own lives so that others could live. It's fitting that the word we use to describe their achievements is "honor."

An individual with *honor* does the following:

- Adheres to a public code of professional Army values
- Identifies with the public code of professional Army values
- Employs honor as a motive for moral action

Developmental Activities/Actions

1. Develop a list with senior NCOs of the daily challenges to honorable behavior that soldiers face and list ways to combat each of them. Conclude by describing how the challenges are the same and different for NCOs and commissioned officers.

2. Facilitate a discussion in your unit about why honor is so important. Together with NCO's, develop some scenarios/vignettes that describe ethical dilemmas faced by soldiers in the unit. Use the vignettes to have soldiers come up with "honorable versus dishonorable" reactions to the dilemmas.

3. With your peers, develop and discuss what you think could be an effective military code of ethics that could be used to guide officers' behavior.

4. Discuss honor openly with your soldiers.

I. Integrity

Do what's right, legally and morally

Integrity, coming from the same Latin root *(integritas)* as the word "integer," refers to a notion of completeness, wholeness, and uniqueness. In this sense, one's completeness or wholeness is dependent on strict adherence to a set of values. Integrity leads to consistency among principles, values, and behaviors.

People of integrity consistently act according to principles—not just what might work at the moment. Leaders of integrity make their principles known and consistently act in accordance with them. The Army requires leaders of integrity who possess high moral standards and are honest in word and deed. Being honest means being truthful and upright all the time, despite pressures to do otherwise. Having integrity means being both morally complete and true to yourself. As an Army leader, you're honest to yourself by committing to and consistently living Army values; you're honest to others by not presenting yourself or your actions as anything other than what they are. Army leaders say what they mean and do what they say. If you can't accomplish a mission, inform your chain of command. If you inadvertently pass on bad information, correct it as soon as you find out it's wrong. People of integrity do the right thing not because it's convenient or because they have no choice. They choose the right thing because their character permits no less.

Conducting yourself with integrity has three parts:

- Separating what's right from what's wrong
- Always acting according to what you know to be right, even at personal cost
- Saying openly that you're acting on your understanding of right versus wrong

An individual is said to have *integrity* when he or she:

- Always acts according to what he or she knows to be right, even at personal cost
- Possesses a high standard of moral values and principles
- Shows good moral judgment and demonstrates consistent moral behavior
- Avoids the wrong and stands up for what is right; abides by principles
- Shows candor and fairness in evaluating subordinates' work
- Shows consistency between words and deeds
- Uses the authority and power that comes with rank to work for mission accomplishment or for soldiers instead of for personal or private gain
- Puts being right ahead of being popular or easy

Developmental Activities and Actions

1. Investigate questionable written or verbal reports. Personally inspect to ensure the report reflects the truth.

2. Facilitate a discussion about the consequences of "stretching the truth" on APFT scores, maintenance records, wpns qualification, and other readiness indicators.

3. Share an ethical dilemma you experience. Discuss them openly with your mentor, leader, or a trusted peer and get their feedback.

4. Develop a short training outline about what the impact on unit mission accomplishment/ cohesion would be if we couldn't accept each other's word as the truth.

5. Share personal values and goals with your commander, peers, family, and friends.

7. Handle sensitive information as if it pertains to you or your family.

8. Read what you put your signature to and ensure it reflects the truth.

P. Personal Courage

Face danger, fear, adversity

Courage includes the notion of taking responsibility for decisions and actions. Additionally, courage involves the ability to perform critical self-assessment, to confront new ideas, and to change. Leaders must make decisions that involve risk and often must take a stand in the face of ambiguity or adversity. Taking risks pertains to the battlefield in war, but more frequently occurs with your boss in peace.

Personal courage isn't the absence of fear; rather, it's the ability to put fear aside and do what's necessary. It takes two forms:

- **Physical courage** means overcoming fears of bodily harm and doing your duty. It's bravery that allows a soldier to take risks in combat in spite of the fear of wounds or death. Physical courage is what gets the soldier at Airborne School out the aircraft door. It's what allows a soldier to assault a bunker to save his buddies.
- **Moral courage**, in contrast, is the willingness to stand firm on your values, principles, and convictions. It enables leaders to stand up for what they believe is right, regardless of the consequences. Leaders who take responsibility for their decisions and actions, even when things go wrong, display moral courage.

A *courageous* leader does the following:

- Controls fear in physical and moral contexts
- Takes responsibility for decisions and actions, mistakes and shortcomings
- Confronts problems directly and takes action based on what he believes is right, regardless of what others may think
- Speaks up for what he believes in and then is gracious whether ideas are accepted or rejected
- Reports on successes and failures with equal candor
- Puts themselves on the line to deal with important problems
- Challenges others to make tough decisions
- Always shares mistakes if it will help the team improve

Developmental Activities/Actions

1. Identify people in your unit whose courage you most admire.

2. Identify and write down one risk you are afraid to take. Carefully analyze its potential benefits and negative consequences. Determine what you should do.

3. Talk with combat veterans about their combat experiences. How did they cope?

4. Do something that you do not really want to do (e.g., provide the commander with a critique of the company training meeting).

5. Read books or watch movies that exemplify true courage.

6. Be the first one in the unit to lead the unit through a physical or mental challenge.

7. Think about and write down the values you want to instill in your soldiers and the unit. What things or qualities do you want them to remember? Evaluate what you currently are doing and make changes to move toward these values.

8. When faced with a difficult dilemma or decision, examine it against your deeply held convictions and values. Use your values to provide direction.

9. Follow uncomfortable issues or actions through to completion.

10. Take action to conquer your physical fears by practicing old skills or developing new physical skills. Enroll in classes such as Tae Kwon Do, Judo, or boxing.

11. Identify the most difficult, demanding task your unit must perform. Once in a while when the soldiers are practicing it, do the task along with them.

Character: What a Leader Must Be

Ib. Attributes

Ref: FM 22-100, chap 2 and ALDH, chap. 2.

Ib. Leader Attributes

1 Mental	**2** Physical	**3** Emotional
A. Will	A. Health Fitness	A. Self-Control
B. Self-Discipline	B. Physical Fitness	B. Balance
C. Initiative	C. Military / Professional	C. Stability
D. Judgment	bearing	
E. Self-Confidence		
F. Intelligence		
G. Cultural Awareness		

Ref: FM 22-100, pp. 2-10 to 2-18.

Attributes are a person's fundamental qualities and characteristics. They capture the pre-dispositional part of the leader that determines, in a large degree, parameters that are more-or-less permanent (or long-standing), yet can develop over time through correct and habitual practices. Attributes are fundamental qualities and characteristics that people possess. Attributes relevant to leadership can be further sub-divided into three groups: mental, physical, and emotional.

Leader attributes influence leader actions; leader actions, in turn, always influence the unit or organization. As an example, if you're physically fit, you're more likely to inspire your subordinates to be physically fit.

1 Mental

The mental attributes of an Army leader include will, self-discipline, initiative, judgment, self-confidence, intelligence and cultural awareness.

Mental Attributes

A. Will
B. Self-Discipline
C. Initiative
D. Judgment
E. Self-Confidence
F. Intelligence
G. Cultural Awareness

Ref: FM 22-100, pp. 2-10 to 2-15.

A. Will

Will is the inner drive that compels soldiers and leaders to keep going when they are exhausted, hungry, afraid, cold, and wet—when it would be easier to quit. Will enables soldiers to press the fight to its conclusion. Yet will without competence is useless. It's not enough that soldiers are willing, or even eager, to fight; they must know how to fight. Likewise, soldiers who have competence but no will don't fight. The leader's task is to develop a winning spirit by building their subordinates' will as well as their skill. That begins with hard, realistic training.

Will is an attribute essential to all members of the Army. Work conditions vary among branches and components, between those deployed and those closer to home. In the Army, personal attitude must prevail over any adverse external conditions. All members of the Army—active, reserve, and DA civilian—will experience situations when it would be easier to quit rather than finish the task at hand. At those times, everyone needs that inner drive to press on to mission completion.

It's easy to talk about will when things go well. But the test of your will comes when things go badly— when events seem to be out of control, when you think your bosses have forgotten you, when the plan doesn't seem to work and it looks like you're going to lose. It's then that you must draw on your inner reserves to persevere—to do your job until there's nothing left to do it with and then to remain faithful to your people, your organization, and your country. The story of the American and Filipino stand on the Bataan Peninsula and their subsequent captivity is one of individuals, leaders, and units deciding to remain true to the end—and living and dying by that decision.

B. Self-Discipline

Self-disciplined people are masters of their impulses. This mastery comes from the habit of doing the right thing. Self-discipline allows Army leaders to do the right thing regardless of the consequences for them or their subordinates. Under the extreme stress of combat, you and your team might be cut off and alone, fearing for your lives, and having to act without guidance or knowledge of what's going on around you. Still, you—the leader—must think clearly and act reasonably. Self-discipline is the key to this kind of behavior.

In peacetime, self-discipline gets the unit out for the hard training. Self-discipline makes the tank commander demand another run-through of a battle drill if the performance doesn't meet the standard—even though every-one is long past ready to quit. Self-discipline doesn't mean that you never get tired or discouraged—after all, you're only human. It does mean that you do what needs to be done regardless of your feelings.

C. Initiative

Initiative is the ability to be a self-starter—to act when there are no clear instructions, to act when the situation changes or when the plan falls apart. In the operational context, it means setting and dictating the terms of action throughout the battle or operation. An individual leader with initiative is willing to decide and initiate independent actions when the concept of operations no longer applies or when an unanticipated opportunity leading to accomplishment of the commander's intent presents itself. Initiative drives the Army leader to seek a better method, anticipate what must be done, and perform without waiting for instructions. Balanced with good judgment, it becomes disciplined initiative, an essential leader attribute. (FM 100-5 discusses initiative as it relates to military actions at the operational level. FM 100-34 discusses the relationship of initiative to command and control. FM 100-40 discusses the place of initiative in the art of tactics.)

As an Army leader, you can't just give orders: you must make clear the intent of those orders, the final goal of the mission. In combat, it's critically important for subordinates to understand their commander's intent. When they are cut off or enemy actions derail the original plan, well-trained soldiers who understand the commander's intent will apply disciplined initiative to accomplish the mission.

Disciplined initiative doesn't just appear; you must develop it within your subordinates. Your leadership style and the organizational climate you establish can either encourage or discourage initiative: you can instill initiative in your subordinates or you can drive it out. If you underwrite honest mistakes, your subordinates will be more likely to develop initiative. If you set a "zero defects" standard, you risk strangling initiative in its cradle, the hearts of your subordinates.

D. Judgment

Leaders must often juggle hard facts, questionable data, and gut-level intuition to arrive at a decision. Good judgment means making the best decision for the situation. It's a key attribute of the art of command and the transformation of knowledge into understanding. (FM 100-34 discusses how leaders convert data and information into knowledge and understanding.)

Good judgment is the ability to size up a situation quickly, determine what's important, and decide what needs to be done. Given a problem, you should consider a range of alternatives before you act. You need to think through the consequences of what you're about to do before you do it. In addition to considering the consequences, you should also think methodically. Some sources that aid judgment are the boss's intent, the desired goal, rules, laws, regulations, experience, and values. Good judgment also includes the ability to size up subordinates, peers, and the enemy for strengths, weaknesses, and potential actions. It's a critical part of problem solving and decision making.

Judgment and initiative go hand in hand. As an Army leader, you must weigh what you know and make decisions in situations where others do nothing. There will be times when you'll have to make decisions under severe time constraints. In all cases, however, you must take responsibility for your actions. In addition, you must encourage disciplined initiative in, and teach good judgment to, your subordinates. Help your subordinates learn from mistakes by coaching and mentoring them along the way.

E. Self-Confidence

Self-confidence is the faith that you'll act correctly and properly in any situation, even one in which you're under stress and don't have all the information you want. Self-confidence comes from competence: it's based on mastering skills, which takes hard work and dedication. Leaders who know their own capabilities and believe in themselves are self-confident. Don't mistake bluster—loudmouthed bragging or self-promotion—for self-confidence. Truly self-confident leaders don't need to advertise; their actions say it all.

Self-confidence is important for leaders and teams. People want self-confident leaders, leaders who understand the situation, know what needs to be done, and demonstrate that understanding and knowledge. Self-confident leaders instill self-confidence in their people. In combat, self-confidence helps soldiers control doubt and reduce anxiety. Together with will and self-discipline, self-confidence helps leaders act—do what must be done in circumstances where it would be easier to do nothing—and to convince their people to act as well.

F. Intelligence

Intelligent leaders think, learn, and reflect; then they apply what they learn. Intelligence is more than knowledge, and the ability to think isn't the same as book learning. All people have some intellectual ability that, when developed, allows them to analyze and understand a situation. And although some people are smarter than others, all people can develop the capabilities they have. Napoleon himself observed how a leader's intellectual development applies directly to battlefield success: It is not genius which reveals to me suddenly and secretly what I should do in circumstances unexpected by others; it is thought and meditation.

Knowledge is only part of the equation. Smart decisions result when you combine professional skills (which you learn through study) with experience (which you gain on the job) and your ability to reason through a problem based on the information available. Reflection is also important. From time to time, you find yourself carefully and thoughtfully considering how leadership, values, and other military principles apply to you and your job. When things don't go quite the way they intended, intelligent leaders are confident enough to step back and ask, "Why did things turn out that way?" Then they are smart enough to build on their strengths and avoid making the same mistake again.

Reflection also contributes to your originality (the ability to innovate, rather than only adopt others' methods) and intuition (direct, immediate insight or understanding of important factors without apparent rational thought or inference).

G. Cultural Awareness

Culture is a group's shared set of beliefs, values, and assumptions about what's important. As an Army leader, you must be aware of cultural factors in three contexts: You must be sensitive to the different backgrounds of your people. You must be aware of the culture of the country in which your organization is operating. You must take into account your partners' customs and traditions when you're working with forces of another nation.

Within the Army, people come from widely different backgrounds: they are shaped by their schooling, race, gender, and religion as well as a host of other influences. Although they share Army values, an African-American man from rural Texas may look at many things differently from, say, a third-generation Irish-American man who grew up in Philadelphia or a Native American woman from the Pacific Northwest. But be aware that perspectives vary within groups as well. That's why you should try to understand individuals based on their own ideas, qualifications, and contributions and not jump to conclusions based on stereotypes.

Army values are part of the Army's institutional culture, a starting point for how you as a member of the Army should think and act. Beyond that, Army leaders not only recognize that people are different; they value them because of their differences, because they are people. Your job as a leader isn't to make everyone the same. Instead, your job is to take advantage of the fact that everyone is different and build a cohesive team.

There's great diversity in the Army—religious, ethnic, and social—and people of different backgrounds bring different talents to the table. By joining the Army, these people have agreed to adopt the Army culture. Army leaders make this easier by embracing and making use of everyone's talents. What's more, they create a team where subordinates know they are valuable and their talents are important.

You never know how the talents of an individual or group will contribute to mission accomplishment. For example, during World War II US Marines from the Navajo nation formed a group of radio communications specialists dubbed the Navajo Code Talkers. The code talkers used their native language unique tal-ent—to handle command radio traffic. Not even the best Japanese code breakers could decipher what was being said.

Understanding the culture of your adversaries and of the country in which your organization is operating is just as important as understanding the culture of your own country and organization. This aspect of cultural awareness has always been important, but today's operational environment of frequent deployments—often conducted by small units under constant media coverage—makes it even more so. As an Army leader, you need to remain aware of current events—particularly those in areas where America has national interests. You may have to deal with people who live in those areas, either as partners, neutrals, or adversaries. The more you know about them, the better prepared you'll be.

You may think that understanding other cultures applies mostly to stability operations and support operations. However, it's critical to planning offensive and defensive operations as well. For example, you may employ different tactics against an adversary who considers surrender a dishonor worse than death than against those for whom surrender is an honorable option. Likewise, if your organization is operating as part of a multinational team, how well you understand your partners will affect how well the team accomplishes its mission.

Cultural awareness is crucial to the success of multinational operations. In such situations Army leaders take the time to learn the customs and traditions of the partners' cultures. They learn how and why others think and act as they do. In multinational forces, effective leaders create a "third culture," which is the bridge or the compromise among partners.

An individual who possesses and applies appropriate mental attributes:

- Thinks and acts quickly and logically
- Analyzes situations; combines complex ideas to generate feasible COAs
- Balances resolve and flexibility
- Adopts better ideas from other sources
- Shows common sense
- Completes mentally demanding endeavors
- Displays cultural awareness

Developmental Activities/Actions

1. Get your superior to commit resources to a junior officer tactical planning OPD. Have him provide a company OPORD to each lieutenant. Each LT plans and produces a platoon OPORD and briefs it to peers and the CO. Each plan is AAR'ed by all.

2. Identify a peer known for having achieved excellence in planning and decision-making. Observe this officer during a planning phase or walk a tactical lane with him/her and observe decision-making in action.

3. Begin a habit of sticking to an action until it is completed. Talk with leaders you respect to get ideas on how to keep from putting off difficult or mundane tasks. Develop a system to help avoid procrastination and use it (e.g., look at each in-box item only once - complete the action, pass it on, or file it away).

4. Identify a role model. Look for a leader who shows appropriate urgency for missions and is concerned for soldiers. Ask that leader to be your mentor. Meet periodically with to discuss your plans and concerns about the unit, your soldiers, and yourself.

5. Run your ideas and potential solutions by peers and NCOs before acting on them. Ask them whether they pass the "Common Sense Test." Allow them to disagree with you without becoming defensive. Listen to their input and consider it before acting.

6. When you feel overwhelmed and think that a task or obstacle is impossible, do the following. Stop yourself from thinking negative thoughts as these block your mental processes and prevent you from thinking creatively. Take the following steps to regain your desire and initiative:

- Tell yourself you've reached a momentary impasse - a solution does exist and you'll eventually find it
- Take a break from the problem and return later
- Avoid judging your ideas
- Identify the problem, redefine it, and look at it from a different perspective
- Ask for help -- others can help you develop a new perspective although they might not be able to solve the issue

2 | Physical

Physical attributes—health fitness, physical fitness, and military and professional bearing—can be developed. Army leaders maintain the appropriate level of physical fitness and military bearing.

Physical Attributes

A. Health Fitness
B. Physical Fitness
C. Military / Professional bearing

Ref: FM 22-100, pp. 2-16 to 2-17.

A. Health Fitness

Health fitness is everything you do to maintain good health, things such as undergoing routine physical exams, practicing good dental hygiene, maintaining deployability standards, and even personal grooming and cleanliness. A soldier unable to fight because of dysentery is as much a loss as one who's wounded. Healthy soldiers can perform under extremes in temperature, humidity, and other conditions better than unhealthy ones. Health fitness also includes avoiding things that degrade your health, such as substance abuse, obesity, and smoking.

B. Physical Fitness

Unit readiness begins with physically fit soldiers and leaders. Combat drains soldiers physically, mentally, and emotionally. To minimize those effects, Army leaders are physically fit, and they make sure their subordinates are fit as well. Physically fit soldiers perform better in all areas, and physically fit leaders are better able to think, decide, and act appropriately under pressure. Physical readiness provides a foundation for combat readiness, and it's up to you, the leader, to get your soldiers ready.

Although physical fitness is a crucial element of success in battle, it's not just for front-line soldiers. Wherever they are, people who are physically fit feel more competent and confident. That attitude reassures and inspires those around them. Physically fit soldiers and DA civilians can handle stress better, work longer and harder, and recover faster than ones who are not fit. These payoffs are valuable in both peace and war.

The physical demands of leadership positions, prolonged deployments, and continuous operations can erode more than just physical attributes. Soldiers must show up ready for deprivations because it's difficult to maintain high levels of fitness during deployments and demanding operations. Trying to get fit under those conditions is even harder. If a person isn't physically fit, the effects of additional stress snowball until their mental and emotional fitness are compromised as well. Army leaders' physical fitness has significance beyond their personal performance and well-being. Since leaders' decisions affect their organizations' combat effectiveness, health, and safety and not just their own, maintaining physical fitness is an ethical as well as a practical imperative.

The Army Physical Fitness Test (APFT) measures a baseline level of physical fitness. As an Army leader, you're required to develop a physical fitness program that enhances your soldiers' ability to complete soldier and leader tasks that support the unit's mission essential task list (METL). (FM 25-101 discusses METL-based integration of soldier, leader, and collective training.) Fitness programs that emphasize training specifically for the APFT are boring and don't prepare soldiers for the varied stresses of combat. Make every effort to design a physical fitness program that prepares your people for what you expect them to do in combat. Readiness should be your program's primary focus; preparation for the APFT itself is secondary. (FM 21-20 is your primary physical fitness resource.)

C. Military and Professional Bearing

As an Army leader, you're expected to look like a soldier. Know how to wear the uniform and wear it with pride at all times. Meet height and weight standards. By the way you carry yourself and through your military courtesy and appearance, you send a signal: I am proud of my uniform, my unit, and myself. Skillful use of your professional bearing—fitness, courtesy, and military appearance—can often help you manage difficult situations. A professional—DA civilian or soldier—presents a professional appearance, but there's more to being an Army professional than looking good. Professionals are competent as well; the Army requires you to both look good and be good.

An individual possessing and applying appropriate *physical fitness*:

- Does his or her fair share
- Appears personally energetic
- Completes physically demanding endeavors
- Keeps trying when hungry, tired, cold/hot, or wet/muddy
- Sets a physical and appearance standard
- Presents a neat, professional appearance
- Does not quit in the face of adversity/copes well with hardship

Developmental Activities/Actions

1. Demonstrate ability to cope with hardship. In the most adverse conditions of weather and sleep deprivation, be visible to your soldiers. Walk around and talk to them, find out their living conditions. Determine what you can do to boost morale by improving living conditions and follow through.

2. Identify unit with a reputation for best PT program. Coordinate to participate in PT with them.

3. Identify the toughest, most physically demanding METL task your soldiers must perform. Participate with them in the completion of this task.

4. Make physical activity a part of your extracurricular activities. Identify seasonal sports that you can progress in and continue throughout your entire lifespan. Routinely participate in sports for fun and improve your performance.

5. Be proactive in controlling your weight. Consult with nutritionists when you first think you might be heading for difficulty with your weight. If necessary, establish fitness goals and objectives with your supervisor and include these on your support form.

6. Seek out a Master Fitness Trainer in your unit. Ask him or her to help you develop an individualized physical fitness program to supplement what you are doing with the unit.

7. Demonstrate genuine interest in the unit PT program. Be an active participant by leading PT sessions and vocally encouraging others to perform their best. Do not simply go through the motions of attending unit PT. Set an enthusiastic example to help others get more benefit from unit PT. Help make the PT program challenging and fun.

8. Set personal physical fitness goals beyond just passing the APFT. Focus goals on measurable aspects of physical fitness such as component scores of the APFT, or your 5K or 10K personal best times. Adjust the goal up a notch each time you achieve it. Include your goals and objectives on your support form.

9. Examine your energy level based on the areas listed below.

- Nutrition: Write down your eating habits for a week and use this information during a session with a nutritionist or physician.
- Exercise: Even brief exercise can make you feel energetic and alert.
- Sleep: Examine your sleep patterns and adjust if necessary.

10. Develop a personal physical fitness program with your peers and support each other to stay involved. Reinforce your peers for their involvement.

11. Present a professional appearance when off duty. Demonstrate your awareness that you represent the U.S. Army on and off duty by your appearance and behavior.

12. Prepare for and attend the Master Physical Fitness Course.

3 | Emotional

As an Army leader, your emotional attributes— self-control, balance, and stability—contribute to how you feel and therefore to how you interact with others. Your people are human beings with hopes, fears, concerns, and dreams. When you understand that will and endurance come from emotional energy, you possess a powerful leadership tool. The feedback you give can help your subordinates use their emotional energy to accomplish amazing feats in tough times.

Self-control, balance, and stability also help you make the right ethical choices. In order to follow the steps of ethical reasoning, you must remain in control of yourself; you can't be at the mercy of your impulses. You must remain calm under pressure, "watch your lane," and expend energy on things you can fix.

Leaders who are emotionally mature also have a better awareness of their own strengths and weaknesses. Mature leaders spend their energy on self-improvement; immature leaders spend their energy denying there's anything wrong. Mature, less defensive leaders benefit from constructive criticism in ways that immature people cannot.

Emotional Attributes

> A. Health Fitness
> B. Physical Fitness
> C. Military / Professional bearing

Ref: FM 22-100, pp. 2-17 to 2-18.

A. Self-Control

Leaders control their emotions. No one wants to work for a hysterical leader who might lose control in a tough situation. This doesn't mean you never show emotion. Instead, you must display the proper amount of emotion and passion—somewhere between too much and too little—required to tap into your subordinates' emotions. Maintaining self-control inspires calm confidence in subordinates, the coolness under fire so essential to a successful unit. It also encourages feedback from your subordinates that can expand your sense of what's really going on.

B. Balance

Emotionally balanced leaders display the right emotion for the situation and can also read others' emotional state. They draw on their experience and provide their subordinates the proper perspective on events. They have a range of attitudes—from relaxed to intense— with which to approach situations and can choose the one appropriate to the circumstances. Such leaders know when it's time to send a message that things are urgent and how to do that without throwing the organization into chaos. They also know how to encourage people at the toughest moments and keep them driving on.

C. Stability

Effective leaders are steady, levelheaded under pressure and fatigue, and calm in the face of danger. These characteristics calm their subordinates, who are always looking to their leader's example. Display the emotions you want your people to display; don't give in to the temptation to do what feels good for you. If you're under great stress, it might feel better to vent—scream, throw things, kick furniture— but that will not help the organization. If you want your subordinates to be calm and rational under pressure, you must be also.

An individual with effective *emotional* attributes displays:

- Low impulsiveness - individuals with good self-control do not react immediately when things go wrong but deliberate intently and sufficiently before responding

- A high hostility tolerance - it takes drastic measures to get great leaders to respond beyond their control

- A high frustration tolerance - emotionally stable leaders have the motivation and ability to delay gratification. They can handle their own frustration at being behind schedule and display the ability to keep trying

- Self-confidence and a persistently positive attitude

- The ability to remain calm, under control, and effective under pressure

- The ability to balance competing demands without complaining

Developmental Activities/Actions

1. Reduce job frustration by improving time management skills. Visit the Education Center or local colleges for time management courses or information.

2. Consciously resist immediate judgment or criticism of others' ideas or explanations. Immediate reactions are often emotionally driven and may be inappropriate. Instead, ask open-ended questions to understand others fully.

3. Develop a one-page questionnaire about aspects of emotional stability. Distribute to your subordinate leaders, respected peers, and superiors. Have the results returned to you anonymously. Develop actions to improve from this assessment.

4. Examine your use of substances that might be having a negative effect on your emotions. Take action to reduce your use of the following:

- Stimulants. Caffeine/tobacco and over-the-counter preparations reduce our ability to deal with pressure and stress. Side effects such as stomachaches, irritability, headaches, and sleeplessness might be influencing your emotions.

- Alcohol. Alcohol can have interpersonal and personal ramifications that create stress and disrupt our ability to control our emotional reactions.

- Nicotine. Nicotine reduces our ability to deal with pressure and stress.

5. Practice thinking optimistically. Anticipating that things will turn out negatively can lead to a "self-fulfilling prophecy." Subordinates may respond to you in ways that validate your negative expectations of them or the situation. Anticipating a positive outcome can increase your chance of success as well as your emotional well-being.

6. Talk with others when you feel unusual or extreme pressure. Talking with others can help you deal with extreme emotions and can provide an outlet for stressful energy. Your discussions may also lead to potentially effective ways of handling the events or situations leading to the pressure.

7. Gain control of your temper or tendency to overreact by taking slow, deep breaths through your nose before responding when angry or upset.

8. Improve your control and display of patience by doing the following. Change your perspective during situations leading to impatience by thinking more positively (for example, "If I wait, I'll understand," or "This will get better with more time"). Then, leave the situation to avoid saying something inappropriate. Carefully look at the strengths and needs of others to gain insight into their behavior and increase your tolerance. Return to the situation when you calm down.

9. Videotape yourself in a leadership role-play situation. Watch the tape to gain insight into facial expressions and voice quality that might send unintended emotional messages. Ask a trusted colleague to watch the tape and give constructive feedback.

Competence: What a Leader Must KNOW

II. Leadership Skills

Ref: FM 22-100, chap. 2 and ALDH, chap. 1.

II. Leadership Skills

1
Interpersonal Skills
affect how you deal with people. They include coaching, teaching, counseling, motivating and enpowering.

2
Conceptual Skills
enable you to handle ideas. They require sound judgment as well as the ability to think creatively and reason analytically, critically and ethically.

3
Technical Skills
are job-related abilities. They include basic soldier skills. As an Army leader, you must possess the expertise necessary to accomplish all tasks and functions you're assigned.

4
Tactical Skills
apply to solving tactical problems, that is, problems concerning employment of units in combat. You enhance tactical skills when you combine them with interpersonal, conceptual and technical skills to accomplish the mission.

Ref: FM 22-100, p. 2-25.

Skills (competencies) define those abilities that people develop and use with other people, with ideas, and with things. Acquiring skill is a prerequisite to acting/behaving with competence. Skill is what soldiers look for in their leaders. Skills are part of a leader's character, along with attributes and values.

Competence results from hard, realistic training. That's why Basic Training starts with simple skills, such as drill and marksmanship. Soldiers who master these skills have a couple of victories under their belts. The message from the drill sergeants—explicit or not—is, "You've learned how to do those things; now you're ready to take on something tougher." When you lead people through progressively more complex tasks this way, they develop the confidence and will—the inner drive—to take on the next, more difficult challenge.

For you as an Army leader, competence means much more than being well-trained. Competence links character (knowing the right thing to do) and leadership (doing or influencing your people to do the right thing). Leaders are responsible for being personally competent, but even that isn't enough: as a leader, you're responsible for your subordinates' competence as well.

Leaders in combat combine interpersonal, conceptual, technical, and tactical skills to accomplish the mission. They use their interpersonal skills to communicate their intent effectively and motivate their soldiers. They apply their conceptual skills to determine viable concepts of operations, make the right decisions, and execute the tactics the operational environment requires. They capitalize on their techni-cal skills to properly employ the techniques, procedures, fieldcraft, and equipment that fit the situation. Finally, combat leaders employ tactical skill, combining skills from the other skill categories with knowledge of the art of tactics appropriate to their level of responsibility and unit type to accomplish the mission. When plans go wrong and leadership must turn the tide, it is tactical skill, combined with character, that enables an Army leader to seize control of the situation and lead the unit to mission accomplishment.

1 | Interpersonal Skills

Developing or improving upon one's ability to work with people. It includes the ability to coach, teach, counsel, motivate, and empower others. Working effectively and developing others is critical because leaders must rely on others to support them in achieving goals.

An individual who possesses and effectively applies *interpersonal skills*:

- Is a good listener; listens more than talks
- Is approachable and interacts well with others
- Is sought out for expertise or counsel
- Provides guidance to subordinates when needed; resists controlling others by allowing autonomy when appropriate

Developmental Activities/Actions

1. Practice using this four step process to empower subordinates:
- Clearly assign responsibility
- Grant them authority to decide issues relevant to the task
- Supply subordinates with resources to accomplish the task
- Look for and remove obstacles that might impede their progress

2. Meet with subordinates within the next 45 days and discuss their strengths and weaknesses.

3. Conduct unit retention/reenlistment interviews with all personnel scheduled to ETS within the next 6 months.

4. Have your subordinates do the following after you have had a few counseling sessions with them. Ask them to review FM 22-101 (Leadership Counseling) and write down five things you do well while counseling. Also have them identify aspects of counseling where you need improvement. Take these lists to an experienced counselor (unit chaplains are a good resource) and ask for feedback and assistance in improving your counseling techniques.

5. Deal with "people problems" when they occur, especially when they are negatively affecting the unit's success or morale.

6. Identify a peer who has good interpersonal skills. Role play a counseling session with him/her as an observer. Ask for and respond to his/her feedback.

7. Investigate professional resources available to your soldiers. Recognize your limits for conducting personal counseling and realize when to refer someone to a professional agency. Visit the following to determine available resources:
- Alcohol and Drug Abuse Prevention and Control Unit
- American Red Cross

- Army Community Service
- Army Emergency Relief
- Chaplain
- Community Mental Health Activity
- Inspector General
- Legal Assistance Office

2 | Conceptual Skills

Developing or improving upon one's ability to reason and judge properly, and to engage effectively in critical and creative thinking and moral reasoning. Having conceptual skills is being able to adjust to new information and to consider a wide range of possibilities when solving problems. Cognition is the cerebral process of being aware, knowing, and thinking. Developing your conceptual skills will increase your ability to reason through problems, develop solutions, and select the most effective one.

To have *conceptual* skill is to have skill with ideas. Leaders often are flooded with too much information and data. Nevertheless, leaders must be capable of sorting through extensive amounts of input in order to make accurate and timely judgments and decisions. In order to do this, leaders need good conceptual skills. There are many types of conceptual skills that leaders require such as critical reasoning, moral reasoning, creative thinking, and problem solving.

Critical reasoning is an especially important skill for leaders to develop. "Critical" means careful, deliberate thinking as opposed to reactionary thinking. Critical reasoning is the ability to use good reasoning and avoid bad reasoning. Leaders can develop this skill throughout their careers. Critical reasoning skills enable leaders to know what to ask for and how to ask the right questions.

An individual possessing and effectively applying *conceptual skills*:
- Recognizes information required for a decision to be made
- When time is available, resists making "snap" decisions or reacting based only on initial information
- Makes decisions based on relevant information
- Doses not demand 100% certainty to make a decision
- Possesses ability to discriminate between information that is important and relevant to a decision, and information that is not important/relevant

Developmental Activities/Actions
1. Procure an operations order or other written directive from your supervisor/ higher headquarters. Highlight information you believe is critical to your implementation of the order/directive. Seek out feedback from a supervisor or peer on the accuracy of your assessment.

2. Make wise use of existing information. Successful creative and innovative thinkers often build on existing ideas. Talk with other leaders who might have worthwhile information that you can build on to solve your problem. Seek out leaders who have dealt with the same issue and learn from what they have done.

3. Conduct a brainstorming session with your subordinates or peers in order to

have ideas build on each other. Follow these guidelines during brainstorming:

- Define the problem
- Don't criticize ideas
- Be free to add to already suggested ideas or combine ideas
- Set a time limit to generate a sense of urgency
- Record all ideas
- Review the ideas to determine which could be implemented

4. Engage in "what-if" thinking with your peers or subordinates. For example, consider the following: "If we do this, what resources will we need, how will soldiers perform, what will be our sister unit's responsibilities, and how will the enemy respond?"

5. Ask peers to provide feedback on situations or issues about which you tend to be overly opinionated or rigid in your thinking. Opinionated or rigid thinking is counterproductive to critical and creative thinking. Recognizing that you are inflexible regarding particular areas is the first step in initiating change.

6. Practice taking a different perspective when facing complex problems. Argue the other side of the issue. This may lead you to commit to your original idea even more strongly, or it may cause you to modify or expand your idea, or abandon it entirely.

7. Tolerate failure. Recognize that people learn from their mistakes best when they are allowed to recover. Increase learning by minimizing the fear of taking risks.

8. Challenge and eliminate thinking and statements that close off alternative solutions. Reward subordinates who have a "can do" attitude and discourage statements such as, "They'll never approve…," or "We can't…" or "We've never done it that way before.."

3 | Technical Skills

Developing or improving upon one's ability to understand and properly use resources, to include equipment, weapons, and systems.

To have *technical* skill is to have skill with things such as equipment, weapon systems, the systems that operate and control weapon systems, computers, and other physical items that leaders operate, manage, and control. Junior leaders in particular work closely with equipment and have a general need to understand the details of operating that equipment.

Junior leaders have several types of technical skills. They are responsible for tending, employing, operating, controlling, and setting up equipment. They are also responsible for training their people to successfully complete these things. Junior leaders also solve the countless problems that arise daily with equipment. New techniques, new equipment, new training methods, and new ideas make it critical for junior leaders to continuously develop their technical skills.

A *technically skilled* leader:

- Correctly sets up, operates, employs, and maintains equipment
- Uses resources efficiently and most effectively to support soldiers and the unit
- Knows his job and the jobs of those who work for him
- Knows standards for task accomplishment
- Strives for mastery of knowledge required for duty performance

Developmental Activities/Actions

1. Visit content/area experts within your unit or installation such as the maintenance, supply, personnel, transportation, or training officer/NCO. Educate yourself regarding their operation/services and think how you can incorporate their resources into your operation.

2. As a staff officer, prepare yourself to be the subject matter expert. Read, highlight and tab the basic regulations and field manuals pertaining to your staff area. Know your own standing operating procedures (SOPs) and those of your higher command. Study copies of the inspection checklists and know what each item is, and where your unit stands regarding it. Get copies of other units' SOPs and see how they do business.

3. Visit the Battalion S-1 and find out how to fix your unit publication system. Publications are important to gaining knowledge required for technical expertise.

4. Set up a junior officer technical proficiency training on METL equipment as part of the unit officer professional development. Administer "hands on" drills that test assembly/disassembly, employment, and maintenance of this equipment.

5. Conduct the next unit Arms Room inspection.

6. Review and update the unit's weakest (or missing) SOP.

7. Develop an SOP to monitor the control, use, and maintenance of unit equipment and equipment records.

8. Learn about and use the following systems to take care of your soldiers: awards, reenlistment, Hometown News Release, leaves and passes, meal cards, promotions and evaluations, and flagging actions (see the Battalion S-1 or read TC 12-17, Adjutant's Call, The S-1 Handbook, for more information).

9. Talk with the Battalion Supply Officer (S-4) and Battalion Property Book Officer to learn about unit supply operations and how to avoid problems within your unit.

10. See your commander and volunteer to conduct a Report of Survey to get hands on experience with the supply system.

11. Shadow the Battalion Motor Officer (BMO) or Battalion/Company Motor Sergeant to examine problems or issues they experience. Explore and discuss things your unit can do to prevent similar problems. Get their perspective regarding what makes a good maintenance program.

12. Identify your weakness among the following resource systems - supply, maintenance, administration. Spend an hour weekly shadowing someone who is particularly competent in that area. Ask for advice regarding a few of the most critical aspects of this system.

13. Subscribe to and read relevant branch magazines such as Armor Magazine or Infantry Magazine. These publications often have valuable information concerning operations and using resources.

14. Research and write a short journal article for your branch magazine.

15. Prepare a development plan to address your technical skills. Ask subordinates to submit "top 5" technical skills you need to improve in. Study the list to determine the types of problems you have and the people to whom you go most often for help. Determine what knowledge or skills these people have that you lack. Work with your mentor to develop a plan to strengthen these weak areas.

16. Enroll yourself or encourage soldiers to enroll in correspondence courses to improve technical deficiencies (see DA PAM 351-20, Correspondence Course Catalog).

Improves upon one's proficiency in warfighting skills. Warfighting skills use each of the three skill groupings above - interpersonal, cognitive, and technical.

Tactical skill is separate from technical skill. To have technical skill is to have skill with things. To have tactical skill is to have far more than skill with things. Technical skill is only one part of tactical skill. Although necessary, technical skill is not sufficient for tactical skill. Tactical skill depends on properly applying skill with people, ideas, and things. Having skill with any one of these three but lacking the ability to apply skill with the others would greatly diminish tactical skill. For example, to have skill with computers and lack skill with people would greatly hamper tactical skill. Or, to understand the principles and theory of war would do no good if the leader had no idea how to operate and employ a unit's weapon systems. A good balance of the three skill groupings is ideal.

A *tactically* skilled leader:
- Understands and properly applies tactical doctrine when appropriate
- Seeks out and applies historical lessons learned to current situations
- Combines skills with people, ideas, and things; applies skills to fight and win

Developmental Activities/Actions

1. Review the After Action Reports (AARs) and Lessons Learned from past tactical exercises to identify training deficiencies. Develop future tactical training to correct these deficiencies.

2. Conduct leader training prior to the execution of tactical collective tasks. Conduct walk throughs, rehearsals, and/or TEWTs with your subordinate leaders, focusing on critical leader tasks.

3. Find out/identify peers with a good reputation for tactical skill. Walk along with this leader during the execution of tactical training.

4. Plan for and allocate time to participate fully in the planning, execution, and assessment of training. Refer to FM 25-100 and FM 25-101 for guidance.

5. Have subordinate, peer, and superior leaders provide you with an assessment of your tactical skill. Improve by visiting the Learning Resource Center or Education Center to view Training Extension Course (TEC) lessons, Soldier Training Programs (STPs), and current regulations, manuals, and correspondence assistance.

6. Coordinate and supervise the unit's advance party movement and or relocation during the next FTX.

7. Volunteer to conduct classes on how to lay out a defensive perimeter to secure and protect an area against enemy attack.

8. Volunteer for unit taskings for observer/controller of other units' tactical exercises.

Leadership: What a Leader Must DO

III. Actions

Ref: FM 22-100, p. 2-26 to 2-28; ALDH, chap. 1.

III. Leader Actions

1 Influencing	**2** Operating	**3** Improving
A. Communicating	A. Plan & Prepare	A. Developing
B. Decision-Making	B. Executing	B. Building
C. Motivating	C. Assessing	C. Learning

Ref: FM 22-100, pp. 2-27 to 2-28.

Actions follow from one or more of the skill groupings previously discussed (i.e., interpersonal, cognitive, technical, and tactical). Acquiring skill competency will help prepare you to behave effectively. The actions of the leader have a major impact on the team, unit, or organization he or she leads. Additionally, they are the reinforcing actions for Army values, attributes, and skills. Consequently, leaders must understand that their actions and the resulting implications of their actions can reinforce standards or destroy what they are trying to establish. Because the actions of the leader have a profound impact on the team, unit or organization he or she leads, it is incumbent on leaders to enjoy leadership. Fun and optimism are contagious as are misery and skepticism.

FM 22-100 identifies nine specific behaviors that a leader of character and competence must be able to do and do well. These behaviors or actions of the leader fall within three major activities - *influencing, operating,* and *improving*. These subordinate actions form the basis for all the activities that a leader must do as leader of a team, unit or organization.

1. Influencing

Influencing demands the act of using appropriate interpersonal styles and methods to guide individuals (subordinates, peers, and superiors) or groups toward task accomplishment or resolution of conflicts and disagreements. When we influence, we prompt others toward task accomplishment. Our ability to influence others in positive ways is dependent on three specific actions:

- How we *communicate*
- How we *motivate*
- How we practice *decision making*

Influencing Actions

A. Communicating
B. Decision-Making
C. Motivating

Ref: FM 22-100, pp. 2-27.

A. Communicating

Communicating comprises the ability to express oneself effectively in individual and group situations, either orally or in writing. Expressing oneself effectively is dependent on the ability to use proper grammar, appropriate gestures, and consistent nonverbal communications. Communicating effectively enhances our ability to influence others by helping to ensure accurate exchanges of information, and by helping to build mutual trust.

Junior leaders spend a lot of their time in face-to-face communication with their people, either with individuals or with small groups. They will, on the whole, spend more time speaking than writing to communicate. Their speaking will more than likely center around directing, coaching, teaching, motivating, and counseling. While they may spend more time speaking than writing, they still need to develop both types of communicating skills. Writing is also an important skill for leaders at all levels. Writing skill generally becomes more important as leaders increase in rank and responsibility. Whether the written work is a hand-written note or a formal staff study, the written work needs to communicate clearly and concisely.

An effective *oral communicator*:

- Conveys ideas and feelings clearly and effectively
- Ensures that his or her spoken word is well thought out and organized
- Uses grammatically correct terms and phrases
- Has appropriate visual aids and few distracting gestures
- Uses a good rate, volume, and inflection in speech
- Determines/recognizes when miscommunication or poor understanding occurs and resolves them
- Listens and watches attentively; makes appropriate notes; conveys the gist of what was said or done
- Maintains eye contact
- Reacts appropriately to verbal/non-verbal feedback from audience
- Engages in effective listening by hearing the speaker's words, understanding the message and its importance to the speaker, and by communicating that understanding to the speaker

Developmental Activities/Actions for *oral communication*

1. Record a briefing rehearsal on video or audio and review it critically with your supervisor, a respected peer, and/or subordinates.

2. Rehearse all briefings/presentations, if possible, in the area in which you'll give it, with the training aids you'll use, and with someone who can give you constructive feedback.

3. Effective communicators recognize and successfully deal with obstacles to quality communication such as incorrect assumptions, word meanings, context, and filtering of the message. Active listening techniques can help you overcome such obstacles to effective communication. Ask a number of peers, subordinates/superiors to anonymously submit the percent of time you listen versus talk. Use these techniques to improve your listening skills:

- Give your honest attention to the speaker
- Let the speaker know you're listening by demonstrating your understanding—restate in your own words what you think the speaker said
- Make implicit assumptions explicit—say what you're thinking
- Listen for intellectual and emotional content to determine any underlying messages
- Avoid criticizing, evaluating, or judging the speaker while he or she is speaking
- Focus on understand the speaker's message instead of thinking about your response while he/she is speaking
- Avoid interrupting others
- When on the phone, avoid sorting through your in box or doing other work
- When disagreeing, summarize what you think the speaker's position is before responding with your view
- Ask open ended questions to get more information. Use phrases beginning with "what," "how," "describe," or "explain." Avoid closed-ended questions that can be answered with "yes" or "no."
- Make good eye contact without staring at the speaker
- Sit or stand squarely facing the other person and lean forward to express interest
- Look and take time to be genuinely interested in the speaker.

4. Observe unit chaplains and how they engage in effective listening. Most Army chaplains have had extensive training and education in communication skills and the art of listening. Watch them and learn.

5. Avoid interrupting by mentally counting to three after others stop talking and before you start talking.

6. Be aware that your speaking style directly influences how convincing you can be. Record yourself as you practice presenting your ideas or stating your position. Ask a peer who has a reputation for a good speaking style to help you analyze how you sound by discussing the following:

- is your tone of voice and inflection consistent with the meaning of your words and the message intent?
- does the pace of speech facilitate understanding?
- is the level of enthusiasm and liveliness appropriate for the topic and setting?
- do you use language that is clear enough for others to easily understand?

7. When talking with soldiers, use open-ended requests or questions to facilitate better communication. Resist using closed-ended questions which can be answered with brief, uninformative responses. For example, instead of asking, "Do you like the dining facility food?", say "Tell me about the last meal you ate in the dining facility." Or, instead of "Does you squad leader tell you when you've done a good job?", ask "How does your squad leader let you know that you've done a good job?"

8. "Wargame" the next meeting/presentation/event at which you will verbally present your viewpoint. Make notes about key points, identify possible challenges to your position, and prepare notes on your response.

9. Barriers may be disrupting your ability to get through to a difficult subordinate, peer, or superior. If you have problems communicating with a particular individual, examine your interaction using the barrier list below.

- Are you failing to understand or appreciate his or her personal motives?
- Are you showing unconcern or not giving feedback?
- Are you trying to protect your prestige or position while communicating?
- Are you withholding relevant information or telling half truths?
- Does either communicator have a hidden agenda or message?
- Is there excessive noise, other distractions, or lack of privacy?
- Are you intimidating subordinates?
- Are you distrusting the speaker or being distrusted?
- Are you talking down to subordinates?
- Are you failing to take the time or devote energy to listening?

An effective *written communicator*:
- Is understood in a single rapid reading by the intended audience
- Puts the "bottom line up front"
- Is grammatically correct
- Uses the active voice
- Uses a reasonably simple style with appropriate format and organization
- Correctly and effectively uses facts and data to support the argument
- Presents ideas in a logical fashion by stating topics, supporting arguments, and conclusions

Developmental Activities/Actions for *written communication*

1. Ask your unit adjutant for copies of well written efficiency report narratives, memorandums, and decision papers. Use these examples as guides in the preparation of your own written work.

2. Put writing resources in your office and use them. At a minimum, all Army writers should regularly refer to a grammar/style reference book, a dictionary, a thesaurus, and AR 25-50 (Preparing and Managing Correspondence).

3. Write a short article for a professional military publication (e.g., your branch magazine). Request feedback from the editor on your writing style.

4. Always use a spell check if available and ensure you proofread your memos or reports two or three times before sending them.

5. Periodically, ask a trusted peer to read and critique your writing. Ask them to interpret your message and intent. Do this especially before forwarding important memorandums.

6. Enroll in a college-level writing course.

B. Decision-Making
Decision-making constitutes the ability to reach sound, logical conclusions based on an analysis of factual information and the readiness to take appropriate actions based on the conclusions.

An effective *decision-maker*:

- Secures and analyzes relevant information about changing situations and emerging problems with the unit and uncovers critical issues affecting decision-making
- Recognizes and generates innovative solutions to problems
- Develops alternative courses of action and weighs their relative costs and benefits
- Exercises judgment to choose the most appropriate alternative for the circumstances

Developmental Activities/Actions for *decision-making*:

1. Formally involve subordinate leaders in deciding what to include in the platoon's training schedule.

2. Provide a formal risk analysis prior to a platoon EXEVAL.

3. Resist making "snap" decisions when time is available. Do the following when presented with your next problem. Define the problem and take time to generate solutions. Before selecting a solution, challenge yourself to think through how you would defend each alternative solution.

4. Before making a decision generate multiple possible decisions by doing the following. View each significant problem from at least three perspectives: your soldiers', a peer's, and a respected senior officer. Prepare notes to briefly outline their perspectives and discuss these with them before making your decision.

5. Make wise use of existing information when considering your decision. Successful decision- makers often look to the past and to others to determine what might be the best course of action. Talk with other leaders who might have worthwhile information regarding your issue. Seek out leaders who have dealt with the same issue and learn from what they've done.

6. Stop yourself from pushing your decision-making responsibilities upward. Take problems to your superior only when you have exhausted your ability to solve the problem. Provide your superior with background information and a recommendation.

7. Conduct a brainstorming session with subordinates or peers in order to understand all the issues affecting a decision. Follow these guidelines for brainstorming:

- Ddefine the problem you're facing
- Don't criticize ideas initially
- Be free to add to already suggested ideas or combine ideas
- Set a time limit to generate a sense of urgency
- Record all ideas
- Review the ideas to determine which could be implemented

8. Have a peer or your mentor observe your speech patterns and word choice for tentative language such as "I believe…," or "I'm not sure this is the best way, but…." Recognize that this approach can undermine confidence in your decisions.

9. Take ownership of your decision and those of your superiors. Refrain from saying, "It's not my idea, but we are going to do it anyway," or "It was the Captain's idea, not mine to do this."

C. Motivating

Motivating embodies using an individual's desires and needs to influence how he thinks and what he does. Motivating uses appropriate incentives and methods to reinforce individuals or groups as they effectively work toward task accomplishment and resolution of conflicts and disagreements. Coupled with influence, motivating involves empowering subordinate leaders to achieve organizational goals and properly rewarding their efforts as they achieve the goals.

An effective *motivator*:

- Continually articulates behavioral expectations of performance
- Assists subordinate leaders in learning how to meet expectations, provides feedback on performance, and holds subordinate leaders responsible to achieve the standard
- Assigns tasks to peers/subordinates with consideration for duty positions, capabilities, and developmental needs
- Provides subordinate leaders the rationale for tasks
- Apportions overall mission into smaller subtasks
- Allocates sufficient time for task completion
- Recognizes the good performance of subordinates at completion of tasks and respond to poor performance appropriately
- Attempts to meet the needs of subordinates
- Provides accurate, timely and (where appropriate) positive feedback
- Solicits and uses subordinate feedback to modify duties, tasks, requirements and goals when appropriate
- Justly applies disciplinary measures IAW prescribed procedures
- Keeps subordinates informed
- Accepts final responsibility for performance of the unit

Developmental Activities/Actions for *motivating*:

1. Get to know your subordinates and their needs. What rewards are important to them; what motivates them?

2. Be creative in rewarding positive performance. Avoid relying on the 3-day pass as a reward for everything. Ask your soldiers and NCOs for ideas, discuss these with your peers and supervisor.

Note: See Alternative Awards on facing page.

3. Make a daily habit of catching people doing something right and reinforce them. Praise can be a powerful motivator. Instead of looking for mistakes to punish, focus on finding examples of desirable behavior and then use praise to reinforce it quickly. For example, during a walk through the barracks or motor pool, focus on and identify more things going well than going wrong.

4. Meet with your NCO's and ask them what, if anything, is preventing them from achieving excellence in their METL tasks. Attempt to provide them the resourcing they need. If this is beyond your control, seek assistance from your higher.

5. Use the Hometown News Release to acknowledge awards, school selection, APFT scores, a safe driving record, participation in exercises, championship sporting events, promotions, Soldier of the Quarter, or assignment to or departure from the unit. See the battalion S-1 or installation PAO for information on how to make this program easy.

Alternative Rewards (Motivating)

Ref: ALDH, app. E, p. 83.

Typically, junior leaders rely on the three or four day pass as the primary means of rewarding soldiers for positive performance. When overly used, this practice can have negative effects on accomplishing the mission, may seem unfair to some soldiers, and may even desensitize soldiers to what, when less frequently used, can be a powerful motivator. Instead of overusing this valuable asset, you may want to try some of the following ideas as alternative ways of rewarding your soldiers. Helpful hint: rewards are most powerful when they are tailored to meet the soldier's needs and desires.

- Use your appreciative words through verbal praise, a formal positive counseling session, or a simple "thank you" card.
- Self-paced PT for a specific amount of time.
- PT Guidon Bearer as an honor.
- Lead the platoon in the PT run.
- Invite chosen soldiers for a "run with the commander."
- Time off for Birthdays.
- Coordinate for airlift of the squad out of the field first.
- Exemption from extra duty or guard.
- Opportunity to attend evening college courses.
- Leave the field exercise early or "first out."
- Post picture on soldier/leader of the month on a recognition board in barracks.
- Recommendation for early promotion to E-4.
- Points for the military schools OML - airborne, AASLT, RGR, NBC, Armorer.
- Recommendation for impact Certificate of Achievement or AAM.
- Additional responsibility or autonomy in job.
- Special assignment for RTO, guidon bearer or CO's driver.
- Participate in planning a training event with leadership.
- Time to explore another MOS for a few days.
- Article in the Post or hometown newspaper.
- Adventure training for the unit - rappelling, pugel sticks.
- LT takes a soldier to lunch at the Community Club.
- Leader shines subordinates boots.
- Hot soup at midnight in the field.
- Leader cleans soldier's weapon or vehicle.
- Permit to name vehicle/weapon system.
- Unit marks duffel bags with hash marks symbolizing deployments.
- Inexpensive gift certificate to "Ranger Joes…"
- Dinner at the LT's house.
- Guard detail preference.
- Leader relieves soldiers of burden in field such as radio or MG.

6. Share your OER Support Form (DA Form 67-9-1) with subordinate leaders, solicit their objectives and goals. Ensure your leadership team is in agreement so you can back each other up! There is nothing worse for motivation of a subordinate leader than to pursue an objective only to not be supported by his /her leader.

7. Visibly display your enthusiasm for the mission and organization. The more excited and energetic you are about the unit and achieving goals, the more committed your subordinates will be in supporting you. Convey how important unit goals and objectives are to you and how pleased you are that soldiers are willing to work with you.

8. State positive expectations to affect better performance. This is the basis for the *Self-fulfilling Prophecy*. Subordinates respond to their perception of our expectations in ways that often make our expectations become true. Examine and note what you say to others during the next 24 hours. Are you expressing positive or negative expectations?

9. Examine how you are reinforcing soldiers and make sure you are following these guidelines:

   • Personalize the reinforcer as much as possible. Observe and communicate with subordinates to determine how they react to reinforcers available to you. Fit the reward to the individual.

   • Use reinforcement that fits the performance. Give small rewards for small successes and big rewards only for big successes.

   • Effective reinforcement should follow closely the desired behavior. Immediate praise from you is likely to be more effective than a letter from the battalion commander that is three weeks old.

10. Constantly work to make your unit climate an environment for high-performance where...

   • the focus is clear

   • the work is challenging

   • soldiers feel appreciated

   • barriers to accomplishing the mission are at a minimum

   • resources are available to accomplish tasks

   • soldiers help and support each other

11. Determine your subordinates' perception of "what exists today" and "what is still needed." Ask subordinates the following to gain a clearer understanding of the current work environment and what is needed to develop a high performance environment:

   • What have you done in the last three months that you are most proud of?

   • What is challenging about your work and what challenges do you like?

   • What duties give you a sense of job satisfaction?

   • Who appreciates the job you do? Where do you get your recognition?

   • What obstacles exist to doing your work?

   • What has motivated you in the past to work harder?

   • What resources are or are not available to do your job?

   • Where do you get your support?

12. Closely examine how you use reinforcement such as recommendations for passes, impact awards, letters of recognition, certificates, etc. Take corrective action if necessary. To maximally increase effective behavior through reinforcement, you should:

- Specify precisely what must be done to get the award (as much as possible, establish and publicize qualitative and quantifiable criteria)
- Recognize positive performance immediately and frequently
- Tailor the reinforcement to the individual (ensure he/she values the award, certificate, praise, etc.)
- Reinforce all who are performing the specified behavior

13. Closely examine any attempts you might be making to motivate through public embarrassment such as a "dirty wrench" award for the weakest motor stables performance, or some other "award" used to recognize and highlight a dumb mistake or error. Public humiliation is a major fear for most and some will lie, cheat, and steal to avoid embarrassment. Poor performers need positive reinforcement , not embarrassment.

14. Analyze your unit and work area(s) to ensure that basic individual needs are taken care of. Look for conditions that undermine motivation such as excessive heat or cold, noisy work areas, poor ventilation or lighting, lack of privacy or security for equipment, or absence of proper and necessary tools and equipment.

15. Deal with subordinates' personal problems immediately. Personal problems might be severely affecting their motivation. Make it a priority for your unit leadership to help soldiers help themselves with problems such as child care conflicts, marital problems, personal or family illness, transportation problems, legal or financial problems, alcohol or drug problems, medical problems such as dental, vision, hearing, and pregnancy, and harassment or equal opportunity issues.

2. Operating

Operating implies a focus on action to meet the immediate situation that requires standard procedures and structures with an expectation of prompt, measurable results. Usually it has a clear linkage between cause and effect and contains much hard data often available for decision-making. Our ability to operate effectively is dependent on specific behaviors:

- How we *plan*
- How we *execute*
- How we *assess*

A. Planning and Preparing

Planning and preparing establishes a course of action for oneself and others to accomplish goals. Planning establishes priorities and appropriately allocates time and resources (to include people).

An effective *planner*:
- Balances competing demands and sets task priorities

Operating Actions
A. Planning and Preparing **B. Executing** **C. Assessing**

Ref: FM 22-100, pp. 2-27.

- Recognizes and resolves time and date conflicts
- Meets deadlines for assigned tasks, mastery of tactical and technical knowledge, and completion of duties
- Develops detailed, executable plans that are feasible, acceptable, and suitable
- Effectively uses planning techniques to develop courses of action based on the desired outcome
- Adequately adapts plan from higher headquarters to own unit
- Prepares and issues orders and directives
- Reasonably adheres to the "1/3 - 2/3 Rule"
- Follows commander's intent
- Sufficiently allocates appropriate resources
- Adequately addresses likely contingencies and remains flexible
- Includes and accomplishes adequate coordination
- Personally arrives on time and meets deadlines
- Delegates work not necessary for the leader (self) to do
- Establishes milestones and conducts interim progress reviews (IPRs) to monitor progress toward goal completion

Developmental Activities/Actions for *planning*

1. Recognize that a 70% plan provided on time to subordinates is preferred to a 100% plan that is late. Ensure you are allowing subordinates sufficient time to respond and adapt to your plan. Follow the "1/3 - 2/3 Rule."

2. Allocate training time for you and your subordinate leaders to conduct a tactical planning exercise. Obtain copy of higher unit OPORD and go through the entire process. Conduct an AAR.

3. When opportunities arise volunteer to serve as an OC of another unit. Make a special effort to observe leaders during the planning process. If appropriate, facilitate an AAR on the planning process.

4. Find out which of your peers is considered to be a good tactical planner. Shadow this person as they conduct the planning process.

5. Involve qualified subordinates in the planning process right from the start to use their experience, skills, and expertise. Participation can also lead to their personal investment in reaching unit goals.

6. Involve your subordinate leaders in developing a plan to accomplish a unit goal. Lead them through the "backward" planning process and identify key milestones.

7. Consult with skilled planners such as company commanders, the S-3, and experienced supply sergeants. Observe and ask about their planning process; review their written plans; observe their tracking systems; and ask them to give feedback regarding your plans.

8. Study the battalion commander's quarterly training guidance and consider its implications for your unit. Discuss these implications with your supervisor, peers, and immediate subordinates.

9. Effective planners cover all bases by ensuring they have answered the questions listed below. Examine a training exercise, program, or event that you are planning right now. Write down answers to these questions and present a briefing or update for your boss organized around your responses.

- **WHAT** must be done to reach our objective?
- **WHY** must it be done? Does the end state justify the investment of resources?
- **WHEN** should it be done? What are the dates, time-frames, and deadlines that should be selected and coordinated?
- **WHO** should do the task(s)?
- **WHERE** should it be done?
- **HOW** should it be done?

10. Ensure you know and understand your commander's vision for the unit. Consider how you incorporate that vision into day-to-day training and operations.

11. Ask to study planning documents (e.g., OPLANs, SOPs, LOIs) created by your peers, especially those who have been in the job for more than six months. Ask them to clarify what works and what doesn't. Use and improve their products.

2. Visit the battalion, brigade, or division S3/G3 shop. Ask to see the long range plans and have someone explain how they are nested within higher level plans.

13. Work closely with the commander or S3 on preparation for the next quarterly training briefing. Start early and follow the entire process through.

14. Ask a trusted peer to play "devil's advocate" by confronting you with all possible things that could go wrong with your plan. Make appropriate changes and contingency plans for issues that are uncovered.

15. Study, refresh, know, and practice troop-leading procedures. These procedures work not only on the battlefield, but also serve as the basic process or general framework to ensure leaders get the right things done during peace.

B. Executing

Execution comprises the ability to complete individual and unit assigned tasks according to specified standards and within certain time criteria or event criteria.

An individuals who *executes* effectively:
- Copes adequately with obstacles, difficulties, and hardships
- Remains committed to excellence even when things get tough
- Puts plans into action
- Completes assigned individual or unit tasks to meet standards and the commander's intent
- Follows plans and adjusts when necessary
- Reports status up the chain of command
- Makes use of available time for preparation, checks and rehearsals
- Maintains good accountability of people and equipment
- Makes necessary spot corrections
- Influences events and makes things happen with available resources
- Handles a fluid environment
- Guides and coaches subordinates
- Establishes and employs procedures for monitoring, coordinating and regulating actions and activities of subordinates
- Keeps track of who is assigned to do what and when; adjusts assignments if necessary; follows up
- Encourages initiative

Developmental Activities/Actions for *executing*

1. Conduct the quarterly M-16 zero and qualification range.

2. Conduct rehearsal of a tactical road march prior to executing.

3. Identify a peer who is acknowledged as an expert at a METL task. Walk along/ shadow this leader during the execution of that task.

4. Have your NCOs describe their responsibilities and the specific duties that they'll be focusing on during an upcoming training event. Look for gaps or areas which may be receiving dual coverage. Use this exercise as a means of focusing your efforts more effectively. Record the lessons learned and use these during subsequent planning.

5. Promote aggressiveness and initiative in subordinates by allowing them to execute as they see fit within your broadly defined intent.

6. Informally and periodically ask your subordinates, "What can I do to help you be more effective?" Show openness and listen carefully to what they tell you.

7. Practice executing effectively by recognizing and eliminating common time wasters:
   - Scheduling too much time and allowing the work to expand to fill the time available
   - Putting off or delaying doing things that you do not like or want to do
   - Having ambiguous or ill-communicated plans, objectives, goals, and priorities
   - Failing to delegate tasks due to fear of losing control or not succeeding
   - Allowing too many interruptions or distractions during training
   - Engaging in or allowing too much socializing by failing to terminate meetings, conversations, or phone calls
   - Failing to assess and measure how time is being spent; this often leads to making the same mistakes
   - Suffering from indecision
   - Attending to details that could be handled by others

C. Assessing

Assessing refers to effectively and appropriately using after action reviews (AARs) and evaluation tools to facilitate continual improvement.

An individual who competently *assesses*:
   - Observes actions in progress
   - Correctly evaluates results based on standards
   - Recognizes poor performance and corrects it
   - Recognizes and reinforces success
   - Sorts out important actual and potential problems
   - Conducts/facilitates after action reviews (AARs) and identifies "lessons learned"
   - Determines cause and effect relationships, and contributing factors for each identified problem
   - Conducts in-progress reviews during long-term preparation

Developmental Activities/Actions for *assessing*

1. Review your METL tasks with subordinate leaders. Come to an agreement as to what "trained", "practice", and "untrained" looks like for each task.

2. Write out your objectives for a specific rating period in terms of clear, measurable outcomes.

3. Review the guidelines and procedures for conducting effective after action reviews (AARs) set forth in FM 25-100 (Training the Force), FM 25-101 (Battle Focused Training), and FC 25-20 (A Leader's Guide to After Action Reviews). Build the AAR process into each significant training event.

4. Become proficient at assessing individual NCO performance. Study and become familiar with the NCOER and how to write administratively correct and influential reports. Ask the 1SG or CSM to review these and provide you with feedback.

5. Observe another unit during a training event and assist battalion observers in developing their assessment.

6. Observe AARs at platoon and company levels during the External Evaluation of another unit.

7. Meet with battalion staff before a unit evaluation (e.g., command inspection, EXEVAL). Ask for copies of the checklists they'll use to evaluate your unit. Assess your unit based on these checklists and focus your training on the identified deficiencies.

8. Assess your unit by conducting an abbreviated unit climate survey. Study DA Pam 600-69, Unit Climate Profile.

9. Communicate your standards and expectations before any event, activity, or performance that you deem worthy of assessment. For example, if you intend to inspect (that is, assess) barracks rooms, then ensure you have established the inspection standards and have communicated them through the chain of command. Then, assess based on the criteria, provide feedback, take corrective action where necessary, and reinforce those who meet or exceed the standard.

10. Discuss with your supervisor opportunities to participate in battalion command inspections as an inspector or during EXEVALS as a controller/evaluator. Use these opportunities to help clarify standards.

3. Improving

Improving implies a focus on sustaining and renewing the development of individuals and the institution (with a time horizon from months to decades) that requires a need for experimentation and innovation. Improving focuses on affecting people, organizations, and systems in ways that positively influence future events.

Improving Actions

A. Developing
B. Building
C. Learning

Ref: FM 22-100, pp. 2-28.

A. Developing

Developing embraces the art of teaching, training, coaching, and counseling subordinates to increase their knowledge, skills, and confidence. We *develop* the competence and self-confidence of subordinate leaders through role modeling and/or training and having them engage in developmental activities related to their current or future duties.

An individual who effectively *develops* subordinates:

- Sets the example by displaying high standards of duty performance, personal appearance, and personal conduct
- Clearly explains tasks and sets realistic standards
- Designs tasks to provide practice for subordinates where needed
- Creates an atmosphere in which good performance is expected, superior performance is recognized, and poor performance is unacceptable
- Guides subordinates in thinking through problems for themselves; coaches, counsels, evaluates and assesses subordinates
- Expands/enhances the competence and self-confidence of subordinates
- Encourages initiative by underwriting honest mistakes
- Builds on success and improves weaknesses
- Clearly articulates expectations and sets realistic standards
- Anticipates mistakes and offers assistance
- Enhances effectiveness and self-esteem of subordinates
- Routinely asks subordinate "how they are doing," or "what is distracting from excellence"

Developmental Activities/Actions for *developing*

1. Prepare a subordinate to stand in for you at a meeting, inspection, or planning session. Observe him or her and provide critical and constructive feedback.

2. Conduct an initial counseling session with all subordinate leaders within 30 days of arrival. Explain the scope of their responsibilities and key tasks.

3. Require subordinate leaders to bring a self-assessment of their leadership to counseling sessions.

4. Stay alert for articles, news reports, and media information that might be useful to others. Discuss them with peers or subordinates and pass them on.

5. Give subordinate leaders assignments or tasks that take them out of their comfort zone. For example, require them to interface directly with the commander to gain experience working directly with senior officers.

6. Prioritize and support developmental activities that are in the best long range interest of the Army: individual Army schools, college courses, warrant officer and OCS applications, self-development activities.

7. Offer to give a presentation to peers and subordinates concerning nonjudicial punishment and administrative options (e.g., extra training, bar to reenlistment, counseling, MOS reclassification, separation, denial of pass privilege) that you can recommend as developmental tools.

8. Discourage upward delegation. Ask subordinates for their recommendation to fix problems. Provide expertise and additional resources if necessary instead of taking over subordinate tasks.

9. Delegate to the lowest level possible. Compare and discuss with your peers the missions and tasks you are delegating. Reassign the work load based on these discussions so that subordinates have greater opportunity to develop.

10. Recognize your responsibility to ensure new soldiers receive an effective orientation to their jobs, their team, section, or squad, and the unit. Closely examine each aspect of the inprocessing/orientation process to ensure they support your goals and objectives for the unit.

11. Together with subordinate leaders, develop and post a succession plan for your unit. Identify the next position each person will move into and a tentative date of the move.

12. Expand subordinate responsibility. Examine the overall picture of your unit to determine which subordinates are not being challenged by their current assignments. Look for ways to provide the skills, resources, and experiences that will enable them to handle more challenging work. Then assign that work to them. Discuss with your peers the specific duties and responsibilities their subordinates have. Look for ways to expand jobs.

13. Lead a discussion with subordinates or peers regarding the organization of your higher headquarters. Use a copy of the organizational chart and assign people to explain the major functions of other units within the command. Have the group identify areas of interdependence, support, and effects on your unit's mission.

14. Stabilize leader time in positions to where individuals remain long enough to achieve excellence as well as fulfill their responsibility to develop subordinates.

15. Identify and mentor soldiers who demonstrate the potential for serving the Army as officers. Help them interpret the appropriate regulations (AR 351-5, Army Officer Candidate Schools; AR 351-17, United States Military Academy and United States Military Academy Preparatory School Admissions Program).

16. Jointly build developmental plans for your subordinates. Use the support form format but ensure the following features are met.

- Specificity: State specifically and concretely each goal and objective. Describe the skills or knowledge that will be gained as a result of each goal or objective.

- Commitment: Subordinates will be more committed to goals they choose and plans they develop. Likewise, you must be committed to providing the opportunities and resources needed by the subordinate to fulfill the plan.

- Small, reasonable steps: Expecting too much too soon can discourage. Divide developmental activities into small steps that lead to the ultimate goal.

- Support and feedback: Provide support in terms of resources, time, feedback, reinforcement, and encouragement.

- Specific time frame for accomplishment: Schedule target dates for completion and dates for in progress reviews.

B. Building

Building focuses on sustaining and renewing the institution. It involves actions that indicate commitment to the achievement of group or organizational goals; timely and effective discharge of operational and organizational duties and obligations; working effectively with others; and compliance with and active support of organizational goals, rules, and policies. Building enhances group cohesion.

An individual who effectively *builds* subordinates and organizations:

- Develops a unit climate based on mutual trust, respect, and confidence
- Participates for the good of the unit in activities, functions, etc.
- Participates in team/mission accomplishment without being specifically requested to do so
- Spends time and resources improving teams, groups, and units
- Gets people to work effectively with each other
- Promotes teamwork and team achievement by setting the example as a "team player"
- Offers suggestions but always supports chain of command
- Volunteers in useful ways that are not self-serving
- Remains positive when situations are confusing or changing
- Properly executes higher headquarters decisions - even unpopular ones
- Gives same good effort whether in charge or not
- Supports equal opportunity and prevention of sexual harrassment programs
- Deliberately plans activities to maximize interaction of soldiers toward a positive outcome; builds cohesion
- Stabilizes key personnel to increase unit cohesion

Developmental Activities/Actions for *building*

1. Publicly acknowledge good team performance during formations or meetings. Let your subordinate teams know that they're making a difference by recognizing them through a personal note, a note on the unit bulletin board, or in formation.

2. Organize one social event per quarter for your platoon, squad, or team (e.g., barbecues, lunches, breakfasts). When possible, coordinate these with the successful completion of actions or training events.

3. Brief your platoon, squad, or team once a month on priorities and mission focus. Emphasize where the unit is headed and why.

4. Invite your subordinate leaders and their families over for a backyard barbecue occasionally, or just take a subordinate leader to lunch occasionally. Instead of talking shop, relax and allow the families to get to know each other. Strengthen your relationship with your most critical team members by getting to know the whole person.

5. Build trust and a positive unit climate by committing yourself to sharing information. Practice these behaviors:

- Use your unit bulletin board to keep people up to date
- Occasionally eat in the dining facility with subordinates or peers and listen
- Keep your supervisor, peers, and subordinates up-to-date by submitting a monthly activity report for your unit. Address where the unit's been, where it's going, and your impressions
- Never "shoot" the messenger of bad news
- Be quick and concise in delivering bad news. Do not think it will go away or wait for a better time. Always report it with a recommendation and accurate status.
- At the end of each day, ask yourself what occurred that should be reported to other people
- Return phone and email messages promptly
- Update your supervisor, peers, and soldiers, even when nothing new has happened

- Allow others to express contrary viewpoints

6. Actively participate in selected squad/section level training activities.

7. In coordination with the platoon NCOs, develop a platoon METL list showing strengths and weaknesses. Brief the CO on your findings and allow NCOs to handle segments of the briefing.

8. Conduct a performance oriented counseling session with each immediate subordinate using a written support form. Allow the NCO to discuss current perceptions of his or her role and the work he/she does. Focus on similarities and differences from your expectations. Arrive at a consensus and record it.

9. As soon as possible, meet with new soldiers or NCOs to discuss your expectations and those of the chain of command, and to identify their expectations. Help the new individual prioritize duties to give job focus and to build support for your mission.

10. Conduct unit leader professional development sessions that focus on topics relevant to officer, warrant officer, and NCO leadership.

11. Lead a discussion with a group of your subordinate leaders using your commander's OER support form and the vision statement of the battalion or brigade commander. During this discussion, develop your own unit vision statement and a collective support form for the unit. Solicit input from subordinates on what they can do.

12. Post your vision and unit mission so that soldiers can see them. Talk about them often. Recognize that making these clear to others is a process, not an event. Continually communicate and clarify your unit's progress toward mission accomplishment.

C. Learning

Learning involves an essential shift or progress of the mind where creation is evident and enjoins activities such as re-engineering, envisioning, changing, adapting, moving into and creating the future.

An individual who is prepared and is open to *learning*:

- Embraces change and is adaptable to a future orientation
- Uses experience to improve both themselves and the unit
- Actively seeks self-improvement
- Fosters a learning environment within the unit
- Acts to expand personal and unit knowledge and capabilities
- Implements needed change
- Applies lessons learned
- Asks incisive questions
- Designs innovative and exciting ways to train
- Endeavors to broaden understanding through teaching and training
- Keep soldiers informed; does not withhold information
- Underwrites honest mistakes

Developmental Activities/Actions for *learning*

1. Allow subordinates to move ahead with their ideas unless you have a major Problem or concern with their plan. Remember that learning from mistakes is an effective and common way for people to develop abilities.

2. When soldiers confront you with a problem, respond with "what would you recommend?" This encourages them to take charge of their learning. Recognize that solutions often take time to develop. Allow people to bring partially developed solutions and then have them struggle with difficult problems and issues before demanding or asking for a more developed solution.

3. Based on AAR comments, work with subordinate leaders to develop a strategy to correct short comings of unit training.

4. Identify and meet with an officer or senior NCO who recently led his or her unit through a MTOE change such as weapon system conversion or upgrade, or moved fixed facilities such as barracks or motor pools. Discuss his or her approach and the problems or issues that were encountered. Present your plans or issues to this person and ask for feedback.

5. Ask newly assigned soldiers to help you evaluate the effectiveness of the unit by providing feedback at designated points - such as during inprocessing, after one month, and after three months in the unit. Write down their feedback and compare it with that from other newly assigned soldiers. Look for trends and learn from them.

6. Seek and generate additional challenges and let your leaders know you are looking for increased responsibility and personal growth.

7. Focus on your learning priorities by keeping a list of things you want to learn during the next three months, year, three years, and five years. Show this list to your mentor and develop a plan that involves continuing effort.

8. Make some form of public commitment to your learning goals so others will encourage you to reach them. Show your goals to others, talk about them, and post them where you'll be reminded daily.

9. Share your mistakes by talking through the mistake with others you trust. This will often increase your understanding of the situation. Solicit their input regarding what you might do differently in the future. Openly discussing mistakes will increase learning and can help build the organization through developing trust.

10. Conduct "exit" briefings with soldiers who are departing your unit (after they have received evaluations). Ask them for a candid opinion of what the unit needs to do to improve.

11. Read the major publications for your branch and specialty. Copy and circulate the most stimulating and relevant articles. Briefly discuss these at staff meetings, OPD sessions, etc.

12. Fight the tendency to respond defensively to criticism. Defensiveness stops others from giving you information you need in order to learn from your performance.

- View defensiveness as the enemy. Don't argue, explain, or debate negative feedback. Ask questions to clarify the feedback you are receiving and to help the person who is giving the feedback to be more precise in his or her feedback.
- Summarize the feedback to ensure that you fully heard and understood it.
- Ask trusted colleagues to tell you when you are reacting defensively. Eliminate the behavior they label as defensive.

13. Set the example for "thinking out of the box" about problems or conditions that require change or action. Reward people for generating ideas by thanking them and telling others about their good ideas.

14. Promote a climate in which people initially encourage, rather than criticize, new ideas.

The Army Leader
IV. The Human Dimension

Ref: FM 22-100, p. 3-1 to 3-19.

A. Leadership Styles

1 Directing Leadership Style

2 Participating Leadership Style

3 Delegating Leadership Style

4 Transformational Leadership Style

5 Transactional Leadership Style

Ref: FM 22-100, p. 3-15 to 3-17.

Regardless of the level, keep in mind one important aspect of leadership: you lead people. This section examines this all-important human dimension.

A. Leadership Styles

All people are shaped by what they've seen, what they've learned, and whom they've met. Who you are determines the way you work with other people. Some people are happy and smiling all the time; others are serious. Some leaders can wade into a room full of strangers and inside of five minutes have everyone there thinking, "How have I lived so long without meeting this person?" Other very competent leaders are uncomfortable in social situations. Most of us are somewhere in between. Although Army leadership doctrine describes at great length how you should interact with your subordinates and how you must strive to learn and improve your leadership skills, the Army recognizes that you must always be yourself; anything else comes across as fake and insincere.

Having said that, effective leaders are flexible enough to adjust their leadership style and techniques to the people they lead. Some subordinates respond best to coaxing, suggestions, or gentle prodding; others need, and even want at times, the verbal equivalent of a kick in the pants. Treating people fairly doesn't mean treating people as if they were clones of one another. In fact, if you treat everyone the same way, you're probably being unfair, because different people need different things from you.

Think of it this way: Say you must teach map reading to a large group of soldiers ranging in rank from private to senior NCO. The senior NCOs know a great deal about the subject, while the privates know very little. To meet all their needs, you must teach the privates more than you teach the senior NCOs. If you train the privates only in the advanced skills the NCOs need, the privates will be lost. If you make the NCOs sit through training in the basic tasks the privates need, you'll waste the NCOs' time. You must fit the training to the experience of those being trained. In the same way, you must adjust your leadership style and techniques to the experience of your people and characteristics of your organization.

Obviously, you don't lead senior NCOs the same way you lead privates. But the easiest distinctions to make are those of rank and experience. You must also take into account personalities, self-confidence, self-esteem—all the elements of the complex mix of character traits that makes dealing with people so difficult and so rewarding. One of the many things that makes your job tough is that, in order to get their best performance, you must figure out what your subordinates need and what they're able to do—even when they don't know themselves.

When discussing leadership styles, many people focus on the extremes: autocratic and democratic. Autocratic leaders tell people what to do with no explanation; their message is, "I'm the boss; you'll do it because I said so." Democratic leaders use their personalities to persuade subordinates. There are many shades in between; the following paragraphs discuss five of them. However, bear in mind that competent leaders mix elements of all these styles to match to the place, task, and people involved. Using different leadership styles in different situations or elements of different styles in the same situation isn't inconsistent. The opposite is true: if you can use only one leadership style, you're inflexible and will have difficulty operating in situations where that style doesn't fit.

1. Directing Leadership Style

The directing style is leader-centered. Leaders using this style don't solicit input from subordinates and give detailed instructions on how, when, and where they want a task performed. They then supervise its execution very closely.

The directing style may be appropriate when time is short and leaders don't have a chance to explain things. They may simply give orders: Do this. Go there. Move. In fast-paced operations or in combat, leaders may revert to the directing style, even with experienced subordinates. If the leader has created a climate of trust, subordinates will assume the leader has switched to the directing style because of the circumstances.

The directing style is also appropriate when leading inexperienced teams or individuals who are not yet trained to operate on their own. In this kind of situation, the leader will probably remain close to the action to make sure things go smoothly.

Some people mistakenly believe the directing style means using abusive or demeaning language or includes threats and intimidation. This is wrong. If you're ever tempted to be abusive, whether because of pressure or stress or what seems like improper behavior by a subordinate, ask yourself these questions: Would I want to work for someone like me? Would I want my boss to see and hear me treat subordinates this way? Would I want to be treated this way?

2. Participating Leadership Style

The participating style centers on both the leader and the team. Given a mission, leaders ask subordinates for input, information, and recommendations but make the final decision on what to do themselves. This style is especially appropriate for leaders who have time for such consultations or who are dealing with experienced subordinates.

The team-building approach lies behind the participating leadership style. When subordinates help create a plan, it becomes—at least in part—their plan. This ownership creates a strong incentive to invest the effort necessary to make the plan work. Asking for this kind of input is a sign of a leader's strength and self-confidence. But asking for advice doesn't mean the leader is obligated to follow it; the leader alone is always responsible for the quality of decisions and plans.

3. Delegating Leadership Style

The delegating style involves giving subordinates the authority to solve problems and make decisions without clearing them through the leader. Leaders with mature and experienced subordinates or who want to create a learning experience for subordinates often need only to give them authority to make decisions, the necessary resources, and a clear understanding of the mission's purpose. As always, the leader is ultimately responsible for what does or does not happen, but in the delegating leadership style, the leader holds subordinate leaders accountable for their actions. This is the style most often used by officers dealing with senior NCOs and by organizational and strategic leaders.

4. Transformational Leadership Style

These words of a distinguished military leader capture the distinction between the transformational leadership style, which focuses on inspiration and change, and the transactional leadership style, which focuses on rewards and punishments. Of course Napoleon understood the importance of rewards and punishments. Nonetheless, he also understood that carrots and sticks alone don't inspire individuals to excellence.

As the name suggests, the transformational style "transforms" subordinates by challenging them to rise above their immediate needs and self-interests. The transformational style is developmental: it emphasizes individual growth (both professional and personal) and organizational enhancement. Key features of the transformational style include empowering and mentally stimulating subordinates: you consider and motivate them first as individuals and then as a group. To use the transformational style, you must have the courage to communicate your intent and then step back and let your subordinates work. You must also be aware that immediate benefits are often delayed until the mission is accomplished.

The transformational style allows you to take advantage of the skills and knowledge of experienced subordinates who may have better ideas on how to accomplish a mission. Leaders who use this style communicate reasons for their decisions or actions and, in the process, build in subordinates a broader understanding and ability to exercise initiative and operate effectively. However, not all situations lend themselves to the transformational leadership style. The transformational style is most effective during periods that call for change or present new opportunities. It also works well when organizations face a crisis, instability, mediocrity, or disenchantment. It may not be effective when subordinates are inexperienced, when the mission allows little deviation from accepted procedures, or when subordinates are not motivated.

Leaders who use only the transformational leadership style limit their ability to influence individuals in these and similar situations.

5. Transactional Leadership Style

In contrast, some leaders employ only the transactional leadership style. This style includes such techniques as—

- Motivating subordinates to work by offering rewards or threatening punishment
- Prescribing task assignments in writing
- Outlining all the conditions of task completion, the applicable rules and regulations, the benefits of success, and the consequences—to include possible disciplinary actions—of failure
- "Management-by-exception," where leaders focus on their subordinates' failures, showing up only when something goes wrong

The leader who relies exclusively on the transactional style, rather than combining it with the transformational style, evokes only short-term commitment from his subordinates and discourages risk-taking and innovation.

There are situations where the transactional style is acceptable, if not preferred. For example, a leader who wants to emphasize safety could reward the organization with a three-day pass if the organization prevents any serious safety-related incidents over a two-month deployment. In this case, the leader's intent appears clear: unsafe acts are not tolerated and safe habits are rewarded.

However, using only the transactional style can make the leader's efforts appear self-serving. In this example, soldiers might interpret the leader's attempt to reward safe practices as an effort to look good by focusing on something that's unimportant but that has the boss's attention. Such perceptions can destroy the trust subordinates have in the leader. Using the transactional style alone can also deprive subordinates of opportunities to grow, because it leaves no room for honest mistakes.

The most effective leaders combine techniques from the transformational and transactional leadership styles to fit the situation. A strong base of transactional understanding supplemented by charisma, inspiration and individualized concern for each subordinate, produces the most enthusiastic and genuine response. Subordinates will be more committed, creative, and innovative. They will also be more likely to take calculated risks to accomplish their mission. Again referring to the safety example, leaders can avoid any misunderstanding of their intent by combining transformational techniques with transactional techniques. They can explain why safety is important (intellectual stimulation) and encourage their subordinates to take care of each other (individualized concern).

B. People, the Team and the Institution

Former Army Chief of Staff John A. Wickham Jr. described the relationship between the people who are the Army and the Army as an institution this way: The Army is an institution, not an occupation. Members take an oath of service to the nation and the Army, rather than simply accept a job…the Army has moral and ethical obligations to those who serve and their families; they, correspondingly, have responsibilities to the Army.

The Army has obligations to soldiers, DA civilians, and their families that most organizations don't have; in return, soldiers and DA civilians have responsibilities to the Army that far exceed those of an employee to most employers. This relationship, one of mutual obligation and responsibility, is at the very center of what makes the Army a team, an institution rather than an occupation.

The Army can't function except as a team. This team identity doesn't come about just because people take an oath or join an organization; you can't force a team to come together any more than you can force a plant to grow. Rather, the team identity comes out of mutual respect among its members and a trust between leaders and subordinates. That bond between leaders and subordinates likewise springs from mutual respect as well as from discipline. The highest form of discipline is the willing obedience of oath or join an organization; you can't force a team to come together any more than you can force a plant to grow. Rather, the team identity comes out of mutual respect among its members and a trust between leaders and subordinates. That bond between leaders and subordinates likewise springs from mutual respect as well as from discipline. The highest form of discipline is the willing obedience of subordinates who trust their leaders, understand and believe in the mission's purpose, value the team and their place in it, and have the will to see the mission through. This form of discipline produces individuals and teams who—in the really tough moments—come up with solutions themselves.

1. Discipline

People are our most important resource; soldiers are in fact our "credentials." Part of knowing how to use this most precious resource is understanding the stresses and demands that influence people.

One sergeant major has described discipline as "a moral, mental, and physical state in which all ranks respond to the will of the [leader], whether he is there or not." Disciplined people take the right action, even if they don't feel like it. True discipline demands habitual and reasoned obedience, an obedience that preserves initiative and works, even when the leader isn't around. Soldiers and DA civilians who understand the purpose of the mission, trust the leader, and share Army values will do the right thing because they're truly committed to the organization.

Discipline doesn't just mean barking orders and demanding an instant response—it's more complex than that. You build discipline by training to standard, using rewards and punishment judiciously, instilling confidence in and building trust among team members, and creating a knowledgeable collective will. The confidence, trust, and collective will of a disciplined, cohesive unit is crucial in combat.

Soldiers persevere in tough situations. They fight through because they have confidence in themselves, their buddies, their leaders, their equipment, and their training—and because they have discipline and will. A young sergeant who participated in Operation Uphold Democracy in Haiti in 1994 asserted this fact when interviewed by the media. The soldier said that operations went well because his unit did things just the way they did them in training and that his training never let him down.

Even in the most complex operations, the performance of the Army comes down to the training and disciplined performance of individuals and teams on the ground. One example of this fact occurred when a detachment of American soldiers was sent to guard a television tower in Udrigovo, Bosnia-Herzegovina.

After the soldiers had assumed their posts, a crowd of about 100 people gathered, grew to about 300, and began throwing rocks at the Americans. However, the soldiers didn't overreact. They prevented damage to the tower without creating an international incident. There was no "Boston Massacre" in Udrigovo. The discipline of American soldiers sent into this and other highly volatile situations in Bosnia kept the lid on that operation. The bloody guerrilla war predicted by some didn't materialize. This is a testament to the professionalism of today's American soldiers—your soldiers—and the quality of their leaders—you.

2. Morale

When military historians discuss great armies, they write about weapons and equipment, training and the national cause. They may mention sheer numbers (Voltaire said, "God is always on the side of the heaviest battalions") and all sorts of other things that can be analyzed, measured, and compared. However, some also write about another factor equally important to success in battle, something that can't be measured: the emotional element called morale.

Morale is the human dimension's most important intangible element. It's a measure of how people feel about themselves, their team, and their leaders. High morale comes from good leadership, shared hardship, and mutual respect. It's an emotional bond that springs from common values like loyalty to fellow soldiers and a belief that the organization will care for families. High morale results in a cohesive team that enthusiastically strives to achieve common goals. Leaders know that morale, the essential human element, holds the team together and keeps it going in the face of the terrifying and dispiriting things that occur in war.

3. Taking Care of Soldiers

Sending soldiers in harm's way, into places where they may be killed or wounded, might seem to contradict all the emphasis on taking care of soldiers. Does it? How can you truly care for your comrades and send them on missions that might get them killed? Consider this important and fundamental point as you read the next few paragraphs.

Whenever the talk turns to what leaders do, you'll almost certainly hear someone say, "Take care of your soldiers." And that's good advice. In fact, if you add one more clause, "Accomplish the mission and take care of your soldiers," you have guidance for a career. But "taking care of soldiers" is one of those slippery phrases, like the word "honor," that lots of people talk about but few take the trouble to explain. So what does taking care of soldiers mean?

Taking care of soldiers means creating a disciplined environment where they can learn and grow. It means holding them to high standards, training them to do their jobs so they can function in peace and win in war. You take care of soldiers when you treat them fairly, refuse to cut corners, share their hardships, and set the example. Taking care of soldiers encompasses everything from making sure a soldier has time for an annual dental exam to visiting off-post housing to make sure it's adequate. It also means providing the family support that assures soldiers their families will be taken care of, whether the soldier is home or deployed. Family support means ensuring there's a support group in place, that even the most junior soldier and most inexperienced family members know where to turn for help when their soldier is deployed.

Taking care of soldiers also means demanding that soldiers do their duty, even at the risk of their lives. It doesn't mean coddling them or making training easy or comfortable. In fact, that kind of training can get soldiers killed. Training must be rigorous and as much like combat as is possible while being safe. Hard training is one way of preparing soldiers for the rigors of combat. Take care of soldiers by giving them the training, equipment, and support they need to keep them alive in combat.

This concept doesn't mean that leaders sit at some safe, dry headquarters and make plans without seeing what their soldiers are going through, counting on them to tough out any situation. Leaders know that graphics on a map symbolize soldiers going forward to fight. Leaders get out with the soldiers to see and feel what they're experiencing as well as to influence the battle by their presence. (Gerhardt and numerous other front-line writers refer to the rear echelon as "anything behind my foxhole.") Leaders who stay a safe distance from the front jeopardize operations because they don't know what's going on. They risk destroying their soldiers' trust, not to mention their Unit.

This example illustrates three points:

- The importance of a leader going to where the action is to see and feel what's really going on
- The importance of a first-line leader telling the boss something he doesn't want to hear
- The importance of a leader accepting information that doesn't fit his preconceived notions

Soldiers are extremely sensitive to situations where their leaders are not at risk, and they're not likely to forget a mistake by a leader they haven't seen. Leaders who are out with their soldiers—in the same rain or snow, under the same blazing sun or in the same dark night, under the same threat of enemy artillery or small arms fire—will not fall into the trap of ignorance. Those who lead from the front can better motivate their soldiers to carry on under extreme conditions.

Taking care of soldiers is every leader's business. A DA civilian engineering team chief volunteered to oversee the installation of six Force Provider troop life support systems in the vicinity of Tuzla, Bosnia-Herzegovina. Using organizational skills, motivational techniques, and careful supervision, the team chief ensured that the sites were properly laid out, integrated, and installed. As a result of thorough planning and the teamwork the DA civilian leader generated, the morale and quality of life of over 5,000 soldiers were significantly improved.

C. Combat Stress

Consider carefully what the squad leader did. First he told his squad to calm down. Then he told them why it was important: they had to continue the fight if they wanted to make it back to their base alive. In this way he jerked his soldiers back to a conditioned response, one that had been drilled during training and that took their minds off the loss. The squad leader demonstrated the calm, reasoned leadership under stress that's critical to mission success. In spite of the loss, the unit persevered.

1. Will and Winning in Battle

The Army's ultimate responsibility is to win the nation's wars. And what is it that carries soldiers through the terrible challenges of combat? It's the will to win, the ability to gut it out when things get really tough, even when things look hopeless. It's the will not only to persevere but also to find workable solutions to the toughest problems. This drive is part of the warrior ethos, the ability to forge victory out of the chaos of battle—to overcome fear, hunger, deprivation, and fatigue and accomplish the mission. And the will to win serves you just as well in peacetime, when it's easy to become discouraged, feel let down, and spend your energy complaining instead of using your talents to make things better. Discipline holds a team together; the warrior ethos motivates its members—you and your people—to continue the mission.

All soldiers are warriors: all need to develop and display the will to win—the desire to do their job well—to persevere, no matter what the circumstances. The Army is a team, and all members' contributions are essential to mission accomplishment. As an Army leader, you're responsible for developing this sense of belonging in your subordinates. Not only that; it's your job to inculcate in your people the winning spirit—the commitment to do their part to accomplish the mission, no matter when, no matter where, no matter what.

Army operations often involve danger and therefore fear. Battling the effects of fear has nothing to do with denying it and everything to do with recognizing fear and handling it. Leaders let their subordinates know, "You can expect to be afraid; here's what we'll do about it." But saying this isn't going to make it happen. Army leaders expect fear to take hold when things go poorly, setbacks occur, the unit fails to complete a mission, or there are casualties. The sights and sounds of the modern battlefield are terrifying. So is fear of the unknown. Soldiers who see their buddies killed or wounded suddenly have a greater burden: they become aware of their own mortality. On top of all these obvious sources of fear is the insecurity before battle that many veterans have written about: "Will I perform well or will I let my buddies down?"

Will and a winning spirit apply in more situations than those requiring physical courage; sometimes you'll have to carry on for long periods in very difficult situations. The difficulties soldiers face may not be ones of physical danger, but of great physical, emotional, and mental strain. Physical courage allowed the soldier in the situation described above to return to the fight; will allowed his leader to say the right thing, to influence his frightened subordinate to do the right thing. Physical courage causes soldiers to charge a machine gun; will empowers them to fight on when they're hopelessly outnumbered, under appalling conditions, and without basic necessities.

2. Stress in Training

Leaders must inject stress into training to prepare soldiers for stress in combat. However, creating a problem for subordinates and having them react to it doesn't induce the kind of stress required for combat training. A meaningful and productive mission, given with detailed constraints and limitations plus high standards of performance, does produce stress. Still, leaders must add unanticipated conditions to that stress to create a real learning environment. Sometimes, you don't even have to add stress; it just happens.

D. The Stress of Change

Since the end of the Cold War, the Army has gone through tremendous change— dramatic decreases in the number of soldiers and DA civilians in all components, changes in assignment policies, base closings, and a host of other shifts that put stress on soldiers, DA civilians, and families. In those same years, the number of deployments to support missions such as peace operations and nation assistance has increased. And these changes have occurred in a peacetime Army. At the same time, Army leaders have had to prepare their soldiers for the stresses of combat, the ultimate crucible.

The stresses of combat you read about earlier in this chapter are classic: they've been the same for centuries. However, there's an aspect of the human dimension that has assumed an increasing importance: the effect of technological advances on organizations and people. Military leaders have always had to deal with the effect of technological changes. What's different today is the rate at which technology, to include warfighting technology, is changing. Rapid advances in new technologies are forcing the Army to change many aspects of the way it operates and are creating new leadership challenges.

1. Technology and Leadership

Technology's presence challenges all Army leaders. Technology is here to stay and you, as an Army leader, need to continually learn how to manage it and make it work for you. The challenges come from many directions. Among them—

- You need to learn the strengths and vulnerabilities of the different technologies that support your team and its mission.

- You need to think through how your organization will operate with organizations that are less or more technologically complex. This situation may take the form of heavy and light Army units working together, operating with elements of another service, or cooperating with elements of another nation's armed forces.

- You need to consider the effect of technology on the time you have to analyze problems, make a decision, and act. Events happen faster today, and the stress you encounter as an Army leader is correspondingly greater.

Technological advances have the potential to permit better and more sustainable operations. However, as an Army leader you must remember the limitations of your people. No matter what technology you have or how it affects your mission, it's still your soldiers and DA civilians—their minds, hearts, courage, and talents—that will win the day.

Advances in electronic data processing let you handle large amounts of information easily. Today's desktop computer can do more, and do it faster, than the room-sized computers of only 20 years ago. Technology is a powerful tool—if you understand its potential uses and limitations. The challenge for all Army leaders is to overcome confusion on a fast-moving battlefield characterized by too much information coming in too fast.

Army leaders and staffs have always needed to determine mission-critical information, prioritize incoming reports, and process them quickly. The volume of information that current technology makes available makes this skill even more important than in the past. Sometimes something low-tech can divert the flood of technological help into channels the leader and staff can manage. For example, a well-understood commander's intent and thought-through commander's critical information requirements (CCIR) can help free leaders from nonessential information while pushing decisions to lower levels. As an Army leader, you must work hard to overcome the attractiveness and potential pitfalls of centralized decision making that access to information will appear to make practical.

Technology is also changing the size of the battlefield and the speed of battle. Instant global communications are increasing the pace of military actions. Global positioning systems and night vision capabilities mean the Army can fight at night and during periods of limited visibility—conditions that used to slow things down. Continuous operations increase the mental and physical stress on soldiers and leaders. Nonlinear operations make it more difficult for commanders to determine critical points on the battlefield. Effective leaders develop techniques to identify and manage stress well before actual conflict occurs. They also find ways to overcome the soldier's increased sense of isolation that comes with the greater breadth and depth of the modern battlefield. (FM 100-34 discusses continuous operations. FM 22-51 discusses combat stress control.)

Modern technology has also increased the number and complexity of skills the Army requires. Army leaders must carefully manage low-density specialties. They need to ensure that critical positions are filled and that their people maintain perishable skills. Army leaders must bring together leadership, personnel management, and training management to ensure their organizations are assigned people with the right specialties and that the entire organization is trained and ready. On top of this, the speed and lethality of modern battle have made mental agility and initiative even more necessary for fighting and winning. As in the past, Army leaders must develop these attributes in their subordinates.

To some, technology suggests a bloodless battlefield that resembles a computer war game more than the battlefields of the past. That isn't true now and it won't be true in the immediate future. Technology is still directed at answering the same basic questions that Civil War leaders tried to answer when they sent out a line of skirmishers: Where am I? Where are the enemy? Where is my buddies? How do I defeat him? Armed with this information, the soldiers and DA civilians of the Army will continue to accomplish the mission with character, using their technological edge to do the job better, faster, and smarter.

Modern digital technology can contribute a great deal to the Army leader's understanding of the battlefield; good leaders stay abreast of advances that enhance their tactical abilities. Digital technology has a lot to offer, but don't be fooled. A video image of a place, an action, or an organization can never substitute for the leader's getting down on the ground with the soldiers to find out what's going on. Technology can provide a great deal of information, but it may not present a completely accurate picture. The only way leaders can see the urgency in the faces of their soldiers is to get out and see them. As with any new weapon, the Army leader must know how to use technology without being seduced by it. Technology may be invaluable; however, effective leaders understand its limits.

Whatever their feeling regarding technology, today's leaders must contend more and more with an increased information flow and operational tempo (OPTEMPO). Pressures to make a decision increase, even as the time to verify and validate information decreases. Regardless of the crunch, Army leaders are responsible for the consequences of their decisions, so they gather, process, analyze, evaluate—and check—information. If they don't, the costs can be disastrous. (FM 100-34 discusses information management and decision making.)

Technology and making the most of it will become increasingly important. Today's Army leaders require systems understanding and more technical and tactical skills. Technical skill: What does this system do? What does it not do? What are its strengths? What are its weaknesses? What must I check? Tactical skill: How do this system's capabilities support my organization? How should I employ it to support this mission? What must I do if it fails? There's a fine line between a healthy questioning of new systems' capabilities and an unreasoning hostility that rejects the advantages technology offers. You, as an Army leader, must stay on the right side of that line, the side that allows you to maximize the advantages of technology. You need to remain aware of its capabilities and shortcomings, and you need to make sure your people do as well.

2. Leadership and the Changing Threat

Another factor that will have a major impact on Army leadership in the near future is the changing nature of the threat. For the Army, the twenty-first century began in 1989 with the fall of the Berlin Wall and subsequent collapse of the Soviet Union. America no longer defines its security interests in terms of a single, major threat. Instead, it faces numerous, smaller threats and situations, any of which can quickly mushroom into a major security challenge.

The end of the Cold War has increased the frequency and variety of Army missions. Since 1989, the Army has fought a large-scale land war and been continually involved in many different kinds of stability operations and support operations. There has been a greater demand for special, joint, and multinational operations as well. Initiative at all levels is becoming more and more important. In many instances, Army leaders on the ground have had to invent ways of doing business for situations they could not have anticipated.

Not only that, the importance of direct leaders—NCOs and junior officers—making the right decisions in stressful situations has increased. Actions by direct-level leaders—sergeants, warrant officers, lieutenants, and captains—can have organizational- and strategic-level implications.

The Army has handled change in the past. It will continue to do so in the future as long as Army leaders emphasize the constants—Army values, teamwork, and discipline—and help their people anticipate change by seeking always to improve. Army leaders explain, to the extent of their knowledge and in clear terms, what may happen and how the organization can effectively react if it does. Change is inevitable; trying to avoid it is futile. The disciplined, cohesive organization rides out the tough times and will emerge even better than it started. Leadership, in a very real sense, includes managing change and making it work for you. To do that, you must know what to change and what not to change.

E. Climate and Culture

Climate and culture describe the environment in which you lead your people. Culture refers to the environment of the Army as an institution and of major elements or communities within it. Strategic leaders maintain the Army's institutional culture. Climate refers to the environment of units and organizations. All organizational and direct leaders establish their organization's climate, whether purposefully or unwittingly.

1. Climate

Taking care of people and maximizing their performance also depends on the climate a leader creates in the organization. An organization's climate is the way its members feel about their organization. Climate comes from people's shared perceptions and attitudes, what they believe about the day-to-day functioning of their outfit. These things have a great impact on their motivation and the trust they feel for their team and their leaders. Climate is generally short-term: it depends on a network of the personalities in a small organization. As people come and go, the climate changes. When a soldier says "My last platoon sergeant was pretty good, but this new one is great," the soldier is talking about one of the many elements that affect organizational climate.

Although such a call seems subjective, some very definite things determine climate. The members' collective sense of the organization—its organizational climate —is directly attributable to the leader's values, skills, and actions. As an Army leader, you establish the climate of your organization, no matter how small it is or how large. Answering the following questions can help you describe an organization's climate:

- Does the leader set clear priorities and goals?

- Is there a system of recognition, rewards and punishments? Does it work?

- Do the leaders know what they're doing? Do they admit when they're wrong?

- Do leaders seek input from subordinates? Do they act on the feedback they're provided?

- In the absence of orders, do junior leaders have authority to make decisions that are consistent with the leader's intent?

- Are there high levels of internal stress and negative competition in the organization? If so, what's the leader doing to change that situation?
- Do the leaders behave the way they talk? Is that behavior consistent with Army values? Are they good role models?
- Do the leaders lead from the front, sharing hardship when things get tough?
- Do leaders talk to their organizations on a regular basis? Do they keep their people informed?

Army leaders who do the right things for the right reasons—even when it would be easier to do the wrong thing—create a healthy organizational climate. In fact, it's the leader's behavior that has the greatest effect on the organizational climate. That behavior signals to every member of the organization what the leader will and will not tolerate.

No matter how they complain about it, soldiers and DA civilians expect to be held to standard; in the long run they feel better about themselves when they do hard work successfully. They gain confidence in leaders who help them achieve standards and lose confidence in leaders who don't know the standards or who fail to demand performance.

2. Culture

Culture is a longer lasting, more complex set of shared expectations than climate. While climate is how people feel about their organization right now, culture consists of the shared attitudes, values, goals, and practices that characterize the larger institution. It's deeply rooted in long-held beliefs, customs, and practices. For instance, the culture of the armed forces is different from that of the business world, and the culture of the Army is different from that of the Navy. Leaders must establish a climate consistent with the culture of the larger institution. They also use the culture to let their people know they're part of something bigger than just themselves, that they have responsibilities not only to the people around them but also to those who have gone before and those who will come after.

Soldiers draw strength from knowing they're part of a tradition. Most meaningful traditions have their roots in the institution's culture. Many of the Army's everyday customs and traditions are there to remind you that you're just the latest addition to a long line of American soldiers. Think of how much of your daily life connects you to the past and to American soldiers not yet born: the uniforms you wear, the martial music that punctuates your day, the way you salute, your title, your organization's history, and Army values such as selfless service. Reminders of your place in history surround you.

This sense of belonging is vitally important. Visit the Vietnam Memorial in Washington, DC, some Memorial Day weekend and you'll see dozens of veterans, many of them wearing bush hats or campaign ribbons or fatigue jackets decorated with unit patches. They're paying tribute to their comrades in this division or that company. They're also acknowledging what for many of them was the most intense experience of their lives.

Young soldiers want to belong to something bigger than themselves. Look at them off duty, wearing tee shirts with names of sports teams and famous athletes. It's not as if an 18-year-old who puts on a jacket with a professional sports team's logo thinks anyone will mistake him for a professional player; rather, that soldier wants to be associated with a winner. Advertising and mass media make heroes of rock stars, athletes, and actors. Unfortunately, it's easier to let some magazine or TV show tell you whom to admire than it is to dig up an organization's history and learn about heroes.

When soldiers join the Army, they become part of a history: the Big Red One, the King of Battle, Sua Sponte. Teach them the history behind unit crests, behind greetings, behind decorations and badges. The Army's culture isn't something that exists apart from you; it's part of who you are, something you can use to give your soldiers pride in themselves and in what they're doing with their lives.

F. Intended and Unintended Consequences

The actions you take as a leader will most likely have unintended as well as intended consequences. Like a chess player trying to anticipate an opponent's moves three or four turns in advance—if I do this, what will my opponent do; then what will I do next?—leaders think through what they can expect to happen as a result of a decision. Some decisions set off a chain of events; as far as possible, leaders must anticipate the second- and third-order effects of their actions. Even lower-level leaders' actions may have effects well beyond what they expect.

Consider the case of a sergeant whose team is manning a roadblock as part of a peace operation. The mission has received lots of media attention (Haiti and Bosnia come to mind), and millions of people back home are watching. Early one morning, a truckload of civilians appears, racing toward the roadblock. In the half-light, the sergeant can't tell if the things in the passengers' hands are weapons or farm tools, and the driver seems intent on smashing through the barricade. In the space of a few seconds, the sergeant must decide whether or not to order his team to fire on the truck.

If the sergeant orders his team to fire because he feels he and his soldiers are threatened, that decision will have international consequences. If he kills any civilians, chances are good that his chain of command from the president on down—not to mention the entire television audience of the developed world—will know about the incident in a few short hours. But the decision is tough for another reason: if the sergeant doesn't order his team to fire and the civilians turn out to be an armed gang, the team may take casualties that could have been avoided. If the only factor involved was avoiding civilian casualties, the choice is simple: don't shoot. But the sergeant must also consider the requirement to protect his force and accomplish the mission of preventing unauthorized traffic from passing the roadblock. So the sergeant must act; he's the leader, and he's in charge. Leaders who have thought through the consequences of possible actions, talked with their own leaders about the commander's intent and mission priorities, and trust their chain of command to support them are less likely to be paralyzed by this kind of pressure.

1. Intended Consequences

Intended consequences are the anticipated results of a leader's decisions and actions. When a squad leader shows a team leader a better way to lead PT, that action will have intended consequences: the team leader will be better equipped to do the job. When leaders streamline procedures, help people work smarter, and get the resources to the right place at the right time, the intended consequences are good.

2. Unintended Consequences

Unintended consequences are the results of things a leader does that have an unplanned impact on the organization or accomplishment of the mission. Unintended consequences are often more lasting and harder to anticipate than intended consequences. Organizational and strategic leaders spend a good deal of energy considering possible unintended consequences of their actions. Their organizations are complex, so figuring out the effects today's decisions will have a few years in the future is difficult.

Unintended consequences are best described with an example, such as setting the morning PT formation time: Setting the formation time at 0600 hours results in soldiers standing in formation at 0600 hours, an intended consequence. To not be late, soldiers living off post may have to depart their homes at 0500 hours, a consequence that's probably also anticipated. However, since most junior enlisted soldiers with families probably own only one car, there will most likely be another consequence: entire families rising at 0430 hours. Spouses must drive their soldiers to post and children, who can't be left at home unattended, must accompany them. This is an unintended consequence.

The Army Leader

Code of Conduct

Ref: ALDH, Appendix A.

Code of Conduct

1 I am an American, fighting in the forces which guard my country and our way of life. I am prepared to give my life in their defense.

2 I will never surrender of my own free will. If in command, I will never surrender the members of my command while they still have the means to resist.

3 If I am captured I will continue to resist by all means available. I will make every effort to escape and aid others to escape. I will accept neither parole nor special favors from the enemy.

4 If I become a prisoner of war, I will keep faith with my fellow prisoners. I will give no information or take part in any action which might be harmful to my comrades. If I am senior, I will take command. If not, I will obey the lawful orders of those appointed over me and will back them up in every way.

5 When questioned, should I become a prisoner of war, I am required to give name, rank, service number and date of birth. I will evade further questions to the utmost of my ability. I will make no oral or written statements disloyal to my country and its allies or harmful to their cause.

6 I will never forget that I am an American fighting for freedom, responsible for my action, and dedicated to the principles which made my country free. I will trust in my God and in the United States of America.

As a member of the Armed Forces of the United States you are protecting your nation. It is your duty to oppose all enemies of the US in combat or, if a captive, in a prisoner of war compound. Your behavior is guided by the Code of Conduct, which has evolved form the heroic lives, experiences and deeds of Americans from the Revolutionary War to the Southeast Asian Conflict.

Your obligations as a US citizen and a member of the Armed Forces result from the traditional values that underlie the American experience as a nation. These values are best expressed in the US Constitution and Bill of Rights, which you have sworn to uphold and defend. You would have these obligations—to your country, your Service and unit, and your fellow Americans—even if the Code of Conduct had never been formulated as a high standard of general behavior.

Just as you have a responsibility to your country under the Code of Conduct, the US Government has a dual responsibility—always to keep faith with you and stand by you as you fight for your country. If you are unfortunate enough to become a prisoner of war, you may rest assured that your Government will care for your dependents and will never forget you. Furthermore, the Government will use every practical means to contact, support and gain release for you and for all other prisoners of war.

To live up to the Code, you must know not only its words but the ideas and principles behind those words. The Code of Conduct is an ethical guide. Its six articles deal with your chief concerns as an American in combat; these concerns become critical when you must evade capture, resist while a prisoner, or escape from the enemy.

Experiences of captured Americans reveal that to survive captivity honorably would demand from you great courage, deep dedication and high motivation. To sustain these personal values throughout captivity requires that you understand and believe strongly in our free and democratic institutions, love your country, trust in the justice of our cause, keep faithful and loyal to your fellow prisoners, and hold firmly to your religious and moral beliefs in time of trial.

Your courage, dedication, and motivation supported by understanding, trust, and fidelity will help you endure the terrors of captivity, prevail over your captors and return to your family, home, and nation with honor and pride.

NOTE: The Code of Conduct for members of the Armed Forces of the US was first promulgated by President Eisenhower August 17, 1955. The Code, including its basic philosophy, was reaffirmed on July 8, 1964, in DOD Directive No. 1300.7. On November 3, 1977, President Carter amended Article V of the Code. On March 28, 1988, President Reagan amended Articles I, II and VI of the Code. The Code, although first expressed in its written form in 1955, is based on time-honored concepts and traditions that date back to the days of the American Revolution.

1. Article 1

I am an American, fighting in the forces which guard my country and our way of life. I am prepared to give my life in their defense.

All men and women in the Armed Forces have the duty at all times and under all circumstances to oppose the enemies of the US and support its national interests. In training or in combat, alone or with others, while evading capture or enduring captivity, this duty belongs to each American defending our nation regardless of circumstances.

2. Article 2

I will never surrender of my own free will. If in command, I will never surrender the members of my command while they still have the means to resist.

As an individual, a member of the Armed Forces may never voluntarily surrender. When isolated and no longer able to inflict casualties on the enemy, the American soldier has an obligation to evade capture and rejoin friendly forces.

Only when evasion by an individual is impossible and further fighting would lead only to death with no significant loss of the enemy should only consider surrender. With all reasonable means of resistance exhausted and with certain death the only alternative, capture does not imply dishonor.

The responsibility and authority of a commander never extends to the surrender of a command to the enemy while the command has the power to fight and evade. When isolated, cut off, or surrounded, a unit must continue to fight until relieved or able to rejoin friendly forces through continued efforts to break out or evade the enemy.

3. Article 3

If I am captured I will continue to resist by all means available. I will make every effort to escape and aid others to escape. I will accept neither parole nor special favors from the enemy.

The duty of a member of the Armed Forces to use all means available to resist the enemy is not lessened by the misfortune of captivity. A POW is still legally bound by the Uniform Code of Military Justice and ethically guided by the Code of Conduct. Under provisions of the Geneva convention, a prisoner of war is also subject to certain rules, such as sanitation regulations. The duty of a member of the Armed Forces to continue to resist does not mean a prisoner should engage in unreasonable harassment as a form of resistance. Retaliation by captors to the detriment of that prisoner and other prisoners is frequently the primary result of such harassment.

The Geneva Convention recognized that a POW may have the duty to attempt escape. In fact, the Geneva Convention prohibits a captor nation from executing a POW simply for attempt escape. Under the authority of the senior official (often called the senior ranking officer, or "SRO") a POW must be prepared to escape whenever the opportunity presents itself. In a POW compound, the senior POW must consider the welfare of those remaining behind after an escape.

However, as a matter of conscious determination, a POW must plan to escape, try to escape, and assist others to escape. Contrary to the spirit of the Geneva Convention, enemies engaged by US forces since 1950 have regarded the POW compound an extension of the battlefield. In doing so, they have used a variety of tactics and pressures, including physical and mental mistreatment, torture and medical neglect to exploit POWs for propaganda purposes, to obtain military information, or to undermine POW organization, communication and resistance.

Such enemies have attempted to lure American POWs into accepting special favors or privileges in exchange for statement, acts, or information. Unless it is essential to the life or welfare of the person or another prisoner of war or to the success of efforts to resist or escape, a POW must neither seek nor accept special favors or privileges.

One such privilege is called parole. Parole is a promise by a prisoner of war to a captor to fulfill certain conditions—such as agreeing not to escape nor to fight again once released—in return for such favors as relief from physical bondage, improved food and living condition, or repatriation ahead of the sick, injured, or longer-held prisoners. Unless specifically directed by the senior American prisoner of war at the same place of captivity, an American POW will never sign nor otherwise accept parole.

4. Article 4

If I become a prisoner of war, I will keep faith with my fellow prisoners. I will give no information or take part in any action which might be harmful to my comrades. If I am senior, I will take command. If not, I will obey the lawful orders of those appointed over me and will back them up in every way.

Informing, or any other action to the detriment of a fellow prisoner, is despicable and is expressly forbidden. Prisoners of war must avoid helping the enemy identify fellow prisoners who may have knowledge of particular value to the enemy and who may, therefore, be made to suffer coercive interrogation.

Strong leadership and communication are essential to discipline. Discipline is the key to camp organization, resistance, and even survival. Personal hygiene, camp sanitation, and care of sick and wounded are imperative. Officers and noncommissioned officers of the United States must continue to carry out their responsibilities and exercise their authority in captivity. The senior, regardless of Service, must accept command. This responsibility, and accountability, may not be evaded.

If the senior is incapacitated or is otherwise unable to act, the next senior person will assume command. Camp leaders should make every effort to inform all PWs of the chain of command and try to represent them in dealing with enemy authorities. The responsibility of subordinates to obey the lawful orders of ranking American military personnel remains unchanged in captivity.

The Geneva convention Relative to Treatment of Prisoners of War provides for election of a "prisoner' representative" in POW camps containing enlisted personnel, but no commissioned officers. American POWs should understand that such a representative is only a spokesman for the actual senior ranking person. Should the enemy appoint a POW chain of command for its of purposes, American POWs should make all efforts to adhere to the principles of Article IV.

As with other provisions of this code, common sense and the conditions of captivity will affect the way in which the senior person and the other POWs organize to carry out their responsibilities. What is important is that everyone support and work within the POW organization.

5. Article 5

When questioned, should I become a prisoner of war, I am required to give name, rank, service number, and date of birth. I will evade answering further questions to the utmost of my ability. I will make no oral or written statements disloyal to my country and its allies or harmful to their cause.

When questioned, a prisoner of war is required by the Geneva Conventions and this Code to give name, rank, service number (SSN) and date of birth. The prison should make every effort to avoid giving the captor and additional information. The prisoner may communicate with captors on matters of health and welfare and additionally may write letters home and fill out a Geneva Convention "capture card."

It is a violation of the Geneva Convention to place a prisoner under physical or mental duress, torture, or any other form of coercion in an effort to secure information. If under such intense coercion, a POW discloses unauthorized information, made an unauthorized statement, or performs an unauthorized act, that prisoner's peace of mind and survival require a quick recovery of courage, dedication, and motivation to resist anew each subsequent coercion.

Actions every POW should resist include making oral or written confessions and apologies, answering questionnaires, providing personal histories, creating propaganda recordings, broadcasting appeals to other prisoners of war, providing any other material readily usable for propaganda purposes., appealing for surrender or parole, furnishing self-criticisms, communicating on behalf of the enemy to the detriment of the United State, its allies, its Armed Forces, or other POWs.

Every POW should also recognize that any confession signed or any statement made may be used by the enemy as a false evidence that the person is a "war criminal" rather than a POW. Several countries have made reservations to the Geneva Convention in which they assert that a "war criminal" conviction deprives the convicted individual of prison of war status, removes that person from protection under the Geneva Convention, and revokes all rights to repatriation until a prison sentence is served.

Recent experiences of American prisoners of war have proved that, although enemy interrogation sessions may be harsh and cruel, one can resist brutal mistreatment when the will to resist remains intact. The best way for prisoner to keep faith with country, fellow prisoners and self is to provide the enemy with as little information as possible.

6. Article 6

I will never forget that I am an American fighting for freedom, responsible for my action, and dedicated to the principles which made my country free. I will trust in my God and in the United States of America.

A member of the Armed Forces remains responsible for personal actions at all times. A member of the Armed Forces who is captured has a continuing obligation to resist and to remain loyal to country, Service, unit and fellow prisoners. Upon repatriation, POWs can expect their actions to be reviewed, both as to circumstances of capture and conduct during detention. The purpose of such review is to recognized meritorious performance as well as to investigate possible misconduct. Each review will be conducted with due regard for the rights of the individual and consideration for the conditions of captivity, for captivity of itself is not a condition of culpability.

Members of the Armed Forces should remember that they and their dependents will be taken care of by the appropriate Service and that pay and allowances, eligibility and procedures for promotion, and benefits for dependents continue while the Service member is detained. Service members should assure that their personal affairs and family matters (such as pay, powers of attorney, current will, and provisions for family maintenance and education) are properly and currently arranged. Failure to so arrange matters can crate a serious sense of guilt for POW and place unnecessary hardship on family members.

The life of a prisoner of war is hard. Each person in this stressful situation must always sustain hope, must resist enemy indoctrination. Prisoners of war standing firm and united against the enemy will support and inspire one another in surviving their ordeal and in prevailing over misfortune with honor.

The Army Leader

Branch Periodicals

Ref: ALDH, app. D, p. 80.

Air Defense Artillery, (quarterly), U.S., Army Air Defense ATSA-TDL-S, Ft. Bliss, TX, 79916.

Armor, (bimonthly), U.S. Army Armor School, Ft. Know, KY, 40121.

Army, (monthly), AUSA, 2425 Wilson Blvd, Arlington, VA, 22201-3385.

Army Aviation, (monthly), 1 Crestwood Road, Westport, CT, 06880.

Army Chemical Review, (monthly), Ft. McClellan, AL 85613-7000.

Army Logistician, (bimonthly), U.S. Army Logistics Management College, Ft. Lee, VA, 23801-6044.

Army Finance, (bimonthly), P.O. Box 793, Alexandria, VA 22218.

Army Personnel Bulletin, (monthly), Marketing and Advertising Office, HQDA, Washington, D.C. 20310-0300.

Army Research, Development and Acquisition, (bimonthly), 5001 Eisenhower Ave., Alexandria, VA, 22333-0001.

Army Times, (weekly), 2201 Main Street, N.W., Washington, D.C., 20037.

Army Trainer, (quarterly), P.O. Drawer A, Ft. Eustis, VA, 23604-0309.

Aviation Digest, (monthly), P.O. Box 699, Ft. Rucker, Al, 36362-5044.

Center for Army Lessons Learned Bulletin, (semiannually), USACATA, Ft. Leavenworth, KS, 66027-7000.

Defense, (bimonthly), American Forces Information Services, 601 N. Fairfax St., Alexandria, VA, 22314-2007.

Defense and Foreign Affairs, (monthly), Copely and Associates, 1777 T. St., N.W., Washington, D.C. 20009.

Engineer, (quarterly), U.S. Army Engineer School, Ft. Belvoir, VA, 22060.

Field Artillery, (bimonthly), Field Artillery Association, P.O. Box 33027, Ft. Sill, OK, 73505.

Infantry, (bimonthly), P.O. Box 2005, Ft. Benning, GA, 31905-0605.

Journal of the Armed Forces, (weekly), 1710 Connecticut Avenue N.W., Washington, D.C., 20009.

Military Affairs, (quarterly), American Military Institute, P.O. Box 568, Washington, D.C., 20044.

Military Engineer, (bimonthly), 607 Prince Street, P.O. Box 180, Alexandria, VA, 22313.

Military Intelligence (quarterly), U.S. Army Intelligence Center, Ft. Huachuca, AZ, 85613-7000.

Military Police, (quarterly), U.S. Army Military Police School, Ft. McClellan, AL, 36205-5030.

Military Review, (monthly), Command and General Staff College, Ft. Leavenworth, KS, 66027-6910.

National Defense, (monthly), Rosslyn Center Suite 900, 1700 N. Moore St., Arlington, VA, 22209.

National Defense Transportation Journal, (bimonthly), 1612 K. Street, N.W., Washington, D.C., 20006.

Officers' Call, (bimonthly), Office Chief of Public Affairs, HQDA, Washington, D.C., 20310-1510.

Ordnance Bulletin, (quarterly), USAOC&S, Aberdeen Proving Ground, MD, 21005-5201.

Parameters, (quarterly), Editor, Parameters, Carlisle Barracks, PA, 17013.

Post Exchange and Commissary, (monthly), 336 Gunderson, Dr., Wheaton, IL, 60187.

Quartermaster Professional Bulletin, (quarterly), Office of the Quartermaster General, Ft. Lee, VA, 23801.

Sergeants' Business, (bimonthly), Office, Chief of Public Affairs, HQDA, Washington, D.C. 20310-1510.

Signal, (monthly), Armed Forces Communications and Electronics Association, 5641 Burke Center Parkway, Burke, VA, 22015.

Soldiers, (monthly), Cameron Station, Alexandria, VA, 22304-5050.

Special Warfare, (quarterly), USAJFKSWCS, Ft. Bragg, NC, 28307-5000.

Strategic Review, (quarterly), U.S. Strategic Institute, 20 Memorial Drive, Cambridge, MA, 02142.

The Army Communicator, (quarterly), U.S. Army Signal School, Ft. Gordon, GA, 30905.

Translog, (monthly), Superintendent of Documents, U.S. Government Printing Office, Washington, D.C. 20402.

Transportation Corps, (quarterly), U.S. Army Transportation School, Ft. Eustis, VA, 23604-5407.

Army Training Support Center Bulletins, U.S. Army Training Support Center, Ft. Eustis, VA, 23604.

International Defense Review, Interavia S. A., 86 Ave Louis Casia, P.O. Box 162, 1216 Cointrin, Geneva, Switzerland.

Leavenworth Papers, Combat Studies Institute, U.S. Army Command and General Staff College, Ft. Leavenworth, KS, 66027.

The Army Officer's Guide. Harris Burg: Stackpole Books.

TRADOC Bulletins, U.S. Army Training and Doctrine Command, ATTN: ATCG-T, Ft Monroe, VA, 23651.

Levels of Leadership

Ref: FM 22-100, chap 4 through chap. 7.

Levels of Leadership

Level		Types of Military Authority
I	Direct Leadership	1. Command Authority
		2. General Military Authority
II	Organizational Leadership	
		Responsibility and Accountability
III	Strategic Leadership	1. Command Responsibility
		2. Indiv. Responsibility

Ref: FM 22-100, chap. 4 through chap. 7.

There are three levels of Army leadership: direct, organizational, and strategic. Factors that determine a position's leadership level can include the position's span of control, its headquarters level, and the extent of the influence the leader holding the position exerts. Other factors include the size of the unit or organization, the type of operations it conducts, the number of people assigned, and its planning horizon.

Sometimes the rank or grade of the leader holding a position does not indicate the position's leadership level. A sergeant first class serving as a platoon sergeant works at the direct leadership level. If the same NCO holds a headquarters job dealing with issues and policy affecting a brigade-sized or larger organization, the NCO works at the organizational leadership level. However, if the NCO's primary duty is running a staff section that supports the leaders who run the organization, the NCO is a direct leader. In fact, most leadership positions are direct leadership positions, and every leader at every level acts as a direct leader when dealing with immediate subordinates.

The headquarters echelon alone doesn't determine a position's leadership level. Soldiers and DA civilians of all ranks and grades serve in strategic-level headquarters, but they are not all strategic-level leaders. The responsibilities of a duty position, together with other factors determine its leadership level. For example, a DA civilian at a training area range control with a dozen subordinates works at the direct leadership level while a DA civilian deputy garrison commander with a span of influence over several thousand people works at the organizational leadership level. Most NCOs, company grade officers, field grade officers, and DA civilian leaders serve at the direct leadership level. Some senior NCOs, field grade officers, and higher-grade DA civilians serve at the organizational leadership level. Most general officers and equivalent Senior Executive Service DA civilians serve at the organizational or strategic leadership levels.

I. Direct Leadership

Direct leadership is face-to-face, first-line leadership. It takes place in those organizations where subordinates are used to seeing their leaders all the time: teams and squads, sections and platoons, companies, batteries, and troops—even squadrons and battalions. The direct leader's span of influence, those whose lives he can reach out and touch, may range from a handful to several hundred people.

Direct leaders develop their subordinates one-on-one; however, they also influence their organization through their subordinates. For instance, a cavalry squadron commander is close enough to his soldiers to have a direct influence on them. They're used to seeing him regularly, even if it is only once a week in garrison; they expect to see him from time to time in the field. Still, during daily operations, the commander guides the organization primarily through his subordinate officers and NCOs.

II. Organizational Leadership

Organizational leaders influence several hundred to several thousand people. They do this indirectly, generally through more levels of subordinates than do direct leaders. The additional levels of subordinates can make it more difficult for them to see results. Organizational leaders have staffs to help them lead their people and manage their organizations' resources. They establish policies and the organizational climate that support their subordinate leaders.

Organizational leadership skills differ from direct leadership skills in degree, but not in kind. That is, the skill domains are the same, but organizational leaders must deal with more complexity, more people, greater uncertainty, and a greater number of unintended consequences. They find themselves influencing people more through policy making and systems integration than through face-to-face contact.

Organizational leaders include military leaders at the brigade through corps levels, military and DA civilian leaders at directorate through installation levels, and DA civilians at the assistant through undersecretary of the Army levels. They focus on planning and mission accomplishment over the next two to ten years.

III. Strategic Leadership

Strategic leaders include military and DA civilian leaders at the major command through Department of Defense levels. Strategic leaders are responsible for large organizations and influence several thousand to hundreds of thousands of people. They establish force structure, allocate resources, communicate strategic vision, and prepare their commands and the Army as a whole for their future roles.

Strategic leaders work in an uncertain environment on highly complex problems that affect and are affected by events and organizations outside the Army. Actions of a theater commander in chief (CINC), for example, may even have an impact on global politics. Strategic leaders focus on planning and mission accomplishment over the next two to ten years.

Strategic leaders concern themselves with the total environment in which the Army functions; their decisions take into account such things as congressional hearings, Army budgetary constraints, new systems acquisition, civilian programs, research, development, and interservice cooperation—just to name a few.

Strategic leaders often do not see their ideas come to fruition during their "watch"; their initiatives may take years to plan, prepare, and execute. This has important implications for long-range planning.

Authority

Authority is the legitimate power of leaders to direct subordinates or to take action within the scope of their positions. Military authority begins with the Constitution, which divides it between Congress and the president. Congress has the authority to make laws that govern the Army. The president, as commander in chief, commands the armed forces, including the Army.

1. Command Authority

Command is the authority that a commander in the armed forces lawfully exercises over subordinates by virtue of rank or assignment. Command includes the authority and responsibility for effectively using available resources to organize, direct, coordinate, employ, and control military forces so that they accomplish assigned missions. It also includes responsibility for health, welfare, morale, and discipline of assigned personnel.

Command authority originates with the president and may be supplemented by law or regulation. It is the authority that a commander lawfully exercises over subordinates by virtue of rank or assignment. Only commissioned & warrant officers may command Army units & installations. DA civilians may exercise general supervision over an Army installation or activity; however, they act under the authority of a military supervisor. DA civilians do not command. (AR 600-20 addresses command authority in more detail.)

Army leaders are granted command authority when they fill command-designated positions. These normally involve the direction and control of soldiers and DA civilians. Ldrs in cmd-designated positions have the inherent authority to issue orders, carry out the unit mission, and care for military members and DA civilians within the ldr's scope of responsibility.

2. General Military Authority

General military authority originates in oaths of office, law, rank structure, traditions, and regulations. This broad-based authority also allows leaders to take appropriate corrective actions whenever a member of any armed service, anywhere, commits an act involving a breach of good order or discipline. AR 600-20, paragraph 4-5, states this specifically, giving commissioned, warrant, and noncommissioned officers authority to "quell all quarrels, frays, and disorders among persons subject to military law"—in other words, to maintain good order and discipline.

All enlisted leaders have general military authority. For example, dining facility managers, platoon sergeants, squad leaders, and tank commanders all use general military authority when they issue orders to direct and control their subordinates. Army leaders may exercise general military authority over soldiers from different units.

For NCOs, another source of general military authority stems from the combination of the chain of command and the NCO support channel. The chain of command passes orders and policies through the NCO support channel to provide authority for NCOs.

Delegation of Authority

Just as Congress and the president cannot participate in every aspect of armed forces operations, most leaders cannot handle every action directly. To meet the organization's goals, officers delegate authority to NCOs and, when appropriate, to DA civilians. These leaders, in turn, may further delegate that authority.

Unless restricted by law, regulation, or a superior, ldrs may delegate any or all of their authority to their subordinate ldrs. However, such delegation must fall within the leader's scope of authority. Ldrs cannot delegate authority they do not have and subordinate ldrs may not assume authority that their superiors do not have, cannot delegate, or have retained. The task or duty to be performed limits the authority of the ldr to which it is assigned.

Roles & Relationships

Ref: FM 22-100, Fig. A-1, p. A-2.

When the Army speaks of soldiers, it refers to commissioned officers, warrant officers, noncommissioned officers (NCOs), and enlisted personnel— both men and women. The roles and responsibilities of Army leaders—commissioned, warrant, noncommissioned, and DA civilian—overlap.

Commissioned Officers

Commissioned officers are direct representatives of the President of the United States. Commissions are legal instruments the president uses to appoint and exercise direct control over qualified people to act as his legal agents and help him carry out his duties. The Army retains this direct-agent relationship with the president through its commissioned officers. The commission serves as the basis for a commissioned officer's legal authority. Commissioned officers command, establish policy, and manage Army resources.

    1. Commands, establishes policy, and manages Army resources.

    2. Integrates collective, leader, and soldier training to accomplish missions.

    3. Deals primarily with units and unit operations.

    4. Concentrates on unit effectiveness and readiness.

Warrant Officers

Warrant officers are highly specialized, single-track specialty officers who receive their authority from the Secretary of the Army upon their initial appointment. However, Title 10 USC authorizes the commissioning of warrant officers (WO1) upon promotion to chief warrant officer (CW2). These commissioned warrant officers are direct representatives of the president of the United States. They derive their authority from the same source as commissioned officers but remain specialists, in contrast to commissioned officers, who are generalists. Warrant officers can and do command detachments, units, activities, and vessels as well as lead, coach, train, and counsel subordinates. As leaders and technical experts, they provide valuable skills, guidance, and expertise to commanders and organizations in their particular field.

    1. Provides quality advice, counsel, and solutions to support the command.

    2. Executes policy and manages the Army's systems.

    3. Commands special-purpose units and task-organized operational elements.

    4. Focuses on collective, leader, and individual training.

    5. Operates, maintains, administers, and manages the Army's equipment, support activities, and technical systems.

    6. Concentrates on unit effectiveness and readiness.

Noncommissioned Officers (NCOs)

NCOs, the backbone of the Army, train, lead, and take care of enlisted soldiers. They receive their authority from their oaths of office, law, rank structure, traditions, and regulations. This authority allows them to direct soldiers, take actions required to accomplish the mission, and enforce good order and discipline. NCOs represent officer, and sometimes DA civilian, leaders. They ensure their subordinates, along with their personal equipment, are prepared to function as effective unit and team members. While commissioned officers command, establish policy, and manage resources, NCOs conduct the Army's daily business.

1. Trains soldiers and conducts the daily business of the Army within established policy.
2. Focuses on individual soldier training.
3. Deals primarily with individual soldier training and team leading.
4. Ensures that subordinate teams, NCOs, and soldiers are prepared to function as effective unit and team members.

The NCO support channel parallels and reinforces the chain of command. NCO leaders work with and support the commissioned and warrant officers of their chain of command. For the chain of command to work efficiently, the NCO support channel must operate effectively. At battalion level and higher, the NCO support channel begins with the command sergeant major, extends through first sergeants and platoon sergeants, and ends with section chiefs, squad leaders, or team leaders. (TC 22-6 discusses the NCO support channel.)

The connection between the chain of command and NCO support channel is the senior NCO. Commanders issue orders through the chain of command, but senior NCOs must know and understand the orders to issue effective implementing instructions through the NCO support channel. Although the first sergeant and command sergeant major are not part of the formal chain of command, leaders should consult them on all individual soldier matters.

Successful leaders have a good relationship with their senior NCOs. Successful commanders have a good leader-NCO relationship with their first sergeants and command sergeants major. The need for such a relationship applies to platoon leaders and platoon sergeants as well as to staff officers and NCOs. Senior NCOs have extensive experience in successfully completing missions and dealing with enlisted soldier issues. Also, senior NCOs can monitor organizational activities at all levels, take corrective action to keep the organization within the boundaries of the commander's intent, or report situations that require the attention of the officer leadership. A positive relationship between officers and NCOs creates conditions for success.

Department of Army Civilians

As members of the executive branch of the federal government, DA civilians are part of the Army. They derive their authority from a variety of sources, such as commanders, supervisors, Army regulations, and Title 5 USC. DA civilians' authority is job-related: they normally exercise authority related to their positions. DA civilians fill positions in staff and base sustaining operations that would otherwise have to be filled by officers and NCOs. Senior DA civilians establish policy and manage Army resources, but they do not have the authority to command.

The complementary relationship and mutual respect between the military and civilian members of the Army is a long-standing tradition. Since the Army's beginning in 1775, military and DA civilian duties have stayed separate, yet necessarily related. Taken in combination, traditions, functions, and laws serve to delineate the particular duties of military and civilian members of the Army.

1. Establishes and executes policy, leads people, and manages programs, projects, and Army systems.
2. Focuses on integrating collective, leader, and individual training.
3. Operates, maintains, administers, and manages Army equipment and support, research, and technical activities.
4. Concentrates on DA civilian individual and organizational effectiveness and readiness.

Responsibility and Accountability

No definitive lines separate officer, NCO, and DA civilian responsibilities. Officers, NCOs, and DA civilians lead other officers, NCOs, and DA civilians and help them carry out their responsibilities. Commanders set overall policies and standards, but all leaders must provide the guidance, resources, assistance, and supervision necessary for subordinates to perform their duties. Similarly, subordinates must assist and advise their leaders. Mission accomplishment demands that officers, NCOs, and DA civilians work together to advise, assist, and learn from each other. Responsibilities fall into two categories: command and individual.

1. Command Responsibility

Command responsibility refers to collective or organizational accountability and includes how well units perform their missions. For example, a company commander is responsible for all the tasks and missions assigned to his company; his leaders hold him accountable for completing them. Military and DA civilian leaders have responsibility for what their sections, units, or organizations do or fail to do.

2. Individual Responsibility

All soldiers and DA civilians must account for their personal conduct. Commissioned officers, warrant officers, and DA civilians assume personal responsibility when they take their oath. DA civilians take the same oath as commissioned officers. Soldiers take their initial oath of enlistment. Members of the Army account for their actions to their fellow soldiers or coworkers, the appointed leader, their unit or organization, the Army, and the American people.

Communications and the Chain of Command

Communication among individuals, teams, units, and organizations is essential to efficient and effective mission accomplishment. Mission accomplishment depends on information passing accurately to and from subordinates and leaders, up and down the chain of command and NCO support channel, and laterally among adjacent organizations or activities. In garrison operations, organizations working on the same mission or project should be considered "adjacent."

The Army has only one chain of command. Through this chain of command, leaders issue orders and instructions and convey policies. A healthy chain of command is a two-way communications channel. Its members do more than transmit orders; they carry information from within the unit or organization back up to its leader. They furnish information about how things are developing, notify the leader of problems, and provide requests for clarification and help. Leaders at all levels use the chain of command—their subordinate leaders—to keep their people informed and render assistance. They continually facilitate the process of gaining the necessary clarification and solving problems.

Beyond conducting their normal duties, NCOs train soldiers and advise commanders on individual soldier readiness and the training needed to ensure unit readiness. Officers and DA civilian leaders should consult their command sergeant major, first sergeant, or NCO assistant, before implementing policy. Commanders, commissioned and warrant officers, DA civilian leaders, and NCOs must continually communicate to avoid duplicating instructions or issuing conflicting orders.

Levels of Leadership

Levels of Leadership

I. Direct Leadership

Ref: FM 22-100, chap 4 and 5.

Direct Leadership

Skills

1 **Interpersonal Skills**
A. Communicating
B. Supervising
C. Counseling

2 **Conceptual Skills**
A. Creative Reasoning
B. Creative Thinking
C. Ethical Reasoning
D. Reflective Thinking

3 **Technical Skills**
A. Knowing Equipment
B. Operating Equipment

4 **Tactical Skills**
A. Doctrine
B. Fieldcraft

Actions

1 **Influencing Actions**
A. Communicating
B. Decision Making
C. Motivating

2 **Operating Actions**
A. Planning & Preparing
B. Executing
C. Assessing

3 **Improving Actions**
A. Developing
B. Building
C. Learning

Ref: FM 22-100, chap. 4 and 5.

This section examines what a direct leader must KNOW and DO. Note the distinction between a skill, knowing something, and an action, doing something. The reason for this distinction bears repeating: knowledge isn't enough. You can't be a leader until you apply what you know, until you act and DO what you must.

Army leaders are grounded in the heritage, values, and tradition of the Army. They embody the warrior ethos, value continuous learning, and demonstrate the ability to lead and train their subordinates. Army leaders lead by example, train from experience, and maintain and enforce standards. They do these things while taking care of their people and adapting to a changing world.

The warrior ethos is the will to win with honor. Despite a thinking enemy, despite adverse conditions, you accomplish your mission. You express your character— the BE of BE, KNOW, DO—when you and your people confront a difficult mission and persevere. The warrior ethos applies to all soldiers and DA civilians, not just those who close with and destroy the enemy. It's the will to meet mission demands no matter what, the drive to get the job done whatever the cost.

Direct Leadership Skills

The Army's direct leaders perform a huge array of functions in all kinds of places and under all kinds of conditions.

1. Interpersonal Skills

Since leadership is about people, it's not surprising to find interpersonal skills, what some call "people skills," at the top of the list of what an Army leader must KNOW.

Interpersonal Skills
A. Communicating **B. Supervising** **C. Counseling**

Ref: FM 22-100, p. 4-3, fig. 4-1.

A. Communicating

Since leadership is about getting other people to do what you want them to do, it follows that communicating—transmitting information so that it's clearly understood—is an important skill. After all, if people can't understand you, how will you ever let them know what you want? The other interpersonal skills—supervising, team building, and counseling—also depend on your ability to communicate.

One-Way and Two-Way Communication

There are two common forms of one-way communication that are not necessarily the best way to exchange information: seeing and hearing. The key difference between one-way and two-way communication is that one-way communication—hearing or seeing something on television, reading a copy of a slide presentation, or even watching a training event unfold— may not give you a complete picture. You may have unanswered questions or even walk away with the wrong concept of what has occurred. That's why two-way communication is preferred when time and resources permit.

Active Listening

An important form of two-way communication is active listening. When you practice active listening, you send signals to the speaker that say, "I'm paying attention." Nod your head every once in a while, as if to say, "Yes, I understands." When you agree with the speaker, you might use an occasional "uh-huh." Look the speaker in the eye. Give the speaker your full attention. Don't allow yourself to be distracted by looking out the window, checking your watch, playing with something on your desk, or trying to do more than one thing at a time. Avoid interrupting the speaker; that's the cardinal sin of active listening.

Be aware of barriers to listening. Don't form your response while the other person is still talking. Don't allow yourself to become distracted by the fact that you're angry, or that you have a problem with the speaker, or that you have lots of other things you need to be thinking about. If you give in to these temptations, you'll miss most of what's being said.

Nonverbal Communication

In face-to-face communication, even in the simplest conversation, there's a great deal going on that has almost nothing to do with the words being used. Nonverbal communication involves all the signals you send with your facial expressions, tone of voice, and body language. Effective leaders know that communication includes both verbal and nonverbal cues.

B. Supervising

Direct leaders check and recheck things. Leaders strike a balance between checking too much and not checking enough. Training subordinates to act independently is important; that's why direct leaders give instructions or their intent and then allow subordinates to work without constantly looking over their shoulders. Accomplishing the mission is equally important; that's why leaders check things— especially conditions critical to the mission (fuel levels), details a soldier might forget (spare batteries for night vision goggles), or tasks at the limit of what a soldier has accomplished before (preparing a new version of a report).

Checking minimizes the chance of oversights, mistakes, or other circumstances that might derail a mission. Checking also gives leaders a chance to see and recognize subordinates who are doing things right or make on-the-spot corrections when necessary. Consider this example: A platoon sergeant delegates to the platoon's squad leaders the authority to get their squads ready for a tactical road march. The platoon sergeant oversees the activity but doesn't intervene unless errors, sloppy work, or lapses occur. The leader is there to answer questions or resolve problems that the squad leaders can't handle. This supervision ensures that the squads are prepared to standard and demonstrates to the squad leaders that the platoon sergeant cares about them and their people.

C. Counseling

Counseling is subordinate-centered communication that produces a plan outlining actions necessary for subordinates to achieve individual or organizational goals. Effective counseling takes time, patience, and practice. As with everything else you do, you must develop your skills as a counselor. Seek feedback on how effective you are at counseling, study various counseling techniques, and make efforts to improve.

Proper counseling leads to a specific plan of action that the subordinate can use as a road map for improvement. Both parties, counselor and counseled, prepare this plan of action. The leader makes certain the subordinate understands and takes ownership of it. The best plan of action in the world does no good if the subordinate doesn't understand it, follow it, and believe in it. And once the plan of action is agreed upon, the leader must follow up with one-on-one sessions to ensure the subordinate stays on track.

Remember the Army values of loyalty, duty, and selfless service require you to counsel your subordinates. The values of honor, integrity, and personal courage require you to give them straightforward feedback. And the Army value of respect requires you to find the best way to communicate that feedback so that your subordinates understand it. These Army values all point to the requirement for you to become a proficient counselor. Effective counseling helps your subordinates develop personally and professionally.

One of the most important duties of all direct, organizational, and strategic leaders is to develop subordinates. Mentoring, which links the operating and improving leader actions, plays a major part in developing competent and confident future leaders. Counseling is an interpersonal skill essential to effective mentoring.

2. Conceptual Skills

Conceptual skills include competence in handling ideas, thoughts, and concepts.

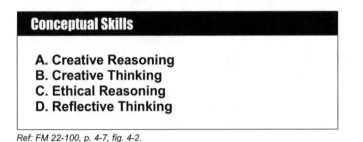

Conceptual Skills

A. Creative Reasoning
B. Creative Thinking
C. Ethical Reasoning
D. Reflective Thinking

Ref: FM 22-100, p. 4-7, fig. 4-2.

A. Critical Reasoning

Critical reasoning helps you think through problems. It's the key to understanding situations, finding causes, arriving at justifiable conclusions, making good judgments, and learning from the experience—in short, solving problems. Critical reasoning is an essential part of effective counseling and underlies ethical reasoning, another conceptual skill.

The word "critical" here doesn't mean finding fault; it doesn't have a negative meaning at all. It means getting past the surface of the problem and thinking about it in depth. It means looking at a problem from several points of view instead of just being satisfied with the first answer that comes to mind. Army leaders need this ability because many of the choices they face are complex and offer no easy solution.

Sometime during your schooling you probably ran across a multiple choice test, one that required you to "choose answer a, b, c, or d" or "choose one response from column a and two from column b." Your job as an Army leader would be a lot easier if the problems you faced were presented that way, but leadership is a lot more complex than that. Sometimes just figuring out the real problem presents a huge hurdle; at other times you have to sort through distracting multiple problems to get to the real difficulty. On some occasions you know what the problem is but have no clue as to what an answer might be. On others you can come up with two or three answers that all look pretty good.

B. Creative Thinking

Sometimes you run into a problem that you haven't seen before or an old problem that requires a new solution. Here you must apply imagination; a radical departure from the old way of doing things may be refreshing. Army leaders prevent complacency by finding ways to challenge subordinates with new approaches and ideas. In these cases, rely on your intuition, experience, and knowledge. Ask for input from your subordinates. Reinforce team building by making everybody responsible for, and shareholders in, the accomplishment of difficult tasks.

Creative thinking isn't some mysterious gift, nor does it have to be outlandish. It's not reserved for senior officers; all leaders think creatively. You employ it every day to solve small problems. A unit that deploys from a stateside post on a peace operation, for instance, may find itself in a small compound with limited athletic facilities and no room to run. Its leaders must devise new ways for their soldiers to maintain physical fitness. These may include sports and games, even games the local nationals play.

C. Ethical Reasoning

Ethical leaders do the right things for the right reasons all the time, even when no one is watching. But figuring out what's the "right" thing is often, to put it mildly, a most difficult task. To fulfill your duty, maintain your integrity, and serve honorably, you must be able to reason ethically.

Occasionally, when there's little or no time, you'll have to make a snap decision based on your experience and intuition about what feels right. For Army leaders, such decisions are guided by Army values, the institutional culture, and the organizational climate. These shared values then serve as a basis for the whole team's buying into the leader's decision. But comfortable as this might be, you should not make all decisions on intuition.

When there's time to consider alternatives, ask for advice, and think things through, you can make a deliberate decision. First determine what's legally right by law and regulation. In gray areas requiring interpretation, apply Army values to the situation. Inside those boundaries, determine the best possible answer from among competing solutions, make your decision, and act on it.

The distinction between snap and deliberate decisions is important. In many decisions, you must think critically because your intuition— what feels right—may lead to the wrong answer. In combat especially, the intuitive response won't always work.

The right action in the situation you face may not be in regulations or field manuals. Even the most exhaustive regulations can't predict every situation. They're designed for the routine, not the exceptional. One of the most difficult tasks facing you as an Army leader is determining when a rule or regulation simply doesn't apply because the situation you're facing falls outside the set of conditions envisioned by those who wrote the regulation.

D. Reflective Thinking

Leader development doesn't occur in a vacuum. All leaders must be open to feedback on their performance from multiple perspectives— seniors, peers, and subordinates. But being open to feedback is only one part of the equation. As a leader, you must also listen to and use the feedback: you must be able to reflect. Reflecting is the ability to take information, assess it, and apply it to behavior to explain why things did or did not go well. You can then use the resulting explanations to improve future behavior. Good leaders are always striving to become better leaders. This means you need consistently to assess your strengths and weaknesses and reflect on what you can do to sustain your strengths and correct your weaknesses. To become a better leader, you must be willing to change.

The Army often places a premium on doing—on the third element of BE, KNOW, DO. All Army leaders are busy dealing with what's on their plates and investing a lot of energy in accomplishing tasks. But how often do they take the time to STOP and really THINK about what they are doing? How often have you seen this sign on a leader's door: Do Not Disturb—Busy Reflecting? Not often. Well, good leaders need to take the time to think and reflect. Schedule it; start really exercising your capacity to get feedback. Then reflect on it and use it to improve. There's nothing wrong with making mistakes, but there's plenty wrong with not learning from those mistakes. Reflection is the means to that end.

C. Ethical Reasoning

Ref: FM 22-100, p. 4-8 to 4-9.

Ethical reasoning isn't a separate process you trot out only when you think you're facing an ethical question. It should be part of the thought process you use to make any decision. Your subordinates count on you to do more than make tactically sound decisions. They rely on you to make decisions that are ethically sound as well. You should always consider ethical factors and, when necessary, use Army values to gauge what's right.

1. Define the Problem

Defining the problem is the first step in making any decision. When you think a decision may have ethical aspects or effects, it's especially important to define it precisely. Know who said what—and what specifically was said, ordered, or demanded. Don't settle for secondhand information; get the details. Problems can be described in more than one way. This is the hardest step in solving any problem. It's especially difficult for decisions in the face of potential ethical conflicts. Too often some people come to rapid conclusions about the nature of a problem and end up applying solutions to what turn out to be only symptoms.

2. Know the Relevant Rules

This step is part of fact gathering, the second step in problem solving. Do your homework. Sometimes what looks like an ethical problem may stem from a misunderstanding of a regulation or policy, frustration, or overenthusiasm. Sometimes the person who gave an order or made a demand didn't check the regulation and a thorough reading may make the problem go away. Other times, a difficult situation results from trying to do something right in the wrong way. Also, some regulations leave room for interpretation; the problem then becomes a policy matter rather than an ethical one. If you do perceive an ethical problem, explain it to the person you think is causing it and try to come up with a better way to do the job.

3. Develop and Evaluate Courses of Action

Once you know the rules, lay out possible courses of action. As with the previous steps, you do this whenever you must make a decision. Next, consider these courses of action in view of Army values. Consider the consequences of your courses of action by asking yourself a few practical questions: Which course of action best upholds Army values? Do any of the courses of action compromise Army values? Does any course of action violate a principle, rule, or regulation identified in Step 2? Which course of action is in the best interest of the Army and of the nation? This part will feel like a juggling act; but with careful ethical reflection, you can reduce the chaos, determine the essentials, and choose the best course—even when that choice is the least bad of a set of undesirable options.

4. Choose the COA That Best Represents Army Values

The last step in solving any problem is making a decision and acting on it. Leaders are paid to make decisions. As an Army leader, you're expected—by your bosses and your people— to make decisions that solve problems without violating Army values.

As a values-based organization, the Army uses expressed values—Army values—to provide its fundamental ethical framework. Army values lay out the ethical standards expected of soldiers and DA civilians. Taken together, Army values and ethical decision making provide a moral touchstone and a workable process that enable you to make sound ethical decisions and take right actions confidently.

3. Technical Skills

Technical Skills

A. Knowing Equipment
B. Operating Equipment

Ref: FM 22-100, p. 4-11, fig. 4-3.

A. Knowing Equipment

Technical skill is skill with things—equipment, weapons, systems—everything from the towing winch on the front of a vehicle to the computer that keeps track of corps personnel actions. Direct leaders must know their equipment and how to operate it. Technical manuals, training circulars, SOPs, and all the other publications necessary for efficient, effective performance explain specific skills more completely. Direct leaders are closer to their equipment than organizational and strategic leaders. Thus, they have a greater need to know how it works and how to use it. In addition, direct leaders are the experts who are called upon to solve problems with the equipment, the ones who figure out how to make it work better, how to apply it, how to fix it—even how to modify it. Sergeants, junior officers, warrant officers, wage grade employees, and journeymen are the Army's technical experts and best teachers. Subordinates expect their first-line leaders to know their equipment and be experts in all the applicable technical skills.

B. Operating Equipment

Direct leaders know how to operate their equipment and make sure their people do as well. They set the example with a hands-on approach. When new equipment arrives, direct leaders find out how it works, learn how to use it themselves, and train their subordinates to do the same.

4. Tactical Skills

Tactical Skills

A. Doctrine
B. Fieldcraft

Ref: FM 22-100, p. 4-12, fig. 4-4.

A. Doctrine

Tactics is the art and science of employing available means to win battles and engagements. The science of tactics encompasses capabilities, techniques, and procedures that can be codified. The art of tactics includes the creative and flexible array of means to accomplish assigned missions, decision making when faced with an intelligent enemy, and the effects of combat on soldiers. Together, FM 100-34, FM 100-40, and branch-specific doctrinal manuals capture the tactical skills that are essential to mastering both the science and the art of tactics.

B. Fieldcraft

Fieldcraft consists of the skills soldiers need to sustain themselves in the field. Proficiency in fieldcraft reduces the likelihood soldiers will become casualties. The requirement to be able to do one's job in a field environment distinguishes the soldier's profession from most civilian occupations. Likewise, the requirement that Army leaders make sure their soldiers take care of themselves and proved them with the means to do so is unique.

The Soldier's Manual of Common Tasks lists the individual skills all soldiers must master to operate effectively in the field. Those skills include everything from how to stay healthy, to how to pitch a tent, to how to run a heater.

Army leaders gain proficiency in fieldcraft through schooling, study, and practice. Once learned, few fieldcraft skills are difficult. However, they are easy to neglect during exercises, when everyone knows that the exercise will end at a specific time, sick and injured soldiers are always evacuated, and the adversary isn't using real ammunition. During peacetime, it's up to Army leaders to enforce tactical discipline, to make sure their soldiers practice the fieldcraft skills that will keep them from becoming casualties— battle or nonbattle—during operations.

C. Tactical Skills and Training

Direct leaders are the Army's primary tactical trainers, both for individuals and for teams. Practicing tactical skills is often challenging. The best way to improve individual and collective skills is to replicate operational conditions. Unfortunately, Army leaders can't always get the whole unit out in the field to practice maneuvers, so they make do with training parts of it separately. Sometimes they can't get the people, the time, and the money all together at the right time and the right place to train the entire team. There are always training distracters. There will always be a hundred excuses not to train together and one reason why such training must occur: units fight as they train.

Direct Leadership Actions

Preparing to be a leader doesn't get the job done; the test of your character and competence comes when you act, when you DO those things required of a leader. Remember that your actions say more about what kind of leader you are than anything else. Your people watch you all the time; you're always on duty. And if there's a disconnect between what you say and how you act, they'll make up their minds about you—and act accordingly—based on how you act. It's not good enough to talk the talk; you have to walk the walk. The most important influence you have on your people is the example you set.

1. Influencing Actions

Leadership is both art and science. It requires constant study, hard work, and frequent practice. Since you're dealing with people and their emotions, dreams, and fears, it also calls for imagination and a positive, upbeat approach.

Effective leaders act competently and confidently. Your attitude sets the tone for the entire unit, and you choose your attitude—day to day, task to task, even minute to minute. Remember that optimism, a positive outlook, and a sense of humor are infectious. This is especially true when you must make unpopular decisions and face the challenge of bringing the team on board. As a leader, you should be asking several questions: What's happening? What should be happening but isn't? Why are these things happening? Then ask yourself: How can I get this team moving toward the goal?

A. Communicating
B. Decision Making
C. Motivating

Ref: FM 22-100, p. 5-1, fig. 5-1.

A. Communicating

Leaders keep their subordinates informed because doing so shows trust, because sharing information can relieve stress, and because information allows subordinates to determine what they need to do to accomplish the mission when circumstances change. By informing them of a decision—and, as much as possible, the reasons for it—you show your subordinates they're important members of the team. Accurate information also relieves unnecessary stress and helps keep rumors under control. (Without an explanation for what's happening, your people will manufacture one—or several—of their own.) Finally, if something should happen to you, the next leader in the chain will be better prepared to take over and accomplish the mission if everyone knows what's going on. Subordinates must understand your intent. In a tactical setting, leaders must understand the intent of their commanders two levels up.

In other situations, leaders use a variety of means to keep people informed, from face-to-face talks to published memos and family newsletters. No matter what the method, keep two things in mind:

- As a leader, you are responsible to make sure your subordinates understand you
- Communication isn't limited to your immediate superiors and subordinates

The success or failure of any communication is the responsibility of the leader. If it appears your subordinates don't understand, check to make sure you've made yourself clear. In fact, even if you think your people understand, check anyway; ask for a back-brief.

Don't assume that communication begins or ends at the next level up or the next level down. If you're a team leader, listen carefully to what your supervisors, platoon sergeants, platoon leaders, and company commanders say. If you're a platoon sergeant, pass the word through your squad leaders or section chiefs, but also watch and listen to the troops to see if the information has made it all the way to where it needs to go. Listen carefully at least two levels up and two levels down.

In combat, subordinates may be out of contact with their leaders. Sometimes the plan falls apart because of something unexpected—weather, terrain, enemy action. Sometimes the leader may be killed or wounded. In those situations, subordinates who know the overall purpose of the mission and the commander's intent have the basic information they need to carry on. And if the leader has established a climate of trust, if the leader has trained the subordinate leaders in how and why decisions are made, one of these subordinates is more likely to step up and take charge.

Communicating also goes on from bottom to top. Leaders find out what their people are thinking, saying, and doing by using that most important communication tool: listening. By listening carefully, you can even hear those messages behind what a person is actually saying, the equivalent of reading between the lines. Practice "leadership by walking around." Get out and coach, listen, teach, and clarify; pass on what you learn to your superiors. They need to know what's going on to make good plans.

B. Decision Making

See Chart 1B. Decision Making: Problem Solving Steps on p. 5-18.

A problem is an existing condition or situation in which what you want to happen is different from what actually is happening. Decision making is the process that begins to change that situation. Thus, decision making is knowing whether to decide, then when and what to decide. It includes understanding the consequences of your decisions.

Every once in a while, you may come across a decision that's easy to make: yes or no, right or left, on or off. As you gain experience as a leader, some of the decisions you find difficult now will become easier. But there will always be difficult decisions that require imagination, that require rigorous thinking and analysis, or that require you to factor in your gut reaction. Those are the tough decisions, the ones you're getting paid to make. As an experienced first sergeant once said to a brand new company commander, "We get paid the big bucks to make the hard calls." The next several paragraphs explain the steps you should use to solve a problem; then you'll read about other factors that affect how you make those hard calls and the importance of setting priorities.

C. Motivating

See chart, Motivating, on facing page.

Motivation involves using word and example to give your subordinates the will to accomplish the mission. Motivation grows out of people's confidence in themselves, their unit, and their leaders. This confidence is born in hard, realistic training; it's nurtured by constant reinforcement and through the kind of leadership—consistent, hard, and fair—that promotes trust. Remember that trust, like loyalty, is a gift your soldiers give you only when you demonstrate that you deserve it. Motivation also springs from the person's faith in the larger mission of the organization— a sense of being a part of the big picture.

(1) Empowering People

People want to be recognized for the work they do and want to be empowered. You empower subordinates when you train them to do a job, give them the necessary resources and authority, get out of their way, and let them work. Not only is this a tremendous statement of the trust you have in your subordinates; it's one of the best ways to develop them as leaders. Coach and counsel them, both when they succeed and when they fail.

(2) Positive Reinforcement

You recognize subordinates when you give them credit for the work they do, from a pat on the back to a formal award or decoration. Don't underestimate the power of a few choice words of praise when a person has done a good job. Don't hesitate to give out awards—commendations, letters, certificates—when appropriate. (Use good judgment, however. If you give out a medal for every little thing, pretty soon the award becomes meaningless. Give an award for the wrong thing and you show you're out of touch.) Napoleon marveled at the motivational power of properly awarded ribbons and medals. He once said that if he had enough ribbon, he could rule the world.

(3) Negative Reinforcement

Of course, not everyone is going to perform to standard. In fact, some will require punishment. Using punishment to motivate a person away from an undesirable behavior is effective, but can be tricky. Sound judgment must guide you when administering punishment.

Motivating

Ref: FM 22-100, p. 5-6 to 5-7.

Positive Reinforcement

When using rewards, leaders have many options. Here are some things to consider:

- Consult the leadership chain for recommendations.
- Choose a reward valued by the person receiving it, one that appeals to personal pride. This may be a locally approved award that's more respected than traditional DA awards.
- Use the established system of awards (certificates, medals, letters of commendation, driver and mechanic badges) when appropriate. These are recognized throughout the Army; when a soldier goes to a new unit, the reward will still be valuable.
- Present the award at an appropriate ceremony. Emphasize its importance. Let others see how hard work is rewarded.
- Give rewards promptly.
- Praise only good work or honest effort. Giving praise too freely cheapens its effect.
- Promote people who get the job done and who influence others to do better work.
- Recognize those who meet the standard and improve performance. A soldier who works hard and raises his score on the APFT deserves recognition, even if the soldier doesn't achieve the maximum score. Not everyone can be soldier of the quarter.

Negative Reinforcement

Not everyone is going to perform to standard. In fact, some will require punishment. Consider these guidelines:

- Before you punish a subordinate, make sure the subordinate understands the reason for the punishment. In most—although not all—cases, you'll want to try to change the subordinate's behavior by counseling or retraining before resulting to punishment.
- Consult your leader or supervisor before you punish a subordinate. They'll be aware of policies and may be able to assist you in changing the subordinate's behavior.
- Avoid threatening a subordinate with punishment. Making a threat puts you in the position of having to deliver on that threat. In such a situation you may end up punishing because you said you would rather than because the behavior merits punishment. This undermines your standing as a leader.
- Avoid mass punishment. Correctly identify the problem, determine if an individual or individuals are responsible, and use an appropriate form of correction.
- With an open mind and without prejudging, listen to the subordinate's side of the story.
- Let the subordinate know that it's the behavior—not the individual—that is the problem. "You let the team down" works; "You're a loser" sends the wrong message.
- Since people tend to live up to their leader's expectations, tell them, "I know you can do better than that. I expect you to do better than that."
- Punish those who are able but unwilling to perform. Retrain a person who's unable to complete a task.
- Respond immediately to undesirable behavior. Investigate fully. Take prompt and prudent corrective action in accordance with established legal or regulatory procedures.
- Never humiliate a subordinate; avoid public reprimand.
- Ensure the person knows exactly what behavior got the person in trouble.
- Make sure the punishment isn't excessive or unreasonable. It's not only the severity of punishment that keeps subordinates in line; it's the certainty that they can't get away with undesirable behavior.
- Control your temper and hold no grudges. Don't let your personal feelings interfere; whether you like or dislike someone has nothing to do with good order and discipline.

1B. Decision Making Problem Solving Steps

Ref: FM 22-100, p. 5-3 to 5-5.

Army leaders usually follow one of two decision-making processes. Leaders at company level and below follow the troop leading procedures (TLP). The TLP are designed to support solving tactical problems. Leaders at battalion level and above follow the military decision making process (MDMP). The MDMP, which FM 101-5 discusses, is designed for organizations with staffs. These established and proven methodologies combine elements of the planning operating action to save time and achieve parallel decision making and planning.

1. Identify the problem

Don't be distracted by the symptoms of the problem; get at its root cause. There may be more than one thing contributing to a problem. The issue you choose to address as the root cause becomes the mission (or restated mission for tactical problems). The mission must include a simple statement of who, what, when, where, and why. It should include your end state, how you want things to look when the mission is complete.

2. Identify facts and assumptions

Get whatever facts you can in the time you have. Facts are statements of what you know about the situation. Assumptions are statements of what you believe about the situation but don't have facts to support. Make only assumptions that are likely to be true and essential to generate alternatives. Some of the many sources of facts include regulations, policies, and doctrinal publications. Your organization's mission, goals, and objectives may also be a source. Sources of assumptions can be personal experiences, members of the organization, subject matter experts, or written observations. Analyze the facts and assumptions you identify to determine the scope of the problem.

3. Generate alternatives

Alternatives are ways to solve the problem. Develop more than one possible alternative. Don't be satisfied with the first thing that comes into your mind. That's lazy thinking; the third or fourth or twentieth alternative you come up with might be the best one. If you have time and experienced subordinates, include them in this step.

4. Analyze the alternatives

Identify intended and unintended consequences, resource or other constraints, and the advantages and disadvantages of each alternative. Be sure to consider all your alternatives. Don't prejudge the situation by favoring any one alternative over the others.

5. Compare the alternatives

Evaluate each alternative for its probability of success and cost. Think past the immediate future. How will this decision change things tomorrow? Next week? Next year?

6. Make and execute your decision

Prepare a leader's plan of action, if necessary, and put it in motion.

7. Assess the results

Check constantly to see how the execution of your plan of action is going. Keep track of what happens. Adjust your plan, if necessary. Learn from the experience so you'll be better equipped next time. Follow up on results and make adjustments as required.

2. Operating Actions

You're operating when you act to achieve an immediate objective, when you're working to get today's job done. Although FM 25-100 is predominantly a training tool, its methodology applies to a unit's overall operational effectiveness. Because operating includes planning, preparing, executing, and assessing, you can use the FM 25-100 principles as a model for operations other than training. Sometimes these elements are part of a cycle; other times they happen simultaneously.

You'll often find yourself influencing after you've moved on to operating. In practice, the nice, neat divisions in this manual are not clear-cut; you often must handle multiple tasks requiring different skills at the same time.

Operating Actions

A. Planning and Preparing
B. Executing
C. Assessing

Ref: FM 22-100, p. 5-8, fig. 5-2.

A. Planning and Preparing

In peacetime training, in actual operations, and especially in combat, your job is to help your organization function effectively—accomplish the mission—in an environment that can be chaotic. That begins with a well thought-out plan and thorough preparation. A well-trained organization with a sound plan is much better prepared than one without a plan. Planning ahead reduces confusion, builds subordinates' confidence in themselves and the organization, and helps ensure success with a minimum of wasted effort—or in combat, the minimum number of casualties.

A plan is a proposal for executing a command decision or project. Planning begins with a mission, specified or implied. A specified mission comes from your boss or from higher headquarters. An implied mission results when the leader, who may be you, sees something within his area of responsibility that needs to be done and, on his own initiative, develops a leader plan of action.

Reverse Planning

When you begin with the goal in mind, you often will use the reverse planning method. Start with the question "Where do I want to end up?" and work backward from there until you reach "We are here right now."

Along the way, determine the basics of what's required: who, what, when, where, and why. You may also want to consider how to accomplish the task, although the "how" is usually not included in a mission to a subordinate. As you plan, consider the amount of time needed to coordinate and conduct each step.

After you have figured out what must happen on the way to the goal, put the tasks in sequence, set priorities, and determine a schedule. Look at the steps in the order they will occur. Make sure events are in logical order and you have allotted enough time for each one. As always, a good leader asks for input from subordinates when time allows. Getting input not only acts as a check on the your plan (you may have overlooked something), but also gets your people involved; involvement builds trust, self-confidence, and the will to succeed.

Preparing

While leaders plan, subordinates prepare. Leaders can develop a plan while their organization is preparing if they provide advance notice of the task or mission and initial guidance for preparation in a warning order. (Warning orders are part of the TLP and MDMP; however, any leader—uniformed or DA civilian—can apply the principle of the warning order by giving subordinates advance notice of an impending requirement and how they'll be expected to contribute to it. FM 101-5 discusses warning orders.) Based on this guidance, subordinates can draw ammunition, rehearse key actions, inspect equipment, conduct security patrols, or begin movement while the leader completes the plan. In the case of a non tactical requirement, preparation may include making sure the necessary facilities and other resources are available to support it. In all cases, preparation includes coordinating with people and organizations that are involved or might be affected by the operation or project. (TC 25-30 discusses preparing for company- and platoon-level training).

Rehearsal is an important element of preparation. Rehearsing key combat actions lets subordinates see how things are supposed to work and builds confidence in the plan for both soldiers and leaders. Even a simple walk-through helps them visualize who's supposed to be where and do what when. Mobilization exercises provide a similar function for DA civilians and reserve component soldiers: they provide a chance to understand and rehearse mobilization and deployment support functions. Execution goes more smoothly because everyone has a mental picture of what's supposed to happen. Rehearsals help people remember their responsibilities. They also help leaders see how things might happen, what might go wrong, how the plan needs to be changed, and what things the leader didn't think of.

Leader plans of action can be used to reinforce positive behavior, improve performance, or even change an aspect of the organizational climate. A leader plan of action may also be personal— as when the leader decides "I need to improve my skills in this area."

No matter what your position is, part of your duty is making your boss's job easier. Just as you loyally provide resources and authority for your subordinates to do their jobs, you leave the boss free to do his. Ask only for decisions that fall outside your scope of authority—not those you want to avoid. Forward only problems you can't fix—not those whose solutions are just difficult. Ask for advice from others with more experience or seek clarification when you don't understand what's required. Do all that and exercise disciplined initiative within your boss's intent.

B. Executing

Executing means acting to accomplish the mission, moving to achieve the leader's goals as expressed in the leader's vision—to standard and on time—while taking care of your people.

Execution, the payoff, is based on all the work that has gone before. But planning and preparation alone can't guarantee success. Things will go wrong. Large chunks of the plan will go flying out the window. At times, it will seem as if everything is working against you. Then you must have the will to fight through, keeping in mind your higher leaders' intent and the mission's ultimate goal. You must adapt and improvise.

In a tactical setting, all leaders must know the intent of commanders two levels up. During execution, position yourself to best lead your people, initiate and control the action, get others to follow the plan, react to changes, keep your people focused, and work the team to accomplish the goal to standard. A well-trained organization accomplishes the mission, even when things go wrong.

(1) Maintaining Standards

The Army has established standards for all military activities. Standards are formal, detailed instructions that can be stated, measured, and achieved. They provide a performance baseline to evaluate how well a specific task has been executed. You must know, communicate and enforce standards. Explain the ones that apply to your organization and give your subordinate leaders the authority to enforce them. Then hold your subordinates responsible for achieving them.

Army leaders don't set the minimum standards as goals. However, everything can't be a number one priority. As an Army leader, you must exercise judgment concerning which tasks are most important. Organizations are required to perform many tasks that are not mission-related. While some of these are extremely important, others require only a minimum effort. Striving for excellence in every area, regardless of how trivial, quickly works an organization to death. On the other hand, the fact that a task isn't a first priority doesn't excuse a sloppy performance. Professional soldiers accomplish all tasks to standard. Competent leaders make sure the standard fits the task's importance.

(2) Setting Goals

The leader's ultimate goal—your ultimate goal—is to train the organization to succeed in its wartime mission. Your daily work includes setting intermediate goals to get the organization ready. Involve your subordinates in goal setting. This kind of cooperation fosters trust and makes the best use of subordinates' talents. When developing goals, consider these points:

- Goals must be realistic, challenging, and attainable
- Goals should lead to improved combat readiness
- Subordinates ought to be involved in the goal setting
- Leaders develop a plan of action to achieve each goal

C. Assessing

Setting goals and maintaining standards are central to assessing mission accomplishment. Whenever you talk about accomplishing the mission, always include the phrase "to standard." When you set goals for your subordinates, make sure they know what the standards are. To use a simple example, the goal might be "All unit members will pass the APFT." The APFT standard tells you, for each exercise, how many repetitions are required in how much time, as well as describing a proper way to do the exercise.

Also central to assessing is spot checking. Army leaders check things: people, performance, equipment, resources. They check things to ensure the organization is meeting standards and moving toward the goals the leader has established. Look closely; do it early and often; do it both before and after the fact. Praise good performance and figure out how to fix poor performance.

(1) In-Process Reviews

Successful assessment begins with forming a picture of the organization's performance early. Anticipate which areas the organization might have trouble in; that way you know which areas to watch closely. Once the organization begins the mission, use IPRs to evaluate performance and give feedback. Think of an IPR as a checkpoint on the way to mission accomplishment.

(2) After-Action Reviews

Note: See Chap. 3 for a full discussion on AARs.

AARs fill a similar role at the end of the mission. Army leaders use AARs as opportunities to develop subordinates. During an AAR, give subordinates a chance to talk about how they saw things. Teach them how to look past a problem's symptoms to its root cause. Teach them how to give constructive, useful feedback. ("Here's what we did well; here's what we can do better.") When subordinates share in identifying reasons for success and failure, they become owners of a stake in how things get done. AARs also give you a chance to hear what's on your subordinates' minds—and good leaders listen closely.

Leaders base reviews on accurate observations and correct recording of those observations. If you're evaluating a ten-day field exercise, take good notes because you won't remember everything. Look at things in a systematic way; get out and see things firsthand. Don't neglect tasks that call for subjective judgment: evaluate unit cohesion, discipline, and morale.

(3) Initial Leader Assessments

Leaders often conduct an initial assessment before they take over a new position. How competent are your new subordinates? What's expected of you in your new job? Watch how people operate; this will give you clues about the organizational climate. Review the organization's SOP and any regulations that apply. Meet with the outgoing leader and listen to his assessment. Review status reports and recent inspection results. After you've been in the position for a while, take the necessary time to make an in-depth assessment.

And in the midst of all this checking and rechecking, don't forget to take a look at yourself. What kind of leader are you? Do you over supervise? Under supervise? How can you improve? What's your plan for working on your weak areas? What's the best way to make use of your strengths? Get feedback on yourself from as many sources as possible: your boss, your peers, even your subordinates.

(4) Assessment of Subordinates

Good leaders provide straightforward feedback to subordinates. Tell them where you see their strengths; let them know where they can improve. Have them come up with a plan of action for self-improvement; offer your help. Leader assessment should be a positive experience that your subordinates see as a chance for them to improve. They should see it as an opportunity to tap into your experience and knowledge for their benefit. To assess your subordinate leaders, you must— Observe and record leadership actions. Compare what you see to performance indicators or the appropriate reference. Determine if the performance meets, exceeds, or falls below standard. Tell your subordinates what you saw; give them a chance to assess themselves. Help your subordinate develop a plan of action to improve performance.

(5) Leader Assessments and Plans of Action

Leader assessment won't help anyone improve unless it includes a plan of action designed to correct weaknesses and sustain strengths. Not only that, you and the subordinate must use the plan; it doesn't do anyone any good if you stick it in a drawer or file cabinet and never think about it again. Here is what you must do:

- Design the plan of action together; let your subordinate take the lead as much as possible

- Agree on the actions necessary to improve leader performance; your subordinate must buy into this plan if it's going to work

- Review the plan frequently, check progress, and change the plan if necessary

3. Improving Actions

Improving actions are things leaders do to leave their organizations better than they found them.

Developing refers to people: you improve your organization and the Army as an institution when you develop your subordinates.

Building refers to team building: as a direct leader, you improve your organization by building strong, cohesive teams that perform to standard, even in your absence.

Learning refers to you, your subordinates, and your organization as a whole. As a leader, you must model self-development for your people; you must constantly be learning. In addition, you must also encourage your subordinates to learn and reward their self-development efforts. Finally, you must establish an organizational climate that rewards collective learning and act to ensure your organization learns from its experiences.

Improving Actions
A. Developing B. Building C. Learning

Ref: FM 22-100, p. 5-14, fig. 5-3.

A. Developing

In the Army, developing means developing people. Your subordinates are the leaders of tomorrow's Army. You have a responsibility to train them, to be the kind of leader they deserve so that they'll see how leading is done. It's your duty to invest the time and energy it takes to help them reach their fullest potential. The driving principle behind Army leader development is that leaders must be prepared before assuming leadership positions; they must be competent and confident in their abilities. This principle applies to all ranks and levels, to soldiers and DA civilians, and to both the active and reserve components.

(1) Institutional Training

The Army school system provides formal education and training for job-related and leadership skills. The American public education system is progressive; that is, children attend primary school before middle school or junior high and then go on to high school. Likewise, the Army school system is progressive. The main difference is that you can expect to go out and use your skills in an assignment before being considered for the next level of schooling. Institutional training is critical in developing leaders and preparing them for increased positions of responsibility throughout the Army.

(2) Operational Assignments

When you take what you've learned in school into the field Army, you continue to learn through on-the-job experience and by watching your leaders, peers, and subordinates. Operational assignments provide opportunities to broaden your knowledge and refine skills you gain during institutional training and previous assignments. You gain and expand your experience base by performing a wide range of duties and tasks under a variety of frequently changing conditions and situations. Operational assignments provide a powerful resource for leader development—an opportunity to learn by doing.

(3) Self-Development

Self-development is a process you should use to enhance previously acquired skills, knowledge, and experience. Its goal is to increase your readiness and potential for positions of greater responsibility. Effective self-development focuses on aspects of your character, knowledge, and capabilities that you believe need developing or improving. You can use the dimensions of the Army leadership framework to help you determine what areas to work on. Self-development is continuous: it takes place during institutional training and operational assignments.

Self-development for junior personnel is very structured and generally narrow in focus. The focus broadens as individuals learn their strengths and weaknesses, determine their individual needs, and become more independent. Everyone's knowledge and perspective increases with age, experience, institutional training, and operational assignments. Specific, goal-oriented self-development actions can accelerate and broaden a person's skills and knowledge. As a member of the Army, you're obligated to develop your abilities to the greatest extent possible. As an Army leader, you're responsible to assist your subordinates in their self-development.

Civilian and military education is part of self-development. Army leaders never stop learning. They seek to educate and train themselves beyond what's offered in formal schooling or even in their duty assignments. Leaders look for educational opportunities to prepare themselves for their next job and future responsibilities. Look for Army off-duty education that interests you and will give you useful skills. Seek civilian education to broaden your outlook on life. Look for things to read that will develop your mind and help you build skills. Challenge yourself and apply the same initiative here as you do in your day-to-day duties.

Mentoring

Mentoring is totally inclusive, real-life leader development for every subordinate. Because leaders don't know which of their subordinates today will be the most significant contributors and leaders in the future, they strive to provide all their subordinates with the knowledge and skills necessary to become the best they can be—for the Army and for themselves. Mentoring techniques include teaching, developmental counseling, and coaching.

Teaching is passing on knowledge and skills to subordinates. It's a primary task for first-line leaders. Teaching focuses primarily on technical and tactical skills. Developmental counseling is better for improving interpersonal and conceptual skills. Technical Teaching gives knowledge or provides skills to others, causing them to learn by example or experience. Mentoring (in the Army) is the proactive development of each subordinate through observing, assessing, coaching, teaching, developmental counseling, and evaluating that results in people being treated with fairness and equal opportunity. Mentoring is an inclusive process (not an exclusive one) for everyone under a leader's charge.

Developmental counseling is central to leader development. It's the means by which you prepare your subordinates of today to be the leaders of tomorrow. It requires you to use all your counseling tools and skills. This means using counseling requirements such as those prescribed in the NCO Evaluation Reporting System (NCOERS), Officer Evaluation Reporting System (OERS), and Total Army Performance Evaluation System (TAPES, which is used to evaluate DA civilians) as more than paper drills. It means face-to-face counseling of individuals you rate. But more important, it means making time throughout the rating period to discuss performance objectives and provide meaningful assessments and feedback. No evaluation report—positive or negative—should be a surprise. A consistent developmental counseling program ensures your people know where they stand and what they should be doing to improve their performance and develop themselves.

Coaching follows naturally from the assessing leader action. As you observe your subordinates at work, you;ll see them perform some tasks to standard and some not to standard. Some of their plans work; some won't. Use each opportunity to teach, counsel or coach from quarterly training briefings to AARs.

B. Building

(1) Building Teams

Note: See Chap. 6, Combat-Ready Teams for a full discussion on building teams.

Regardless of other issues, soldiers perform for the other people in the squad or section, for others in the team or crew, for the person on their right or left. This is a fundamental truth: soldiers perform because they don't want to let their buddies down.

If the leaders of the small teams that make up the Army are competent, and if their members trust one another, those teams and the larger team of teams will hang together and get the job done. People who belong to a successful team look at nearly everything in a positive light; their winners' attitudes are infectious, and they see problems as challenges rather than obstacles. Additionally, a cohesive team accomplishes the mission much more efficiently than a group of individuals. Just as a football team practices to win on the gridiron, so must a team of soldiers practice to be effective on the battlefield.

Training together builds collective competence; trust is a product of that competence. Subordinates learn to trust their leaders if the leaders know how to do their jobs and act consistently— if they say what they mean and mean what they say. Trust also springs from the collective competence of the team. As the team becomes more experienced and enjoys more successes, it becomes more cohesive.

Developing teams takes hard work, patience, and quite a bit of interpersonal skill on the part of the leader, but it's a worthwhile investment. Good teams get the job done. People who are part of a good team complete the mission on time with the resources given them and a minimum of wasted effort; in combat, good teams are the most effective and take the fewest casualties.

Good teams—

- Work together to accomplish the mission
- Execute tasks thoroughly and quickly
- Meet or exceed the standard
- Thrive on demanding challenges
- Learn from their experiences and are proud of their accomplishments

(2) Building the Ethical Climate

As an Army leader, you are the ethical standard bearer for your organization. You're responsible for building an ethical climate that demands and rewards behavior consistent with Army values. The primary factor affecting an organization's ethical climate is its leader's ethical standard. Leaders can look to other organizational or installation personnel—for example, the chaplain, staff judge advocate, inspector general, and equal employment opportunity manager—to assist them in building and assessing their organization's ethical climate, but the ultimate responsibility belongs to the leader—period.

C. Learning

The Army is a learning organization, one that harnesses the experience of its people and organizations to improve the way it does business. Based on their experiences, learning organizations adopt new techniques and procedures that get the job done more efficiently or effectively. Likewise, they discard techniques and procedures that have outlived their purpose. However, you must remain flexible when trying to make sense of your experiences. The leader who works day after day after day and never stops to ask "How can I do this better?" is never going to learn and won't improve the team.

"Zero Defects" and Learning

There's no room for the "zero-defects" mentality in a learning organization. Leaders willing to learn welcome new ways of looking at things, examine what's going well, and are not afraid to look at what's going poorly. When direct leaders stop receiving feedback from subordinates, it's a good indication that something is wrong. If the message you hammer home is "There will be no mistakes," or if you lose your temper and "shoot the messenger" every time there's bad news, eventually your people will just stop telling you when things go wrong or suggesting how to make things go right. Then there will be some unpleasant surprises in store. Any time you have human beings in a complex organization doing difficult jobs, often under pressure, there are going to be problems. Effective leaders use those mistakes to figure out how to do things better and share what they have learned with other leaders in the organization, both peers and superiors.

Barriers to Learning

Fear of mistakes isn't the only thing that can get in the way of learning; so can rigid, lockstep thinking and plain mental laziness. These habits can become learning barriers leaders are so used to that they don't even notice them. Fight this tendency. Challenge yourself. Use your imagination. Ask how other people do things. Listen to subordinates.

Helping People Learn

Certain conditions help people learn. First, you must motivate the person to learn. Explain to the subordinate why the subject is important or show how it will help the individual perform better. Second, involve the subordinate in the learning process; make it active. For instance, you would never try to teach someone how to drive a vehicle with classroom instruction alone; you have to get the person behind the wheel. That same approach applies to much more complex tasks; keep the lecture to a minimum and maximize the hands-on time.

After-Action Reviews and Learning

Individuals benefit when the group learns together. The AAR is one tool good leaders use to help their organizations learn as a group. Properly conducted, an AAR is a professional discussion of an event, focused on performance standards, that enables people to discover for themselves what happened, why it happened, and how to sustain strengths and improve on weaknesses. Like warning orders and rehearsals, the AAR is a technique that all leaders—military or DA civilian—can use in garrison as well as field environments.

Organizational Climate and Learning

It takes courage to create a learning environment. When you try new things or try things in different ways, you're bound to make mistakes. Learn from your mistakes and the mistakes of others. Pick your team and yourself up, determine what went right and wrong, and continue the mission. Be confident in your abilities.

II. Organizational Ldrshp

Ref: FM 22-100, p. 6-1 to -32.

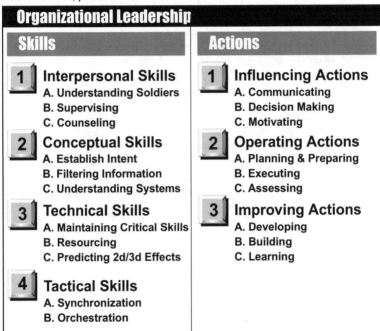

Organizational Leadership

Skills

1 Interpersonal Skills
A. Understanding Soldiers
B. Supervising
C. Counseling

2 Conceptual Skills
A. Establish Intent
B. Filtering Information
C. Understanding Systems

3 Technical Skills
A. Maintaining Critical Skills
B. Resourcing
C. Predicting 2d/3d Effects

4 Tactical Skills
A. Synchronization
B. Orchestration

Actions

1 Influencing Actions
A. Communicating
B. Decision Making
C. Motivating

2 Operating Actions
A. Planning & Preparing
B. Executing
C. Assessing

3 Improving Actions
A. Developing
B. Building
C. Learning

Ref: FM 22-100, chap. 6.

As Army leaders mature and assume greater responsibilities, they must also learn new skills, develop new abilities, and act in more complex environments. Organizational and strategic leaders maintain their own personalities and propensities, but they also expand what they know and refine what they do.

Whether for key terrain in combat or for results in peacetime training, leaders in units and organizations translate strategy into policy and practice. They develop programs, plans, and systems that allow soldiers in teams, like the infantryman in the All-American Division, to turn plans and orders into fire and maneuver that seize victory at the least possible cost in sweat and blood. By force of will and application of their leadership skills, organizational leaders build teams with discipline, cohesion, trust, and proficiency. They clarify missions throughout the ranks by producing an intent, concept, and systematic approach to execution.

Organizational leadership builds on direct leader actions. Organizational leaders apply direct leader skills in their daily work with their command and staff teams and, with soldiers and subordinate leaders, they influence during their contacts with units. But to lead complex organizations like brigades, divisions, and corps at today's OPTEMPO and under the stresses of training, contingency operations, and combat, organizational leaders must add a whole new set of skills and actions to their leadership arsenal. They must practice direct and organizational leadership simultaneously.

Communicating to NCOs, like the airborne soldier at the Battle of the Bulge, occurs through individual subordinates, the staff, and the chain of command. Organizational leaders divide their attention between the concerns of the larger organization and their staffs and those of their subordinate leaders, units, and individuals. This tradeoff requires them to apply interpersonal and conceptual skills differently when exercising organizational leadership than when exercising direct leadership.

Organizational leaders rely heavily on mentoring subordinates and empowering them to execute their assigned responsibilities and missions. They stay mentally and emotionally detached from their immediate surroundings so they can visualize the larger impact on the organization and mission. Soldiers and subordinate leaders look to their organizational leaders to establish standards for mission accomplishment and provide resources (conditions) to achieve that goal. Organizational leaders provide direction and programs for training and execution that focus efforts on mission success.

Due to the indirect nature of their influence, organizational leaders assess interrelated systems and design long-term plans to accomplish the mission. They must sharpen their abilities to assess their environments, their organization, and their subordinates. Organizational leaders determine the cause and effect of shortcomings, translate these new understandings into plans and programs, and allow their subordinate leaders latitude to execute and get the job done.

Organizational demands also differ as leaders develop a systems perspective. At the strategic level, the Army has identified six imperatives: quality people, training, force mix, doctrine, modern equipment, and leader development. In organizations these imperatives translate into doctrine, training, leader development, organization, materiel, and soldiers—commonly called DTLOMS. Together with Army values, these systems provide the framework for influencing people and organizations at all levels, conducting a wide variety of operations, and continually improving the force. Doctrine includes techniques to drive the functional systems in Army organizations. FMs 25-100, 25-101, and 101-5 lay out procedures for training management and military decision making that enable and focus execution. The training management and military decision-making processes provide a ready-made, systemic approach to planning, preparing, executing, and assessing.

Organizational Skills

Organizational leaders continue to use the direct leader skills discussed in section I, however their larger organizations and spans of authority require them to master additional skills. As with direct leader skills, these span four areas: interpersonal, conceptual, technical, and tactical.

1. Interpersonal Skills

Interpersonal Skills

A. Understanding Soldiers
B. Supervising
C. Counseling

Ref: FM 22-100, p. 6-3, fig. 6-1.

A. Understanding Soldiers

Good organizational leaders understand the human dimension. They use that understanding to motivate subordinates and to encourage initiative. Motivation means much more than an individual willingness to do what's directed. It imparts a desire on the part of individuals and organizations to do what's needed without being directed. This collective desire to accomplish the mission underlies good organizational discipline: good soldiers and competent DA civilians adhere to standards because they understand that doing so, even when it's a nuisance or hardship, leads to success.

This understanding, along with Army values, forms the foundation of great units. Units that have solid discipline can take tremendous stress and friction yet persevere, fight through, and win. Fostering initiative builds on motivation and discipline. It requires subordinates' confidence that in an uncertain situation, when they know the commander's intent and develop a competent solution, the commander will underwrite the risk they take. While this principle applies to both direct and organizational leaders, the stakes are usually higher in larger, more complex organizations. Additionally, organizational leaders may be more remote in time and distance and subordinates' ability to check back with them is diminished. Therefore, organizational leaders' understanding must develop beyond what they can immediately and personally observe.

B. Communicating

Persuasion is a communication skill important to organizational leaders. Well-developed skills of persuasion and an openness to working through controversy in a positive way help organizational leaders overcome resistance and build support. These characteristics are particularly important in dealing with other organizational leaders. By reducing grounds for misunderstanding, persuasion reduces time wasted in overcoming unimportant issues. It also ensures involvement of others, opens communication with them, and places value on their opinions—all team-building actions. Openness to discussing one's position and a positive attitude toward a dissenting view often diffuses tension and saves time and resistance in the long run. By demonstrating these traits, organizational leaders also provide an example that subordinates can use in self-development.

In some circumstances, persuasion may be inappropriate. In combat, all leaders make decisions quickly, modifying the decision-making process to fit the circumstances. But this practice of using the directing leadership styles as opposed to more participatory ones should occur when situations are in doubt, risks are high, and time is short—circumstances that often appear in combat. No exact blueprints exist for success in every context; leadership and the ability to adapt to the situation will carry the day. Appropriate style, seasoned instinct, and the realities of the situation must prevail.

C. Supervising

Organizations pay attention to things leaders check. Feedback and coaching enhance motivation and improve performance by showing subordinates how to succeed. But how much should you check and how much is too much? When are statistics and reports adequate indicators and when must you visit your front-line organizations, talk to your soldiers and DA civilians and see what's going on yourself?

Overcentralized authority and oversupervising undermine trust and empowerment. Undersupervising can lead to failure, especially in cases where the leader's intent wasn't fully understood or where subordinate organizations lack the training for the task. Different subordinate commanders need different levels of supervision: some need a great deal of coaching and encouragement, though most would just as soon be left alone. As always, a good leader knows his subordinates and has the skill to supervise at the appropriate level.

2. Conceptual Skills

The complexity of the organizational leader's environment requires patience, the willingness to think before acting. Furthermore, the importance of conceptual and analytical skills increases as an organizational leader moves into positions of greater responsibility. Organizational environments with multiple dimensions offer problems that become more abstract, complex, and uncertain.

For organizational leaders, reasoning skills are crucial for developing intent and direction toward common goals. Critical thinking requires understanding systems and an increased ability to filter information, that is, to identify quickly information that applies to the task at hand and separate the important from the unimportant. Organizational leaders use this analytical ability to assess ambiguous environments and to calculate and manage risk. Their experience may allow them to see and define problems more easily—but not necessarily fix them quickly. Therefore, they also dedicate time to think and generate alternative ways of organizing their organizations and resources for maximum effect. It's important for organizational leaders to encourage critical thinking in subordinates because subordinates also assess organizational challenges, analyze indicators, and recommend courses of action. It's also important, time and mission permitting, to allow subordinates' solutions to bear fruit.

Conceptual Skills
A. Establish Intent **B. Filtering Information** **C. Understanding Systems**

Ref: FM 22-100, p. 6-5, fig. 6-2.

A. Establishing Intent

Intent is the leader's personal expression of a mission's end state and the key tasks the organization must accomplish to achieve it. During operations and field training, it's a clear, concise statement of what the force must do to succeed with respect to the enemy and the terrain and to the desired end state. By describing their intent, organizational leaders highlight the key tasks that, along with the mission, are the basis for subordinates to exercise initiative when unanticipated opportunities arise or when the original concept of operations no longer applies. Clear and concise, the leader's intent includes a mission's overall purpose and expected results. It provides purpose, motivation, and direction, whether the leader is commanding a division or running a staff directorate. An organizational leader visualizes the sequence of activities that will move the organization from its current state to the desired end state and expresses it simply and clearly.

After establishing a clear and valid intent, the art of organizational leadership lies in having subordinates take actions on their own to transform that intent into reality. Since organizational leaders are likely to be farther away from the point of execution in time and space, they must describe the collective goal rather than list tasks for individual subordinates. With clearly communicated purpose and direction, subordinates can then determine what they must do and why. Within that broad framework, leaders empower subordinates, delegating authority to act within the intent: "Here's where we're headed, why we're going there, and how we're going to get there."

B. Filtering Information

Organizational leaders deal with a tremendous amount of information. Some information will make sense only to someone with a broad perspective and an understanding of the entire situation. Organizational leaders communicate clearly to their staffs what information they need and then hold the staff accountable for providing it. Then, they judge—based on their education, training, and experience—what's important and make well-informed, timely decisions.

Analysis and synthesis are essential to effective decision-making and program development. Analysis breaks a problem into its component parts. Synthesis assembles complex and disorganized data into a solution. Often, data must be processed before it fits into place.

Commander's Critical Information Requirements (CCIR) are the commander's most important information filters. Commanders Must know the environment, the situation, their organizations, and themselves well enough to articulate what they need to know to control their organizations and accomplish their missions. They must also ensure they have thought through the feedback systems necessary to supervise execution. Organizational-level commanders must not only establish CCIR but also train their staffs to battle drill proficiency in information filtering. (FM 101-5 discusses CCIR, mission analysis, information management, and other staff operations.)

C. Understanding Systems

Organizational leaders think about systems in their organization: how they work together, how using one affects the others, and how to get the best performance from the whole. They think beyond their own organizations to how what their organization does affects other organizations and the team as a whole. Whether coordinating fires among different units or improving sponsorship of new personnel, organizational leaders use a systems perspective. While direct leaders think about tasks, organizational leaders integrate, synchronize, and fine-tune systems and monitor outcomes. If organizational leaders can't get something done, the flaw or failure is more likely systemic than human. Being able to understand and leverage systems increases a leader's ability to achieve organizational goals and objectives.

Organizational leaders also know how effectively apply all available systems to achieve mission success. They constantly make sure that the systems for personnel, administration, logistical support, resourcing, and training work effectively. They know where to look to see if the critical parts of the system are functioning properly.

Organizational leaders analyze systems and results to determine why things happened the way they did. Performance indicators and standards for systems assist them in their analysis. Once an assessment is complete and causes of a problem known, organizational leaders develop appropriate solutions that address the problem's root cause.

3. Technical Skills

The external responsibilities of organizational leaders are greater than those of direct leaders, both vertically and horizontally. Their organizations have more levels than direct-level organizations and, depending on the organization's role, command interest may reach to the CINC or national command authority. There are more requirements to coordinate with other organizations, which may include agencies outside the Department of Defense (DOD). To make full use of their organizations' capabilities, organizational leaders must continue to master technical skills outside their original area of expertise.

Technical Skills

A. Maintaining Critical Skills
B. Resourcing
C. Predicting 2d/3d Order Effects

Ref: FM 22-100, p. 6-9, fig. 6-3.

A. Maintaining Critical Skills

Organizational leaders have fewer opportunities to practice many of the technical skills they mastered as direct leaders. However, that doesn't mean they can forget about them. In every organization there are certain skills in which all members must be proficient. Soldiers know what they are and expect their leaders to be able to perform them. This doesn't mean that organizational leaders must be able to perform every specialty-related skill as well as an individual holding that specialty. The Army is too complex for that. It does, however, mean that organizational leaders must identify and be proficient in those critical, direct-leader skills they need to assess tactical training and set the example.

B. Resourcing

In addition to using the technical skills they learned as direct leaders, organizational leaders must also master the skill of resourcing. Resources—which include time, equipment, facilities, budgets, and people—are required to achieve organizational goals. Organizational leaders must aggressively manage the resources at their disposal to ensure their organizations' readiness. The leader's job grows more difficult when unprogrammed costs—such as an emergency deployment—shift priorities.

Organizational leaders are stewards of their people's time and energy and their own will and tenacity. They don't waste these resources but skillfully evaluate objectives, anticipate resource requirements, and efficiently allocate what's available. They balance available resources with organizational requirements and distribute them in a way that best achieves organizational goals—in combat as well as peacetime. For instance, when a cavalry squadron acting as the division flank guard makes contact, its commander asks for priority of fires. The division commander considers the needs of the squadron but must weigh it against the overall requirements of the current and future missions.

C. Predicting Second- and Third-Order Effects

Because the decisions of organizational leaders have wider-ranging effects than those of direct leaders, organizational leaders must be more sensitive to how their own actions affect the organization's climate. These actions may be conscious, as in the case of orders and policies, or unconscious, such as requirements for routine or unscheduled reports and meetings. The ability to discern and predict second-and third-order effects helps organizational leaders assess the health of the organizational climate and provide constructive feedback to subordinates. It can also result in identifying resource requirements and changes to organizations and procedures.

4. Tactical Skills

Organizational leaders must master the tactical skills of synchronization and orchestration.

Tactical Skills

A. Synchronization
B. Orchestration

Ref: FM 22-100, p. 6-10, fig. 6-4.

A. Synchronization

Synchronization applies at the tactical level of war; orchestration is an operational-level term. Synchronization arranges activities in time, space, and purpose to focus maximum relative military power at a decisive point in space and time. Organizational leaders synchronize battles, each of which may comprise several synchronized engagements. (FM 100-40 discusses synchronization. FM 100-5 discusses orchestration.)

B. Orchestration

Organizational leaders at corps and higher levels orchestrate by applying the complementary and reinforcing effects of all military and nonmilitary assets to overwhelm opponents at one or more decisive points. Both synchronization and orchestration require leaders to put together technical, interpersonal, and conceptual skills and apply them to Warfighting tasks.

Tactical skill for direct leaders involves employing individuals and teams of company size and smaller. In contrast, tactical skill for organizational leaders entails employing units of battalion size and larger. Organizational leaders get divisions, brigades, and battalions to the right place, at the right time, and in the right combination to fight and win battles and engagements. (FM 100-40 discusses battles and engagements.) They project the effects of their decisions further out—in time and distance—than do direct leaders.

The operational skill of orchestrating a series of tactical events is also more demanding and far-reaching. Time horizons are longer. Effects take more time to unfold. Decision sets are more intricate.

Organizational leaders know doctrine, tactics, techniques, and procedures. Their refined tactical skills allow them to understand, integrate, and synchronize the activities of systems, bringing all resources and systems to bear on war fighting tasks.

Organizational Leadership Actions

Actions by organizational leaders have far greater consequences for more people over a longer time than those of direct leaders. Because the connections between action and effect are sometimes more remote and difficult to see, organizational leaders spend more time thinking about what they're doing and how they're doing it than direct leaders do. When organizational leaders act, they must translate their intent into action through the larger number of people working for them.

1. Influencing Actions

Influencing is achieved through communicating, decision making, and motivating. At the organizational level, influencing means not only getting the order or concept out; it means marshaling the activities of the staff and subordinate leaders to move towards the organization's objective. Influencing involves continuing to reinforce the intent and concept, continually acquiring and assessing available feedback, and inspiring subordinates with the leader's own presence and encouragement.

The chain of command provides the initial tool for getting the word out from, and returning feedback to, the commander. In training, commanders must constantly improve its functioning. They must stress it in training situations, pushing it to the point of failure. Combat training centers (CTCs) offer tremendous opportunities to exercise and assess the chain of command in their communicating and monitoring tasks. Programs for officer and NCO professional development based on either terrain walks or seminars can reinforce chain of command functioning. Checking organizational functions daily ("leading by walking around") can reveal whether the commander's intent is getting to the lowest level.

Communication becomes more complex for organizational leaders because of their increased span of control and separation from elements actually executing the mission. Whatever organizational leaders ask for, explicitly or implicitly, causes ripples throughout the organization. Therefore, they must consider how subordinates might interpret their wishes. Directives and actions must be clear and issued in a manner that discourages overreaction. The installation commander who remarks out loud about bland walls may cause an entire organization's soldiers to paint all weekend (it has happened).

Influencing Actions

**A. Communicating
B. Decision Making
C. Motivating**

Ref: FM 22-100, p. 6-12, fig. 6-5.

A. Communicating

Ironically, organizational leaders' face-to-face communication must be more powerful, more focused, and more unequivocal than direct leaders' communication. Because organizational leaders move quickly from one project to another and one part of the organization to the other, they must be careful that the right message goes out the first time. Poor communication can have tremendously negative consequences.

(1) Know Yourself

Even before assuming an organizational, leadership position, leaders must assess themselves, understand their strengths and weaknesses, and commit to an appropriate leadership philosophy. Organizational leaders must realize that some techniques that worked in direct-level positions may no longer work at the organizational level. They must resist the temptation to revert to their old role and thus preempt their subordinates by making decisions for them.

That said, personal qualities that contributed to their previous success are still important for organizational leaders. They must be themselves. They must know their biases, frustrations, and desires and try to keep these factors from negatively influencing their communication. It's not enough to be careful about what they say. Nonverbal communication is so powerful that organizational leaders need to be aware of personal mannerisms, behavioral quirks, and demeanor that reinforce or contradict a spoken message.

(2) Know the Purpose

Organizational leaders know themselves, the mission, and the message. They owe it to their organization and their people to share as much as possible. People have to know what to do and why. At the most basic level, communication provides the primary way that organizational leaders show they care. If subordinates are to succeed and the organization is to move forward, then the organizational leader must work hard at maintaining positive communication. Encouraging open dialogue, actively listening to all perspectives, and ensuring that subordinate leaders and staffs can have a forthright, open, and honest voice in the organization without fear of negative consequences greatly fosters communication at all levels. Organizational leaders who communicate openly and genuinely reinforce team values, send a message of trust to subordinates, and benefit from subordinates' good ideas.

(3) Know the Environment

Before organizational leaders can effectively communicate, they must assess the environment—people, events, and systems— and tailor their message to the target audience. Organizational leaders constantly communicate by persuading and conveying intent, standards, goals, and priorities at four levels within the Army: their people, their own and higher staffs, their subordinate leaders and commanders, and their superiors. They may have to repeat the message to different audiences and retune it for different echelons, but only leaders can reinforce their true intent.

(4) Know the Boss

Working to communicate consistently with the boss is especially important for organizational leaders. Organizational leaders have to figure out how to reach the boss. They must assess how the boss communicates and how the boss receives information. For some leaders, direct and personal contact is best; others may be more comfortable with weekly meetings, e-mail, or letters. Knowing the boss's intent, priorities, and thought processes greatly enhances organizational success. An organizational leader who communicates well with the boss minimizes friction between the organization and the higher headquarters and improves the overall organizational climate.

(5) Know the Subordinates

The mere presence of an organizational leader somewhere communicates the leader's character and what the leader values. The organizational leader who hurries through a talk about caring for subordinates, then passes up an opportunity to speak face-to-face with some soldiers, does more than negate the message; he undercuts whatever trust his subordinates may have had.

(6) Know the Staff

Organizational leaders must understand what's going on within their own and the next-higher echelon staff. Networking allows them to improve communication and mission accomplishment by giving them a better understanding of the overall environment. Informed staffs can then turn policies, plans, and programs into realities.

(7) Know the Best Method

To disseminate information accurately and rapidly, organizational leaders must also develop an effective communications network. Some of these networks—such as the chain of command, the family support network, the NCO support channel, and staff relationships— simply need to be recognized and exploited. Other informal chains must be developed. Different actions may require different networks.

The more adept organizational leaders become in recognizing, establishing, and using these networks, the more successful the outcome, especially as they become comfortable using a wider range of communications forums. Memorandums, notes, and e-mail as well as formal and informal meetings, interactions, and publications are tools of an effective communicator. Organizational leaders must know the audiences these methods reach and use them accordingly.

B. Decision Making

Organizational leaders are far more likely than direct leaders to be required to make decisions with incomplete information. They determine whether they have to decide at all, which decisions to make themselves, and which ones to push down to lower levels. To determine the right course of action, they consider possible second- and third-order effects and think far-ther into the future—months, or even years, out in the case of some directorates.

During operations, the pace and stress of action increase over those of training. Organizational leaders use the MDMP to make tactical decisions; however, they must add their conceptual skill of systems understanding to their knowledge of tactics when considering courses of action. Organizational leaders may be tempted—because of pressure, the threat, fear, or fatigue—to abandon sound decision making by reacting to short-term demands. The same impulses may result in focusing too narrowly on specific events and losing their sense of time and timing. But there's no reason for organizational leaders to abandon proven decision-making processes in crises, although they shouldn't hesitate to modify a process to fit the situation. In combat, success comes from creative, flexible decision making by leaders who quickly analyze a problem, anticipate enemy actions, and rapidly execute their decisions. Leaders who delay or attempt to avoid a decision may cause unnecessary casualties and even mission failure.

Effective and timely decision making— both the commander's and subordinates'— is crucial to success. As part of decision making, organizational leaders establish responsibility and accountability among their subordinates. They delegate decision making authority as far as it will go, empowering and encouraging subordinates to make decisions that affect their areas of responsibility or to further delegate that authority to their own subordinates.

Effective organizational leaders encourage initiative and risk-taking. They remember that they are training leaders and soldiers; the goal is a better-trained team, not some ideal outcome. When necessary, they support subordinates' bad decisions, but only those made attempting to follow the commander's intent. Failing through want of experience or luck is forgivable. Negligence, indecision, or attempts to take an easy route should never be tolerated.

Coping with uncertainty is normal for all leaders, increasingly so for organizational leaders. Given today's information technology, the dangerous temptation to wait for all available information before making a decision will persist. Even though this same technology may also bring the unwanted attention of a superior, leaders should not allow it to unduly influence their decisions. Organizational leaders are where they are because of their experience, intuition, initiative, and judgment. Events move quickly, and it's more important for decisive organizational leaders to recognize and seize opportunities, thereby creating success, than to wait for all the facts and risk failure.

In the end, leaders bear ultimate responsibility for their organizations' success or failure. If the mission fails, they can't lay the blame elsewhere but must take full responsibility. If the mission succeeds, good leaders give credit to their subordinates. While organizational leaders can't ensure success by being all-knowing or present everywhere, they can assert themselves throughout the organization by being decisive in times of crisis and quick to seize opportunities. In combat, leaders take advantage of fleeting windows of opportunity: they see challenges rather than obstacles; they seek solutions rather than excuses; they fight through uncertainty to victory.

C. Motivating

Interpersonal skills involved in creating and sustaining ethical and supportive climates are required at the organizational as well as the direct leadership level. The organizational, unit, or command climate describes the environment in which subordinates work. While direct leaders are responsible for their organizations' climate, their efforts are constrained (or reinforced) by the larger organization's climate. Organizational leaders shape that larger environment. Their primary motivational responsibility is to establish and maintain the climate of their entire organization.

Disciplined organizations evolve within a positive organizational climate. An organization's climate springs from its leader's attitudes, actions, and priorities. Organizational leaders set the tone most powerfully through a personal example that brings Army values to life. Upon assuming an organizational leadership position, a leader determines the organizational climate by assessing the organization from the bottom up. Once this assessment is complete, the leader can provide the guidance and focus required to move the organizational climate to the desired end state.

A climate that promotes Army values and fosters the warrior ethos encourages learning and promotes creative performance. The foundation for a positive organizational climate is a healthy ethical climate, but that alone is insufficient. Characteristics of successful organizational climates include a clear, widely known intent; well-trained and confident soldiers; disciplined, cohesive teams; and trusted, competent leadership.

To create such a climate, organizational leaders recognize mistakes as opportunities to learn, create cohesive teams, and reward leaders of character and competence. Organizational leaders value honest feedback and constantly use all available means to maintain a feel for the environment. Staff members who may be good sources for straightforward feedback may include equal opportunity advisors and chaplains. Methods may include town hall meetings, surveys, and councils. And of course, personal observation—getting out and talking to DA civilians, soldiers, and family members— brings organizational leaders face-to-face with the people affected by their decisions and policies. Organizational leaders' consistent, sincere effort to see what's really going on and fix things that are not working right can result in mutual respect throughout their organizations. They must know the intricacies of the job, trust their people, develop trust among them, and support their subordinates.

2. Operating Actions

Organizational leaders see, decide, and act as they perform the operating actions. They emphasize teamwork and cooperation over competition. They provide their intent so subordinates can accomplish the mission, no matter what happens to the original plan. Because organizational leaders primarily work through subordinates, empowerment and delegation are indispensable. As a result of communicating with subordinates, listening to their responses, and obtaining feedback from their assessments, organizational leaders are better equipped to make decisions.

A. Planning and Preparing
B. Executing
C. Assessing

Ref: FM 22-100, p. 6-18, fig. 6-6.

A. Systems Planning and Preparing

Planning, getting ready for the future by laying out how leaders aim to turn their intent into reality, is something leaders do every day and something the Army does very well. However, organizational leaders plan for the systems that support training and operations as well as for the actual training event or operation. Systems planning involves seven steps:

(1) Establish Intent

The first step in systems planning is for the organizational leader to have a clear intent for what he wants the organization to be. What will it look like at some future point? Spending extra time visualizing the end state up front is more important than quickly jumping into the mechanics of planning. Obviously, the actual mission is critical in determining this end state. The organizational leader's intent should be announced at the earliest practicable time after it has been formulated so the staff and subordinate commanders can have maximum time to plan. For a division, the intent might be—

- The best infantry division in the world
- Supported by the finest installation in the Army
- Trained and ready to deploy anywhere in the world to fight and win
- But flexible enough to accomplish any other mission the nation asks us to perform
- A values-based organization that takes care of its soldiers, DA civilians, and families

Organizational leaders must determine how this intent affects the various systems for which they are responsible. By their actions and those of their subordinates and by using their presence to be heard, organizational leaders bring meaning for their intent to their people.

(2) Set Goals

Once they have established their intent, organizational leaders, with the help of their team of subordinate leaders and staffs, set specific goals for their organizations. Goals frame the organizational leader's intent. For instance, the goal "Improve fire control and killing power" could support that part of the intent that states the division will be "trained and ready to deploy anywhere in the world to fight and win." Organizational leaders are personally involved in setting goals and priorities to execute their intent and are aware that unrealistic goals punish subordinates.

(3) Determine Objectives

In the third step, organizational leaders establish objectives that are specific and measurable. For example, an objective that supports the goal of improving fire control and killing power could be "Fifty percent of the force must fire expert on their personal weapons." Establishing objectives is difficult because the process requires making precise calls from a wide variety of options. Since time and resources are limited, organizational leaders make choices about what can and cannot be accomplished. They check key system nodes to monitor subsystem functions.

(4) Determine Tasks

The fourth step involves determining the measurable, concrete steps that must be taken on the way to the objective. For example, the commander of a forward-stationed division might ensure family readiness by ordering that any newly arriving soldier with a family may not be deployed without having a vehicle in country and household goods delivered.

(5) Establish Priorities

The fifth step is to establish a priority for the tasks. This crucial step lets subordinates know how to spend one of their most critical resources: time.

(6) Prepare

Though organizational leaders have more complex missions than direct leaders, they also have more assets: a staff and additional subordinate leaders, specialists, and equipment allow their preparation to be diverse and complete. Direct leaders prepare by getting individuals moving in the right direction; organizational leaders take a step back and check to make sure the systems necessary to support the mission are in place and functioning correctly.

(7) Follow Up

The final step in systems planning is to follow up: Does the team understand the tasks? Is the team taking the necessary actions to complete them? Check the chain of command again: does everyone have the word? Organizational leader involvement in this follow up validates the priorities and demonstrates that the leader is serious about seeing the mission completed. Organizational leaders who fail to follow up send a message that the priorities are not really that important and that their orders are not really binding.

Keeping their intent in mind, organizational leaders fight distracters, make time to reflect, and seek to work more efficiently. Despite the pressure of too much to do in too little time, they keep their sense of humor and help those around them do the same.

The Creative Staff Process

The size and complexity of the organizations led by organizational leaders requires well-trained, competent staffs. Training these staffs is a major responsibility of organizational leaders. The chief of staff or executive officer is the organizational leader's right hand in that effort.

Building a creative, thinking staff requires the commander's time, maturity, wisdom, and patience. Although managing information is important, the organizational leader needs to invest in both quality people and in training them to think rather than just process information. Several factors contribute to building a creative, thinking staff.

The Right People

A high-performing staff starts with putting the right people in the right places. Organizational leaders are limited to their organization's resources, but have many choices about how to use them. They assemble, from throughout their organizations, people who think creatively, possess a vast array of technical skills, are trained to solve problems, and can work together. They take the time to evaluate the staff and implement a training program to improve it as a whole. They avoid micromanaging the staff, instead trusting and empowering it to think creatively and provide answers.

The Chief of Staff

The staff needs its own leader to take charge—someone who can focus it, work with it, inspire it, and move it to decisive action in the absence of the commander. The sections of the staff work as equals, yet without superb leadership they won't perform exceptionally. To make a staff a true team, an empowered deputy must be worthy of the staff and have its respect. The chief of staff must have the courage to anticipate and demand the best possible quality. On the other hand, the chief must take care of the hardworking people who make up the staff and create an environment that fosters individual initiative and develops potential. (FM 100-34 discusses the role of the chief of staff.)

Challenging Problems

A staff constantly needs challenging problems to solve if it's to build the attitude that it can overcome any obstacle. Tackling problems with restricted time and resources improves the staff members' confidence and proficiency, as long as they get an opportunity to celebrate successes and to recharge their batteries. Great confidence comes from training under conditions more strenuous than they would likely face otherwise.

Clear Guidance

The commander constantly shares thoughts and guidance with the staff. Well-trained staffs can then synthesize data according to those guidelines. Computers, because of their ability to handle large amounts of data, are useful analytical tools, but they can do only limited, low-order synthesis. There's no substitute for a clear commander's intent, clearly understood by every member of the staff.

B. Executing

Planning and preparation for branches and sequels of a plan and contingencies for future operations may continue, even during execution. However, execution is the purpose for which the other operating actions occur; at some point, the organizational leader commits to action, spurs his organization forward, and sees the job through to the end. (FM 100-34 and FM 101-5 discuss branches and sequels.)

In combat, organizational leaders integrate and synchronize all available elements of the combined arms team, empower subordinates, and assign tasks to accomplish the mission. But the essence of war fighting for organizational leaders is their will. They must persevere despite limitations, setbacks, physical exhaustion, and declining mental and emotional reserves. They then directly and indirectly energize their units—commanders and soldiers—to push through confusion and hardship to victory.

Whether they're officers, NCOs, or DA civilians, the ultimate responsibility of organizational-level leaders is to accomplish the mission. To this end, they must mass the effects of available forces on the battlefield, to include supporting assets from other services. The process starts before the fight as leaders align forces, resources, training, and other supporting systems.

(1) Combined Arms and Joint Warfighting

Brigades and battalions usually conduct single-service operations supported by assets from other services. In contrast, the large areas of responsibility in which divisions and corps operate make division and corps fights joint by nature. Joint task forces (JTFs) are also organizational-level formations. Therefore, organizational leaders and their staffs at division-level and higher must understand joint procedures and concerns at least as well as they understand Army procedures and concerns. In addition, it's not unusual for a corps to control forces of another nation; divisions do also, but not as frequently. This means that corps and division headquarters include liaison officers from other nations. In some cases, these staffs may have members of other nations permanently assigned: such a staff is truly multinational.

Today's operations present all Army leaders—but particularly organizational leaders—with a nonlinear, dynamic environment ranging the full spectrum of continuous operations. These dispersed conditions create an information-intense environment that challenges leaders to synchronize their efforts with nonmilitary and often nongovernmental agencies.

(2) Empowering

To increase the effects of their will, organizational leaders must encourage initiative in their subordinates. Although unity of command is a principle of war, at some level a single leader alone can no longer control all elements of an organization and personally direct the accomplishment of every aspect of its mission. As leaders approach the brigade or directorate level, hard work and force of personality alone cannot carry the organization. Effective organizational leaders delegate authority and support their subordinates' decisions, while holding subordinates accountable for their actions.

Delegating successfully involves convincing subordinates that they're empowered, that they indeed have the freedom to act independently. Empowered subordinates have, and know they have, more than the responsibility to get the job done. They have the authority to operate in the way they see fit and are limited only by the leader's intent.

To do that, the organizational leader gives subordinates the mission, motivates them, and lets them go. Subordinates know that the boss trusts them to make the right things happen; this security motivates them, in turn, to lead their people with determination. They know the boss will underwrite honest mistakes, well-intentioned mistakes—not stupid, careless, or repeated ones. So for the boss, empowering subordinates means building the systems and establishing the climate that gives subordinates the rein to do the job within the bounds of acceptable risk. It means setting organizational objectives and delegating tasks to ensure parallel, synchronized progress.

C. Assessing

The ability to assess a situation accurately and reliably—a critical tool in the leader's arsenal—requires instinct and intuition based on experience and learning. It also requires a feel for the reliability and validity of information and its sources. Organizational assessment is necessary to determine organizational weaknesses and preempt mishaps. Accurately determining causes is essential to training management, developing subordinate leadership, and process improvement.

There are several different ways to gather information: asking subordinates questions to find out if the word is getting to them, meeting people, and checking for synchronized plans are a few. Assessing may also involve delving into the electronic databases upon which situational understanding depends. Assessment techniques are more than measurement tools; in fact, the way a leader assesses something can influence the process being assessed. The techniques used may produce high quality, useful feedback; however, in a dysfunctional command climate, they can backfire and send the wrong message about priorities.

A leader's preconceived notions and opinions (such as "technology undermines basic skills" or "technology is the answer") can interfere with objective analysis. It's also possible to be too analytical, especially with limited amounts of information and time. Therefore, when analyzing information, organizational leaders guard against dogmatism, impatience, or overconfidence that may bias their analysis.

The first step in designing an assessment system is to determine the purpose of the assessment. While purposes vary, most fall into one of the following categories:

- Evaluate progress toward organizational goals (using an emergency deployment readiness exercise to check unit readiness or monitoring progress of units through stages of reception, staging, onward movement, and integration)
- Evaluate the efficiency of a system, that is, the ratio of the resources expended to the results gained (comparing the amount of time spent performing maintenance to the organization's readiness rate)
- Evaluate the effectiveness of a system, that is, the quality of the results it produces (analyzing the variation in Bradley gunnery scores)
- Compare the relative efficiency or effectiveness against standards
- Compare the behavior of individuals in a group with the prescribed standards (APFT or gunnery scores)
- Evaluate systems supporting the organization (following up "no pay dues" to see what the NCO support channel did about them)

Organizational leaders consider the direct and indirect costs of assessing. Objective costs include the manpower required to design and administer the system and to collect, analyze, and report the data. Costs may also include machine-processing times and expenses related to communicating the data. Subjective costs include possible confusion regarding organizational priorities and philosophies, misperceptions regarding trust and decentralization, fears over unfair use of collected data, and the energy expended to collect and refine the data.

3. Improving Actions

Improving actions are what all leaders do today to make their organization and subordinates better tomorrow, next month, next year, five years from now. The responsibility for how the Army fights the next war lies with today's leaders; the work to improve the organization in the long term never ends. Leaders teaching subordinates to do the leader's job in combat is the hallmark of the profession of arms.

The payoff for improving actions might not be evident for years. In fact, leaders at all levels may never see the benefit of developing subordinates, since those subordinates go on to work for someone else. But this doesn't stop them from taking pride in their subordinates' development and performance; a subordinate's success is a great measure of a leader's success. Further, it's often difficult to draw a cause-and-effect line from what leaders do today to how it pays off tomorrow. Precisely because of these difficulties, organizational leaders ensure the goals they establish include improving people and organizations. They also make sure they communicate this to their subordinates.

Improving Actions

A. Developing
B. Building
C. Learning

Ref: FM 22-100, p. 6-25, fig. 6-7.

A. Developing

Just as leadership begins at the top, so does developing. Organizational leaders keep a focus on where the organization needs to go and what all leaders must be capable of accomplishing. They continually develop themselves and mentor their subordinate leaders. Leaders search for and take advantage of opportunities to mentor their subordinates. At the organizational level, commanders ensure that systems and conditions are in place for the mentoring of all organizational members.

Effective organizational leaders grow leaders at all levels of their organization. Just as they prepare their units for in-stride breaches, for example, they combine existing opportunities into a coherent plan for leadership development. Leaders get much of their development when they practice what they've learned and receive straightforward feedback in rigorously honest AARs. Feedback also comes from self-assessments as well as from peers, subordinates, and supervisors.

Organizational leaders design and integrate leader development programs into everyday training. They aim to capture learning in common duties, ensure timely feedback, and allow reflection and analysis. As Frederick the Great said, "What good is experience if you do not reflect?" Simply scheduling officer and NCO professional development sessions isn't enough for genuine, lasting leader development. Letting "operating" overwhelm "improving" threatens the future.

Organizational leaders assess their organizations to determine organization-specific developmental needs. They analyze their mission, equipment, and long-term schedule as well as the experience and competence of their subordinate leaders to determine leadership requirements. In addition to preparing their immediate subordinates to take their place, organizational leaders must also prepare subordinate leaders selected for specific duties to actually execute them.

Based on their assessment, organizational leaders define and clearly articulate their goals and objectives for leadership development within the organization. They create program goals and objectives to support their focus as well as to communicate specific responsibilities for subordinate leaders. These subordinate leaders help bring leadership development to life through constant mentoring and experiential learning opportunities. Leadership development is an important responsibility shared by leaders at every level. It becomes their greatest contribution—their legacy.

B. Building
(1) Building Combat Power

Emphasis on winning can't waver during training, deploying, and fighting. By developing the right systems and formulating appropriate contingency plans, organizational leaders ensure that the organization is prepared for a variety of conditions and uncertainties. In wartime, building combat power derives from task organization, resourcing, and preparing for execution while still meeting the human needs of the organization. Commanders must preserve and recycle organizational energy throughout the campaign. In peacetime, the main component of potential combat power is embedded collective skill and organizational readiness stemming from hard, continuous, and challenging training to standard.

(2) Building Teams

Note: See chapter 6 for more information on building teams.

Organizational leaders rely on others to follow and execute their intent. Turning a battlefield vision or training goals into reality takes the combined efforts of many teams inside and outside of the leader's organization. Organizational leaders build solid, effective teams by developing and training them and sustain those teams by creating healthy organizational climates.

Organizational leaders work consistently to create individual and team ownership of organizational goals. By knowing their subordinates—their aspirations, fears, and concerns—organizational leaders can ensure their subordinate organizations and leaders work together. Taking time to allow subordinates to develop ways to meet organizational missions fosters ownership of a plan. The FM 25-100 training management process, in which subordinate organizations define supporting tasks and suggest the training required to gain and maintain proficiency, is an example of a process that encourages collective investment in training. That investment leads to a commitment that not only supports execution but also reduces the chances of internal conflict.

Subordinates work hard and fight tenaciously when they're well-trained and feel they're part of a good team. Collective confidence comes from winning under challenging and stressful conditions. People's sense of belonging comes from technical and tactical proficiency—as individuals and then collectively as a team—and the confidence they have in their peers and their leaders. As cohesive teams combine into a network, a team of teams, organizations work in harness with those on the left and right to fight as a whole. The balance among three good battalions is more important than having a single outstanding one. Following that philosophy necessarily affects resource allocation and task assignment.

C. Learning

Organizational leaders create an environment that supports people within their organizations learning from their own experiences and the experiences of others. How leaders react to failure and encourage success now is critical to reaching excellence in the future. Subordinates who feel they need to hide mistakes deprive others of valuable lessons. Organizational leaders set the tone for this honest sharing of experiences by acknowledging that not all experiences (even their own) are successful. They encourage subordinates to examine their experiences, and make it easy for them to share what they learn.

Learning is continuous and occurs throughout an organization: someone is always experiencing something from which a lesson can be drawn. For this reason, organizational leaders ensure continual teaching at all levels; the organization as a whole shares knowledge and applies relevant lessons. They have systems in place to collect and disseminate those lessons so that individual mistakes become organizational tools. This commitment improves organizational programs, processes, and performances.

III. Strategic Leadership

Ref: FM 22-100, p. 7-1 to 7-28.

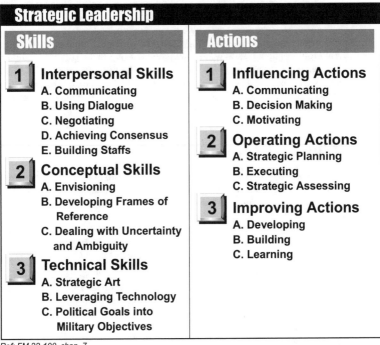

Strategic Leadership

Skills

1 Interpersonal Skills
A. Communicating
B. Using Dialogue
C. Negotiating
D. Achieving Consensus
E. Building Staffs

2 Conceptual Skills
A. Envisioning
B. Developing Frames of Reference
C. Dealing with Uncertainty and Ambiguity

3 Technical Skills
A. Strategic Art
B. Leveraging Technology
C. Political Goals into Military Objectives

Actions

1 Influencing Actions
A. Communicating
B. Decision Making
C. Motivating

2 Operating Actions
A. Strategic Planning
B. Executing
C. Strategic Assessing

3 Improving Actions
A. Developing
B. Building
C. Learning

Ref: FM 22-100, chap. 7.

Strategic leaders are the Army's highest-level thinkers, warfighters, and political-military experts. Some work in an institutional setting within the United States; others work in strategic regions around the world. They simultaneously sustain the Army's culture, envision the future, convey that vision to a wide audience, and personally lead change. Strategic leaders look at the environment outside the Army today to understand the context for the institution's future role. They also use their knowledge of the current force to anchor their vision in reality.

Strategic leadership requires significantly different techniques in both scope and skill from direct and organizational leadership. In an environment of extreme uncertainty, complexity, ambiguity, and volatility, strategic leaders think in multiple time domains and operate flexibly to manage change.

Strategic leaders are not only experts in their own domain—warfighting and leading large military organizations—but also are astute in the departmental and political environments of the nation's decision-making process. They're expected to deal competently with the public sector, the executive branch, and the legislature. The complex national security environment requires an in-depth knowledge of the political, economic, informational, and military elements of national power as well as the interrelationship among them.

Because strategic leaders implement the National Military Strategy, they deal with the elements that shape that strategy. The most important of these are Presidential Decision Memorandums, Department of State Policies, the will of the American people, US national security interests, and the collective strategies—theater and functional—of the combatant commanders (CINCs). Strategic leaders operate in intricate networks of competing constituencies and cooperate in endeavors extending beyond their establishments. As institutional leaders, they represent their organizations to soldiers, DA civilians, citizens, statesmen, and the media, as well as to other services and nations. Communicating effectively with these different audiences is vital to the organization's success.

While direct and organizational leaders have a short-term focus, strategic leaders have a "future focus." Strategic leaders spend much of their time looking toward the mid-term and positioning their establishments for long-term success, even as they contend with immediate issues. With that perspective, strategic leaders seldom see the whole life span of their ideas; initiatives at this level may take years to come to fruition. Strategic leaders think, therefore, in terms of strategic systems that will operate over extended time periods.

Strategic Leadership Skills

The values and attributes demanded of Army leaders are the same at all leadership levels. Strategic leaders live by Army values and set the example just as much as direct and organizational leaders, but they face additional challenges. Strategic leaders affect the culture of the entire Army and may find themselves involved in political decision making at the highest national or even global levels. Therefore, nearly any task strategic leaders set out to accomplish requires more coordination, takes longer, has a wider impact, and produces longer-term effects than a similar organizatvel task.al-le

Strategic leaders understand, embody, and execute values-based leadership. The political and long-term nature of their decisions doesn't release strategic leaders from the current demands of training, readiness, and unforeseen crises; they are responsible to continue to work toward the ultimate goals of the force, despite the burden of those events. Army values provide the constant reference for actions in the stressful environment of strategic leaders. Strategic leaders understand, embody, and execute leadership based on Army values.

1. Interpersonal Skills

Interpersonal Skills

A. Communicating
B. Using Dialogue
C. Negotiating
D. Achieving Consensus
E. Building Staffs

Ref: FM 22-100, p. 7-3, fig. 7-1.

Strategic leaders continue to use interpersonal skills developed as direct and organizational leaders, but the scope, responsibilities, and authority of strategic positions require leaders with unusually sophisticated interpersonal skills. Internally, there are more levels of people to deal with; externally, there are more interactions with outside agencies, with the media, even with foreign governments. Knowing the Army's needs and goals, strategic leaders patiently but tenaciously labor to convince the proper people about what the Army must have and become.

A. Communicating

Communication at the strategic level is complicated by the wide array of staff, functional, and operational components interacting with each other and with external agencies. These complex relationships require strategic leaders to employ comprehensive communications skills as they represent their organizations. One of the most prominent differences between strategic leaders and leaders at other levels is the greater importance of symbolic communication. The example strategic leaders set, their decisions, and their actions have meaning beyond their immediate consequences to a much greater extent than those of direct and organizational leaders.

Thus, strategic leaders identify those actions that send messages. Then they use their positions to send the desired messages to their organizations and ensure that the right audiences hear them. The messages strategic leaders send set the example in the largest sense. For instance, messages that support traditions, Army values, or a particular program indicate the strategic leader's priorities.

Thus, strategic leaders communicate not only to the organization but also to a large external audience that includes the political leadership, media, and the American people. To influence those audiences, strategic leaders seek to convey integrity and win trust.

Strategic leaders commit to a few common, powerful, and consistent messages and repeat them over and over in different forms and settings. They devise a communications campaign plan, written or conceptual, that outlines how to deal with each target group. When preparing to address a specific audience, they determine its composition and agenda so they know how best to reach its members. Finding some apparent success with the medium, frequency, and words of the message, strategic leaders determine the best way to measure the message's effectiveness and continually scan and assess the environment to make sure that the message is going to all the right groups.

B. Using Dialogue

One of the forms of communication that strategic leaders use to persuade individuals, rather than groups, is dialogue. Dialogue is a conversation between two or more people. It requires not only active listening, but carefully considering what's said (and not said), logically assessing it without personal bias, and specifying issues that are not understood or don't make sense within the strategic leader's frame of reference. By using dialogue to thoroughly exchange points of view, assumptions, and concepts, strategic leaders gather information, clarify issues, and enlist support of subordinates and peers.

C. Negotiating

Many relationships between strategic-level organizations are lateral and without clear subordination. Often, strategic leaders rely heavily on negotiating skills to obtain the cooperation and support necessary to accomplish a mission or meet the command's needs. For example, commanders of the national contingents that made up the North Atlantic Treaty Organization (NATO) implementation force (IFOR) sent to Bosnia to support the 1995 Dayton peace accords all had limitations imposed on the extent of their participation. In addition, they all had direct lines to their home governments, which they used when they believed IFOR commanders exceeded those limits. NATO strategic leaders had to negotiate some actions that ordinarily would have required only issuing orders. They often had to interpret a requirement to the satisfaction of one or more foreign governments.

Successful negotiation requires a range of interpersonal skills. Good negotiators are also able to visualize several possible end states while maintaining a clear idea of the best end state from the command's perspective. One of the most important skills is the ability to stand firm on nonnegotiable points while simultaneously communicating respect for other participants and their negotiating limits. In international forums, firmness and respect demonstrate that the negotiator knows and understands US interests. That understanding can help the negotiator persuade others of the validity of US interests and convince others that the United States understands and respects the interests of other states.

A good negotiator is particularly skilled in active listening. Other essential personal characteristics include perceptiveness and objectivity. Negotiators must be able to diagnose unspoken agendas and detach themselves from the negotiation process. Successful negotiating involves communicating a clear position on all issues while still conveying willingness to bargain on negotiable issues, recognizing what's acceptable to all concerned, and achieving a compromise that meets the needs of all participants to the greatest extent possible.

D. Achieving Consensus

Strategic leaders are skilled at reaching consensus and building and sustaining coalitions. They may apply these skills to tasks as diverse as designing combatant commands, JTFs, and policy working groups or determining the direction of a major command or the Army as an institution. Strategic leaders routinely weld people together for missions lasting from months to years. Using peer leadership rather than strict position authority, strategic leaders oversee progress toward their visualized end state and monitor the health of the relationships necessary to achieve it. Interpersonal contact sets the tone for professional relations: strategic leaders are tactful and discreet.

E. Building Staffs

Until Army leaders reach the highest levels, they cannot staff positions and projects as they prefer. Strategic leaders have not only the authority but also the responsibility to pick the best people for their staffs. They seek to put the right people in the right places, balancing strengths and weaknesses for the good of the nation. They mold staffs able to package concise, unbiased information and build networks across organizational lines. Strategic leaders make so many wide-ranging, interrelated decisions that they must have imaginative staff members who know the environment, foresee consequences of various courses of action, and identify crucial information accordingly.

With their understanding of the strategic environment and vision for the future, strategic leaders seek to build staffs that compensate for their weaknesses, reinforce their vision, and ensure institutional success. Strategic leaders can't afford to be surrounded by staffs that blindly agree with everything they say. Not only do they avoid surrounding themselves with "yes-men," they also reward staff members for speaking the truth. Strategic leaders encourage their staffs to participate in dialogue with them, discuss alternative points of view, and explore all facts, assumptions, and implications. Such dialogue assists strategic leaders to fully assess all aspects of an issue and helps clarify their intent and guidance.

2. Conceptual Skills

Strategic leaders, more than direct and organizational leaders, draw on their conceptual skills to comprehend national, national security, and theater strategies, operate in the strategic and theater contexts, and improve their vast, complex organizations. The variety and scope of their concerns demand the application of more sophisticated concepts.

Strategic leaders need wisdom—and wisdom isn't just knowledge. They routinely deal with diversity, complexity, ambiguity, change, uncertainty, and conflicting policies. They are responsible for developing well-reasoned positions and providing their views and advice to our nation's highest leaders. For the good of the Army and the nation, strategic leaders seek to determine what's important now and what will be important in the future. They develop the necessary wisdom by freeing themselves to stay in touch with the force and spending time thinking, simply thinking.

Conceptual Skills

A. Envisioning
B. Developing Frames of Reference
C. Dealing with Uncertainty and Ambiguity

Ref: FM 22-100, p. 7-7, fig. 7-2.

A. Envisioning

Strategic leaders design compelling visions for their organizations and inspire a collaborative effort to articulate the vision in detail. They then communicate that vision clearly and use it to create a plan, gain support, and focus subordinates' work. Strategic leaders have the further responsibility of defining for their diverse organizations what counts as success in achieving the vision. They monitor their progress by drawing on personal observations, review and analysis, strategic management plans, and informal discussions with soldiers and DA civilians.

Strategic leaders look realistically at what the future may hold. They consider things they know and things they can anticipate. They incorporate new ideas, new technologies, and new capabilities. The National Security Strategy and National Military Strategy guide strategic leaders as they develop visions for their organizations. From a complicated mixture of ideas, facts, conjecture, and personal experience they create an image of what their organizations need to be.

Once strategic leaders have developed a vision, they create a plan to reach that end state. They consider objectives, courses of action to take the organization there, and resources needed to do the job. The word "vision" implies that strategic leaders create a conceptual model of what they want. Subordinates will be more involved in moving the organization forward if they can "see" what the leader has in mind. And because moving a large organization is often a long haul, subordinates need some sign that they're making progress. Strategic leaders therefore provide intermediate objectives that act as milestones for their subordinates in checking their direction and measuring their progress.

The strategic leader's vision provides the ultimate sense of purpose, direction, and motivation for everyone in the organization. It is at once the starting point for developing specific goals and plans, a yardstick for measuring what the organization accomplishes, and a check on organizational values. Ordinarily, a strategic leader's vision for the organization may have a time horizon of years, or even decades. In combat, the horizon is much closer, but strategic leaders still focus far beyond the immediate actions.

The strategic leader's vision is a goal, something the organization strives for (even though some goals may always be just out of reach). When members understand the vision, they can see it as clearly as the strategic leader can. When they see it as worthwhile and accept it, the vision creates energy, inspiration, commitment, and a sense of belonging.

Strategic leaders set the vision for their entire organization. They seek to keep the vision consistent with the external environment, alliance or coalition goals, the National Security Strategy, and the National Military Strategy. Subordinate leaders align their visions and intent with their strategic leader's vision. A strategic leader's vision may be expressed in everything from small acts to formal, written policy statements.

B. Developing Frames of Reference

All Army leaders build a personal frame of reference from schooling, experience, self-study, and reflection on current events and history. Strategic leaders create a comprehensive frame of reference that encompasses their organization and places it in the strategic environment. To construct a useful frame, strategic leaders are open to new experiences and to comments from others, including subordinates. Strategic leaders are reflective, thoughtful, and unafraid to rethink past experiences and to learn from them. They are comfortable with the abstractions and concepts common in the strategic environment. Moreover, they understand the circumstances surrounding them, their organization, and the nation.

Much like intelligence analysts, strategic leaders look at events and see patterns that others often miss. These leaders are likely to identify and understand a strategic situation and, more important, infer the outcome of interventions or the absence of interventions. A strategic leader's frame of reference helps identify the information most relevant to a strategic situation so that the leader can go to the heart of a matter without being distracted. In the new information environment, that talent is more important than ever. Cosmopolitan strategic leaders, those with comprehensive frames of reference and the wisdom that comes from thought and reflection, are well equipped to deal with events having complex causes and to envision creative solutions.

A well-developed frame of reference also gives strategic leaders a thorough understanding of organizational subsystems and their interacting processes. Cognizant of the relationships among systems, strategic leaders foresee the possible effects on one system of actions in others. Their vision helps them anticipate and avoid problems.

C. Dealing with Uncertainty and Ambiguity

Strategic leaders operate in an environment of increased volatility, uncertainty, complexity, and ambiguity. Change at this level may arrive suddenly and unannounced. As they plan for contingencies, strategic leaders prepare intellectually for a range of uncertain threats and scenarios. Since even great planning and foresight can't predict or influence all future events, strategic leaders work to shape the future on terms they can control, using diplomatic, informational, military, and economic instruments of national power.

Strategic leaders fight complexity by encompassing it. They must be more complex than the situations they face. This means they're able to expand their frame of reference to fit a situation rather than reducing a situation to fit their preconceptions. They don't lose sight of Army values and force capabilities as they focus on national policy. Because of their maturity and wisdom, they tolerate ambiguity, knowing they will never have all the information they want. Instead, they carefully analyze events and decide when to make a decision, realizing that they must innovate and accept some risk. Once they make decisions, strategic leaders then explain them to the Army and the nation, in the process imposing order on the uncertainty and ambiguity of the situation. Strategic leaders not only understand the environment themselves; they also translate their understanding to others.

In addition to demonstrating the flexibility required to handle competing demands, strategic leaders understand complex cause-and-effect relationships and anticipate the second-and third-order effects of their decisions throughout the organization. The highly volatile nature of the strategic environment may tempt them to concentrate on the short term, but strategic leaders don't allow the crisis of the moment absorb them completely. They remain focused on their responsibility to shape an organization or policies that will perform successfully over the next 10 to 20 years. Some second-and third-order effects are desirable; leaders can design and pursue actions to achieve them. For example, strategic leaders who continually send—through their actions—messages of trust to subordinates inspire trust in themselves. The third-order effect may be to enhance subordinates' initiative.

3. Technical Skills

Technical Skills
A. Strategic Art B. Leveraging Technology C. Translating Political Goals into Miltary Objectives

Ref: FM 22-100, p. 7-10, fig. 7-3.

A. Strategic Art

The strategic art, broadly defined, is the skillful formulation, coordination, and application of ends, ways, and means to promote and defend the national interest. Masters of the strategic art competently integrate the three roles performed by the complete strategist: strategic leader, strategic practitioner, and strategic theorist.

Using their understanding of the systems within their own organizations, strategic leaders work through the complexity and uncertainty of the strategic environment and translate abstract concepts into concrete actions. Proficiency in the science of leadership—programs, schedules, and systems, for example—can bring direct or organizational leaders success. For strategic leaders, however, the intangible qualities of leadership draw on their long and varied experience to produce a rare art.

By reconciling political and economic constraints with the Army's needs, strategic leaders navigate to move the force forward using the strategy and budget processes. They spend a great deal of time obtaining and allocating resources and determining conceptual directions, especially those judged critical for future strategic positioning and necessary to prevent readiness shortfalls. They're also charged with overseeing of the Army's responsibilities under Title 10 of the United States Code.

Strategic leaders focus not so much on internal processes as on how the organization fits into the DOD and the international arena: What are the relationships among external organizations? What are the broad political and social systems in which the organization and the Army must operate? Because of the complex reporting and coordinating relationships, strategic leaders fully understand their roles, the boundaries of these roles, and the expectations of other departments and agencies. Understanding those interdependencies outside the Army helps strategic leaders do the right thing for the programs, systems, and people within the Army as well as for the nation.

Theater CINCs, with their service component commanders, seek to shape their environments and accomplish long-term national security policy goals within their theaters. They operate through congressional testimony, creative use of assigned and attached military forces, imaginative bilateral and multilateral programs, treaty obligations, person-to-person contacts with regional leaders, and various joint processes. These actions require strategic leaders to apply the strategic art just as much as does designing and employing force packages to achieve military end states.

B. Leveraging Technology

Leveraging technology—that is, applying technological capabilities to obtain a decisive military advantage—has given strategic leaders advantages in force projection, in command and control, and in the generation of overwhelming combat power. Leveraging technology has also increased the tempo of operations, the speed of maneuver, the precision of firepower, and the pace at which information is processed. Ideally, information technology, in particular, enhances not only communications, but also situational understanding. With all these advantages, of course, comes increasing complexity: it's harder to control large organizations that are moving quickly. Strategic leaders seek to understand emerging military technologies and apply that understanding to resourcing, allocating, and exploiting the many systems under their control.

Emerging combat, combat support, and combat service support technologies bring more than changes to doctrine. Technological change allows organizations to do the things they do now better and faster, but it also enables them to do things that were not possible before. So a part of leveraging technology is envisioning the future capability that could be exploited by developing a technology. Another aspect is rethinking the form the organization ought to take in order to exploit new processes that previously were not available. This is why strategic leaders take time to think "out of the box."

C. Translating Political Goals into Military Objectives

Leveraging technology takes more than understanding; it takes money. Strategic leaders call on their understanding and their knowledge of the budgetary process to determine which combat, combat support, and combat service support technologies will provide the leap-ahead capability commensurate with the cost. Wise Army leaders in the 1970s and 1980s realized that superior night systems and greater standoff ranges could expose fewer Americans to danger yet kill more of the enemy. Those leaders committed money to developing and procuring appropriate weapons systems and equipment. Operation Desert Storm validated these decisions when, for example, M1 tanks destroyed Soviet-style equipment before it could close within its maximum effective range. However strategic leaders are always in the position of balancing budget constraints, technological improvements, and current force readiness against potential threats as they shape the force for the future.

Strategic leaders identify military conditions necessary to satisfy political ends desired by America's civilian leadership. They must synchronize the efforts of the Army with those of the other services and government agencies to attain those conditions and achieve the end state envisioned by America's political leaders. To operate on the world stage, often in conjunction with allies, strategic leaders call on their international perspective and relationships with policy makers in other countries.

Since the end of the Cold War, the international stage has become more confused. Threats to US national security may come from a number of quarters: regional instability, insurgencies, terrorism, and proliferation of weapons of mass destruction to name a few. International drug traffickers and other transnational groups are also potential adversaries. To counter such diverse threats, the nation needs a force flexible enough to execute a wide array of missions, from warfighting to peace operations to humanitarian assistance. And of course, the nation needs strategic leaders with the sound perspective that allows them to understand the nation's political goals in the complex international environment and to shape military objectives appropriate to the various threats.

Strategic Leadership Actions

Operating at the highest levels of the Army, the DOD, and the national security establishment, military and DA civilian strategic leaders face highly complex demands from inside and outside the Army. Constantly changing global conditions challenge their decision-making abilities. Strategic leaders tell the Army story, make long-range decisions, and shape the Army culture to influence the force and its partners inside and outside the United States. They plan for contingencies across the range of military operations and allocate resources to prepare for them, all the while assessing the threat and the force's readiness. Steadily improving the Army, strategic leaders develop their successors, lead changes in the force, and optimize systems and operations. This section addresses the influencing, operating, and improving actions they use.

1. Influencing Actions

Strategic leaders act to influence both their organization and its outside environment. Like direct and organizational leaders, strategic leaders influence through personal example as well as by communicating, making decisions, and motivating.

Because the external environment is diverse and complex, it's sometimes difficult for strategic leaders to identify and influence the origins of factors affecting the organization. This difficulty applies particularly to fast-paced situations like theater campaigns. Strategic leaders meet this challenge by becoming masters of information, influence, and vision.

Strategic leaders also seek to control the information environment, consistent with US law and Army values. Action in this area can range from psychological operations campaigns to managing media relationships. Strategic leaders who know what's happening with present and future requirements, both inside and outside the organization, are in a position to influence events, take advantage of opportunities, and move the organization toward its goals.

Influencing Actions

A. Communicating
B. Decision Making
C. Motivating

Ref: FM 22-100, p. 7-13, fig. 7-4.

A. Communicating

(1) Communicating a Vision

The skill of envisioning is vital to the strategic leader. But forming a vision is pointless unless the leader shares it with a broad audience, gains widespread support, and uses it as a compass to guide the organization. For the vision to provide purpose, direction, and motivation, the strategic leader must personally commit to it, gain commitment from the organization as a whole, and persistently pursue the goals and objectives that will spread the vision throughout the organization and make it a reality

(2) Telling the Army Story

Whether by nuance or overt presentation, strategic leaders vigorously and constantly represent who Army is, what it's doing, and where it's going. The audience is the Army itself as well as the rest of the world. There's an especially powerful responsibility to explain things to the American people, who support their Army with money and lives. Whether working with other branches of government, federal agencies, the media, other militaries, the other services, or their own organizations, strategic leaders rely increasingly on writing and public speaking (conferences and press briefings) to reinforce the Army's central messages. Because so much of this communication is directed at outside agencies, strategic leaders avoid parochial language and remain sensitive to the Army's image.

Strategic leaders of all times have determined and reinforced the message that speaks to the soul of the nation and unifies the force. In 1973 Army leaders at all levels knew about "The Big Five," the weapons systems that would transform the Army (a new tank, an infantry fighting vehicle, an advanced attack helicopter, a new utility helicopter, and an air defense system). Those programs yielded the M1 Abrams, the M2/M3 Bradley, the AH-64 Apache, the UH-60 Blackhawk, and the Patriot. But those initiatives were more than sales pitches for newer hardware; they were linked to concepts about how to fight and win against a massive Soviet-style force. As a result, fielding the new equipment gave physical form to the new ideas being adopted at the same time. Soldiers could see improvements as well as read about them. The synergism of new equipment, new ideas, and good leadership resulted in the Army of Excellence.

A recent example of successfully telling the Army story occurred during Operation Desert Shield. During the deployment phase, strategic leaders decided to get local reporters to the theater of war to report on mobilized reserve component units from their communities. That decision had several effects. The first-order effect was to get the Army story to the citizens of hometown America. That publicity resulted in an unintended second-order effect: a flood of mail that the nation sent to its deployed soldiers. That mail, in turn, produced a third-order effect felt by American soldiers: a new pride in themselves.

B. Strategic Decision Making

Strategic leaders have great conceptual resources; they have a collegial network to share thoughts and plan for the institution's continued success and well being. Even when there's consensual decision making, however, everyone knows who the boss is. Decisions made by strategic leaders—whether CINCs deploying forces or service chiefs initiating budget programs—often result in a major commitment of resources. They're expensive and tough to reverse. Therefore, strategic leaders rely on timely feedback throughout the decision-Army making process in order to avoid making a decision based on inadequate or faulty information. Their purpose, direction, and motivation flow down; information and recommendations surface from below.

Strategic leaders use the processes of the DOD, Joint Staff, and Army strategic planning systems to provide purpose and direction to subordinate leaders. These systems include the Joint Strategic Planning System (JSPS), the Joint Operation Planning and Execution System (JOPES), and the Planning, Programming and Budgeting System (PPBS). However, no matter how many systems are involved and no matter how complex they are, providing motivation remains the province of the individual strategic leader.

C. Motivating

Strategic leaders inspire great effort. To mold morale and motivate the entire Army, strategic leaders cultivate a challenging, supportive, and respectful environment for soldiers and DA civilians to operate in. An institution with a history has a mature, well-established culture—a shared set of values and assumptions that members hold about it. At the same time, large and complex institutions like the Army are diverse; they have many subcultures, such as those that exist in the civilian and reserve components, heavy and light forces, and special operations forces. Gender, ethnic, religious, occupational, and regional differences also define groups within the force.

(1) Culture and Values

The challenge for strategic leaders is to ensure that all these subcultures are part of the larger Army culture and that they all share Army values. Strategic leaders do this by working with the best that each subculture has to offer and ensuring that subcultures don't foster unhealthy competition with each other, outside agencies, or the rest of the Army. Rather, these various subcultures must complement each other and the Army's institutional culture. Strategic leaders appreciate the differences that characterize these subcultures and treat all members of all components with dignity and respect. They're responsible for creating an environment that fosters mutual understanding so that soldiers and DA civilians treat one another as they should.

Like organizational and direct leaders, strategic leaders model character by their actions. Only experience can validate Army values: subordinates will hear of Army values, then look to see if they are being lived around them. If they are, the Army's institutional culture is strengthened; if they are not, the Army's institutional culture begins to weaken. Strategic leaders ensure Army values remain fundamental to the Army's institutional culture.

(2) Culture and Leadership

A healthy culture is a powerful leadership tool strategic leaders use to help them guide their large diverse organizations. Strategic leaders seek to shape the culture to support their vision, accomplish the mission, and improve the organization. A cohesive culture molds the organization's morale, reinforcing an ethical climate built on Army values, especially respect. As leaders initiate changes for long-range improvements, soldiers and DA civilians must feel that they're valued as persons, not just as workers or program supporters.

2. Operating Actions

Operating at the strategic level can involve both short-term and long-term actions. The most agile organizations have standing procedures and policies to take the guesswork out of routine actions and allow leaders to concentrate their imagination and energy on the most difficult tasks. Strategic leaders coordinate their organizations' actions to accomplish near-term missions, often without the benefit of direct guidance. Strategic leaders receive general guidance—frequently from several sources, including the national command authority.

Although they perform many of the same operating actions as organizational and direct leaders, strategic leaders also manage joint, multinational, and interagency relationships. For strategic leaders, planning, preparing, executing, and assessing are nearly continuous, more so than at the other leadership levels, because the larger organizations they lead have continuing missions. In addition, the preparing action takes on a more comprehensive meaning at the strategic leadership level. Leaders at all levels keep one eye on tomorrow. Strategic leaders, to a greater extent than leaders at other levels, must coordinate their organizations' actions, positioning them to accomplish the current mission in a way that will feed seamlessly into the next one. The Army doesn't stop at the end of a field exercise—or even after recovering from a major deployment; there's always another mission about to start and still another one on the drawing board.

Operating Actions

A. Strategic Planning
B. Executing
C. Strategic Assessing

Ref: FM 22-100, p. 7-18, fig. 7-5.

A. Strategic Planning

Strategic-level plans must balance competing demands across the vast structure of the DOD, but the fundamental requirements for strategic-level planning are the same as for direct-and organizational-level planning. At all levels, leaders establish priorities and communicate decisions; however, at the strategic level, the sheer number of players who can influence the organization means that strategic leaders must stay on top of multiple demands. To plan coherently and comprehensively, they look at the mission from other players' points of view. Strategic planning depends heavily on wisely applying interpersonal and conceptual skills. Strategic leaders ask, What will these people want? How will they see things? Have I justified the mission? The interaction among strategic leaders' interpersonal and conceptual skills and their operating actions is highly complex.

B. Executing

(1) Allocating Resources

Because lives are precious and materiel is scarce, strategic leaders make tough decisions about priorities. Their goal is a capable, prepared, and victorious force. In peacetime, strategic leaders decide which programs get funded and consider the implications of those choices. Allocating resources isn't simply a matter of choosing helicopters, tanks, and missiles for the future Army. Strategic resourcing affects how the Army will operate and fight tomorrow. For example, strategic leaders determine how much equipment can be pre-positioned for contingencies without degrading current operational capabilities.

(2) Managing Joint, Interagency, and Multinational Relationships

Strategic leaders oversee the relationship between their organizations, as part of the nation's total defense force, and the national policy apparatus. They use their knowledge of how things work at the national and international levels to influence opinion and build consensus for the organization's missions, gathering support of diverse players to achieve their vision. Among their duties, strategic leaders—

• Provide military counsel in national policy forums
• Interpret national policy guidelines and directions

- Plan and maintain the military capability required to implement national policy
- Present the organization's resource requirements
- Develop strategies to support national objectives
- Bridge the gap between political decisions made as part of national strategy and the individuals and organizations that must carry out those decisions

As part of this last requirement, strategic leaders clarify national policy for subordinates and explain the perspectives that contribute to that national policy. They develop policies reflecting national security objectives and prepare their organizations to respond to missions across the spectrum of military actions.

To operate effectively in a joint or multinational environment, strategic leaders exercise a heightened multiservice and international sensitivity developed over their years of experience. A joint perspective results from shared experiences and interactions with leaders of other services, complemented by the leader's habitual introspection. Similar elements in the international arena inform an international perspective. Combing those perspectives with their own Army and national perspectives, strategic leaders—

- Influence opinions of those outside the Army and help them understand Army needs
- Interpret the outside environment for people on the inside, especially in the formulation of plans and policies

Strategic leaders take the time to learn about their partners' cultures—including political, social and economic aspects—so that they understand how and why the partners think and act as they do. Strategic leaders are also aware that the successful conduct of multinational operations requires a particular sensitivity to the effect that deploying US forces may have on the laws, traditions, and customs of a third country.

(3) Military Actions Across the Spectrum

Since the character of the next war has not been clearly defined for them, today's strategic leaders rely on hints in the international environment to provide information on what sort of force to prepare. Questions they consider include these: Where is the next threat? Will we have allies or contend alone? What will our national and military goals be? What will the exit strategy be? Strategic leaders address the technological, leadership, and moral considerations associated with fighting on an asymmetrical battlefield. They're at the center of the tension between traditional warfare and the newer kinds of multiparty conflict emerging outside the industrialized world. Recent actions like those in Bosnia, Somalia, Haiti, Grenada, and the Persian Gulf suggest the range of possible military contingencies.

C. Strategic Assessing

There are many elements of their environment that strategic leaders must assess. Like leaders at other levels, they must first assess themselves: their leadership style, strengths and weaknesses, and their fields of excellence. They must also understand the present operational environment—to include the will of the American people, expressed in part through law, policy, and their leaders. Finally, strategic leaders must survey the political landscape and the international environment, for these affect the organization and shape the future strategic requirements.

Strategic leaders also cast a wide net to assess their own organizations. They develop performance indicators to signal how well they're communicating to all levels of their commands and how well established systems and processes are balancing the six imperatives. Assessment starts early in each mission and continues through its end. It may include monitoring such diverse areas as resource use, development of subordinates, efficiency, effects of stress and fatigue, morale, and mission accomplishment.

3. Improving Actions

Improving is institutional investment for the long haul, refining the things we do today for a better organization tomorrow. A fundamental goal of strategic leaders is to leave the Army better than they found it. Improving at this level calls for experimentation and innovation; however, because strategic-level organizations are so complex, quantifying the results of changes may be difficult.

Improving the institution and organizations involves an ongoing tradeoff between today and tomorrow. Wisdom and a refined frame of reference are tools to understand what improvement is and what change is needed. Knowing when and what to change is a constant challenge: what traditions should remain stable, and which long-standing methods need to evolve? Strategic leaders set the conditions for long-term success of the organization by developing subordinates, leading change, building the culture and teams, and creating a learning environment.

One technique for the Army as a learning institution is to decentralize the learning and other improving actions to some extent. That technique raises the questions of how to share good ideas across the entire institution and how to incorporate the best ideas into doctrine (thus establishing an Army-wide standard) without discouraging the decentralized learning process that generated the ideas in the first place. Those and other questions face the strategic leaders of the learning organization the Army seeks to become.

Improving Actions
A. Developing
B. Building
C. Learning

Ref: FM 22-100, p. 7-22, fig. 7-6.

A. Developing
(1) Mentoring

Strategic leaders develop subordinates by sharing the benefit of their perspective and experience. People arriving at the Pentagon know how the Army works in the field, but regardless of what they may have read, they don't really know how the institutional Army works. Strategic leaders act as a kind of sponsor by introducing them to the important players and pointing out the important places and activities. But strategic leaders actually become mentors as they, in effect, underwrite the learning, efforts, projects, and ideas of rising leaders. The moral responsibility associated with mentoring is compelling for all leaders; for strategic leaders, the potential significance is enormous.

More than a matter of required forms and sessions, mentoring by strategic leaders means giving the right people an intellectual boost so that they make the leap to operations and thinking at the highest levels. Because those being groomed for strategic leadership positions are among the most talented Army leaders, the manner in which leaders and subordinates interact also changes. Strategic leaders aim not only to pass on knowledge but also to grow wisdom in those they mentor.

(2) Developing Intellectual Capital

What strategic leaders do for individuals they personally mentor, they also seek to provide to the force at large. They invest in the future of the force in several ways. Committing money to programs and projects and investing more time and resources in some actions than others are obvious ways strategic leaders choose what's important. They also value people and ideas as investments in the future. The concepts that shape the thinking of strategic leaders become the intellectual currency of the coming era; the soldiers and DA civilians who develop those ideas become trusted assets themselves. Strategic leaders must choose wisely the ideas that bridge the gap between today and tomorrow and skillfully determine how best to resource important ideas and people.

Strategic leaders make difficult decisions about how much institutional development is enough. They calculate how much time it will take to plant and grow the seeds required for the Army's great leaders and ideas in the future. They balance today's operational requirements with tomorrow's leadership needs to produce programs that develop a core of Army leaders with the required skills and knowledge.

Programs like training with industry, advanced civil schooling, and foreign area officer education complement the training and education available in Army schools and contribute to shaping the people who will shape the Army's future. Strategic leaders develop the institution using Army resources when they are available and those of other services or the public sector when they are not.

After Vietnam the Army's leadership thought investing in officer development so important that new courses were instituted to revitalize professional education for the force. The establishment of the Training and Doctrine Command revived Army doctrine as a central intellectual pillar of the entire service. The Goldwater-Nichols Act of 1986 provided similar attention and invigoration to professional joint education and joint doctrine.

Likewise, there has been a huge investment in and payoff from developing the NCO corps. The Army has the world's finest noncommissioned officers, in part because they get the world's best professional development. The strategic decision to resource a robust NCO education system signaled the Army's investment in developing the whole person—not just the technical skills—of its first-line leaders.

The Army Civilian Training and Education Development System is the Army's program for developing DA civilian leaders. Like the NCO education system, it continues throughout an individual's career. The first course integrates interns into the Army by explaining Army values, culture, customs, and policies. The Leadership Education and Development Course helps prepare leaders for supervisory demands with training in communication, counseling, team building, problem solving, and group development. For organizational managers, the Organizational Leadership for Executives course adds higher-order study on topics such as strategic planning, change management, climate, and culture. DA civilians in the Senior Executive Service have a variety of leadership education options that deal with leadership in both the military and civilian contexts. Together, these programs highlight ways that leadership development of DA civilians parallels that of soldiers.

B. Building
(1) Building Amid Change

The Army has no choice but to face change. It's in a nearly constant state of flux, with new people, new missions, new technologies, new equipment, and new information. At the same time, the Army, inspired by strategic leaders, must innovate and create change. The Army's customs, procedures, hierarchical structure, and sheer size make change especially daunting and stressful.

Nonetheless, the Army must be flexible enough to produce and respond to change, even as it preserves the core of traditions that tie it to the nation, its heritage and its values.

Strategic leaders deal with change by being proactive, not reactive. They anticipate change even as they shield their organizations from unimportant and bothersome influences; they use the "change-drivers" of technology, education, doctrine, equipment, and organization to control the direction and pace of change. Many agencies and corporations have "futures" groups charged with thinking about tomorrow; strategic leaders and their advisory teams are the Army's "futures people."

(2) Leading Change

Strategic leaders lead change by—

- Identifying the force capabilities necessary to accomplish the National Military Strategy
- Assigning strategic and operational missions, including priorities for allocating resources
- Preparing plans for using military forces across the spectrum of operations
- Creating, resourcing, and sustaining organizational systems, including— force modernization programs; requisite personnel and equipment; essential command, control, communications, computers, and intelligence systems
- Developing and improving doctrine and the training methods to support it
- Planning for the second- and third-order effects of change
- Maintaining an effective leader development program and other human resource initiatives

C. Learning

The nation expects military professionals as individuals and the Army as an institution to learn from the experience of others and apply that learning to understanding the present and preparing for the future. Such learning requires both individual and institutional commitments. Each military professional must be committed to self-development, part of which is studying military history and other disciplines related to military operations. The Army as an institution must be committed to conducting technical research, monitoring emerging threats, and developing leaders for the next generation. Strategic leaders, by their example and resourcing decisions, sustain the culture and policies that encourage both the individual and the Army to learn.

Efficient and effective operations require aligning various initiatives so that different factions are not working at cross-purposes. Strategic leaders focus research and development efforts on achieving combined arms success. They deal with questions such as: Can these new systems from various sources communicate with one another? What happens during digitization lapses—what's our residual combat capability? Strategic leaders coordinate time lines and budgets so that compatible systems are fielded together. However, they are also concerned that the force have optimal capability across time; therefore, they prepare plans that integrate new equipment and concepts into the force as they're developed, rather than waiting for all elements of a system to be ready before fielding it. Finally, learning what the force should be means developing the structure, training, and leaders those future systems will support and studying the variety of threats they may face.

Combat-Ready Teams

Ref: FM 22-102, chap 1.

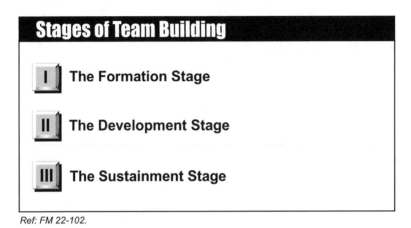

Stages of Team Building

I The Formation Stage

II The Development Stage

III The Sustainment Stage

Ref: FM 22-102.

A. BE Characteristics

The BE of BE-KNOW-DO deals with inner qualities—the heart of the team and its members. These inner qualities are expressed in soldiers' actions. Successful soldier teams reflect a winning spirit and a professional attitude.

1. Spirit

When we try to determine the probable winner of a sports contest, we weigh the participants' strengths and weaknesses. We add them up and normally choose the strongest as the probable winner. But experience shows that this system does not always work. A team, outnumbered and overpowered, can overcome lack of strength and win when it has a strong desire to do so. That strong desire is called spirit—a most critical element of a combat-ready team. Soldiers in a unit with spirit believe in the cause for which they are fighting, they believe in themselves, and they fight for one another. They have a will to win and believe they are winners. They act as one in accomplishing the units' tasks and missions.

Leadership that nurtures and builds this kind of spirit reinforces the pride in service critical for cohesive teams.

2. Professionalism

In effective units prepared for the air-land battlefield, each soldier is a respected professional. Others believe that he can get the job done and can be trusted. Professional soldiers are mature and share the values of their profession and their unit.

Stages of Team Building

Ref: FM 22-100, p. 5-20 to 5-23.

Teams, like individuals, have different personalities. As with individuals, the leader's job isn't to make teams that are clones of one another; the job is to make best use of the peculiar talents of the team, maximize the potential of the unit climate, and motivate aggressive execution.

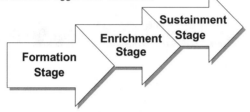

1. Formation Stage

Teams work best when new members are brought on board quickly, when they're made to feel a part of the team. The two steps—reception and orientation— are dramatically different in peace and war. In combat, this sponsorship process can literally mean life or death to new members and to the team.

Reception is the leader's welcome: the orientation begins with meeting other team members, learning the layout of the workplace, learning the schedule and other requirements, and generally getting to know the lay of the land. In combat, leaders may not have time to spend with new members. In this case, new arrivals are often assigned a buddy who will help them get oriented and keep them out of trouble until they learn their way around.

In combat, Army leaders have countless things to worry about; the mental state of new arrivals might seem low on the list. But if those soldiers can't fight, the unit will suffer needless casualties and may fail to complete the mission.

One way to ensure cohesion is to build it during peacetime. Team building begins with receiving new members; you know how important first impressions are when you meet someone new. The same thing is true of teams; the new member's reception and orientation creates that crucial first impression that colors the person's opinion of the team for a long time. A good experience joining the organization will make it easier for the new member to fit in and contribute. Even in peacetime, the way a person is received into an organization can have long-lasting effects—good or bad—on the individual and the team.

	Subordinate Challenges	Leader & Unit / Organization Actions
Generic	• Achieve belonging and acceptance • Set personal & family concerns • Learn about leaders and other members	• Listen to and care for subordinates • Design effective reception and orientation • Communicate • Reward positive contributions • Set example
Soldier Critical	• Face the uncertainty of war • Cope with fear of unknown injury and death • Adjust to sights and sounds of war • Adjust to separation from family and home	• Talk with each soldier • Reassure with calm presence • Communicate vital safety tips • Provide stable situation • Establish buddy system • Assist soldiers to deal with immediate problems

2. Enrichment stage

New teams and new team members gradually move from questioning everything to trusting themselves, their peers, and their leaders. Leaders earn that trust by listening, following up on what they hear, establishing clear lines of authority, and setting standards. By far the most important thing a leader does to strengthen the team is training. Training takes a group of individuals and molds them into a team while preparing them to accomplish their missions. Training occurs during all three team building stages, but is particularly important during enrichment; it's at this point that the team is building collective proficiency.

	Subordinate Challenges	Leader & Unit / Organization Actions
Generic	• Trust leaders & other members • Find close freinds • Learn who is in charge • Accept the way things are done • Adjust to feelings about how things ought to be done • Overcome family-versus-unit conflict	• Trust and encourage trust • Allow growth while keeping control • Identify and channel emerging leaders • Establish clear lines of authority • Establish individual and unit goals • Train as a unit for mission • Build pride through accomplishment • Acquire self-evaluation / self-assessment habits • Be fair and give responsibility
Soldier Critical	• Survive • Demonstrate competence • Become a team member quickly • Learn about the enemy • Learn about the battlefield • Avoid life-threatening mistakes	• Train as a unit for combat • Demonstrate competence • Know the soldiers • Pace subordinate battlefield integration • Provide stable unit climate • Emphasize safety awareness for improved readiness

3. Sustainment stage

When a team reaches this stage, its members think of the team as "their team." They own it, have pride in it, and want the team to succeed. At this stage, team members will do what needs to be done without being told. Every new mission gives the leader a chance to make the bonds even stronger, to challenge the team to reach for new heights. The leader develops his subordinates because they're tomorrow's team leaders. He continues to train the team so that it maintains proficiency in the collective and individual tasks it must perform to accomplish its missions. Finally, the leader works to keep the team going in spite of the stresses and losses of combat.

	Subordinate Challenges	Leader & Unit / Organization Actions
Generic	• Trust others • Share ideas and feelings freely • Assist other team members • Sustain trust and confidence • Share mission and values	• Demonstrate trust • Focus on teamwork, training and maintaining • Respond to subordinate problems • Devise more challenging training • Build pride and spirit through unit sports, social & spiritual activities
Soldier Critical	• Adjust to continuous operations • Cope with casualties • Adjust to enemy actions • Overcome boredom • Avoid rumors • Control fear, anger, despair and panic	• Observe and enforce sleep discipline • Sustain safety awareness • Inform soldiers • Know and deal with soldier's perceptions • Keep soldier's productively busy • Use in-process reviews (IPRs) and after-action reviews (AARs) • Act decisively in face of panic

Combat-Ready Teams

a. Maturity

A mature soldier develops physically, socially, emotionally, and spiritually. Physical fitness and development provide the stamina necessary for sustained action and intense stress. Social maturity provides the willingness to work with others in cohesive teams. Emotional maturity gives stability to deal with the stress of combat. Spiritual maturity gives the soldier hope and purpose to face the dangers and uncertainty of combat. Signs of maturity that are important in combat-ready teams include self-discipline, initiative and judgment, and confidence.

Self-discipline enables clear thinking and reasonable action in the moment of combat with its isolation, high leadership casualties, continuous stress, and need for independent actions. Self-disciplined soldiers realize that success and survival depend on working together, and they are able to undergo extreme hardship to achieve team goals. In peacetime, self-discipline helps the team engage in more difficult training, develop trust more quickly, and handle more tasks with ease.

Initiative and Judgment are essential in both peacetime and combat. On the battlefield soldiers need initiative to operate within the intent of their commander and to move decisively in accomplishing their mission. This is true whether "combat action" involves firing at the enemy, performing maintenance and repairs on combat equipment, or driving a truck that takes essential food, ammunition, or fuel to the battle. However, initiative does not mean "do something even if it's wrong." It must be tempered by good judgment-the ability to size up a situation quickly and to know what is important and how to accomplish what needs to be done. Soldiers with initiative tempered by good judgment act on their assessments quickly and decisively with little or no supervision. They accept responsibility and take thoughtful action to operate successfully and to execute difficult missions.

Confidence. To remove doubt and anxiety in combat, the soldier must first have confidence in his own professional ability. Then he must be confident that his fellow team members, as well as other supporting soldiers, can do their jobs effectively. For example, when a forward observer calls for "danger close" fires, the soldier needs confidence in the accuracy of the forward observer and of those delivering the fire. The soldier needs to feel confidence in his leader. The leader earns his soldiers' confidence as he demonstrates his ability to do his job. Soldiers and leaders develop mutual confidence by sharing difficult, challenging, and realistic training, as well as the rigors and dangers of combat. Mutual confidence multiplies combat power as it welds individuals into cohesive teams.

b. Values

The values of the professional Army ethic—loyalty, duty, selfless service, and integrity–are stated in FM 100-1. These values, based on the Army's relationship to the nation, form the bedrock of the soldier's values and provide guidelines for his behavior. They are time-tested, and they work. Each soldier has his own set of values developed in his home, place of worship, school, and community. But when an individual leaves civilian life and puts on the Army uniform, he incurs new obligations based on the Army values. Through strengthening individual values of candor, competence, courage, and commitment, these values of the professional Army ethic can be developed as the working values of all soldier teams. The role of the leader is not to change long-held personal values, but to impress upon the soldier the importance of these professional values. If, however, a soldier holds values that significantly conflict with these Army values, the leader must seek some resolution with the soldier.

(1) The Professional Army Ethic

The values of the professional Army ethic are discussed below as they relate to developing effective military teams. when team members share these values, they have the basis for a cohesive team committed to the unit, the Army, and the nation.

Loyalty to the nation, to the Army, and to the unit is inherent in the oath which every soldier takes upon entry into the service of his country. If the leader shows loyalty to his soldiers, he earns their loyalty. He trains his soldiers before battle to ensure they have the best possible chance for survival. He cares for their well-being and for that of their families. He demonstrates genuine concern for their problems. He protects them from ill-conceived and unnecessary tasks from outside elements. In turn, loyal soldiers follow legitimate orders without explanation because they have confidence in their leader. They stand up for their unit and its leadership in discussions with other soldiers.

Duty is obedience and disciplined performance. A sense of duty in each soldier, even in the face of difficulty and change, is indispensable to soldier team development. Soldiers with a sense of duty accomplish tasks given them, seize opportunities for self-improvement, and accept responsibility for their actions. They recognize their place on the team and work to earn and maintain the respect and loyalty of their peers, leaders, and subordinates.

Selfless Service is evident in the cohesive, combat-ready team; soldiers and leaders operate with the view that "we're in this thing together." Soldiers are primarily committed to mission accomplishment rather than to self-interest.

Integrity is the cornerstone of the professional Army ethic. Integrity involves honesty, but more than honesty, it is a way of life. When a soldier has integrity, others know that what he says and what he does are the same and that he is absolutely dependable. In both preparing for, and fighting in, combat, demonstrated integrity is the basis for dependable information, decision making, and delegation of authority.

Trust and Loyalty will more likely develop in a unit where integrity is an accepted way of life. Trust allows the leader to give critical tasks to the soldier, confident that he will accomplish them responsibly. The soldier who trusts his leader's integrity follows his orders willingly, even in the heat of battle. He trusts that the leader has good reasons for his actions. Mutual trust leads to mutual loyalty between soldiers and their leaders.

(2) Soldier Values

The development of four basic values in each soldier can help strengthen the acceptance of the values of the Army ethic. These soldier values are candor, competence, courage, and commitment.

Candor is honesty and faithfulness to the truth. The combat-ready team develops only when its members realize that honesty is absolutely essential. Team members must be able to trust one another and their leaders. Without truthfulness, this will not occur. When soldiers see their leaders or peers lying about status reports, or other unit situations, they wonder if they can be trusted to be truthful in a crisis. The question arises "Will they be honest about the wartime situation?" There is no time for such second-guessing in combat.

Competence is imperative for the combat-ready team. Soldiers accept one another and their leaders when they are satisfied with their leaders' knowledge of the job and ability to apply that knowledge in the working situation. Nothing deteriorates teamwork quicker than the perception that soldiers do not know how to soldier and leaders do not know how to lead. Further, the soldier's competence is the basis for the self-confidence critical to feeling accepted by the team.

Courage, both moral and physical, is displayed by soldiers in cohesive, combat-ready teams. They understand that fear in combat is natural and to be expected. This helps them retain control and accomplish their objectives in spite of the risk. Moral courage helps the combat-ready team to do the right thing in a difficult situation, even when some might strongly feel that the wrong is more attractive.

Both physical and moral courage requires that soldiers do their part lest they lose face with their buddies. Courage on the part of one or two soldiers is contagious and becomes a way of life in the cohesive, combat-ready unit.

Commitment to the unit, the Army, and the nation occurs when soldiers accept and demonstrate the values discussed above. When soldiers show that unit accomplishment takes priority over personal inconveniences, when they willingly spend extra time to get the job done for the unit, when they spend time developing their competence to be the best possible soldier to make their unit combat-effective, they are demonstrating commitment to the unit and to the Army.

The values discussed are more than nice-sounding words; they apply in sections, squads, and crews and in platoons and companies. They are important in combat, combat support, and combat service support units. Soldiers may not think of them in terms of the Army or of the nation. Instead they may think of their buddies with whom they eat and sleep and share dangerous situations. These values and the actions they cause set the climate for a team prepared for battle.

B. KNOW Characteristics

What the soldier knows about his profession has made the difference between winning and losing since the first two warriors met in the days before recorded history. It is even more imperative on the complex, fast-moving, and high-technology battlefield of today and tomorrow. Competence is necessary if trust and confidence are to develop in cohesive, combat-ready teams. A soldier or leader new to a unit is not automatically accepted. He earns his way as others become confident that he knows how to do his job. Certain key knowledge is necessary for effective teams.

1. Soldier Knowledge

All soldiers, regardless of military occupational specialty, must master skills necessary for survival in combat. These skills apply to all soldiers, from the engineer platoon leader to the finance clerk to the infantry squad member. In addition, each soldier is trained to do certain tasks that when combined with tasks of other soldiers accomplish the objectives of the commander. Each soldier is depended on for his expertise. Winning on the modern battlefield depends on harmonizing the skills of many soldiers.

2. Battlefield Knowledge

For units to be cohesive and combat-ready, soldiers must know what to expect on the battlefield. This knowledge will support them during the shock of the first few days of battle as well as during the sustained stress of continuous operations. In the effective team, soldiers want to know as much as possible about the enemy and the battle environment in order to anticipate the enemy, make decisions quickly, favorably exploit the terrain, and win the battle.

3. Ethical Knowledge

Soldiers in cohesive, combat-ready units take pride in successfully accomplishing their mission with honor. Violating the basic principles of American life and the rules of warfare while defending them leads to tainted victory.

4. People Knowledge

In cohesive, combat-ready units, soldiers and leaders know one another. Realizing that others have similar fears and needs helps each soldier overcome his own fears and assists unit members in creating the necessary spirit and "oneness."

C. DO Characteristics

What soldiers and teams DO is the concrete expression of who they ARE and what they KNOW. In every situation, units of excellence display character and knowledge as they successfully accomplish their mission. Following are key actions performed by soldiers and teams in units of excellence.

1. Assess

Teamwork assessment is critical for an effective, combat-ready unit. Most leaders know a great deal about the status of their unit's teamwork and cohesion. They gather impressions by listening, observing, and monitoring soldiers' problems. But even the best leader can be blind to problems; the communication system may fail; the pressure of other work may cause inattention to danger signs; or the actual status of teamwork may be misinterpreted or misrepresented. For these reasons the leader should create a guide to assess teamwork similar to checklists used to determine unit readiness. The assessment process is continual. Units grow and change, leaders come and go, and the uncertainties of combat impinge on unit teamwork and, consequently, on combat readiness. In each new situation, leaders and soldiers of effective, combat-ready units reassess and correct to retain and enhance teamwork.

2. Communicate

Communication is the process of sending and receiving information both verbally and nonverbal. Clear, uncluttered communication is especially critical for teams on the modern battlefield. The complexity of the battlefield, dispersion of soldiers, actions of small teams, and disruption of conventional means of communication demand innovative communications between soldiers in squads, sections, and crews. To operate within the commander's intent, soldiers and leaders in combat-ready teams practice both verbal and nonverbal communication. They practice it in training, in day-to-day activities, and in social activities. When combat comes, they practice it in the heat of battle. Team members know one another well enough to anticipate the actions of the other. They also develop a set of words—a short cut—that communicates large pieces of information in brief form. In critical situations, they use hand signals or other forms of nonverbal communication. They communicate within their team as well as with surrounding units.

3. Make Decisions

Decisions are made at every level of the Army. For example, on the battlefield, a squad member has to decide what he can do to help other team members when he becomes aware of an enemy threat. When the squad member reports to the squad leader, the squad leader then has to make critical decisions and respond to the enemy so that his squad can take the initiative and make the enemy fight on his terms. Once the squad leader notifies the platoon leader of the situation, the platoon leader has to make decisions about taking the initiative on a larger scale. At each higher level, the problems become more complex. The use of the chain of command allows these decisions to take place at the proper place and time. Leaders in cohesive units use the initiative and creative efforts of team members by giving them planning and decision-making responsibilities. When this is done, soldiers know the operation and learn to do the right thing within the commander's intent when necessary.

4. Train

The teamwork necessary for cohesive, combat-ready teams requires training. It involves mastering set procedures, such as battle drills or map reading. It also requires training in the processes of doing things, such as communicating or thinking on one's feet. Teams will more likely react without hesitation in combat when they have practiced what to do in realistic training. All training should be accomplished without unnecessarily risking the safety of soldiers or equipment. Careless accidents can significantly harm unit cohesion and teamwork.

D. Team Characteristics

Effective teams possess most of the BE-KNOW-DO characteristics described above. Of course teams vary from crew to crew, section to section, and squad to squad. Each has its own character and unique ways of doing things. Each finds itself in different situations with different people.

Cohesive teams that are already effective receive new soldiers and leaders from time to time. When this happens, the teams have to regroup and spend time integrating the new members. Occasionally, groups of people are together for some time but never form an effective team. Other situations involve COHORT units in which an already-formed team of soldiers joins an already-formed leadership team. When this happens, time must be spent in joining these two teams into one effective combat-ready team.

Regardless of how the unit is formed, it is important to remember that all units go through a fairly well-defined process of development. The stages of this process are formation, development, and sustainment. While these stages follow in sequence, they have flexible boundaries, and many things can cause a unit to move back and forth from one stage to another. For example, third squad, first platoon, has been together for some time and functions as an effective combat-ready team. The team members are used to, and trust, one another, and their squad is a source of pride to them.

The squad leader's job is to sustain the squad's high performance level. This squad is in the sustainment stage. As frequently happens, two of the squad members are transferred, one leaves active duty, and three new soldiers arrive to take their places. Now the team is faced with breaking in three new team members. It will take time for each of the new soldiers to feel at home and to be accepted. Each must learn the way the team operates. Each must demonstrate the ability to contribute to the team before he is accepted. It will take time to trust and be trusted. Gradually, as the team shares experiences, the new members will begin to share its values and goals. Such shared experiences are necessary for soldier integration. In short, it will be some time before the team is in the sustainment stage again.

The leader must realize that developing into a team is not an easy or a rapid process for people who are basically strangers. His primary role is to encourage acceptance, open communication, develop team members' reliance on one another, and promote team acceptance of shared standards and values. Further, he must become involved in bonding between team members and bonding of team members to himself as the leader. He must set and enforce standards and set the example in the development of closer relationships.

I. Forming Combat-Ready Teams

Ref: FM 22-102, chap 2.

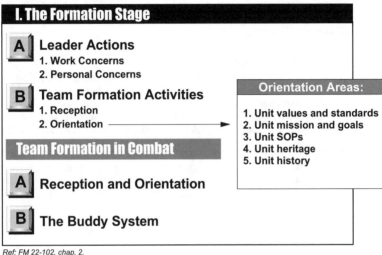

I. The Formation Stage

A **Leader Actions**
1. Work Concerns
2. Personal Concerns

B **Team Formation Activities**
1. Reception
2. Orientation ————————————→

Team Formation in Combat

A Reception and Orientation

B The Buddy System

Orientation Areas:
1. Unit values and standards
2. Unit mission and goals
3. Unit SOPs
4. Unit heritage
5. Unit history

Ref: FM 22-102, chap. 2.

The first events in the new soldier's life in the unit make critical and lasting impressions. Good impressions created by an effective reception begin to build the soldier's trust and confidence in his new team. This chapter discusses what the leader can expect during the formation of a combat-ready team, what actions the leader can take to guide this process, how combat changes the process, and what the leader can do in combat to form a combat-ready team.

The Formation Stage

Initially, the new soldier is concerned about fitting in and belonging. He wants a place on the team, but he is not sure how others will accept him. Any person who moves into a new community with new schools and new friends experiences these growing pains. Every soldier experiences this adjustment when he enters the Army and learns to live with many different types of people. He goes through a process of checking out other soldiers and his leaders. The more he gets to know them, the more he realizes how much they have in common and the more comfortable he feels with them. He reexperiences the same feelings and uncertainty every time he moves into a new unit. Each soldier adjusts to this new experience differently. Some soldiers "come on strong, " bragging about past exploits or telling "war stories" from past Army experiences. Others adjust by withdrawing and watching quietly until they begin to trust others in the unit. As trust develops, they participate more actively. Others achieve a balance somewhere between. Some adjust quickly while others fit in more slowly. A few need considerable help from the leader; occasionally, a soldier is not able to adjust to the team at all. But all soldiers go through some concern about whether or not they belong in the unit.

A. Leader Actions

The leader assists a new soldier's entry into a team by realizing that the soldier is searching for answers to some basic questions concerning the team's activities. What are the goals of this group? To be the best in the field? To have the lowest deadline rate? To be the best in post softball? Where do I fit in? What is going to be required of me by my friends and by my leaders? How much effort am I going to have to put in to accomplish my daily duties? The leader also understands the soldier's concerns as he attempts to become a team member. With these questions in mind, the leader develops a systematic reception and orientation program designed to ease the new soldier's transition into the team.

1. Work Concerns

For the leader, it is not enough to simply give each new soldier a quick in-briefing and assign him to a sponsor and a duty position. The leader takes the time and effort necessary to coordinate the reception of the new member into the team. This concern for the processing of the soldier takes place from the fire team or section level on up and requires that the leader speak to the new soldier daily to see if he is doing the assigned tasks as energetically as required. The leader spends time talking to the new soldier in a systematic manner for weeks after the initial reception to ensure he is developing the appropriate goals and understands how his actions contribute to the overall performance of the team. This may require that the leader sit down with the soldier after duty hours or during lunch breaks to ask him questions about the standards of the team. The soldier may have questions or suggestions concerning the operation of the team. They may discuss the new soldier's responsibilities and how they fit into the overall goals of the team. This exchange of information ensures that the new soldier understands what the team is trying to accomplish.

Further, the leader checks on the new soldier to see if there is a problem with fitting in or abiding by formal and informal rules, such as meeting appearance standards, yelling unit mottos when saluting, or joining the unit's athletic teams. Time spent by the leader on these activities helps the soldier become a functioning member of the team. It also allows the leader to check on the team to see if the group is maintaining its motivation to be the best and to accomplish the organization's goals.

2. Personal Concerns

Leaders recognize that most soldiers have an initial desire to contribute to the team, to be part of the team effort. They build on this personal motivation by realizing that each soldier is different. Each has different abilities, and each learns things in different ways at different speeds. Some soldiers are challenged by progressively more difficult, yet achievable, goals. As they become more competent and reliable, leaders reward their achievements and give them more responsibility.

The leader who looks for positive contributions and gives praise, who takes the position that every soldier is a good soldier until proven otherwise, and who understands that each soldier has strengths that can fit in with the strengths of others to form a strong team, establishes a climate for success.

The new soldier is concerned with whether the leader really "cares about me and my situation." If seemingly uncaring things are done during the soldier's first days in the unit (being left out of major training events, brushed off by supposedly "busy" leaders, left waiting for days to be unprocessed), they will be remembered and could harm the soldier's integration into the team. When it is said that the "leader cares for his soldiers," it means that he is genuinely concerned about the problems that the soldier faces from day one. He cares "bone deep" not just "skin deep."

FORMATION: Teamwork Assessment

Ref: FM 22-100, app. A, p. 58 - 59.

Kind of Leader

1. As a leader, are you sensitive to the personal problems of your soldiers? Do the soldiers feel that you care?

2. Do you know your soldiers? The way the soldier reacts and thinks? Personal data? Strengths and weaknesses? Reliability?

3. Are you fair in the assignment and treatment of all soldiers regardless of race, sex, or religious belief?

4. Are your soldiers confident that you know what you are doing?

5. Do you know enough about the job of your subordinates to teach and guide them as they develop?

Reception

1. Does your soldier reception address the needs of both single and married soldiers?

2. Are sponsors carefully selected to ensure they are good role models for new soldiers?

3. Are your soldiers given adequate time to deal with administrative and personal details involved in moving into the unit?

4. Are you taking action to make the family feel welcomed into the unit?

Orientation

Values and Standards

1. Do you know and live by Army ethical values?

2. Do you know how to communicate appropriate Army and unit values to the soldier?

3. Do you communicate standards of conduct clearly to the soldier during orientation?

4. Do you recognize and reward soldiers for exemplifying unit values and standards?

5. Does your team accept the values and standards of the unit?

6. Do your team members require acceptance of the unit values and standards?

Mission and Goals

1. Do you communicate unit mission/ goals to your soldiers during the orientation period?

2. Do you spend personal time with each of your soldiers to tell him what is expected and to find out what he expects?

Standing Operating Procedure

1. Does your unit have a simple, clear SOP that soldiers are required to read?

2. Do you communicate the way the squad, section, and platoon do business?

Unit Heritage

1. Do you utilize unit patches, colors, crests, and mottoes to develop pride and spirit?

2. Do you teach the unique history of the unit as a source of pride and identification?

3. Are your soldiers required to learn important facts about unit heritage? Are questions about these subjects included on soldier of the month boards, promotion boards, guard mounts, and other prominent places?

4. Do your soldiers talk with pride about successful accomplishments of the recent past?

Team Formation in Combat

1. Do you take care in combat to reassure the new soldier and welcome him to the unit?

2. Is your team prepared to orient the soldier in combat procedures/guidance for survival?

3. Does your unit have a working buddy system to assist the new soldier as he adjusts to the uncertainties of combat?

If the soldier has personal problems, caring means that the leader strives to assist him in dealing with them, whether they are uncovered during his reception or occur during his stay in the unit. Assisting soldiers in dealing with their feelings and concerns not only reflects caring leadership, it also enhances their effectiveness.

B. Team Formation Activities

Whether the group has been together for some time or is concerned with inducting new members, the above principles apply. Leaders at every level must take the time necessary to properly receive and orient the members of the team toward the agreed upon goals while balancing individual needs of team members. Well-developed reception and orientation activities make the leader's team building efforts more efficient.

1. Reception

A well-planned reception is an important first step in creating a cohesive team. Although often thought of as primarily a family program, the reception should address the needs of all soldiers. It is true that the presence of family members adds to the complexity of "getting settled," but the single soldier who lives in the barracks has questions, problems, and concerns that are equally important. Units must reinforce soldier confidence so that no matter what happens, soldiers feel they can always depend on their leaders for assistance for themselves and, if appropriate, their families. If they trust the leader, confidence begins to build immediately.

Personnel and administrative problems associated with moving into a new unit are handled promptly and successfully by assigning sponsors to assist new members. Effective leaders recognize that sponsors do more than ensure that the personal needs of soldiers are met. Sponsors also model for new soldiers what the team leader expects of members of the team. The team leader selects and briefs the sponsor in such a manner that he realizes the importance of the assignment. The leader tells the sponsor exactly what is to be done and that being chosen as a sponsor means he represents what members of the team should look and act like. Anything less than proper behavior is unacceptable.

A successful reception includes being sure that the soldier's pay is accurately pro-cessed in a timely manner; that his personnel, medical, and other records are in their proper place; that he has all his personal equipment; that he has an adequate place to sleep; that he knows where key places such as the dining facility, hospital, chapel, and recreational facilities are located; and that he is shown the kind of caring essential for developing his loyalty to the team.

The Army family is linked to the unit not only by the soldier but also by the opportunities it has to participate in unit activities. The unit leader should strive to develop bonds between the families in the unit to enhance each family's identification with the unit.

It is important that family members understand the service member's duties and the unit's specific mission. They should have the chance to learn about the uniqueness of life in the military, to include information about the unit and its history and about available services and benefits. Such activities as family day programs or organization days allow the family to visit the unit and learn firsthand about soldier and unit activities. A well-informed family is usually more willing to make the personal sacrifices required to adequately support the soldier and his unit. An uninformed family is likely to see itself as an unwilling victim of military life. An informed family is more likely to view itself as contributing to the service member's career and the unit's mission.

A family's attitude toward the Army is often based on perceptions of how the leader treats the soldier and his family. Therefore, the unit leader develops and conveys to the soldier and his family an attitude that clearly recognizes the importance and legitimacy of family needs. This begins with the leader's appreciation of the impact of unit and mission requirements on family life. It also includes his awareness of how family needs affect the soldier and the unit.

The Army family can expect to make sacrifices in support of the soldier's career and even of the unit's mission. But the unit and family relationship is a partnership, and the leader takes every opportunity to promote family well-being, This is more than saying the right words or expressing good intentions. Actions which clearly express the leader's commitment to family well-being must be implemented. The more welcomed family members feel and the more informed they are about the unit, the more likely the soldier will commit himself to the unit's goals and missions.

2. Orientation

Early in his time in the unit, after accomplishing most of the administrative and family details, the soldier goes through an orientation process. During orientation he receives information that is common knowledge among the soldiers already in the unit. Orientation varies from unit to unit, depending on the time, leadership, and situation. But no matter how it is done, this is a time for the unit to tell the soldier about life in the unit and explain the rules.

Orientation may be done in a group or individually. If a leader uses a group method, it is important that he also spend time in face-to-face conversation with the soldier. Getting to know each soldier begins to build the trust necessary for team membership. Also, information communicated by the leadership team is reinforced by unit members as the new soldier begins to fit into the unit. Some important areas to cover in the orientation include—

- **Unit values and standards.** The leader begins to communicate the values and standards of the unit during the orientation process and reinforces them often during the soldier's stay in the unit. These values will become the standards of the unit. Other standards of behavior to which soldiers are held are saluting, promptness, proper haircuts, and proper wear of the uniform. These standards support the value of discipline.

- **Unit mission and goals.** Unit mission and goals need to be firmly established in the soldier's mind so that he has no question about what the unit is trying to accomplish. As each soldier accepts and commits himself to the mission and goals of the unit, cohesive teamwork will develop. The soldier's contribution to mission accomplishment is learning, practicing, and becoming proficient in his job.

- **Unit standing operating procedures.** Another area the leader must explain during orientation is the unit's standing operating procedure— the way the unit operates. The company has a written SOP that each soldier reads when he first enters the unit. It describes how the unit conducts day-to-day business. Beyond that, the platoon and squad have added requirements that help accomplish the mission. These are communicated directly by the platoon sergeant and the squad leader. This process is important because it shortens the time needed to become a working member of the team.

- **Unit heritage.** Instilling unit heritage can begin during the orientation process. This heritage, which includes the unit's symbols and history, is the heart of its spirit and identity. It develops morale and esprit and it builds pride and loyalty. Traditionally, unit symbols such as unit insignia, mottos, colors, and guidons serve two purposes. First, they identify the soldier as a member of an exclusive group. Second, and more important, they instill a "we" feeling among members and help

Combat-
Ready Teams

instill within each team member a commitment to a unit with its own unique identity. In short, symbols instill and maintain unit cohesion.

- **Unit history.** The more positive things the soldier knows about his unit, the easier it is for him to identify with it, but these need not focus only on easy success. The following information is important for inclusion in unit histories: origin of the unit, participation in battles and significant results, major accomplishments, heroes and their achievements, and development of customs and traditions.

Team Formation in Combat

Combat presents unique challenges to team formation. While the formation process remains basically the same, combat alters the way it is accomplished. Variations because of type of unit, type of battlefield, and combat situation make exact predictions difficult. But the goal of the process remains the same—to help the soldier become a member of the team as quickly as possible. This benefits both the team and the soldier.

To preclude disastrous situations, the leader must consider the different dimensions that combat introduces. First, the time that the unit has to receive the new soldier is compressed. That which occurs in hours and days in peacetime is shortened to minutes and hours in combat. Next, the space in which things happen is altered. For instance, in peacetime the formal orientation process takes place close to the soldier's company. In combat, the place of his first orientation to the theater of operations may be far removed from his company. Furthermore, the soldier feels more restricted in his movement in combat than in peacetime.

The soldier's concerns and feelings are also different. In peacetime, he is concerned with getting physically settled in his home, be it in the barracks or in an apartment with his family. In combat, although he remains concerned about things back home, his focus shifts to the fear and uncertainty of war. He fears the unknown as well as death in a strange place among strange people. Getting himself emotionally settled with friendly faces in his new unit is very important.

Further, the environment is different. Death and injury are commonplace on the battlefield. The real noises and confusion of war and isolation from friendly faces are not easily simulated in peacetime.

Finally, the level at which important information is transmitted is different. In peacetime, information important to the soldier is transmitted at post, division, battalion, and company levels. In combat, however, this may not necessarily be the case. As the new soldier processes through the theater, division, brigade, battalion, and company levels, leaders need to be actively involved in the orientation process to ensure that the soldier is provided with the most important information —what he needs to know to be effective in the combat zone. This will make the jobs of the company commander, platoon leader, squad leader, and team leader easier. These leaders will ultimately be the ones who ensure the success of the soldier's orientation.

A. Reception and Orientation

Let us now discuss what might be covered at the various levels of command as the soldier passes through the integration process. The soldier will probably begin at the theater level once he enters the overall combat area. The information the soldier receives here will be very general, covering the mission, overall situation, and theater policies such as leave and hospitalization procedures. As the soldier moves from theater to corps to division and on down, the information will become more specific. A key point, however, is that the messages presented should be positive and show concern for the soldier's well-being. Commanders, staff officers, and leaders must also check with each other to make sure that the information they present at the various levels is not contradictory.

When the new soldier joins his company in combat, he comes with a variety of questions. He is thinking of such things as "What will the people be like? Will the leaders and other soldiers be people whom I can trust and depend on? Will they take care of me? Will they accept me? What will my job be like?" There may not be a great deal of time available before the unit faces combat, so a quick, positive welcome from the entire chain of command is crucial. A positive reception and welcome to the unit will help the soldier feel secure.

The company commander should greet the new soldier personally if at all possible. He should welcome the soldier and cover several topics with him. For example, it might be useful for the company commander to discuss the current tactical situation, the company's recent activities, and the upcoming events. He should reassure each soldier that he will be taken care of in all areas, including mail and proper medical care and evacuation in case he should be wounded. The first sergeant could assist the company commander by explaining various company SOPs to the soldier. The company commander or first sergeant then assigns the soldier to his platoon and hands the soldier off to his platoon leader and platoon sergeant. The platoon leader covers platoon SOPs and basic information the soldier needs to know to work and survive in the platoon. Of course, at platoon level and below, the leader will get right down to the basic information the soldier needs to know to stay alive.

The squad leader will cover the numerous details the soldier needs to know to operate in the squad. The squad leader is the key individual involved in successfully orienting the new soldier, for he probably has more direct influence on the soldier than anyone in the unit. The squad leader must present a calm, unhurried, and confident presence that will help calm the soldier down and make him feel at ease in this new situation. The squad leader must also be alert to the many thoughts and feelings that are probably churning inside the new team member. The squad leader should encourage the soldier to talk about his concerns; he should listen to the soldier and reassure him. Further, the squad leader needs to give the soldier specific guidance about how the squad operates SOPs and safety tips on how to minimize his chances of being killed or wounded. The squad leader needs to stress that the squad works together and that he must do his job well in order to protect other squad and team members. The squad leader can use other experienced, positive soldiers in the squad to work the soldier into the unit. It is critical that the members of the squad personally welcome the new soldier and help him "learn the ropes." They must understand that everyone's safety is at stake. The soldier must be quickly brought "on board" to develop the teamwork necessary for combat survival.

B. The Buddy System

The squad leader will probably be extremely busy in the midst of combat operations. To help with the integration of the new soldier, he can use a "buddy system" approach. He must be careful to place the soldier with a buddy team who will be positive role models. They should be experienced combat soldiers who will teach the new soldier the right things to do to stay alive. They should be soldiers who wholeheartedly support the chain of command. This buddy team should also teach the soldier how to work as part of the overall team. These experienced soldiers are actually serving as mentors to the new soldier.

When the soldier is ready to pull his weight, he and another soldier will become a buddy team. They will assist one another in many ways on the battlefield. In the NBC environment, for example, they will assist one another in putting on protective equipment and in conducting decontamination activities. Administering first aid in case of injury and sharing security duties during periods of rest, eating, and personal hygiene are other examples.

Soldiers will work with their buddies and, at the same time, actively function as part of the larger squad team. They will go to others in the squad for support based on each soldier's unique skills and strengths. As time passes, both the pairs and the squad will develop more cohesive teamwork.

Buddies will intimately know each other and pick up cues from one another just by watching. When a soldier on patrol moves a certain way, his buddy will know what it means and react accordingly with no words being said. This is just as true if the buddies are working together to repair a burned-out transmission on a tank or using forklifts to load supplies from the depot onto a truck. Buddies will know the other's strengths and weaknesses and will complement one another, the strengths of both enhancing combat power and team effectiveness. They can exchange data to make accurate judgments quickly. They will cross train each other in their specialized skills, each expecting the other to pick up and use those skills if one is disabled.

A properly selected buddy team causes several positive things to happen. First, the new soldier begins to develop close ties of loyalty and friendship to the buddy and other squad members and sees how he and his buddy are part of the team effort at fire team and squad levels. He develops a strong sense of commitment to his unit from the bottom up: buddy team, fire team, squad, section, and platoon. If the chain of command has done this right, the new soldier will rapidly become "combat smart," committed to his fellow soldiers and his unit. In the long run, this should greatly improve his effectiveness in combat. Leaders in combat support and combat service support units should also practice these principles. They are key to ensuring successful integration of all soldiers into combat situations.

II. Developing Combat-Ready Teams

Ref: FM 22-102, chap 3.

II. The Development Stage

A **Leader Actions**
1. Listen
2. Establish Clear Lines of Authority
3. Develop Soldier and Unit Goals

B **Training Principles**
1. Train as a Unit
2. Train for Combat
3. Build Pride in Accomplishment
4. Develop Self-Evaluation Habits

Team Development in Combat

A **Leader Actions**
1. Know the Job
2. Know the Soldiers
3. Develop the Soldier
4. Structure the Situation for the Soldier

Ref: FM 22-102, chap. 3.

The leader must be ready to use the new soldiers as soon as possible after reception and orientation. Although proper integration requires ample time for reception and orientation activities, boredom will set in if soldiers are not put into productive training and work quickly. Therefore, the leader . . . must take the initiative and get the soldiers involved in the team's day-to-day activities as soon as possible.

The soldier's first day in the routine activities of the unit is important. The relationships begun that day set the tone for the remainder of the time a soldier works within the team. It is best for both the soldier and the unit that his integration proceed smoothly. The leader needs to guide the soldier's progress both through training for combat and in combat. To assist the leader, this chapter discusses the development stage of soldier teams. It discusses important leader actions and unit training. Further, it discusses the changes demanded by the combat situation and actions the leader can take in combat to develop his soldier team.

Combat-Ready Teams

The Development Stage

Team leaders share responsibility for both soldier and team development. After the soldier goes through reception and orientation, he begins to establish relationships of trust with his leaders and fellow soldiers. He begins the journey from outsider to team member. There is no clean break between the formation and development stages. The amount of time required for the process varies, based on such factors as leadership, nature of the group's task, member personalities and abilities, and goals of the team.

The development stage is characterized by questioning and sometimes by resistance. Some have called this the "storming" stage. The soldier exerts his independence during this critical stage, trying to determine just what he can expect from the unit and the leader as well as from the members of the team. His attempt to resolve these issues may take many forms. He may ask "Who's in charge?" As he becomes more comfortable with his surroundings, he also feels more at home challenging and questioning those around him, including the leadership. He may openly criticize leaders and other team members to his trusted associates.

The leader can see this stage occurring when he feels resistance to his leadership. He may notice smaller groups with their own informal leaders forming apart from the leadership team. Team members may disrupt meetings by arguing over minor or unrelated subjects. If soldiers do not like the task they are given, if they do not feel that their needs are met, if they do not understand why they are training the way they are, or if they do not understand the mission they are given, they question, criticize, or resist in some way.

The issues involved in this stage of development will not be restricted to the work place or to dealings between team members. As the soldier becomes more involved in the life of the unit, tensions may arise between his family and the unit. These tensions will cause stress for the soldier who, on the one hand, tries his best to fit into the unit and, on the other, wants to take care of his family.

As time passes and the unit works together more effectively, trust begins to develop and team bonding occurs. The process takes time and happens in predictable steps. First, the soldier accepts himself as a new member with a new role and set of responsibilities. He then gradually develops trust for the other soldiers and the leader based on their willingness to accept and trust him. The soldier's fear and distrust of other team members disappear as he realizes their competence, worth, and concern.

As members share their thoughts and feelings about the unit and about each other, the initial caution and stiff formal communication turn into more relaxed conversation. The soldier feels freer to express his feelings and ideas. Within the team, individuals begin to pass information more rapidly and accurately to help one another adjust to new situations and requirements.

As the soldier sees his goals and needs being met within the team, he begins to depend on other team members, and they on him, thus increasing the level of trust. As members of the team begin to depend on one another, cohesion develops. This process makes relationships become more predictable and motivates soldiers to accept team goals and to contribute to mission accomplishment.

A. Leader Actions

As the leader detects signs of team growth in his unit, it is important to exert wise leadership as he guides the developing team. He must retain unquestionable control without alienating soldiers. Firmness of direction and respect for his soldiers will help the leader direct the entire unit toward mission accomplishment.

DEVELOPMENT: Teamwork Assessment

Ref: FM 22-100, app. A, p. 60 - 61.

Leader Actions

1. Are your soldiers allowed time to get their personal affairs and their families settled before they are put to work?

2. Do you use the new soldier in productive activity as soon as he finishes his initial inprocessing and orientation?

3. Do you take time to listen to your soldiers?

4. Do you retain control and respect of your soldiers as you allow them to express their questions and concerns?

5. Do team members know who is next in line for leadership in case of leader casualties?

6. Are all team members involved in the unit goal-setting process?

7. Do you periodically spend time with each soldier to help clarify his expectations of you and the team and to help him understand your expectations of him?

8. Do soldiers trust one another, you, and other leaders?

9. Do your policies and practices communicate trust to the soldier?

10. Do your actions and words encourage acceptance?

11. Do you attempt to protect your unit from taskings beyond available resources?

12. Are you concerned about each soldier's development so that the soldier is best equipped to become a productive team member?

Training

1. Does unit training challenge the soldier? Is he actively involved?

2. Do you productively use lulls in the training scenario?

3. What benefits do your soldiers feel they get from training experiences?

4. When you give missions or tasks, are they unit missions?

5. Do you reward your unit for team accomplishments in training?

6. Does your unit keep training detractors to a minimum?

7. When talking about a tng experience, do they view it as "we" and "our" rather than "I"?

8. Do you continually upgrade the training situation to ensure the soldier is challenged?

9. Do you emphasize safety awareness for all training activities?

10. Are you present for training events?

11. Does your unit realistically train for combat?

12. Do you train your soldiers to cope with fear through training?

13. Do you give leadership responsibilities to soldiers during training?

14. Does your unit utilize and reinforce the chain of command in all training exercises?

15. Do your soldiers develop pride in their training accomplishments?

16. Do you reward your soldiers for unit accomplishment in training events?

17. Do your soldiers criticize themselves and seek better ways of doing things?

Development in Combat

1. Do you demonstrate competence that wins the respect of your soldiers?

2. Do you know your soldiers? Do you continuously assess them for leadership potential?

3. Do you have a plan to pace the new soldier's integration into combat activity?

4. Are your soldiers prepared to receive and assist new soldiers who enter the unit?

5. Do you do things in combat to ensure that the team retains its focus as a team?

6. Do you keep the soldiers informed?

7. Do you make your presence known to your soldiers during combat?

8. Do your soldiers have a realistic picture of the enemy, or do they tend to overestimate?

1. Listen
2. Establish Clear Lines of Authority
3. Develop Soldier and Unit Goals

Ref: FM 22-102, p. 30-32.

1. Listen

The leader must listen and respond fairly to criticisms or questions while retaining a firm grasp of the situation. When team members question authority or form into smaller groups, conflict is likely to occur within the team. Overreaction to these developments will likely harm more than help. The leader must listen and interfere only when the conflicts become disruptive or when the small groups threaten to destroy the cohesion of the team. By listening, the leader can discover the soldier's individual needs and can attempt to guide him into accepting team goals.

During this phase, the leader has an opportunity to identify and channel potential leaders in ways productive to the entire team. As he observes and listens, the leader can increase his knowledge about the strengths of individual soldiers—what they like to do and what they do well. He can then place them in the jobs they do best.

2. Establish Clear Lines of Authority

To deal with possible conflicts over team members' responsibilities and goals, the leader needs to establish clear policies about who has what authority and under what conditions each team member can exercise authority or make decisions for the team. The leader should clearly establish these lines of authority with new soldiers immediately and constantly monitor the situation to ensure that they are being adhered to.

The leader should explain that as the new soldiers gain knowledge and experience on the team, their responsibilities and authority will likely increase. In preparing for combat, all team members must know who is responsible to take over if the leader becomes a casualty. Practicing this in training—simulating leader casualties and forcing the new leadership to work effectively—will pay dividends in combat.

3. Develop Soldier and Unit Goals

Soldiers look to their leadership to establish goals for the unit. They want a positive direction that will challenge them and provide a chance for reaching their potential. The leader also has the responsibility to accomplish the mission and directives given to the team by the senior leader. He must attempt to show the soldiers of the team how their own goals and needs can be satisfied as a direct result of working toward team goals.

To do this, the leader needs to sit down with each soldier and find out what he expects from the team both personally and professionally. The leader must also get the same information from his boss. The team's goals must effectively integrate the goals of the organization and the needs of the individuals, to include the leader. If soldier and team expectations differ, this is the time to find out. If the soldier perceives that his needs are not important to the leader, the process of developing a cohesive team will seriously bog down and may never advance to more productive stages of development.

A personal discussion between the leader and the soldiers serves five important purposes:

• It establishes communication between the leader and the members of the team

- It lets the soldiers know what goals can realistically be achieved through membership as an active team member
- It helps the leader know more about the soldiers and their needs
- It establishes clear goals throughout the chain of command that are achievable and support the goals of the higher headquarters
- It assures the soldiers that their individual thoughts and feelings are at least being considered by the team and its leadership

Periodically, the leader needs to get the soldiers together as a team to check on progress. This allows them to share with others what their goals are. As they begin to understand that they share common goals for themselves and their unit, a cohesive team begins to develop. They will establish personal ownership of the unit goals. More and more, they will feel like a family and will think and act as one. This process is important before combat because it lays a foundation for teamwork that will be indispensable when the unit deploys.

B. Training Principles

Training is the heart of soldier team development, and all unit tasks and missions are training opportunities. The good leader capitalizes on every event, from the most exciting to the most boring, in combat and in peacetime. Cohesive teamwork is developed through training activities that motivate and challenge team members. In planning these activities, the leader needs to think constantly of developing each of his soldiers and his unit. Safety awareness should become a "sixth sense" as the soldiers execute this realistic training.

Training Principles

1. Train as a Unit
2. Train for Combat
3. Build Pride in Accomplishment
4. Develop Self-Evaluation Habits

Ref: FM 22-102, p. 32-37.

Combat-Ready Teams

1. Train as a Unit

The only way to develop teamwork is for team members to do things together. This applies to training. When a training mission is assigned to a unit as a team, soldiers are given the opportunity to work together; the chain of command is strengthened; and the team is given an opportunity to experience accomplishment and growth. When the team works together to accomplish the mission, soldiers experience a deepening sense of unit identity. As training standards are met, unit pride develops.

Involving the total group in a unit activity means that the activity must in some way benefit each part of the unit and ultimately each soldier. Sometimes the benefit may occur in the future, something that the soldiers can anticipate, such as victory in combat. More often the benefit is closer at hand, such as completing the field exercise successfully. Some benefits are intangible, such as the feeling of pride that a soldier has in a job well done. Other benefits may be quite tangible, such as praise from the commander or time off for a job well done.

For leaders and soldiers to learn their part in unit operations, both must be present for training. This means that during training exercises, participation must be first priority for all soldiers.

The most tangible benefit of training is the realization by all soldiers that the unit is either combat ready or close to that goal. Combat readiness is best achieved by training exercises that approximate combat, lead to achieving higher standards, and involve all unit members in coordinated actions. When this training is handled well, leaders and team members become more involved in the effort, become more aware of the strengths and competence of one another, and learn more about the particular needs, concerns, and interests of each soldier.

In training, small teams should be given as much responsibility as possible. Combat requires both coordinated action and individual responsibility from the smaller teams that make up the unit. When such training occurs, small-unit leaders develop needed skills to ensure proper action in the absence of instructions from seniors in the combat situation. This kind of training also reinforces the development of the noncommissioned officers, increasing the respect their soldiers have for them. It is primarily in this way that leaders become respected and valued by their sections, crews, teams, and squads.

To achieve maximum cohesion, training goals and objectives must be defined as unit goals and objectives. The pronoun "our" should be used instead of "my." To achieve "our" objective, "we" have to move through this area and secure this high ground, while protecting "our" flanks from the reported enemy in this area. Or, "we" have to get these five vehicles ready tonight so that "our" unit can move the ammunition to the soldiers who need it. "Our" unit should emerge from the training with the feeling that "we" did this well and "we" have to work on this. Unit members share both the praise and criticism as one.

2. Train for Combat

Training must prepare the unit for combat. Self-confidence during stressful times, ability to control fear, communication in combat, and initiative in the absence of orders need to be integral parts of the training environment.

One thing that leaders have at their constant disposal is the opportunity for challenging and realistic training. The training needs to be hard yet safe. Specific training activities that strengthen teamwork and soldier confidence include obstacle and confidence courses and military skills competition. Other team activities are patrolling; independent squad missions; and survival, evasion, resistance, and escape training. These activities are of special value to combat service support units because they help reinforce the fact that they are soldiers as well as mechanics, clerks, and technicians. On the battlefield, every soldier needs the confidence that he, others on the team, and team leaders have the physical strength and the combat skills to defend each other and the unit.

Challenging and worthwhile training both creates and reflects unit cohesion. The soldier gains confidence in himself, his fellow soldiers, and his leaders, as well as personal competence and confidence in his weapons and equipment, through successful completion of challenging training. Such training results in shared experiences among unit members that directly contribute to increased unit and personal pride. Soldiers need to know that they can depend on their buddies and other units and that together they can achieve objectives and accomplish the mission. Soldiers need to know that as a cohesive team they can carry the fight to the enemy and win.

More experienced leaders may not feel the same sense of excitement and adventure that younger team members feel. However, the experienced leader should never forget the lessons of his own youth and work hard to provide the excitement that can shape younger soldiers into a cohesive team.

An important aspect of training for combat is to help the soldier learn how to deal with fear. The leader can first teach the soldier about the physical effects of fear. Each soldier must consciously think about what happens to him when he is afraid so that when he feels fear in combat, he will know what to expect. He must be trained to recognize fear as a normal reaction that prepares the body to respond to a threatening situation.

Second, when planning training, the leader can develop training tasks that require moral and physical courage. The soldier should face situations in training that generate fear and anxiety so that he can learn to deal with them.

Third, the leader should tell the soldier that extreme fear occurs in combat and he must prepare for it in advance; that fear is greatest just before the action; that fear is greater when in defense, when under artillery attack, when under bombing attack, when attacking at night, when helpless to retaliate, or when uninformed about the situation. Knowing what the symptoms of fear are and when to expect fear makes the soldier's situation more predictable. He can determine in advance how to cope with it. All men feel fear in combat; it is a normal human response.

Soldiers should also practice in training the type of communications required in combat. Person-to-person communication is perhaps the first familiar element of the training environment that is lost in the combat situation. In the midst of deafening noise, the voices of other soldiers are extremely difficult to hear. The new, inexperienced soldier may find himself alone in a hostile and dangerous environment, out of contact with those who directed his movements in training. Such loss of contact can only be practiced in training, but it needs to be done. The soldier must be aware that loss of communication may occur, taught what to do when it occurs, and given a chance to react to it in field exercises.

During training, the leader needs to assign increased responsibility to soldiers who will take it. On the battlefield of the future, the successful accomplishment of a mission may very well hinge on the actions of isolated teams led by new leaders. Leaders must be soldiers who have shown a willingness to assume responsibility in training. Training gives the leader the opportunity to identify potential leaders.

The soldier who gives his best on the battlefield does so, in part, because he feels responsible for the success of his unit. To the extent that soldiers feel such responsibility for winning, they actually feel that the danger is less—and it is! A crucial task of the leader is to instill and develop pride and spirit in the unit by building personal responsibility through assigning responsibility and holding the soldiers accountable for their actions.

3. Build Pride in Accomplishment

Pride comes from respect for the unit's ability. Being part of a team that performs well in challenging training instills confidence and pride like no other experience short of combat. Thus training must be unit training that all soldiers can be proud of.

Performance must be rewarded on a unit basis. When it is good, the unit should be rewarded as a unit. When performance is not good, the unit should work together as a unit to improve. The leader must instill the belief that it is important for all soldiers who are performing well to help those who are having difficulty so that the team, as a unit, can perform better. The leader must further instill the belief that all soldiers have the responsibility to accept assistance if it helps the unit do better.

The measurement of successful training should be meeting an attainable, realistic standard rather than just completing a block of training hours. Even if a unit must stay on the range or in the woods for an extra half day to achieve a training goal, the unit pride that results is well worth the disrupted schedule. Or better yet, if the unit accomplishes all training objectives before the planned time, the soldiers can come home early.

Finally, for the soldier to respect the unit, he must feel that the unit respects him. A soldier who lacks pride in himself and his own performance feels no pride in his unit or his leaders. Thus, it is imperative that the leader show respect for each soldier to encourage self-esteem and pride so that the soldier can have a sense of pride in his unit.

4. Develop Self-Evaluation Habits

In training, the unit works toward specific performance standards. Unit self-evaluation that focuses on these standards is a must. Cohesion can be enhanced if the unit conducts its own after action review with individual soldiers participating in problem-solving situations. After action reviews conducted on a unit basis, especially those in which team members discuss their own performances, help develop the feeling that improvement is important to leaders and soldiers alike.

Team Development in Combat

The dimensions of time and space, the feelings of soldiers, the level of critical information, and the environment affect the development stage in combat. In terms of time and space, the team literally develops under fire. In peacetime, the unit has time to practice training missions. In combat, the time available to practice for an actual mission is greatly diminished or even nonexistent. The leader must use any available time to sharpen basic combat skills. Rarely, if ever, will the team be far enough from the combat zone for concentrated training and practice.

In peacetime training, the soldier learns technical and tactical skills and has time to apply them to unit operations. In wartime, he brings these skills when he joins the unit, but he has to learn their application in the specific unit and battle environment. The soldier will have to learn what the realistic threat is, how the enemy thinks and operates, and how to react in the real situation in response to enemy movement and activity. Training in combat usually involves conducting actual operations. The quicker the soldier learns specific techniques, the quicker he will be accepted as a team member.

The soldier will find it difficult at times to be accepted. The more experienced soldiers have shared difficult and dangerous times that have created a bond between them. The new soldier will gradually be accepted as he also shares experiences in the unit and proves his competence.

There is a sense of urgency about the battlefield. Time is critical; soldiers' lives are at stake. One fear of the soldier is that he will somehow cause serious injury or death to other soldiers. He also fears being wounded or killed himself.

All the dynamics of this new situation cause stress on the soldier. The leader and other soldiers can help him find ways to cope with this stress. Normal outlets for tension and stress may not be available to him, thereby requiring stress reduction efforts on his part. Some soldiers will become hardened to the situation. Others will talk about their fears and concerns to a buddy or a leader. Yet others will try to put these fears and problems out of their minds. The key is that they deal with the stress in some manner. (FM 26-2 provides information on dealing with stress.)

A. Leader Actions

The leader plays a key role throughout the development stage. By attentiveness to the team and individual soldiers, he can make a significant difference. The leader actions that were discussed earlier for the "storming" stage of development in peacetime apply in combat as well. The major differences are that the focus of the soldier's needs changes in combat; the time span for team development is highly constricted; and the increased rate of personnel turnover places a larger burden on the orientation and reception process as well as on the fire team, crew, or section leader.

The realities of combat suggest several leader actions that will assist the leader in developing effective fighting and supporting teams in combat. The easy way out would be to say that team building cannot be done in the confusion of combat. The most effective leaders will realize that team building can be, and must be, made to work in any environment if the leader follows some basic principles.

Leader Actions (Combat)

1. Know the Job
2. Know the Soldiers
3. Develop the Soldier
4. Structure the Situation for the Soldier

Ref: FM 22-102, p. 37-41.

1. Know the Job

The primary concern of most soldiers is the leader's competence— "Does he know what he is doing?" It is the responsibility of the leader to know the tasks required of his level of rank and experience as well as the tasks of his subordinates. When he can demonstrate such competence in combat, he gains the confidence and respect of his soldiers.

2. Know the Soldiers

As the leader gets to know the soldiers, he determines their reliability. He discovers those he can turn to in a crisis. He gives them responsibility where possible to develop them as potential leaders. He identifies those soldiers who may need more intensive training to increase their competence and self-confidence. He also encourages those few soldiers who do not seem to fit in by pointing out that being effective team members is important to their survival and to the survival of the unit in critical war situations.

3. Develop the Soldier

In combat, the soldier's job expectations will be strongly influenced by his need to survive. The leader needs to establish a phased program that gradually works the soldier into his combat role without endangering his life or the lives of those around him. On the basis of his own experience, the leader considers the time it takes to get used to the combat environment and gives the soldier time lines within which to develop. He paces the integration process based on the soldier's progress. It is critical that the leader get feedback from soldiers with whom the new member is placed as well as that he personally observe the soldier's progress. Continual feedback to the soldier from both the leader and the team members is also essential during this process to ensure orderly integration into the team. Guiding this progress is the responsibility of the leader.

4. Structure the Situation for the Soldier

When in contact with the enemy, the soldier's greatest need is the feeling of structure that his team members and leaders provide. This group solidarity and coordinated team action are possible only if the soldier knows where his buddies are, what they are doing, and what the leader wants each soldier to do.

The leader structures the situation by ensuring that soldiers are adequately informed. The soldier wants to know all he can about his situation. As time permits, the leader needs to tell the soldier as much as he can about the what and why of his situation to counteract the fear and uncertainty of the unknown. There will be enough inaccuracies and inadequate information on the battlefield. It is no place for poor transmission and reception of information because of lack of aggressiveness in communicating.

The leader must use every possible means to structure the situation. He must make his presence known by moving among his soldiers, issuing verbal instructions, using arm and hand signals, using flares, or simply standing up and leading his soldiers when appropriate. Soldiers feel structure when they know that all share the dangers and burdens equally. Dangerous jobs must be rotated among all the men. And it must be evident that leaders share the dangers too. After any disorganization occurs, no matter how slight, the leader must restructure the situation as quickly as possible.

Finally, the leader can structure the situation by realistically minimizing the perceived threat. The soldier must be calmly and convincingly reminded not to over dramatize critical situations. The leader cultivates calmness in the soldiers by personal example. He can use existing feelings of pride in accomplishments under fire to build unit confidence. The leader and the men must be constantly aware that suppressing fearful behavior during combat is critical because it can spread from soldier to soldier and paralyze an entire unit.

III. Sustaining Combat-Ready Teams

Ref: FM 22-102, chap 4.

III. The Sustainment Stage

A. Leader Actions
1. Deal with Change
2. Reassess Goals and Priorities
3. Focus on Teamwork
4. Focus on Training
5. Focus on Maintaining
6. Ensure Timely Supply
7. Respond to Soldier Concerns

B. Unit Activities
1. Military Ceremonies
2. Sports Activities
3. Social Activities
4. Spiritual Activities

Sustainment in Combat

A. Deal with the Situation
1. Continuous Operations
2. Enemy Actions
3. Casualites
4. Boredom
5. Rumors

B. Soldier's Inner Feelings

C. Deal with Panic

D. Restructure Situation

Ref: FM 22-102, chap. 4.

The sustainment stage is characterized by accomplishing the mission through teamwork and cohesion. It begins when soldiers and leaders emerge from the questioning and challenging stage and begin to work together as a team. Soldiers now feel more comfortable about themselves and their leaders. They trust leaders to be fair in assigning work and in dealing with differences between team members. During this stage, the team, rather than individuals, accomplishes tasks and missions. The team, thinking, acting, and working as one, knows the requirements and gets better results more quickly and efficiently.

As soldiers share common goals, interests, and experiences, they feel pride in shared experiences and begin to develop a sense of comradeship. Comradeship describes the bonding process necessary for total trust in and acceptance by fellow team members and the leader. While comradeship develops slowly, it is necessary for high cohesion and effectiveness. It is enhanced as the team works together and succeeds in achieving high standards.

Comradeship occurs as team members realize that they share the same goals and are committed to the mission. It is important that team members orient on mission accomplishment because comradeship can also form around influences that harm team loyalty. One combat expression of comradeship is the buddy team. The leader's challenge is to focus individual soldiers, buddy teams, and fire teams on total unit teamwork. With this focus, comradeship will be realized through cooperative accomplishment of team goals.

In peacetime and in combat, the team experiences personnel turbulence. With each change, the leader also observes a change in team effectiveness. For example, when a squad receives one or more new soldiers, the automatic way it accomplishes complex team tasks is degraded. The shortcuts that the team has established by members working together have to be established with the new soldiers. Soldiers feel less secure in the effectiveness of the team and focus on relationships with more established team members rather than with new soldiers.

Soldiers continually encounter problems that range from financial hardships to professional differences to severe family crisis. They are distressed from time to time about disturbing news from home and frustrated when they cannot handle things from a distance. Such situations deteriorate teamwork and move the team black to an earlier stage of development. The result can be a minor decrease in efficiency when performing a previously routine task, or an outbreak of minor petty arguments which keep the team from performing up to an agreed upon standard. The leader must be aware that this can happen, alert to the signs, and prepared to smoothly ease the team back to the sustainment stage of development.

A. Leader Actions

Leadership is the key to sustaining cohesive teamwork. The leader must understand and respond to problems that affect quality teamwork over a long period. Certain leader actions associated with the sustaining process become necessary as well as some unit activities that support the process.

1. Deal with Change

As the leader responds to situations that threaten sustained teamwork, he needs to realize that team growth and stability will be uneven at best. The unit will reach a peak of teamwork and then seem to slump; then it will build to a new peak of performance. This natural process will continue throughout the life of the unit. The successful leader guides his unit to peak performance when it faces critical tasks or combat action.

As new soldiers gain knowledge and experience, the need for leader control decreases. Using team members to establish objectives and procedures bonds members to one another and to the leader. They become more committed to the team and its operations, resulting in a more cohesive team.

2. Reassess Goals and Priorities

A vital part of the sustaining process occurs when the leader rechecks the progress of each soldier in satisfying personal and professional goals. The soldier should now see that his goals and the goals of other members in the unit are compatible. Team members now use team expectations and standards as the measurement by which they accept new soldiers into the team.

When new members join the team, or a new team leader is designated, the leader reviews the short-term goals of the team, the responsibilities and expectations of the team members, and the procedures and rules by which they operate. Similarly, as the leader is given new taskings, or as situations change, he ensures that each team member understands clearly what must be done, what is expected of him, and how well he is expected to do it. At the same time, the leader identifies long-term goals and the time needed for the team to perform them to standard. If several things need to be completed in the same time period, he sets priorities and allocates time to complete each task. Additionally, the leader coordinates these plans with his superior to ensure that they agree with the priorities set by the higher unit.

SUSTAINMENT: Teamwork Assessment

Ref: FM 22-100, app. A, p. 62 - 63.

Leader Actions

1. Are you aware of the effects of change on teamwork? Do you actively work to minimize its impact?

2. Do you periodically check on the progress of each soldier to ensure that personal goals and team goals are compatible?

3. Do your team members use team expectations and standards as a measurement by which they accept new soldiers into the team?

4. Do your team members share a commitment to the team mission?

5. Do you reassess team goals often to ensure timely adjustment to the changing situation of combat?

6. Do you listen for suggestions, concerns, or complaints of soldiers that can assist in maintaining a high level of team work?

7. Do you assess your training program to challenge your soldiers and minimize boredom?

8. Is maintenance a day-to-day routine with your soldiers? Do they see its value?

9. Are you continually sensitive to soldiers' personal concerns?

Unit Activities

1. Does your unit plan and utilize activities that build unit spirit and identity?

2. Do you use military ceremonies to build and reinforce soldier spirit, identification and pride?

3. Do your sports teams reinforce the identity and teamwork of the unit? Do your soldiers view their unit teams as "our team"?

4. Does your unit sponsor social events for your soldiers and their families that build identification of the soldier and his family with the unit?

5. Do you encourage the spiritual development of your soldiers and their families?

Sustainment in Combat

1. Do your soldiers observe and learn from actual experiences in combat?

2. Does your unit have a realistic plan for sleep discipline in continuous combat operations?

3. Are your soldiers prepared to react to enemy movement in conjunction with other team members?

4. Do your soldiers spend time talking about immediately prior combat action in order to adjust to and overcome enemy actions?

5. Do team members know what to do in case of a casualty?

6. Are you prepared for team member reactions to injury or death of a team member?

7. Are you prepared to counteract boredom during lulls in combat activity?

8. Are your soldiers aware of stress-reduction techniques?

9. Do you take decisive steps to deal with rumors?

10. Do you discuss aspects of combat, such as fear and panic, with your soldiers?

11. Are your soldiers prepared to deal with fear as a normal reaction to the dangers of combat?

12. Are you alert to critical incidents that might trigger panic among your soldiers?

13. Do you take decisive action to prevent/ cope with despair and panic among soldiers?

14. Are you alert to disruptions in your unit that might cause teamwork to suffer? Do you take decisive action to restructure the unit situation?

Combat-Ready Teams

3. Focus on Teamwork

Sustaining cohesive teams requires that the leader focus continually on teamwork and on those things which he and his soldiers have in common, rather than on their differences. To do this, the leader must listen to what the soldier says, how it is said, and what the soldier does not say. He must continually evaluate the communication channels within the team to ensure that they are open. Even in a well-run team, soldiers have legitimate concerns, complaints, safety considerations, and recommendations for better ways to do things. Listening and then acting to improve the situation are powerful means of gaining trust and developing cohesion. The good leader is always alert to suggestions, complaints, and input from soldiers. The attitude that plans and procedures always need to be defended can separate the leader from the rest of his team and harm team readiness.

4. Focus on Training

As soldiers develop their personal skills and blend them into team training, they become more and more proficient as a team. Unit movements and activities become second nature, and the danger of boredom arises. Boredom challenges the leader to reinforce the basics while providing increasingly complex and demanding training. Realistic training can be conducted as the leader analyzes the risks involved and integrates safety considerations into the training scenario. The leader needs imagination and innovation, particularly in garrison situations, where the inevitable details and duties can undermine the morale of a high-performing unit.

Besides relieving boredom and developing teamwork, demanding team training enables soldiers and leaders to feel more competent to do their job in combat. This competence increases mutual respect among all team members. As the leader shows his ability to use his team effectively in realistic training or in combat, soldiers and leaders become one in accomplishing team missions.

5. Focus on Maintaining

While maintenance of personal and organizational equipment seems far afield to soldier team development, nothing could be further from the truth. It is essential to sustaining the fighting spirit of combat-ready teams. In such teams, soldiers develop special relationships with their weapons and equipment. At times they even give them names.

The leader should develop good maintenance habits as part of the unit training routine. The loss of firepower because of dirty weapons or the loss of mobility because of vehicle failure can seriously demoralize a tightly-knit team. If the unit goes into combat, there will be no time to stand down for maintenance. It will have to be done as routinely as other critical tasks necessary for day-to-day survival. Properly accomplished, maintenance builds confidence of soldiers in their equipment, thus enhancing teamwork.

6. Ensure Timely Supply

The leader must also do all in his power to ensure timely delivery of supplies to his team. If soldiers expect resupply of critical items such as ammunition or food at a certain time, delay can cause serious repercussions. The leader who ensures timely resupply of his team, or who takes time to explain the problem if resupply is delayed, develops the trust of his soldiers in his leadership and in the units responsible for resupply. This also reduces the fear of isolation that soldiers might feel.

7. Respond to Soldier Concerns

To sustain his team, the leader must demonstrate caring leadership through his entire time in the unit. Significant to caring leadership is the way the leader responds to the legitimate concerns of his soldier. One only has to assess the impact of an unexpected financial hardship, a troubled relationship with a loved one, or an illness or a death in his own family to understand how another soldier might feel in such a case. If the leader is insensitive to crisis events in the soldier's life, or takes the stance that the immediate Army "necessity" is more important than the soldier's concern, he can harm the soldier's morale and damage unit teamwork. If military necessity does dictate some hardship for the soldier, the leader first needs to show an understanding attitude and then communicate precisely why the soldier cannot be allowed to do all that he might want to do to alleviate his personal concern.

B. Unit Activities

Unit activities are events that involve all the soldiers and, in most cases, their families. When challenging and positive, they are vital to sustaining cohesive teams by encouraging mutual acceptance. They can take place during duty or nonduty hours. In the company, their purpose is to develop relationships among the participants. Regardless of size, unit activities provide a focus around which members come together and create an atmosphere for emerging relationships and unit cohesion.

Care must be taken, however, to avoid overemphasizing unit activities. Overemphasis can be damaging if it takes the focus of the unit away from mission accomplishment. When done successfully, military ceremonies, sports activities, social activities, and spiritual activities enhance pride and spirit in the unit.

1. Military Ceremonies

Participation in military ceremonies, such as retreat formations, parades, and battalion and company awards ceremonies, fosters pride and spirit in the unit and in the Army. Such unit spirit is essential in building cohesive teamwork. Likewise, when a death occurs in the unit, it is equally important to give soldiers an opportunity to express their feelings at a memorial ceremony or funeral. Such ceremonies help unit members deal with their feelings and contribute significantly to unit cohesion. This is especially important in combat. Such unit spirit is essential in building cohesive teamwork.

Recognizing soldiers and their families during unit formations provides formal and public recognition of their valued membership in the unit. For example, a new soldier, along with his family if appropriate, can be recognized as a new team member during such a ceremony. Departing team members and their families can also be recognized for their contribution to the unit. Such ceremonies show all soldiers that the unit appreciates a job well done.

The unit formation also provides the opportunity to reinforce the history of the unit and the Army. A short reading from the unit's history, or the soldier's creed, might be used to instill pride in the unit and its heritage.

2. Sports Activities

A unit sports program can give all the soldiers a sense of membership in the unit. While only a few soldiers can actively participate in sports teams, the excitement and pride in competition and the prestige of a winning team can be shared by all the soldiers. Soldiers begin to refer to the company team as "our" softball, volleyball, or touch football team. When they do so, they identify with their unit. These activities should be organized at company level to reinforce cohesion and a sense of identity among the smaller teams that make up the company. Soldiers recall and talk about highlights of competition, reinforcing mutual feelings and building cohesion. Participation in several sports should produce enough winners to avoid a loser image that could be harmful.

3. Social Activities

The variety of social activities is limited only by time, imagination of the planner, and good taste. The unit party, at any level and in any appropriate form, provides a relaxed atmosphere for soldiers to develop positive relationships among themselves and with their leaders. It also provides an opportunity for families to meet families and enhances family belonging to and involvement in the unit.

4. Spiritual Activities

Encouraging soldiers to develop their spiritual lives is another way in which the leader can influence the cohesion of his unit. Because of our rich American religious heritage, soldiers have many and varied religious backgrounds. Each faith provides for its member soldier the strength to cope with difficult situations in combat. Through encouraging his soldiers to practice and develop their faith, the leader shows another facet of his concern for their well-being. The unit chaplain can assist in answering any question the leader may have in this area. The Unit Ministry Team provides religious services, rites, and activities for unit members and is a valuable resource for all leaders.

Team Sustainment in Combat

Keeping unit spirit and teamwork at a high level during combat operations depends in part on the tide of battle, but it also requires work on the part of the leader and the team. Combat affects soldiers as individuals and the unit as a team. It is critical that the leader overcome conditions that deteriorate teamwork and, consequently, combat effectiveness.

A. Deal With the Situation

Conditions in combat exert pressure on the leader's efforts to sustain his team. The leader must know how to deal with each situation if his team is to successfully accomplish combat operations.

1. Continuous Operations

The continuous operations anticipated on the modern battlefield cause effects such as decreased vigilance, reduced attention, slowed perception, inability to concentrate, mood changes, communication difficulties, and inability to accomplish manual tasks. Over time, these effects can lead to apathy in both leaders and their soldiers. If left unchecked, they can deteriorate the most cohesive teams and damage their will to fight.

Proper sleep and rest are necessary to keep soldiers functioning at their best. The leader needs to develop sleep discipline routines for his soldiers and particularly for himself. His soldiers cannot operate efficiently without proper sleep and he needs to be fresh to make necessary decisions. The battlefield is no place for the leader who stays awake for long periods because he feels that the unit cannot operate without him. (FM 22-9 provides valuable information to assist the leader during continuous operations.)

2. Enemy Actions

The movement of the enemy and the necessary countermoves of the friendly force can be confusing and frightening. The appearance of the enemy in force, or fire from an enemy that cannot be seen, can affect the soldier's performance as a team member. Discussion of real situations, along with battle drills practiced until they are automatic, can prepare the soldier for quick reaction to the situations that he will face. The more he knows about what to expect and how to react, the more confident he will be in the moment of crisis.

During breaks in combat, the team should spend time discussing recent combat actions, their performance, and ways they can improve. These after action reviews will increase the confidence of the soldier and help him develop a sense of responsibility for his own performance. They will also help eliminate the feeling that he is alone and allow him to vent possible feelings of anger, fear, and despair.

3. Casualties

Casualties create personnel turbulence and have a psychological effect on the soldier. They are a serious and continuous threat to sustained teamwork and cohesion. Proper safety precautions can assist in minimizing unnecessary casualties and their psychological impact on the soldier. But even with sound leadership, and by the leader doing all that he can do to reduce casualties, the team will still sustain casualties in combat. Soldiers must have no doubt that if they are injured they will not be deserted because of hostile fire.

Further, when a casualty occurs, the leader must also counsel the casualty's buddies as promptly as the situation allows. Talk relieves tension and they may be feeling anger and fear. It is the leader's task to reassure the remaining men that their whole supporting unit structure is not collapsing. The quicker the unit can adjust to these casualties, the less damage to unit teamwork. More experienced soldiers can be invaluable in helping new soldiers to deal with the injury and death around them and in reassuring them. On a personal level, the Unit Ministry Team, consisting of chaplain and chaplain's assistant, can assist leaders, soldiers, and the team in coping with feelings caused by casualties.

The loss of a leader because of injury or death will even more seriously affect teamwork, Soldiers look to the leader as a stabilizing force in a chaotic situation. When the leader is hurt or killed, the spirit and teamwork of the unit can be severely degraded.

When a new leader is appointed, other leaders need to back and support him. Even if he has combat experience, he still has to fit into the new unit. His successful integration requires close supervision by the next higher leader and an intensive on-the-job training program that develops his tactical and technical competence. Each new leader has to depend on the soldiers and on other leaders to assist him in adapting his training and peacetime experience to combat.

4. Boredom

Combat activity will vary from periods of intense and violent conflict to times of boredom. Dealing with boredom is essential for combat effectiveness. In Vietnam some units spent days in the jungles and rice paddies without enemy contact. The only diversion was their constant alertness for booby traps. After a while, in its boredom, the unit would let its guard down and become careless. The unit then lacked combat sharpness when attacked, even failing to detect booby traps. Effective leaders found ways to occupy their units while they spent those days in the jungle. They focused on security, resupply, personal hygiene, patrol activities, equipment maintenance, and mission-related training activities such as cross training and radio procedures. Such activities helped develop and maintain unit cohesion and combat effectiveness.

5. Rumors

Rumors are bits of information that are not based on definite knowledge. They can spread quickly throughout the unit, increasing uncertainty and destroying confidence. To sustain teamwork, the leader must constantly use truth to deal with rumors and put them to rest. Following are ways that help control rumors:

- **Stress honesty**. When soldiers discover that their leaders have lied to them once, they stop believing. Soldiers must be absolutely convinced that all information coming from their leader is true to the best of his knowledge. Honesty is a prerequisite for mutual confidence.

- **Inform.** The leader must start an effective information program and pass out as much information. as possible. Soldiers must be confident that they are getting the whole story, the good and the bad.

- **Identify and counsel** those who spread rumors. The way rumors are communicated, however, makes identifying the source extremely difficult. Leaders should be careful to avoid wrongly accusing team members of starting rumors as this creates distrust.

B. Deal with Soldier's Inner Feelings

When a soldier is threatened, he may feel anger, despair, or fear. When a soldier is angry, the anger may indicate a high confidence level. In this case, the leader's problem is how to direct the soldier's anger in the right direction. When a soldier is apathetic or despairing, it usually indicates he has an extremely low confidence level. The leader's problem with the apathetic soldier is how to keep him alive until the battle is over and he can get appropriate treatment. If a soldier is afraid, the fear is neither a good nor a bad sign in itself. It simply indicates that the soldier may, or may not, take action to eliminate the threat. It may depend on whether the soldier has learned to deal with fear or how skillful the leader is in controlling the undesirable effect of fear on himself and his soldiers.

Fear can come from many directions in combat. The sights and sounds of the battlefield frighten many. Others fear the unexpected or the unknown. Still others are afraid of dying or of being crippled or disfigured for life. And some fear being a coward or failing as a soldier. Whatever the source, these fears can immobilize soldiers, destroy a team's will to fight, and even lead to despair and panic.

If the leader can reduce fear levels, he can inspire effective action. In controlling fear in combat, the leader must emphasize that these fears are very normal. An open discussion of fear can best be conducted by either the team leader, or a combat veteran, who admits to fear in combat. Further, he can tell how he coped with it and went on to do his job in spite of it. The unit's chaplain and chaplain's assistant can assist in this effort.

Finally, leaders must use fear-control techniques. A powerful method for controlling fear in combat is to concentrate on each step of the task at hand. The soldiers must be trained to concentrate on specific aspects of the job, not the danger. A soldier who is concentrating on firing his weapon and on selecting his next firing position is not concentrating on fear. Once the soldier takes action to alleviate his situation, his fear usually subsides. Fear control is a central function of combat leadership.

C. Deal with Panic

In combat, many situations cause despairing behavior in individuals. The well-prepared leader can cope with such behavior as it occurs. A much more difficult and complicated leadership problem arises, however, when individual despairing behavior leads to group despairing behavior, or panic. Soldiers in panic have intense fear, are easily spooked, and tend to flee the battlefield. Two battlefield conditions that are primary causes of panic are—

- Belief by the group that all escape routes are rapidly closing
- Group feelings of helplessness and anxiety caused by an unclear situation or by what the group perceives as an immediate threat

When these conditions exist, a "trigger" incident can cause soldiers to panic. A trigger incident confirms the belief of soldiers that the situation is out of control, causing them to give in to their worst fears and suspicions. Examples of trigger incidents are a soldier fleeing to the rear, fire coming from an exposed flank, or a respected leader or soldier being killed.

Also, combat troops tend to relate all previous and subsequent information to the trigger incident. If the trigger incident was an exceptionally heavy artillery barrage in the friendly rear area, soldiers may interpret the lack of an ammunition resupply as evidence that all ammunition has been destroyed. The trigger incident, and other reinforcing evidence, lead to uncontrollable fear that, in turn, can lead to hysterical behavior on the part of one or more soldiers. If a soldier turns and runs, others may follow and the action may snowball until the entire unit is in flight.

To prevent panic, the leader must focus on and control what the soldiers believe to be true. If soldiers believe that their escape routes are rapidly closing, if they believe that uncertain situations lead to uncontrollable events, or if they believe in their most pessimistic appraisals of the situation, then the seeds of panic are firmly planted. It is what the soldiers think is true that counts, not what is actually true.

Soldiers in combat are regularly exposed to death and battle wounds. They are subject to all the fears that lead to panic. Experienced soldiers who are well trained, organized, and led seldom give way to panic because they are confident in their ability to cope with difficult situations.

The reverse is true for the inexperienced, inadequately trained, poorly led soldiers. In either case, the leader must constantly evaluate the confidence level of his team, strive to increase soldier confidence, eliminate the conditions that lead to panic, and decrease troop despair.

A leader should be on the alert for incidents that soldiers may interpret as critical. When trigger incidents occur, the leader must follow with prompt and calm action. He can—

- Keep the soldiers busy with routine tasks that are simple and repetitive but meaningful. If the troops are concentrating intently on a routine task such as firing their weapons, they will pay less attention to their own fears.
- Move from position to position, reassuring the soldiers that the situation is not critical. When the leader does this, he not only reassures the men but also adds structure to the situation.
- Slow the soldiers down so that they can act instead of react. This is especially important if they are showing early hysterical behaviors such as extreme agitation or confusion.
- Set a personal example of fearlessness, even though he feels fear, and insist that all on the leadership team do the same
- Explain the reasons for withdrawals and delaying actions
- Stress the unit's ability, as a unit, to cope with all battlefield situations
- Assure the unit that it is in command of the situation and not in an inescapable situation
- Assure the unit that its flanks, rear, and supplies are secure, if this is the case

If panic develops in spite of all the leader's efforts, he must take firm and decisive action to stop it as soon as possible. Remember, panic is contagious! The leader can often restore unity of action by standing with a few volunteers in the path of fleeing soldiers, ordering them to return to their positions. These volunteers must be ready to take firm action, manhandling or restraining those men who come within reach, or threatening the others. The overriding consideration is to stop the panic. Once panic is stopped, the leader must immediately restructure the situation and give the panicked soldiers something constructive to do as part of the larger unit. The work will distract them from their fears, and the stability of the unit will restore their confidence.

D. Restructure the Situation

The leader must work constantly to restructure the situation and keep the unit organized, together, and working. His main concern is that the unit does not disintegrate. When the unit is disrupted, members are preoccupied with individual physical survival and the attraction to remain a member of the team is minimized. Following are actions the leader can take to help restructure:

- Use the chain of command wherever possible to avoid conflicting orders and to prevent rumors
- Manage time efficiently to prevent prolonged waits
- Avoid false alarms
- Train subordinate leaders to take command immediately in the event of the death or incapacitation of their leader
- Prevent surprise by stressing security
- Keep the soldiers informed on all matters, especially on their own location and that of the enemy
- Never express dissension in the presence of the soldiers
- Forcefully correct those soldiers who are increasing fear by irresponsible talk. A soldier who is inflating the accuracy and lethality of enemy weapons or exaggerating the strength of the enemy increases soldier despair. He must be warned about his irresponsible behavior

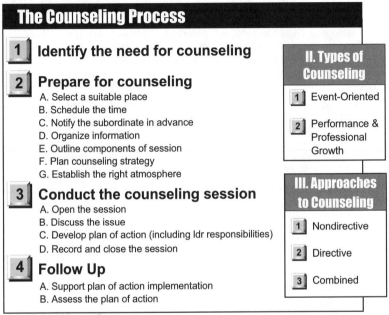

Developmental Counseling

Ref: FM 22-100, pp. C-1 to C-6.

The Counseling Process

1 **Identify the need for counseling**

2 **Prepare for counseling**
A. Select a suitable place
B. Schedule the time
C. Notify the subordinate in advance
D. Organize information
E. Outline components of session
F. Plan counseling strategy
G. Establish the right atmosphere

3 **Conduct the counseling session**
A. Open the session
B. Discuss the issue
C. Develop plan of action (including Idr responsibilities)
D. Record and close the session

4 **Follow Up**
A. Support plan of action implementation
B. Assess the plan of action

II. Types of Counseling
1 Event-Oriented
2 Performance & Professional Growth

III. Approaches to Counseling
1 Nondirective
2 Directive
3 Combined

Ref: FM 22-100, app. C.

Subordinate leadership development is one of the most important responsibilities of every Army leader. Developing the leaders who will come after you should be one of your highest priorities. Your legacy and the Army's future rests on the shoulders of those you prepare for greater responsibility.

Leadership development reviews are a means to focus the growing of tomorrow's leaders. Think of them as AARs with a focus of making leaders more effective every day. These important reviews are not necessarily limited to internal counseling sessions; leadership feedback mechanisms also apply in operational settings such as the CTCs.

Just as training includes AARs and training strategies to fix shortcomings, leadership development includes performance reviews. These reviews result in agreements between leader and subordinate on a development strategy or plan of action that builds on the subordinate's strengths and establishes goals to improve. Leaders conduct performance reviews and create plans of action during developmental counseling.

Leadership development reviews are a component of the broader concept of developmental counseling. Developmental counseling is subordinate-centered communication that produces a plan outlining actions subordinates must take to achieve individual and organizational goals. During developmental counseling, subordinates are not merely passive listeners; they're actively involved. The Developmental Counseling Form (DA Form 4856-E) provides a framework to prepare for almost any counseling. Use it to help mentally organize issues and isolate important, relevant items to cover

Developmental counseling is a shared effort. As a leader, you assist your subordinates in identifying strengths and weaknesses and creating plans of action. Then you support them throughout the plan implementation and assessment. However, to achieve success, your subordinates must be forthright in their commitment to improve and candid in their own assessment and goal setting.

The Leader's Responsibilities

Organizational readiness and mission accomplishment depend on every member's ability to perform to established standards. Supervisors must mentor their subordinates through teaching, coaching, and counseling. Leaders coach subordinates the same way sports coaches improve their teams: by identifying weaknesses, setting goals, developing and implementing plans of action, and providing oversight and motivation throughout the process. To be effective coaches, leaders must thoroughly understand the strengths, weaknesses, and professional goals of their subordinates.

Army leaders evaluate DA civilians using procedures prescribed under the Total Army Performance Evaluation System (TAPES). Although TAPES doesn't address developmental counseling, you can use DA Form 4856-E to counsel DA civilians concerning professional growth and career goals. DA Form 4856-E is not appropriate for documenting counseling concerning DA civilian misconduct or poor performance. The servicing civilian personnel office can provide guidance for such situations.

Soldiers and DA civilians often perceive counseling as an adverse action. Effective leaders who counsel properly can change that perception. Army leaders conduct counseling to help subordinates become better members of the team, maintain or improve performance, and prepare for the future. Just as no easy answers exist for exactly what to do in all leadership situations, no easy answers exist for exactly what to do in all counseling situations.

However, to conduct effective counseling, leaders should develop a counseling style with the following characteristics:

A. Purpose
Clearly define the purpose of the counseling. Flexibility: Fit the counseling style to the character of each subordinate and to the relationship desired.

B. Respect
View subordinates as unique, complex individuals, each with a distinct set of values, beliefs, and attitudes.

C. Communication
Establish open, two-way communication with subordinates using spoken language, nonverbal actions, gestures, and body language. Effective counselors listen more than they speak.

D. Support
Encourage subordinates through actions while guiding them through their problems.

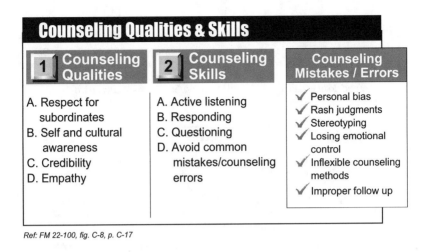

Counseling Qualities & Skills

1 Counseling Qualities	**2** Counseling Skills	Counseling Mistakes / Errors
A. Respect for subordinates B. Self and cultural awareness C. Credibility D. Empathy	A. Active listening B. Responding C. Questioning D. Avoid common mistakes/counseling errors	✓ Personal bias ✓ Rash judgments ✓ Stereotyping ✓ Losing emotional control ✓ Inflexible counseling methods ✓ Improper follow up

Ref: FM 22-100, fig. C-8, p. C-17

1. Leader Counseling Qualities

Army leaders must demonstrate certain qualities to be effective counselors. These qualities include respect for subordinates, self-awareness and cultural awareness, empathy, and credibility.

A. Respect for Subordinates

As an Army leader, you show respect for subordinates when you allow them to take responsibility for their own ideas and actions. Respecting subordinates helps create mutual respect in the leader-subordinate relationship. Mutual respect improves the chances of changing (or maintaining) behavior and achieving goals.

B. Self Awareness and Cultural Awareness

As an Army leader, you must be fully aware of your own values, needs, and biases prior to counseling subordinates. Self-aware leaders are less likely to project their biases onto subordinates. Also, aware leaders are more likely to act consistently with their own values and actions.

Cultural awareness is a mental attribute. As an Army leader, you need to be aware of the similarities and differences between individuals of different cultural backgrounds and how these factors may influence values, perspectives, and actions. Don't let unfamiliarity with cultural backgrounds hinder you in addressing cultural issues, especially if they generate concerns within the organization or hinder team-building. Cultural awareness enhances your ability to display empathy.

C. Empathy

Empathy is the action of being understanding of and sensitive to the feelings, thoughts, and experiences of another person to the point that you can almost feel or experience them yourself. Leaders with empathy can put themselves in their subordinate's shoes; they can see a situation from the other person's perspective. By understanding the subordinate's position, you can help a subordinate develop a plan of action that fits the subordinate's personality and needs, one that works for the subordinate. If you don't fully comprehend a situation from your subordinate's point of view, you have less credibility and influence and your subordinate is less likely to commit to the agreed upon plan of action.

Developmental Counseling

D. Credibility

Leaders achieve credibility by being honest and consistent in their statements and actions. To be credible, use a straightforward style with your subordinates. Behave in a manner that your subordinates respect and trust. You can earn credibility by repeatedly demonstrating your willingness to assist a subordinate and being consistent in what you say and do. If you lack credibility with your subordinates you'll find it difficult to influence them.

2. Leader Counseling Skills

One challenging aspect of counseling is selecting the proper approach to a specific situation. To counsel effectively, the technique you use must fit the situation, your capabilities, and your subordinate's expectations. In some cases, you may only need to give information or listen. A subordinate's improvement may call for just a brief word of praise. Other situations may require structured counseling followed by definite actions.

All leaders should seek to develop and improve their own counseling abilities. You can improve your counseling techniques by studying human behavior, learning the kinds of problems that affect your subordinates, and developing your interpersonal skills. The techniques needed to provide effective counseling will vary from person to person and session to session. However, general skills that you'll need in almost every situation include active listening, responding, and questioning.

A. Active Listening

During counseling, you must actively listen to your subordinate. When you're actively listening, you communicate verbally and non-verbally that you've received the subordinate's message. To fully understand a subordinate's message, you must listen to the words and observe the subordinate's manners. Elements of active listening you should consider include—

- **Eye contact.** Maintaining eye contact without staring helps show sincere interest. Occasional breaks of contact are normal and acceptable. Subordinates may perceive excessive breaks of eye contact, paper shuffling, and clock-watching as a lack of interest or concern. These are guidelines only. Based on cultural background, participants in a particular counseling session may have different ideas about what proper eye contact is.

- **Body posture.** Being relaxed and comfortable will help put the subordinate at ease. However, a too-relaxed position or slouching may be interpreted as a lack of interest.

- **Head nods.** Occasionally nodding your head shows you're paying attention and encourages the subordinate to continue.

- **Facial expressions.** Keep your facial expressions natural and relaxed. A blank look or fixed expression may disturb the subordinate. Smiling too much or frowning may discourage the subordinate from continuing.

- **Verbal expressions.** Refrain from talking too much and avoid interrupting. Let the subordinate do the talking while keeping the discussion on the counseling subject. Speaking only when necessary reinforces the importance of what the subordinate is saying and encourages the subordinate to continue. Silence can also do this, but be careful. Occasional silence may indicate to the subordinate that it's okay to continue talking, but a long silence can sometimes be distracting and make the subordinate feel uncomfortable.

Active listening also means listening thoughtfully and deliberately to the way a subordinate says things. Stay alert for common themes. A subordinate's opening and closing statements as well as recurring references may indicate the subordinate's priorities. Inconsistencies and gaps may indicate a subordinate's avoidance of the real issue. This confusion and uncertainty may suggest additional questions.

While listening, pay attention to the subordinate's gestures. These actions complete the total message. By watching the subordinate's actions, you can "see" the feelings behind the words. Not all actions are proof of a subordinate's feelings, but they should be taken into consideration. Note differences between what the subordinate says and does. Nonverbal indicators of a subordinate's attitude include—

- **Boredom**. Drumming on the table, doodling, clicking a ball-point pen, or resting the head in the palm of the hand.
- **Self-confidence**. Standing tall, leaning back with hands behind the head, and maintaining steady eye contact.
- **Defensiveness.** Pushing deeply into a chair, glaring at the leader, and making sarcastic comments as well as crossing or folding arms in front of the chest.
- **Frustration.** Rubbing eyes, pulling on an ear, taking short breaths, wringing the hands, or frequently changing total body position.
- **Interest, friendliness, and openness.** Moving toward the leader while sitting.
- **Openness or anxiety.** Sitting on the edge of the chair with arms uncrossed and hands open.

Consider these indicators carefully. Although each indicator may show something about the subordinate, don't assume a particular behavior absolutely means something. Ask the subordinate about the indicator so you can better understand the behavior and allow the subordinate to take responsibility for it.

B. Responding

Responding skills follow-up on active listening skills. A leader responds to communicate that the leader understands the subordinate. From time to time, check your understanding: clarify and confirm what has been said. Respond to subordinates both verbally and nonverbal. Verbal responses consist of summarizing, interpreting, and clarifying the subordinate's message. Nonverbal responses include eye contact and occasional gestures such as a head nod.

C. Questioning

Although questioning is a necessary skill, you must use it with caution. Too many questions can aggravate the power differential between a leader and a subordinate and place the subordinate in a passive mode. The subordinate may also react to excessive questioning as an intrusion of privacy and become defensive. During a leadership development review, ask questions to obtain information or to get the subordinate to think about a particular situation. Generally, the questions should be open-ended so as to evoke more than a yes or no answer. Well-posed questions may help to verify understanding, encourage further explanation, or help the subordinate move through the stages of the counseling session.

D. Counseling Errors

Effective leaders avoid common counseling mistakes. Dominating the counseling by talking too much, giving unnecessary or inappropriate "advice," not truly listening, and projecting personal likes, dislikes, biases, and prejudices all interfere with effective counseling. You should also avoid other common mistakes such as rash judgments, stereotypes, loss of emotional control, inflexible methods of counseling and improper follow-up.

Support Activities

Ref: FM 22-100, fig. C-3. p. C-6.

Activity	Description
Adjutant General	Provides personnel and administrative services support such as orders, ID cards, retirement assistance, deferments, and in- and out-processing.
American Red Cross	Provides communications support between soldiers and families and assistance during or after emergency or compassionate situations.
Army Community Service	Assists military families through their information and referral services, budget and indebtedness counseling, household item loan closet, information on other military posts, and welcome packets for new arrivals.
Army Substance Abuse Program	Provides alcohol and drug abuse prevention and control programs for DA civilians.
Better Opportunities to Single Soldiers (BOSS)	Serves as a liaison between upper levels of command and single soldiers.
Army Education Center	Provides services for continuing education and individual learning.
Army Emergency Relief	Provides financial assistance and personal budget counseling; coordinates student loans through Army Emergency Relief education loan programs.
Career Counselor	Explains reenlistment options and provides current information on prerequisites for reenlistment and selective reenlistment bonuses.
Chaplain	Provides spiritual and humanitarian counseling to soldiers and DA civilians.
Claims Section, SJA	Handles claims for and against the government, most often those for the loss and damage of household goods.
Legal Assistance Office	Provides legal information or assistance on matters of contracts, citizenship, adoption, marital problems, taxes, wills, and powers of attorney.
Community Counseling Center	Provides alcohol& drug abuse prevention and control programs for soldiers.
Community Health Nurse	Provides preventive health care services.
Community Mental Health	Provides assistance and counseling for mental health problems.
Employees Assistance Pgm	Provides health nurse, mental health and social work services for DA Civilians.
Equal Opportunity Office	Provides assistance for matters involving discrimination in race, color, national origin, gender, and religion. Provides, information on procedures
Family Advocacy Office	Coordinates programs supporting children and families including abuse and neglect investigation, counseling, and educational programs.
Finance and Accouting Office	Handles inquiries for pay, allowances, and allotments.
Housing Referral Office	Provides assistance with housing on and off post.
Inspector General	Renders assistance to soldiers and DA civilians. Corrects injustices affecting individuals and eliminates conditions determined to be detrimental to the efficiency, economy, morale, and reputation of the Army. Investigates fraud, waste & abuse.
Social Work Office	Provides services dealing with social problems: crisis intervention, family therapy, marital counseling, and parent or child management assistance.
Transition Office	Provides assistance and information on separation from the Army.

Guidelines to Improve Counseling

Ref: FM 22-100, fig. C-2. p. C-5.

1. Determine the subordinate's role in the situation and what the subordinate has done to resolve the problem or improve performance.

2. Draw conclusions based on more than the just what the suborindate states.

3. Try to understand what the subordinate says and feels; listen to how they say it.

4. Show empathy when discussing the problem.

5. When asking questions, be sure you need the info.

6. Keep the conversation open-ended; avoid interrupting.

7. Give the subordinate your full attention.

8. Be receptive to the subordinate's feelings without feeling responsible to save the subordinate from hurting.

9. Encourage subordinate to take initiative and to say what he/she wants to say.

10. Avoid interrogating.

11. Keep your personal experiences out of the counseling session unless you believe your experiences will really help.

12. Remain objective -- Listen more; talk less.

13. Avoid confirming a subordinate's prejudices.

14. Help the subordinate help himself.

15. Know what to keep confidential and what to present to the chain of command.

Counseling Mistakes / Errors

✓ Personal bias
✓ Rash judgments
✓ Stereotyping
✓ Losing emotional control
✓ Inflexible counseling methods
✓ Improper follow up

Developmental Counseling

I. Types of Counseling

Ref: FM 22-100, pp. C-7 to C-9.

You can often categorize developmental counseling based on the topic of the session. The two major categories of counseling are event-oriented and performance/professional growth .

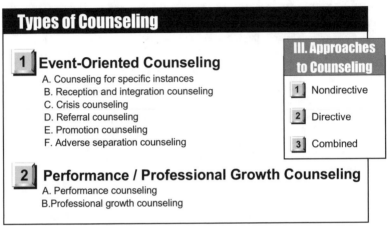

Types of Counseling

1 **Event-Oriented Counseling**
A. Counseling for specific instances
B. Reception and integration counseling
C. Crisis counseling
D. Referral counseling
E. Promotion counseling
F. Adverse separation counseling

III. Approaches to Counseling
1 Nondirective
2 Directive
3 Combined

2 **Performance / Professional Growth Counseling**
A. Performance counseling
B.Professional growth counseling

Ref: FM 22-100, pp. C-7 to C-9.

1. Event-Oriented Counseling

Event-oriented counseling involves a specific event or situation. It may precede events, such as going to a promotion board or attending a school; or it may follow events, such as a noteworthy duty performance, a problem with performance or mission accomplishment, or a personal problem.

A. Counseling for Specific Instances

Sometimes counseling is tied to specific instances of superior or substandard duty performance. You tell your subordinate whether or not the performance met the standard and what the subordinate did right or wrong. The key to successful counseling for specific performance is to conduct it as close to the event as possible.

Many leaders focus counseling for specific instances on poor performance and miss, or at least fail to acknowledge, excellent performance. You should counsel subordinates for specific examples of superior as well as substandard duty performance. To measure your own performance and counseling emphasis, you can note how often you document counseling for superior versus substandard performance.

You should counsel subordinates who don't meet the standard. If the subordinate's performance is unsatisfactory because of a lack of knowledge or ability, you and the subordinate should develop a plan to improve the subordinate's skills. Corrective training may be required at times to ensure the subordinate knows and achieves the standard. Once the subordinate can achieve the standard, you should end the corrective training.

When counseling a subordinate for a specific performance, take the following actions:

- Tell the subordinate the purpose of the counseling, what was expected, and how the subordinate failed to meet the standard
- Address the specific unacceptable behavior or action, not the person's character
- Tell the subordinate the effect of the behavior, action, or performance on the rest of the organization
- Actively listen to the subordinate's response
- Remain unemotional
- Teach the subordinate how to meet the standard
- Be prepared to do some personal counseling, since a failure to meet the standard may be related to or the result of an unresolved personal problem

Explain to the subordinate what will be done to improve performance (plan of action). Identify your responsibilities in implementing the plan of action; continue to assess and follow up on the subordinate's progress. Adjust plan of action as necessary.

B. Reception and Integration Counseling

As the leader, you must counsel new team members when they arrive at your organization. This reception and integration counseling serves two purposes. First, it identifies and helps fix any problems or concerns that new members may have, especially any issues resulting from the new duty assignment. Second, it lets them know the organizational standards and how they fit into the team. It clarifies job titles and sends the message that the chain of command cares. Reception and integration counseling should begin immediately upon arrival so new team members can quickly become integrated into the organization.

C. Crisis Counseling

You may conduct crisis counseling to get a subordinate through the initial shock after receiving negative news, such as notification of the death of a loved one. You may assist the subordinate by listening and, as appropriate, providing assistance. Assistance may include referring the subordinate to a support activity or coordinating external agency support. Crisis counseling focuses on the subordinate's immediate, short-term needs.

D. Referral Counseling

Referral counseling helps subordinates work through a personal situation and may or may not follow crisis counseling. Referral counseling may also act as preventative counseling before the situation becomes a problem. Usually, the leader assists the subordinate in identifying the problem and refers the subordinate to the appropriate resource, such as Army Community Services, a chaplain, or an alcohol and drug counselor.

E. Promotion Counseling

Leaders must conduct promotion counseling for all specialists and sergeants who are eligible for advancement without waivers but not recommended for promotion to the next higher grade. Army regulations require that soldiers within this category receive initial (event-oriented) counseling when they attain full eligibility and then periodic (performance/ personal growth) counseling thereafter.

F. Adverse Separation Counseling

Adverse separation counseling may involve informing the soldier of the administrative actions available to the commander in the event substandard performance continues and of the consequences associated with those administrative actions (see AR 635-200).

Developmental counseling may not apply when an individual has engaged in more serious acts of misconduct. In those situations, you should refer the matter to the commander and the servicing staff judge advocate. When the leader's rehabilitative efforts fail, counseling with a view towards separation fills an administrative prerequisite to many administrative discharges and serves as a final warning to the soldier to improve performance or face discharge. In many situations, it may be beneficial to involve the chain of command as soon as you determine that adverse separation counseling might be required. A unit first sergeant or commander should be the person who informs the soldier of the notification requirements outlined in AR 635-200.

2. Performance/Professional Growth Counseling

A. Performance Counseling

During performance counseling, you conduct a review of a subordinate's duty performance during a certain period. You and the subordinate jointly establish performance objectives and standards for the next period. Rather than dwelling on the past, you should focus the session on the subordinate's strengths, areas needing improvement, and potential.

Performance counseling is required under the officer, NCO, and DA civilian evaluation reporting systems. The OER process requires periodic performance counseling as part of the OER Support Form requirements. Mandatory, face-to-face performance counseling between the ratter and the rated NCO is required under the NCOERS. TAPES includes a combination of both of these requirements.

Counseling at the beginning of and during the evaluation period facilitates a subordinate's involvement in the evaluation process. Performance counseling communicates standards and is an opportunity for leaders to establish and clarify the expected values, attributes, skills, and actions. Part IVb (Leader Attributes/ Skills/ Actions) of the OER Support Form (DA Form 67-9-1) serves as an excellent tool for leaders doing performance counseling. For lieutenants and warrant officers one, the major performance objectives on the OER Support Form are used as the basis for determining the developmental tasks on the Junior Officer Developmental Support Form (DA Form 67-9-1a). Quarterly face-to-face performance and developmental counseling is required for these junior officers as outlined in AR 623-105.

As an Army leader, you must ensure you've tied your expectations to performance objectives and appropriate standards. You must establish standards that your subordinates can work towards and must teach them how to achieve the standards if they are to develop.

Developmental Counseling

B. Professional Growth Counseling

Professional growth counseling includes planning for the accomplishment of individual and professional goals. You conduct this counseling to assist subordinates in achieving organizational and individual goals. During the counseling, you and your subordinate conduct a review to identify and discuss the subordinate's strengths and weaknesses and create a plan of action to build upon strengths and overcome weaknesses. This counseling isn't normally event-driven.

As part of professional growth counseling, you may choose to discuss and develop a "pathway to success" with the subordinate. This future-oriented counseling establishes short- and long-term goals and objectives. The discussion may include opportunities for civilian or military schooling, future duty assignments, special programs, and reenlistment options. Every person's needs are different, and leaders must apply specific courses of action tailored to each individual.

Career field counseling is required for lieutenants and captains before they're considered for promotion to major. Raters and senior raters, in conjunction with the rated officer, need to determine where the officer's skills best fit the needs of the Army. During career field counseling, consideration must be given to the rated officer's preference and his abilities (both performance and academic). The ratter and senior ratter should discuss career field designation with the officer prior to making a recommendation on the rated officer's OER.

While these categories can help you organize and focus counseling sessions, they should not be viewed as separate, distinct, or exhaustive. For example, a counseling session that focuses on resolving a problem may also address improving duty performance. A session focused on performance may also include a discussion on opportunities for professional growth. Regardless of the topic of the counseling session, leaders should follow the same basic format to prepare for and conduct it.

II. Approaches & Techniques

Ref: FM 22-100, pp. C-10 to C-11.

III. Approaches to Counseling

		Advantages	Disadvantages
1	**Nondirective**	- Encourages maturity - Encourages communication - Develops responsiblity	- More time-consuming - Requires greatest skill
2	**Directive**	- Quickest method - Good for people who need clear direction - Allows counselors to actively use their experience	- Doesn't encourage subords to be part of solution - Tends to treat symptons, not problems - Tends to discourage subordinates from talking freely - Solution is the counselor's, not the subordinate's
3	**Combined**	- Moderately quick - Encourages maturity - Encourages communication - Allows counselors to actively use their experience	- May take too much time for some situations

Ref: FM 22-100, fig. C-5, p. C-11.

Approaches to Counseling

An effective leader approaches each subordinate as an individual. Different people and different situations require different counseling approaches. Three approaches to counseling include non directive, directive, and combined. These approaches differ in the techniques used, but they all fit the definition of counseling and contribute to its overall purpose. The major difference between the approaches is the degree to which the subordinate participates and interacts during a counseling session.

1. Nondirective

The nondirective approach is preferred for most counseling sessions. Leaders use their experienced insight and judgment to assist subordinates in developing solutions. You should partially structure this type of counseling by telling the subordinate about the counseling process and explaining what you expect. During the counseling session, listen rather than make decisions or give advice. Clarify what's said. Cause the subordinate to bring out important points, so as to better understand the situation. When appropriate, summarize the discussion. Avoid providing solutions or rendering opinions; instead, maintain a focus on individual and organizational goals and objectives. Ensure the subordinate's plan of action supports those goals and objectives.

Developmental Counseling

2. Directive

The directive approach works best to correct simple problems, make on-the-spot corrections, and correct aspects of duty performance. The leader using the directive style does most of the talking and tells the subordinate what to do and when to do it. In contrast to the nondirective approach, the leader directs a course of action for the subordinate. Choose this approach when time is short, when you alone know what to do, or if a subordinate has limited problem-solving skills. It's also appropriate when a subordinate needs guidance, is immature, or is insecure.

3. Combined

In the combined approach, the leader uses techniques from both the directive and nondirective approaches, adjusting them to articulate what's best for the subordinate. The combined approach emphasizes the subordinate's planning and decision-making responsibilities. With your assistance, the subordinate develops the subordinate's own plan of action. You should listen, suggest possible courses, and help analyze each possible solution to determine its good and bad points. You should then help the subordinate fully understand all aspects of the situation and encourage the subordinate to decide which solution is best.

Counseling Techniques

As an Army leader, you may select from a variety of techniques when counseling subordinates. These counseling techniques, when appropriately used, cause subordinates to do things or improve upon their performance. You can use these methods during scheduled counseling sessions or while simply coaching a subordinate.

A. Nondirective or combined approaches include—
- **Suggesting alternatives.** Discuss alternative actions that the subordinate may take, but both you and the subordinate decide which course of action is most appropriate.
- **Recommending.** Recommend one course of action, but leave the decision to accept the recommended action to the subordinate.
- **Persuading.** Persuade the subordinate that a given course of action is best, but leave the decision to the subordinate. Successful persuasion depends on the leader's credibility, the subordinate's willingness to listen, and their mutual trust.
- **Advising.** Advise the subordinate that a given course of action is best. This is the strongest form of influence not involving a command.

B. Directive approaches to counseling include—
- **Corrective training.** Teach and assist the subordinate in attaining and maintaining the standards. The subordinate completes corrective training when the subordinate attains the standard.
- **Commanding.** Order the subordinate to take a given course of action in clear, exact words. The subordinate understands that he has been given a command and will face the consequences for failing to carry it out.

Developmental Counseling
III. The Counseling Process

Ref: FM 22-100, pp. C-12 to C-16.

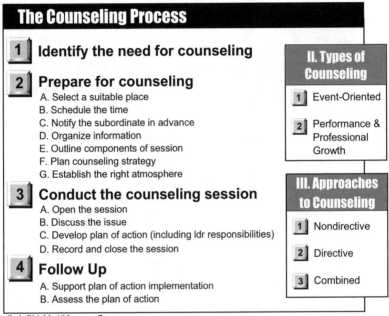

The Counseling Process

1 **Identify the need for counseling**

2 **Prepare for counseling**
   A. Select a suitable place
   B. Schedule the time
   C. Notify the subordinate in advance
   D. Organize information
   E. Outline components of session
   F. Plan counseling strategy
   G. Establish the right atmosphere

3 **Conduct the counseling session**
   A. Open the session
   B. Discuss the issue
   C. Develop plan of action (including ldr responsibilities)
   D. Record and close the session

4 **Follow Up**
   A. Support plan of action implementation
   B. Assess the plan of action

II. Types of Counseling
1 Event-Oriented
2 Performance & Professional Growth

III. Approaches to Counseling
1 Nondirective
2 Directive
3 Combined

Ref: FM 22-100, app. C.

---

1. Identify the Need for Counseling

Quite often organizational policies, such as counseling associated with an evaluation or counseling required by the command, focus a counseling session. However, you may conduct developmental counseling whenever the need arises for focused, two-way communication aimed at subordinate development. Developing subordinates consists of observing the subordinate's performance, comparing it to the standard, and then providing feedback to the subordinate in the form of counseling.

Developmental Counseling

2. Prepare for Counseling

Successful counseling requires preparation. To prepare for counseling, do the following:

A. Select a Suitable Place

Schedule counseling in an environment that minimizes interruptions and is free from distracting sights and sounds.

B. Schedule the Time

When possible, counsel a subordinate during the duty day. Counseling after duty hours may be rushed or perceived as unfavorable. The length of time required for counseling depends on the complexity of the issue. Generally a counseling session should last less than an hour. If you need more time, schedule a second session. Additionally, select a time free from competition with other activities and consider what has been planned after the counseling session. Important events can distract a subordinate from concentrating on the counseling.

C. Notify the Subordinate Well in Advance

For a counseling session to be a subordinate-centered, two-person effort, the subordinate must have time to prepare for it. The subordinate should know why, where, and when the counseling will take place. Counseling following a specific event should happen as close to the event as possible. However, for performance or professional development counseling, subordinates may need a week or more to prepare or review specific products, such as support forms or counseling records.

D. Organize Information

Solid preparation is essential to effective counseling. Review all pertinent information. This includes the purpose of the counseling, facts and observations about the subordinate, identification of possible problems, main points of discussion, and the development of a plan of action. Focus on specific and objective behaviors that the subordinate must maintain or improve as well as a plan of action with clear, obtainable goals.

E. Outline the Components of the Counseling Session

Using the information obtained, determine what to discuss during the counseling session. Note what prompted the counseling, what you aim to achieve, and what your role as a counselor is. Identify possible comments or questions to help you keep the counseling session subordinate-centered and help the subordinate progress through its stages. Although you never know what a subordinate will say or do during counseling, a written outline helps organize the session and enhances the chance of positive results.

F. Plan Counseling Strategy

As many approaches to counseling exist as there are leaders. The directive, nondirective, and combined approaches to counseling were addressed earlier. Use a strategy that suits your subordinates and the situation.

G. Establish the Right Atmosphere

The right atmosphere promotes two-way communication between a leader and subordinate. To establish a relaxed atmosphere, you may offer the subordinate a seat or a cup of coffee.

Some situations make an informal atmosphere inappropriate. For example, during counseling to correct substandard performance, you may direct the subordinate to remain standing while you remain seated behind a desk. This formal atmosphere, normally used to give specific guidance, reinforces the leader's rank, position in the chain of command, and authority.

3. Conduct the Counseling Session

Be flexible when conducting a counseling session. Often counseling for a specific incident occurs spontaneously as leaders encounter subordinates in their daily activities. Such counseling can occur in the field, motor pool, barracks—wherever subordinates perform their duties. Good leaders take advantage of naturally occurring events to provide subordinates with feedback.

Counseling Session Steps

A. Opening the Session
B. Discussing the Issues
C. Developing the Plan of Action
D. Recording and Closing the Session

Ref: FM 22-100, p. C-14.

A. Open the Session

In the session opening, state the purpose of the session and establish a subordinate-centered setting. Establish the preferred setting early in the session by inviting the subordinate to speak. The best way to open a counseling session is to clearly state its purpose. For example, an appropriate purpose statement might be: "The purpose of this counseling is to discuss your duty performance over the past month and to create a plan to enhance performance and attain performance goals." If applicable, start the counseling session by reviewing the status of the previous plan of action.

You and the subordinate should attempt to develop a mutual understanding of the issues. You can best develop this by letting the subordinate do most of the talking. Use active listening; respond, and question without dominating the conversation. Aim to help the subordinate better understand the subject of the counseling.

Both you and the subordinate should provide examples or cite specific observations to reduce the perception that either is unnecessarily biased or judgmental. However, when the issue is substandard performance, you should make clear how the performance didn't meet the standard. The conversation, which should be two-way, then addresses what the subordinate needs to do to meet the standard. It's important that you define the issue as substandard performance and don't allow the subordinate to define the issue as an unreasonable standard—unless you consider the standard negotiable or are willing to alter the conditions under which the subordinate must meet the standard.

B. Develop a Plan of Action

A plan of action identifies a method for achieving a desired result. It specifies what the subordinate must do to reach the goals set during the counseling session. The plan must be specific: it should show the subordinate how to modify or maintain his behavior. It should avoid vague intentions such as "Next month I want you to improve your land navigation skills." The plan must use concrete and direct terms. For example, you might say: "Next week you'll attend the map reading class with 1st Platoon. After the class, SGT Dixon will coach you through the land navigation course. He will help you develop your skill with the compass. I will observe you going through the course with SGT Dixon, and then I will talk to you again and determine where and if you still need additional training." A specific and achievable plan sets the stage for successful development.

C. Record and Close the Session

Although requirements to record counseling sessions vary, a leader always benefits by documenting the main points of a counseling session. Documentation serves as a reference to the agreed upon plan of action and the subordinate's accomplishments, improvements, personal preferences, or problems. A complete record of counseling aids in making recommendations for professional development, schools, promotions, and evaluation reports.

Additionally, Army regulations require written records of counseling for certain personnel actions, such as a barring a soldier from reenlisting, processing a soldier for administrative separation, or placing a soldier in the overweight program. When a soldier faces involuntary separation, the leader must take special care to maintain accurate counseling records. Documentation of substandard actions conveys a strong corrective message to subordinates.

To close the session, summarize its key points and ask if the subordinate understands the plan of action. Invite the subordinate to review the plan of action and what's expected of you, the leader. With the subordinate, establish any follow-up measures necessary to support the successful implementation of the plan of action. These may include providing the subordinate with resources and time, periodically assessing the plan, and following through on referrals. Schedule any future meetings, at least tentatively, before dismissing the subordinate.

4. Follow Up

Leader's Responsibilities

The counseling process doesn't end with the counseling session. It continues through implementation of the plan of action and evaluation of results. After counseling, you must support subordinates as they implement their plans of action. Support may include teaching, coaching, or providing time and resources. You must observe and assess this process and possibly modify the plan to meet its goals. Appropriate measures after counseling include follow-up counseling, making referrals, informing the chain of command, and taking corrective measures.

Assess the Plan of Action

The purpose of counseling is to develop subordinates who are better able to achieve personal, professional, and organizational goals. During the assessment, review the plan of action with the subordinate to determine if the desired results were achieved. You and the subordinate should determine the date for this assessment during the initial counseling session. The assessment of the plan of action provides useful information for future follow-up counseling sessions.

IV. Developmental Counseling Form

Ref: FM 22-100, pp. C-18 to C-23.

The Developmental Counseling Form (DA Form 4856-E) is designed to help Army leaders conduct and record counseling sessions.

The following form shows a blank DA Form 4856-E with instructions on how to complete each block. Additional examples can be found in FM 22-100, App. C.

DEVELOPMENTAL COUNSELING FORM
For use of this form see FM 22-100

DATA REQUIRED BY THE PRIVACY ACT OF 1974

AUTHORITY: 5 USC 301, Departmental Regulations; 10 USC 3013, Secretary of the Army and E.O. 9397 (SSN)
PRINCIPAL PURPOSE: To assist leaders in conducting and recording counseling data pertaining to subordinates.
ROUTINE USES: For subordinate leader development IAW FM 22-100. Leaders should use this form as necessary.
DISCLOSURE: Disclosure is voluntary.

PART I - ADMINISTRATIVE DATA

Name (Last, First, MI)	Rank / Grade	Social Security No.	Date of Counseling
Organization		Name and Title of Counselor	

PART II - BACKGROUND INFORMATION

Purpose of Counseling: (Leader states the reason for the counseling, e.g. performance/professional or event-oriented counseling and includes the leader's facts and observations prior to the counseling):

See paragraph C-68, Open the Session

The leader should annotate pertinent, specific, and objective facts and observations made. If applicable, the leader and subordinate start the counseling session by reviewing the status of the previous plan of action.

PART III - SUMMARY OF COUNSELING
Complete this section during or immediately subsequent to counseling.

Key Points of Discussion:

See paragraphs C-69 and C-70, Discuss the Issues.

The leader and subordinate should attempt to develop a mutual understanding of the issues. Both the leader and the subordinate should provide examples or cite specific observations to reduce the perception that either is unnecessarily biased or judgmental.

OTHER INSTRUCTIONS
This form will be destroyed upon: reassignment (other than rehabilitative transfers), separation at ETS, or upon retirement. For separation requirements and notification of loss of benefits/consequences see local directives and AR 635-200.

DA FORM 4856-E, JUN 99   EDITION OF JUN 85 IS OBSOLETE

Developmental Counseling

Plan of Action: (Outlines actions that the subordinate will do after the counseling session to reach the agreed upon goals(s). The actions must be specific enough to modify or maintain the subordinate's behavior and include a specific time line for implementation and assessment (Part IV below)).

See paragraph C-71, Develop a Plan of Action

The plan of action specifies what the subordinate must do to reach the goals set during the counseling session. The plan of action must be specific and should contain the outline, guideline(s), and time line that the subordinate follows. A specific and achievable plan of action sets the stage for successful subordinate development.

Remember, event-oriented counseling with corrective training as part of the plan of action can't be tied to a specified time frame. Corrective training is complete once the subordinate attains the standard.

Session Closing: (The leader summarizes the key points of the session and checks if the subordinate understands the plan of action. The subordinate agrees/disagrees and provides remarks if appropriate).

Individual counseled: I agree/ <u>disagree</u> with the information above

Individual counseled remarks:

See paragraph C-72 through C-74, Close the Session

Signature of Individual Counseled:_____ Date: _____

Leader Responsibilities: (Leader's responsibilities in implementing the plan of action).

See paragraph C76, Leader's Responsibilities

To accomplish the plan of action, the leader must list the resources necessary and commit to providing them to the soldier.

Signature of Counselor: _____ Date: _____

PART IV - ASSESSMENT OF THE PLAN OF ACTION

Assessment (Did the plan of action achieve the desired results? This section is completed by both the leader and the individual counseled and provides useful information for follow-up counseling):

The assessment of the plan of action provides useful information for future follow-up counseling. This block should be completed prior to the start of a follow-up counseling session. During an event-oriented counseling session, the counseling session is not complete until this block is completed.

During performance/professional growth counseling, this block serves as the starting point for future counseling sessions. Leaders must remember to conduct this assessment based on resolution of the situation or the established time line discussed in the plan of action block above.

Counselor:_____ Individual Counseled: _____ Date of Assessment: _____

Note: Both the counselor and the individual counseled should retain a record of the counseling.

DA FORM 4856-E (Reverse)

Developmental Counseling

The Leader's SMARTbook (2nd Rev. Ed.)

Index

Index

Speak the Language of Your Profession
Military SMARTbooks

The Leader's SMARTbook (2nd Rev. Ed.)
Step-by-Step Guide to Training, Leadership, Team Building & Counseling

Updated with the new FM 7-0! Covers the complete doctrinal series on training management, team building, leadership and developmental counseling. Topics include FM 7-0 Training the Army, company-level training management (TC 25-30), after action reviews (TC 25-20), the Army leader (FM 22-100) and levels of leadership (FM 22-100), combat-ready teams (FM 22-102) and developmental counseling.

The Battle Staff SMARTbook (2nd Rev. Ed.)
Doctrinal Guide to Military Decision Making & Tactical Operations

Completely updated with the new FM 5-0, FM 6-0 and FM 1-02! Covers the entire spectrum of planning and conducting military operations. Topics include fundamentals of planning, the military decision making process (MDMP & TLP), intelligence preparation of the battlefield (IPB), plans and orders (WARNOs/OPORDs/FRAGOs), mission command, rehearsals and AARs, and operational terms and graphics.

The Operations SMARTbook (3rd Rev. Ed.)
FM 3-0 Full Spectrum Operations and the Battlefield Operating Systems

Fully updated! Guide to FM 3-0 Full Spectrum Operations and the battlefield operating systems (BOSs): intelligence, surveillance & reconnaissance (ISR); maneuver and U.S. Army organization; fire support; air defense and Army airspace command and control (A2C2); mobility, countermobility & survivability (MCS) to include NBC operations; combat service support (CSS); and command & control (C2).

The Joint Forces & Operational Warfighting SMARTbook
Guide to Joint Doctrine, Operational Warfighting and Theater/Campaign Planning

Applicable to ALL Services plus the Dept of Defense and Joint Staff. Covers fundamentals of joint ops; joint structure and org; joint strategy & resource development (DPS, NSC, JSPS, PPBS); Joint Operations Planning & Execution System (JOPES); campaign/theater planning; joint task forces (JTFs); log spt to joint ops; and joint doctrine resources.

The Combat Service Support & Deployment SMARTbook
Doctrinal Guide to Combat Service Support, RSO&I and Unit Movement Operations

Complete guide to FM 4-0 Combat Service Support; joint force logistics (JP 4-0); CSS operations (FSB, DSB, DASB, DISCOM, TSC, rear area defensive ops, transformation); CSS planning; unit movement ops (FM 4-01.011); reception, staging, onward movement and integration (RSO&I - FM 100-17-3); and combat service support resources.

www.TheLightningPress.com
Purchase/Order Form

Indicate quantity desired ($29.95 each + shipping):

_____ The Leader's SMARTbook (2nd Ed.)

_____ The Battle Staff SMARTbook (2nd Ed.)

_____ The Operations SMARTbook (3rd Ed.)

_____ The Joint Forces & Operational
Warfighting SMARTbook

_____ The Combat Service Support &
Deployment SMARTbook

Order SECURE Online:
Place your order online at **www.TheLightningPress.com**

24-hour Voicemail/Fax/Order:
Record your order by voicemail at 1-800-997-8827

Business Fax:
Fax your completed order to 1-800-997-8827

Mail:
Mail this order form to 2227 Arrowhead Blvd., Lakeland, FL 33813

For up-to-date pricing and ordering details, visit www.TheLightningPress.com

Shipping Information

Name _____

Address _____

Address _____

City _____ State _____ Zip _____

Phone _____ E-mail _____

If ordering by credit card (Mastercard, Visa, American Express)

Card Holder's Name _____ Card Type _____

Card Number _____ Expiration Date _____

Card Holder's Signature _____

Billing Address (if different from above) _____

In addition to Mastercard, Visa and American Express, we also accept qualified purchase orders, government IMPAC cards, personal checks and money orders.

Shipping

____ Standard ($5.00 first book, +$1.50 each additional book). Allow 2-3 weeks.

____ APO ($5.50 first book, +$1.50 each additional book). Allow 2-4 weeks.

All published prices (to include postage), specifications and services are subject to change without notice. This includes preprinted order forms included in books.